Kraków, Warsaw & Gdańsk

CONTENTS

INTRODUCTION

This Snapshot guide, excerpted from my guidebook *Rick Steves Eastern Europe,* introduces you a trio of grand Polish cities: historic Kraków, thriving Warsaw, and gorgeous Gdańsk. Covering the best of Poland, this book offers an enjoyable cross-section of this proud nation.

Poland's historical capital, Kraków, clusters around one of Europe's biggest and most inviting market squares. Explore Kraków's picture-perfect Old Town—filled with museums, restaurants, university life, and Old World charm—and head to the Kazimierz neighborhood to learn about Poland's Jewish story. Side-trip to the world's most powerful memorial to the victims of the Holocaust at Auschwitz-Birkenau concentration camp.

For a look at today's Poland, visit Warsaw—leveled in World War II, rebuilt soon after, and now rapidly gentrifying. Stroll through Warsaw's reconstructed Old Town, promenade along newly spiffed-up boulevards, gape up at the communist-style Palace of Culture and Science, and dip into engaging museums on WWII history, native son Fryderyk Chopin, Polish painters, and much more.

On the Baltic Coast, Gdańsk offers a vibrantly colorful main drag fronted by opulent old Hanseatic facades, plus inspiring tales from the toppling of communism at the shipyard where the Solidarity trade union was born. Nearby in Pomerania is a pair of medieval red-brick sights: the imposing Gothic headquarters of the Teutonic Knights, Malbork Castle; and the appealing, gingerbread-scented town of Toruń.

To help you have the best trip possible, I've included the following topics in this book:

• **Planning Your Time,** with advice on how to make the most of your limited time

- **Orientation,** including tourist information offices (abbreviated as TI), tips on public transportation, local tour options, and helpful hints
- **Sights** with ratings:
  - ▲▲▲—Don't miss
  - ▲▲—Try hard to see
  - ▲—Worthwhile if you can make it
  - No rating—Worth knowing about
- **Sleeping** and **Eating,** with good-value recommendations in every price range
- **Connections,** with tips on trains, buses, and boats

Practicalities, near the end of this book, has information on money, staying connected, lodging, restaurants, transportation, and more, plus Polish survival phrases.

To travel smartly, read this little book in its entirety before you go. It's my hope that this guide will make your trip more meaningful and rewarding. Traveling like a temporary local, you'll get the absolute most out of every mile, minute, and dollar.

Szczęśliwej podróży—happy travels!

Rick Steves

POLAND

POLAND

Polska

Poland is a land of surprises. Many people imagine Poland as a backwards, impoverished land of rusting factories, smoggy cities, and gloomy natives. But these people are left speechless when they step into Kraków's vibrant main square, Gdańsk's colorful Royal Way, or Warsaw's lively Old Town. While parts of the country still do feel like a time warp, today's Poland also has a vibrant urbanity, an enticing food and design culture, dynamic history, and kindhearted natives.

The Poles are a proud people—as moved by their spectacular failures as by their successes. Their quiet elegance has been tempered by generations of abuse by foreign powers. You'll find fewer scams and con artists here than in other Eastern European countries.

In a way, there are two Polands: lively, cosmopolitan urban centers, and countless tiny farm villages in the countryside. A societal tension exists between city-dwelling progressives and what they call the "simple people" of Poland: hardworking small-town Poles descended from generations of farmers, who still live an uncomplicated, agrarian lifestyle. There's a large contingent of these salt-of-the-earth folks, who like things the way they are and tend to be politically conservative and staunchly Euroskeptic.

Poland is arguably Europe's most devoutly Catholic country. Their profound faith has united the Poles through many tough times. Squeezed between Protestant Germany (originally Prussia) and Eastern Orthodox Russia, Poland wasn't even a country for generations (1795-1918)—but its Catholicism helped keep its spirit alive. Under communism, Poles found their religion a source of strength as well as rebellion—they could express dissent against the atheistic regime by going to church. Be sure to step into some serene church interiors. These aren't museums—you'll almost certainly see locals in prayer.

(Be careful to show the proper respect: Maintain silence, keep a low profile, and if you want to snap pictures, do so discreetly.)

Much of Poland's story is a Jewish story. Before World War II, 80 percent of Europe's Jews lived in Poland. Warsaw was the world's second-largest Jewish city (after New York), with 380,000 Jews (out of a total population of 1.2 million). Poland was a magnet for Jewish refugees because of its relatively welcoming policies. Still, Jews were forbidden from owning land; that's why they settled mostly in the cities. But the Holocaust (and a later Soviet policy of sending "troublemaking" Jews to Israel) decimated the Jewish population. This tragic chapter, combined with postwar border shifts and population movements, made Poland one of Europe's most ethnically homogeneous countries. Today, virtually everyone in the country is an ethnic Pole, and only a few thousand Polish Jews remain.

Poland has long been extremely pro-America. Of course, their big neighbors (Russia and Germany) have been their historic enemies. And when Hitler invaded in 1939, the Poles felt let down by their supposed European friends (France and Britain), who declared war on Germany but provided virtually no military support to the Polish resistance. America, meanwhile, is seen as the big ally from across the ocean—and the home of the largest population of Poles outside of Poland. In 1989, when Poland finally won its freedom, many Poles half-joked that they should apply to become the 51st state.

On my first visit to Poland, I had a poor impression of Poles, who seemed brusque and often elbowed ahead of me in line. I've since learned that all it takes is a smile and a cheerful greeting—preferably in Polish—to break through the thick skin that helped

Poland Almanac

Official Name: Rzeczpospolita Polska (Republic of Poland), or Polska for short.

Snapshot History: This thousand-year-old country has been dominated by foreigners for much of the past two centuries, finally achieving true independence (from the Soviet Union) in 1989.

Population: 38.5 million people, slightly more than California. About 97 percent are ethnic Poles who speak Polish (though English is also widely spoken). Three out of every four Poles are practicing Catholics. The population is younger than most European countries, with an average age of 39 (Germany's is 46).

Latitude and Longitude: 52°N and 20°E (similar latitude to Berlin, London, and Edmonton, Alberta).

Area: 121,000 square miles, the same as New Mexico (or Illinois and Iowa put together).

Geography: Because of its overall flatness, Poland has been a corridor for invading armies since its infancy. The Vistula River (650 miles) runs south-to-north up the middle of the country, passing through Kraków and Warsaw, and emptying into the Baltic Sea at Gdańsk. Poland's climate is generally cool and rainy—40,000 storks love it.

Biggest Cities: Warsaw (the capital, 1.7 million), Kraków (757,000), and Łódź (747,000).

Economy: The Gross Domestic Product recently surpassed $1 trillion, with a GDP per capita of $26,500. The 1990s saw an aggressive and successful transition from state-run socialism to privately-owned capitalism. Still, Poland's traditional potato-and-pig-farming society is behind the times, with 16 percent of the country's workers producing less than 3 percent of its GDP. About one in ten Poles is unemployed, and nearly one in five lives in poverty. Poland weathered the economic crisis better than most European countries; some believe it's thanks to their relatively primitive economic model.

these kind people survive the difficult communist times. With a friendly *Dzień dobry!*, you'll turn any grouch into an ally.

It may help to know that, because of the distinct cadence of Polish, Poles speaking English sometimes sound more impatient, gruff, or irritated than they actually are. Part of the Poles' charm is that they're not as slick and self-assured as many Europeans: They're kind, soft-spoken, and quite shy. On a recent train trip in Poland, I offered my Polish seatmate a snack—and spent the rest of trip enjoying a delightful conversation with a new friend.

Currency: 1 złoty (zł, or PLN) = 100 groszy (gr) = about 25 cents; 4 zł = about $1.

Government: Poland's mostly figurehead president selects the prime minister and cabinet, with legislators' approval. They govern along with a two-house legislature (Sejm and Senat) of 560 seats. Prime Minister Beata Szydło—already Poland's third female PM in less than 30 years of democracy—represents the majority political party, the right-wing Law and Justice (Prawo i Sprawiedliwość). President Andrzej Duda, formerly of the Law and Justice party (but currently a conservative-leaning independent), began his five-year term in 2015. (For more on Polish politics, see page 14.)

Flag: The upper half is white, and the lower half is red—the traditional colors of Poland. Poetic Poles claim the white represents honor, and the red represents the blood spilled by the Poles to honor their nation. The flag sometimes includes a coat of arms with a crowned eagle (representing Polish sovereignty). Under Poland's many oppressors (including the Soviets), the crown was removed from the emblem, and its talons were trimmed. On regaining its independence, Poland coronated its eagle once more.

Not-so-Average Poles: Poland's three big airports offer a rundown of just a few of the country's biggest names: St. John Paul II (in Kraków), Fryderyk Chopin (in Warsaw), and Lech Wałęsa (in Gdańsk). And, despite the many "Polack jokes" you've heard (and maybe repeated), you're already familiar with many other famous Polish intellectuals—you just don't realize they're Polish. The "Dumb Polack" Hall of Fame includes Mikołaj Kopernik **(Nicolas Copernicus),** scientist **Marie Curie** (née Skłodowska), writer Teodor Józef Korzeniowski (better known as **Joseph Conrad,** author of *Heart of Darkness*), filmmaker **Roman Polański** (*Chinatown, The Pianist*), **Daniel Libeskind** (the master architect for redeveloping the 9/11 site in New York City)...and one of this book's co-authors.

HELPFUL HINTS

Restroom Signage: To confuse tourists, the Poles have devised a secret way of marking their WCs. You'll see doors marked with *męska* (men) and *damska* (women)—but even more often, you'll simply see a triangle (for men) or a circle (for women). A sign with a triangle, a circle, and an arrow is directing you to the closest WCs.

Pay to Pee: Many Polish bathrooms charge a small fee (around 1 zł). Don't be surprised if you're even charged at a restaurant where you're paying to dine.

Train Station Lingo: "PKP" is the abbreviation for Polish National Railways ("PKS" is for buses). In larger towns with sev-

POLAND

Top 10 Dates that Changed Poland

A.D. 966: The Polish king, Mieszko I, is baptized a Christian, symbolically uniting the Polish people and founding the nation.

1385: The Polish queen (called a "king" by sexist aristocrats of the time) marries a Lithuanian duke, starting the two-century reign of the Jagiełło family.

1410: Poland defeats the Teutonic Knights at the Battle of Grunwald, part of a Golden Age of territorial expansion and cultural achievement.

1572: The last Jagiellonian king dies, soon replaced by bickering nobles and foreign kings. Poland declines.

1795: In the last of three Partitions, the country is divvied up by its more-powerful neighbors: Russia, Prussia, and Austria.

1918: Following World War I, Poland gets back its land and sovereignty.

1939: The Free City of Gdańsk (then called Danzig) is invaded by Nazi Germany, starting World War II. At war's end, the country is "liberated" (i.e., occupied) by the Soviet Union.

1980: Lech Wałęsa leads a successful strike, demanding more freedom from the communist regime.

1989: Poland gains independence under its first president—Lech Wałęsa. Fifteen years later, Poland joins the European Union.

2010: President Lech Kaczyński and 95 other high-level government officials are killed in a plane crash in Russia.

eral train stations, you'll normally use the one called Główny (meaning "Main"—except in Warsaw, where it's Centralna). *Dworzec główny* means "main train station." Most stations have several platforms *(peron),* each of which has two tracks *(tor).* Departures are generally listed by the *peron,* so keep your eye on both tracks for your train. Arrivals are *przyjazdy,* and departures are *odjazdy.* Left-luggage counters or lockers are marked *przechowalnia bagażu. Kasy* are ticket windows. These can be marked (sometimes only in Polish) for specific needs—domestic tickets, international tickets, and so on; ask fellow travelers to be sure you select the right line. The line you choose will invariably be the slowest one—leave plenty of time to buy your ticket. On arriving at a station, to get into town, follow signs for *wyjście* (sometimes followed by *do centrum* or *do miasta).*

Transit Route Planner: For a good public transit route planner for most Polish cities, try www.jakdojade.pl.

Busy May: Be prepared for crowds and closures in the month of

May. May 1 is May Day and May 3 is Constitution Day, so
the entire country gets closed up for several days. Later in the
month, younger kids get out of school, so families go on vacation (and Kraków is one of the most popular domestic destinations).

Telephones: Remember these Polish prefixes: 800 is toll-free,
and 70 is expensive (like phone sex). Many Poles use mobile
phones (which come with the prefix 50, 51, 53, 60, 66, 69, 72,
78, 79, or 88). For details on how to dial, see page 302.

POLISH HISTORY

Poland is flat. Take a look at a topographical map of Europe, and
you'll immediately appreciate the Poles' historical dilemma: The

path of least resistance from northern Europe to Russia leads right
through Poland. Over the years,
many invaders—from Genghis
Khan to Napoleon to Hitler—have
taken advantage of Poland's strategic
location. The country is nicknamed
"God's playground" for the many
wars that have rumbled through its
territory. Poland has been invaded
by Soviets, Nazis, French, Austrians, Russians, Prussians, Swedes,
Teutonic Knights, Tatars, Bohemians, Magyars—and, about 1,300
years ago, Poles.

Medieval Greatness

The first Poles were the Polonians ("people of the plains"), a Slavic
band that arrived here in the eighth century. In 966, Mieszko I,
Duke of the Polonian tribe, adopted Christianity and founded the
Piast dynasty (which would last for more than 400 years). Centuries before Germany, Italy, or Spain first united, Poland was born.

Poland struggled against two different invaders in the 13th
century: the Tatars (Mongols who ravaged the south) and the Teutonic Knights (Germans who conquered the north—see page 290).
But despite these challenges, Poland persevered. The last king of
the Piast dynasty was also the greatest: Kazimierz the Great, who
famously "found a Poland made of wood and left one made of brick
and stone," and helped bring Poland (and its then-capital, Kraków)
to international prominence (see page 45). The progressive Kazimierz also invited Europe's much-persecuted Jews to settle here, establishing Poland as a haven for the Jewish people, which it would
remain until the Nazis arrived.

Kazimierz the Great died at the end of the 14th century
without a male heir. His grand-niece, Princess Jadwiga, became

"king" (the Poles weren't ready for a "queen") and married Lithuanian Prince Władysław Jagiełło, uniting their countries against a common enemy, the Teutonic Knights. Their marriage marked the beginning of the Jagiellonian dynasty and set the stage for Poland's Golden Age.

During this time, Poland expanded its territory, the Polish nobility began to acquire more political influence, Italy's Renaissance (and its architectural styles) became popular, and the Toruń-born astronomer Nicholas Copernicus shook up the scientific world with his bold new heliocentric theory. Up on the Baltic coast, the port city of Gdańsk took advantage of its Hanseatic League trading partnership to become one of Europe's most prosperous cities.

Foreign Kings and Partitions

When the Jagiellonians died out in 1572, political power shifted to the nobility. Poland became a republic of nobles governed by its wealthiest 10 percent—the *szlachta*, who elected a series of foreign kings. In the 16th and 17th centuries—with its territory spanning from the Baltic Sea to the Black Sea—the Polish-Lithuanian Commonwealth was the largest state in Europe.

But over time, many of the elected kings made poor diplomatic decisions and squandered the country's resources. To make matters worse, the nobles' parliament (Sejm) introduced the concept of *liberum veto* (literally "I freely forbid"), whereby any measure could be vetoed by a single member of parliament. This policy, which effectively demanded unanimous approval for any law to be passed, paralyzed the Sejm's waning power.

Sensing the Commonwealth's weakness, in the mid-17th century forces from Sweden rampaged through Polish and Lithuanian lands in the devastating "Swedish Deluge." While Poland eventually reclaimed its territory, a third of its population was dead. The Commonwealth continued to import self-serving foreign kings, including Saxony's Augustus the Strong and his son, who drained Polish wealth to finance vanity projects in their hometown of Dresden.

By the late 18th century, the Commonwealth was floundering...and surrounded by three land-hungry empires (Russia, Prussia, and Austria). The Poles were unaware that these neighbors had entered into an agreement now dubbed the "Alliance of the Three Black Eagles" (since all three of those countries, coincidentally, used that bird as their symbol); they began to circle Poland's white eagle like vultures. Stanisław August Poniatowski, elected king with Russian support in 1764, would be Poland's last.

Over the course of less than 25 years, Russia, Prussia, and Austria divided Polish territory among themselves in a series of three Partitions. In 1772 and again in 1790, Poland was forced into ceding large chunks of land to its neighbors. Desperate to reform their government, Poles enacted Europe's first democratic constitution (and the world's second, after the US Constitution) on May 3, 1791—still celebrated as a national holiday. This visionary document protected the peasants, dispensed with both *liberum veto* and the election of the king, and set up something resembling a modern nation. But the constitution alarmed Poland's neighbors, who swept in soon after with the third and final Partition in 1795. "Poland" disappeared from Europe's maps, not to return until 1918.

Even though Poland was gone, the Poles wouldn't go quietly. As the Partitions were taking place, Polish soldier Tadeusz Kościuszko (also a hero of the American Revolution) returned home to lead an unsuccessful military resistance against the Russians in 1794.

Napoleon offered a brief glimmer of hope to the Poles in the early 19th century, when he marched eastward through Europe and set up the semi-independent "Duchy of Warsaw" in Polish lands. But that fleeting taste of freedom lasted only eight years; with Napoleon's defeat, Polish hopes were dashed. The Congress of Vienna, which again redistributed Polish territory to Prussia, Russia, and Austria, is sometimes called (by Poles) the "Fourth Partition." In a classic case of "my enemy's enemy is my friend," the Poles still have great affection for Napoleon for how fiercely he fought against their mutual foes.

The Napoleonic connection also established France as a safe haven for refugee Poles. After another failed uprising against Russia in 1830, many of Poland's top artists and writers fled to Paris—including pianist Fryderyk Chopin and Romantic poet Adam Mickiewicz (whose statue adorns Kraków's main square and Warsaw's Royal Way). These Polish artists tried to preserve the nation's spirit with music and words; those who remained in Poland continued to fight with swords and fists. By the end of the 19th century, the image of the Pole as a tireless, idealistic insurgent emerged. During this time, some Romantics—with typically melodramatic flair—dubbed Poland "the Christ of nations" for the way it was misunderstood and persecuted by the world, despite its nobility.

Poles didn't just flock to France during the Partitions. Untold numbers of Polish people uprooted their lives to pursue a better future in the New World. About 10 million Americans have Polish ancestry, and most of them came stateside from the mid-19th to early 20th centuries. Because the sophisticated and educated tended to remain in Poland, these new arrivals were mostly poor farmers who were (at first) unschooled and didn't speak English, placing them on a bottom rung of American society. It was during this time that the tradition of insulting "Polack jokes" emerged. Some claim these originated in Chicago, which was both a national trendsetter in humor and a magnet for Polish immigrants. Others suggest that German immigrants to America imported insulting stereotypes of their Polish neighbors from the Old World. Either way, the jokes only became more vicious through the 20th century, until the Polish government actually lobbied the US State Department to put a stop to them.

As the map of Europe was redrawn following World War I, Poland emerged as a reborn nation, under the war hero-turned-head of state, Marshal Józef Piłsudski. The newly reformed "Second Polish Republic," which patched together the bits and pieces of territory that had been under foreign rule for decades, enjoyed a diverse ethnic mix—including Germans, Russians, Ukrainians, Lithuanians, and an enormous Jewish minority. A third of Poland spoke no Polish.

This interwar period was a time of particular flourishing for the Jewish culture. Jews were, for the first time, legally protected citizens of Poland, with full voting rights. Cities like Warsaw, Kraków, and Wilno (today's Vilnius, Lithuania)—where Jews made up a quarter to a third of the population—saw the blossoming of a rich Jewish culture.

Meanwhile, the historic Baltic port city of Gdańsk—which was bicultural (German and Polish)—was granted the special "Free City of Danzig" status to avoid dealing with the prickly issue of whether to assign it to Germany or Poland. But the peace was not to last.

World War II

On September 1, 1939, Adolf Hitler began World War II by attacking Danzig to bring it into the German fold. Before the month was out, Hitler's forces had overrun Poland, and the Soviets had taken over a swath of eastern Poland (today still part of Ukraine, Belarus, and Lithuania).

The Nazis considered the Poles *slawische Untermenschen,* "Slavic sub-humans" who were useful only for manual labor. And Poland was also home to a huge population of Jewish people. Nazi Germany annexed Polish regions that it claimed historic ties to, while the rest (including "Warschau" and "Krakau") became a puppet state ruled by the *Generalgouvernement* and Hitler's handpicked governor, Hans Frank. The Nazis considered this area *Lebensraum*—"living space" that wasn't nice enough to actually incorporate into Germany, but served perfectly as extra territory for building things that Germans didn't want in their backyards...such as the notorious death camp, Auschwitz-Birkenau.

The Poles anxiously awaited the promised military aid of France and Britain; when help failed to arrive, they took matters into their own hands, forming a ragtag "Polish Home Army" and staging incredibly courageous but lopsided battles against their powerful German overlords (such as the Warsaw Uprising—see page 207). Throughout the spring of 1945, as the Nazis retreated from their failed invasion of the Soviet Union, the Red Army gradually "liberated" the rubble of Poland from Nazi oppression—guaranteeing it another four decades of oppression under another regime.

During World War II, occupied Poland had the strictest laws in the Nazi realm: This was the only place where, if you were caught trying to help Jews escape, your entire family could be executed. And yet, many Poles risked their lives to help escapees.

With six million deaths over six years—including both Polish Jews and ethnic Poles—Poland suffered the worst per-capita WWII losses of any nation. By the war's end, one out of every five Polish citizens was dead—and 90 percent of those killed were civilians. While the human and infrastructure loss of World War II was incalculable, that war's cultural losses were also devastating—for example, some 60,000 paintings were lost.

At the war's end, the victorious Allies shifted Poland's borders significantly westward—folding historically German areas into Polish territory and appropriating previously Polish areas for the USSR. This prompted a massive movement of populations—which today we'd decry as "ethnic cleansing"—as Germans were forcibly removed from western Poland, and Poles from newly Soviet territory were transplanted to Poland proper. Entire cities were repopulated (such as the formerly German metropolis of Breslau, which was renamed Wrocław and filled with refugee Poles from Lwów, now Lviv, in Ukraine). After millions died in the war, millions more were displaced from their ancestral homes. When the dust settled, Poland was almost exclusively populated by Poles.

Saddle on a Cow: Poland Under Communism

Poland suffered horribly under the communists. A postwar intimidation regime was designed to frighten people "on board" and coincided with government seizure of private property, rationing, and food shortages. The country enjoyed a relatively open society under Premier Władysław Gomułka in the 1960s, but the impractical, centrally planned economy began to unravel in the 1970s. Stores were marked by long lines stretching around the block.

The little absurdities of communist life—which today seem almost comical—made every day a struggle. For years, every elderly woman in Poland had hair the same strange magenta color. There was only one color of dye available, so if you had dyed hair, the choice was simple: Let your hair grow out (and look clownishly half red and half white), or line up and go red.

During these difficult times, the Poles often rose up—staging

The Heritage of Communism

Poland has been free, democratic, and capitalist since 1989, but some adults carry lots of psychological baggage from living under communism. While the vast majority of Poles much prefer the current system to the old one, even the gloomiest memories are tinged with nostalgia. A friend who was 13 in 1989 recalled those days this way:

"My childhood is filled with happy memories. Under communism, life was family-oriented. Careers didn't matter. There was no way to get rich, no reason to rush, so we had time. People always had time.

"But there were also shortages—many things were 'in defi-cit.' We stood in line not knowing what would be for sale. We'd buy whatever shoes were available and then trade. At grocery stores, vinegar and mustard were always on the shelf, along with plastic cheese to make it seem less empty. Milk and bread were very low quality—it wasn't unusual to find a cigarette butt in your loaf. We had to carry ration coupons, which we'd present when buying a staple that was in short supply. They'd snip a corner off the coupon after making the sale. We didn't necessarily buy what we needed—just anything that could be bartered on the black market. I remember my mother and fa-

major protests in 1956, 1968, 1970, and 1976. Stalin famously noted that introducing communism to the Poles was like putting a saddle on a cow.

When an anticommunist Polish cardinal named Karol Wojtyła was elected pope in 1978, then visited his homeland in 1979, it was a sign to his countrymen that change was in the air. (For more on St. John Paul II, see page 54.) In 1980, Lech Wałęsa, an electrician at the shipyards in Gdańsk, became the leader of the Solidarity movement, the first workers' union in communist Eastern Europe. After an initial 18-day strike at the Gdańsk shipyards, the communist regime gave in, legalizing Solidarity (for more on Solidarity, see page 251).

But the union grew too powerful, and the communists felt their control slipping away. On Sunday, December 13, 1981, Poland's head of state, General Wojciech Jaruzelski, declared martial law in order to "forestall Soviet intervention." (Whether the Soviets actually would have invaded remains a hotly debated issue.) Tanks ther had to 'organize' for special events...somehow find a good sausage and some Coca-Cola.

"Instead of a tidy roll of toilet paper, bathrooms came with a wad of old newspapers. Sometimes my uncle would bring us several toilet paper rolls, held together with a string—absolutely the best gift anyone could give.

"Boys in my neighborhood collected pop cans. Since drinks were very limited in Poland, cans from other countries represented a world of opportunities beyond our borders. Parents could buy their children these cans on the black market, and the few families who were allowed to travel returned home with a treasure trove of cans. One boy up the street from me went to Italy, and proudly brought home a Pepsi can. All of the boys in the neighborhood wanted to see it—it was a huge status symbol. But a month later, communism ended, you could buy whatever you wanted, and everyone's can collections were worthless.

"We had real chocolate only for Christmas. The rest of the year, for treats we got something called 'chocolate-like product,' which was sweet, dark, and smelled vaguely of chocolate. And we had oranges from Cuba for Christmas, too. Everybody was excited when the newspapers announced, 'The boat with the oranges from Cuba is just five days from Poland.' We waited with excitement all year for chocolate and those oranges. The smell of Christmas was so special. Now we have that smell every day. Still, my happiest Christmases were under communism."

ominously rolled through the streets of Poland on that snowy December morning, and the Poles were terrified.

Martial law lasted until 1983. Each Pole has his or her own chilling memories of this frightening time. During riots, the people would flock into churches—the only place they could be safe from the ZOMO (riot police). People would go for their evening walks during the 19:30 government-sanctioned national news as a sign of protest. But Solidarity struggled on, going underground and becoming a united movement of all demographics, 10 million members strong (more than a quarter of the population).

In July of 1989, the ruling Communist Party agreed to hold open elections (reserving 65 percent of representatives for themselves). Their goal was to appease Solidarity, but the plan backfired: Communists didn't win a single contested seat. These elections helped spark the chain reaction across Eastern Europe that eventually tore down the Iron Curtain. Lech Wałęsa became Poland's first postcommunist president. (For more on Lech Wałęsa, see page 254.)

POLAND

Poland in the 21st Century

When 10 new countries joined the European Union in May 2004, Poland was the most ambivalent of the bunch. After centuries of being under other empires' authority, the Poles were hardly eager to relinquish some of their hard-fought autonomy to Brussels. Many Poles thought that EU membership would make things worse (higher prices, a loss of traditional lifestyles) before they got better. But most people agreed that their country had to join to survive in today's Europe. Today most Poles begrudgingly acknowledge that the benefits of EU membership have outweighed the drawbacks.

The most obvious initial impact of EU membership was the droves of job-seeking young Poles who migrated to other EU countries (mostly Britain, Ireland, and Sweden, which were the first to waive visa requirements for Eastern European workers). Many found employment at hotels and restaurants. Visitors to London and Dublin noticed a surprising language barrier at hotel front desks, and Polish-language expat newspapers joined British gossip rags on newsstands. Those who remained in Poland were concerned about the "brain drain" of bright young people flocking out of their country. But with the economic crisis, quite a few Polish expats returned home. And the 2016 Brexit vote has placed UK-Polish relations in doubt, likely prompting another wave of returnees.

Poland is by far the most populous of the recent EU members, with nearly 39 million people (about the same as Spain, or about half the size of Germany). This makes Poland the sixth-largest of the 26 EU member states—giving it serious political clout, which it has already asserted...sometimes to the dismay of the EU's more established powers.

On the American political spectrum, Poland may be the most "conservative" country in Europe. Poles are phobic when it comes to "big government"—likely because they've been subjugated and manipulated by so many foreign oppressors over the centuries. For most of the 2000s, the country's right wing was represented by a pair of twin brothers, Lech and Jarosław Kaczyński. (The Kaczyński brothers were child actors who appeared in several popular movies together.) Their conservative Law and Justice Party is pro-tax cuts, fiercely Euroskeptic (anti-EU), and very Catholic. In the 2005 presidential election, Lech Kaczyński emerged as the victor; several months later, he took the controversial step of appointing his identical twin brother Jarosław as Poland's prime minister.

The political pendulum swung back toward the center in October of 2007, when the Kaczyński brothers' main political rival, the pro-EU Donald Tusk, led his Civic Platform Party to victory in the parliamentary elections. The name Kaczyński loosely means

Polish Jokes

Through the dreary communist times, the Poles managed to keep their sense of humor. A popular target of jokes was the riot police, called the ZOMO. Here are just a few of the things Poles said about these unpopular cops:

- It's better to have a sister who's a whore than a brother in the ZOMO.
- ZOMO police are hired based on the 90-90 principle: They have to weigh at least 90 kilograms (200 pounds), and their I.Q. must be less than 90.
- ZOMO are dispatched in teams of three: one who can read, one who can write, and a third to protect those other two smart guys.
- A ZOMO policeman was sitting on the curb, crying. Someone came up to him and asked what was wrong. "I lost my dog!" he said. "No matter," the person replied. "He's a smart police dog. I'm sure he can find his way back to the station." "Yes," the ZOMO said. "But without him, I can't!"

The communists gave their people no options at elections: If you voted, you voted for the regime. Poles liked to joke that in some ways, this made communists like God—who created Eve, then said to Adam, "Now choose a wife." It was said that communists could run a pig as a candidate, and it would still win; a popular symbol of dissent became a pig painted with the words "Vote Red."

There were even jokes about jokes. Under communism, Poles noted that there was a government-sponsored prize for the funniest political joke: 15 years in prison.

"duck"—so the Poles quipped that they were led by "Donald and the Ducks."

Tragically, the levity wasn't to last. On April 10, 2010, a plane carrying President Lech Kaczyński crashed in a thick fog near the city of Smolensk, Russia. All 96 people on board—including top government, military, and business officials, high-ranking clergy, and others—were killed, plunging the nation into a period of stunned mourning. Poles wondered why, yet again, an unprecedented tragedy had befallen their nation. (Ironically, the group's trip was intended to put a painful chapter of Poland's history to rest: a commemoration of the Polish officers and enlisted men killed in the Soviet massacre at Katyń.)

Meanwhile, Poland's economy has kept chugging along, even as the rest of Europe and much of the world were bogged down by the economic crisis. More than a quarter of Poland's trade is with neighboring Germany—another of Europe's healthiest economies—and Poland was the only European Union country that didn't have a recession in 2009. Why? Poland is a big,

POLAND

Bar Mleczny (Milk Bar)

When you see a "bar" in Poland, it doesn't mean alcohol—it means cheap grub. Eating at a bar mleczny (bar MLECH-neh) is an essential Polish sightseeing experience. These cafeterias, which you'll see all over the country, are an incredibly cheap way to get a good meal...and, with the right attitude, a fun cultural experience.

In the communist era, the government subsidized the food at milk bars, allowing workers to enjoy a meal out. The name comes from the cheese cutlets that were sold here, back in a time when good meat was rare. The tradition continues today, as milk-bar prices remain astoundingly low: My bill for a filling meal usually comes to about $5. And, while communist-era fare was gross, today's milk-bar cuisine is usually quite tasty.

Milk bars usually offer many of the traditional tastes listed in the "Polish Food" section. Common items are soups (like żurek and barszcz), a variety of cabbage-based salads, kotlet (fried pork chops), pierogi (like ravioli, with various fillings), and naleśniki (pancakes). You'll see glasses of juice and (of course) milk, but most milk bars also stock bottles of water and Coke.

There are two types of milk bars: updated, modern cafeterias that cater to tourists (English menus), add some modern twists to their traditional fare, and charge about 50 percent more; and time-machine dives that haven't changed for decades. At truly traditional milk bars, the service is aimed at locals, which means no English menu and a confusing ordering system.

Every milk bar is a little different, but here's the general procedure: Head to the counter, wait to be acknowledged, and point to what you want. Handy vocabulary: to (sounds like "toe") means "this"; i (pronounced "ee") means "and."

If the milk-bar lady asks you any questions, you have three options: Nod stupidly until she just gives you something; repeat one of the things she just said (assuming she's asked you to choose between two options, like meat or cheese in your pierogi); or hope that a kindly English-speaking Pole in line will leap to your rescue. If nothing else, ordering at a milk bar is an adventure in gestures. Smiling seems to slightly extend the patience of milk-bar staffers.

Once your tray is all loaded up, pay the cashier, do a double-take when you realize how cheap your bill is, then find a table. After the meal, bus your own dishes to the little window.

self-sustaining, insular economy. In recent years, Poland's relatively weak currency ("cheaper" than the euro, yet also shielded from euro volatility) and robust economy are luring foreign investment, paradoxically threatening the very autonomy that has buffered it so far.

In recent years, the political pendulum has just kept on swinging, as key governmental posts have gone back and forth between the two dominant parties—the Civic Platform and Law and Justice. It seems the Poles are getting the hang of this whole democracy thing.

POLISH FOOD

Polish food is hearty and tasty. Because Poland is north of the Carpathian Mountains, its weather tends to be chilly, limiting the kinds of fruits and vegetables that flourish here. As in other northern European countries (such as Russia or Scandinavia), dominant staples include potatoes, dill, berries, beets, and rye. Much of what you might think of as "Jewish cuisine" turns up on Polish menus (gefilte fish, potato pancakes, chicken soup, and so forth)—which makes sense, given that Poles and Jews lived in the same area for centuries.

Polish soups are a highlight. The most typical are *żurek* and *barszcz*. *Żurek* (often translated as "sour soup" on menus) is a light-colored soup made from a sourdough base, usually containing a hard-boiled egg and pieces of *kiełbasa* (sausage). *Barszcz*, better known to Americans as borscht, is a savory beet soup that you'll see in several varieties: *Barszcz czerwony* (red borscht) is a thin, flavorful broth with a deep red color, sometimes containing dumplings or a hard-boiled egg. *Barszcz ukraiński* (Ukrainian borscht) is thicker, with cream and vegetables (usually cabbage, beans, and carrots). In summer, try the "Polish gazpacho"—*chłodnik*, a savory cream soup with beets, onions, and radishes that's served cold. I never met a Polish soup I didn't like...until I was introduced to *flaki* (sometimes *flaczki*)—tripe soup.

Another familiar Polish dish is pierogi. These ravioli-like dumplings come with various fillings. The most traditional are minced meat, sauerkraut, mushroom, cheese, and blueberry; many restaurants also experiment with more exotic fillings. Pierogi are often served with specks of fatty bacon to add flavor. Pierogi are a budget traveler's dream: Restaurants serving them are everywhere, and they're generally cheap, tasty, and very filling.

Bigos is a rich and delicious sauerkraut stew cooked with

meat, mushrooms, and whatever's in the pantry. *Gołąbki* is a dish of cabbage leaves stuffed with minced meat and rice in a tomato or mushroom sauce. *Kotlet schabowy* (fried pork chop)—once painfully scarce in communist Poland—remains a local favorite to this day. *Kaczka* (duck) is popular, as is freshwater fish: Look for *pstrąg* (trout), *karp* (carp, beware of bones), and *węgorz* (eel). On the Baltic Coast (such as in Gdańsk), you'll also see *łosoś* (salmon), *śledź* (herring), and *dorsz* (cod). Poles eat lots of potatoes, which are served with nearly every meal. Look for *placki ziemniaczane*—potato pancakes.

Several foods—both new and old—are popular in today's Poland. Herring-and-vodka bars are extremely trendy, many following the "4/8 model"—4 zł for a shot of vodka, 8 zł for a herring snack. The Polish street food *zapiekanka*—a toasted baguette with melted cheese, rubbery mushrooms from a can, and a drizzle of ersatz ketchup—began life as a "hardship food" under communism, as a pale imitation of pizza. But these days it has been reborn as a foodie staple, with *zapiekanka* vendors topping them with a world of creative flavors. The bagel-like rings you'll see sold on the street, *obwarzanki* (singular *obwarzanek*), are also cheap, and usually fresh and tasty. And, as throughout Europe, gourmet hamburgers are in—including a trend for vegan burgers.

Poland has good pastries—look for a *cukiernia* (pastry shop). The classic Polish treat is *pączki*, glazed jelly doughnuts. They can have different fillings, but most typical is a wild-rose jam. *Szarlotka* is apple cake—sometimes made with chunks of apples (especially in season), sometimes with apple filling. *Sernik* is cheesecake, and *makowiec* is poppy-seed cake. *Winebreda* is an especially gooey Danish. *Babeczka* is like a cupcake filled with pudding. And *Napoleonka* is a French-style treat with layers of crispy wafers and custard.

Lody (ice cream) is popular. The tall, skinny cones of soft-serve ice cream are called *świderki,* sometimes translated as "American ice cream." The most beloved traditional candy is *ptasie mleczko* (birds' milk), which is like a semisour marshmallow covered with chocolate. E. Wedel is the country's top brand of chocolate, with outlets in all the big cities (see page 217).

Thirsty? *Woda* is water, *woda mineralna* is bottled water (*gazowana* is with gas, *niegazowana* is without), *kawa* is coffee, *herbata* is tea, *sok* is juice, and *mleko* is milk. Żywiec, Okocim, and Lech are the best-known brands of *piwo* (beer).

Wódka (vodka) is a Polish staple—the word means, roughly, "precious little water." Żubrówka, the most famous brand of vodka, comes with a blade of grass from the bison reserves in eastern Poland (look for the bottle with the bison). The bison "flavor" the grass...then the grass flavors the vodka. Poles often mix Żubrówka with apple juice, and call this cocktail *szarlotka* ("apple cake"); it also goes by the name *tatanka* (a Native American word for "bison"). For "Cheers!" say, *"Na zdrowie!"* (nah ZDROH-vyeh).

Unusual drinks to try if you have the chance are *kwas* (a cold, fizzy, Ukrainian-style nonalcoholic beverage made from day-old rye bread) and *kompot* (a hot drink made from stewed berries). Poles are unusually fond of carrot juice (often cut with fruit juice); Kubuś is the most popular brand.

"Bon appétit" is *"Smacznego"* (smatch-NEH-goh). To pay, ask for the *rachunek* (rah-KHOO-nehk).

POLISH LANGUAGE

Polish is closely related to its neighboring Slavic languages (Slovak and Czech), with the biggest difference being that Polish has lots of fricatives (hissing sounds—"sh" and "ch"—often in close proximity).

Polish intimidates Americans with long, difficult-to-pronounce words. But if you take your time and sound things out, you'll quickly develop an ear for it. One rule of thumb to help you out: The stress is always on the next-to-last syllable.

Polish has some letters that don't appear in English, and some letters and combinations are pronounced differently than in English:

ć, ci, and cz all sound like "ch" as in "church"
ś, si, and sz all sound like "sh" as in "short"
ż, ź, zi, and rz all sound like "zh" as in "leisure"
dż and dź both sound like the "dj" sound in "jeans"
ń and ni sound like "ny" as in "canyon"
ę and ą are pronounced nasally, as in French: "en" and "an"
c sounds like "ts" as in "cats"
ch sounds like "kh" as in the Scottish "loch"
j sounds like "y" as in "yellow"
w sounds like "v" as in "Victor"
ł sounds like "w" as in "with"

So to Poles, "Lech Wałęsa" isn't pronounced "lehk wah-LEH-sah," as Americans tend to say—but "lehkh vah-WEHN-sah."

The Polish people you meet will be impressed and flattered if you take the time to learn a little of their language. To get started, check out the selection of Polish survival phrases on the following pages.

As you're tracking down addresses, these words will help: *miasto* (mee-AH-stoh, town), *plac* (plahts, square), *rynek* (REE-nehk, big market square), *ulica* (OO-leet-sah, road), *aleja* (ah-LAY-yah, avenue), and *most* (mohst, bridge). And that long word you see everywhere—*zapraszamy*—means "welcome."

POLAND

Polish Survival Phrases

Keep in mind a few Polish pronunciation tips: **w** sounds like "v," **ł** sounds like "w," **ch** is a back-of-your-throat "kh" sound (as in the Scottish "loch"), and **rz** sounds like the "zh" sound in "pleasure." The vowels with a tail (**ą** and **ę**) have a slight nasal "n" sound at the end, similar to French.

English	Polish	Pronunciation
Hello. (formal)	Dzień dobry.	jehn **doh**-brih
Hi. / Bye. (informal)	Cześć.	cheshch
Do you speak English? (asked of a man)	Czy Pan mówi po angielsku?	chih pahn **moo**-vee poh ahn-**gyehl**-skoo
Do you speak English? (asked of a woman)	Czy Pani mówi po angielsku?	chih **pah**-nee **moo**-vee poh ahn-**gyehl**-skoo
Yes. / No.	Tak. / Nie.	tahk / nyeh
I (don't) understand.	(Nie) rozumiem.	(nyeh) roh-**zoo**-myehm
Please. / You're welcome. / Can I help you?	Proszę.	**proh**-sheh
Thank you (very much).	Dziękuję (bardzo).	jehn-**koo**-yeh (**bard**-zoh)
Excuse me. / I'm sorry.	Przepraszam.	psheh-**prah**-shahm
(No) problem.	(Żaden) problem.	(**zhah**-dehn) **proh**-blehm
Good.	Dobrze.	**dohb**-zheh
Goodbye.	Do widzenia.	doh veed-**zay**-nyah
one / two / three	jeden / dwa / trzy	**yeh**-dehn / dvah / tzhih
four / five / six	cztery / pięć / sześć	**chteh**-rih / pyench / sheshch
seven / eight	siedem / osiem	**shyeh**-dehm / **oh**-shehm
nine / ten	dziewięć / dziesięć	**jeh**-vyench / **jeh**-shench
hundred / thousand	sto / tysiąc	stoh / **tih**-shants
How much?	Ile?	**ee**-leh
local currency	złoty (zł)	**zwoh**-tih
Write it.	Napisz to.	**nah**-peesh toh
Is it free?	Czy to jest za darmo?	chih toh yehst zah **dar**-moh
Is it included?	Czy jest to wliczone?	chih yehst toh vlee-**choh**-neh
Where can I find / buy...?	Gdzie mogę dostać / kupić...?	guh-**dyeh** moh-geh doh-**statch** / **koo**-peech
I'd like... (said by a man)	Chciałbym...	**khchaw**-beem
I'd like... (said by a woman)	Chciałabym...	**khchah**-wah-beem
We'd like...	Chcielibyśmy...	**khchehl**-ee-bish-mih
...a room.	...pokój.	**poh**-kooey
...a ticket to ___.	...bilet do ___.	**bee**-leht doh ___
Is it possible?	Czy jest to możliwe?	chih yehst toh mohzh-**lee**-veh
Where is...?	Gdzie jest...?	guh-**dyeh** yehst
...the train station	...dworzec kolejowy	**dvoh**-zhehts koh-leh-**yoh**-vih
...the bus station	...dworzec autobusowy	**dvoh**-zhehts ow-toh-boos-**oh**-vih
...the tourist information office	...informacja turystyczna	een-for-**maht**-syah too-ris-**titch**-nah
...the toilet	...toaleta	toh-ah-**leh**-tah
men / women	męska / damska	**mehn**-skah / **dahm**-skah
loft / right / straight	lewo / prawo / prosto	lch voh / **prah** voh / **proh**-stoh
At what time...?	O której godzinie...?	oh kuh-**too**-ray gohd-**zhee**-nyeh
...does this open / close	...będzie otwarte / zamknięte	**bend**-zheh oht-**vahr**-teh / zahm-**knyehn**-teh
Just a moment.	Chwileczkę.	khvee-**letch**-keh
now / soon / later	eraz / niedługo / później	**teh**-rahz / nyed-**woo**-goh / **poozh**-nyey
today / tomorrow	dzisiaj / jutro	**jee**-shigh / **yoo**-troh

In a Polish Restaurant

English	Polish	Pronunciation
I'd like to reserve... (said by a man)	Chciałbym zarezerwować...	khchaw-beem zah-reh-zehr-**voh**-vahch
I'd like to reserve... (said by a woman)	Chciałabym zarezerwować...	**khchah**-wah-beem zah-reh-zehr-**voh**-vahch
We'd like to reserve...	Chcielibyśmy zarezerwować...	khchehl-ee-bish-mih zah-reh-zehr-**voh**-vahch
...a table for one person / two people.	...stolik na jedną osobę / dwie osoby.	**stoh**-leek nah **yehd**-now oh-**soh**-beh / dvyeh oh-**soh**-bih
Is this table free?	Czy ten stolik jest wolny?	chih tehn **stoh**-leek yehst **vohl**-nih
Can I help you?	W czym mogę pomóc?	vchim **moh**-geh **poh**-moots
The menu (in English), please.	Menu (po angielsku), proszę.	**meh**-noo (poh ahn-**gyehl**-skoo) **proh**-sheh
service (not) included	usługa (nie) wliczona	oos-**woo**-gah (nyeh) **vlee**-choh-nah
cover charge	wstęp	vstenp
"to go"	na wynos	nah **vih**-nohs
with / without	z / bez	z / behz
and / or	i / lub	ee / loob
milk bar (cheap cafeteria)	bar mleczny	bar **mletch**-nih
fixed-price meal (of the day)	zestaw (dnia)	**zehs**-tahv (dih-**nyah**)
specialty of the house	specjalność zakładu	speht-**syahl**-nohshch zah-**kwah**-doo
half portion	pół porcji	poow **ports**-yee
daily special	danie dnia	**dah**-nyeh dih-**nyah**
appetizers	przystawki	pshih-**stahv**-kee
bread	chleb	khlehb
cheese	ser	sehr
sandwich	kanapka	kah-**nahp**-kah
soup	zupa	**zoo**-pah
salad	sałatka	sah-**waht**-kah
meat / poultry	mięso / drób	**myehn**-soh / droob
fish / seafood	ryba / owoce morza	**rih**-bah / oh-**voht**-seh **moh**-zhah
fruit / vegetables	owoce / warzywa	oh-**voht**-seh / vah-**zhih**-vah
dessert	deser	**deh**-sehr
(tap) water	woda (z kranu)	**voh**-dah (**skrah**-noo)
mineral water	woda mineralna	**voh**-dah mee-neh-**rahl**-nah
carbonated / not carbonated	gazowana / niegazowana	gah-zoh-**vah**-nah / **nyeh**-gah-zoh-vah-nah
milk	mleko	**mleh**-koh
(orange) juice	sok (pomarańczowy)	sohk (poh-mah-rayn-**choh**-vih)
coffee / tea	kawa / herbata	**kah**-vah / hehr-**bah**-tah
wine	wino	**vee**-noh
red / white	czerwone / białe	chehr-**voh**-neh / bee-**ah**-weh
sweet / dry / semi-dry	słodkie / wytrawne / półwytrawne	**swoht**-kyeh / vih-**trahv**-neh / poow-vih-**trahv**-neh
glass / bottle	szklanka / butelka	**shklahn**-kah / boo-**tehl**-kah
beer	piwo	**pee**-voh
vodka	wódka	**vood**-kah
Cheers!	Na zdrowie!	nah **zdroh**-vyeh
Enjoy your meal.	Smacznego.	smatch-**neh**-goh
More. / Another.	Więcej. / Inny.	**vyehnt**-say / **ee**-nih-nih
The same.	Taki sam.	**tah**-kee sahm
the bill	rachunek	rah-**khoo**-nehk
I'll pay.	Ja płacę.	yah **pwaht**-seh
tip	napiwek	nah-**pee**-vehk
Delicious!	Pyszne!	**pish**-neh

KRAKÓW

Kraków is easily Poland's best destination: a beautiful, old-fashioned city buzzing with history, enjoyable sights, tourists, and college students. Even though the country's capital moved from here to Warsaw 400 years ago, Kraków remains Poland's cultural and intellectual center. Of all the Eastern European cities laying claim to the boast, "the next Prague," Kraków is for real.

What's so special about it? First off, Kraków is simply charming; more than any town in Europe, it seems made for aimless strolling. And its historic walls and former moat corral an unusually full range of activities and interests: bustling university life; thought-provoking museums; breathtaking churches that evoke a powerful faith (and include many sights relating to Poland's favorite son, St. John Paul II); sprawling parks that invite you to just relax; vivid Jewish heritage sights; a burgeoning foodie and nightlife scene; and compelling side-trips to the most notorious Holocaust site anywhere (Auschwitz-Birkenau), a communist-planned workers town, and a mine filled with salty statues. With so many opportunities to learn, to have fun, or to do both at once, it's no surprise that Kraków has become the darling of Polish tourism.

PLANNING YOUR TIME

Don't skimp on your time in Kraków. It takes a minimum of two days to experience the city, and a third or fourth day lets you dig in and consider a world of fascinating side-trips.

Almost everyone coming to Kraków also visits the Auschwitz-Birkenau Concentration Camp Memorial—and should. As it's about an hour and a half away, this demands the better part of a

Kraków: A Snapshot History

Kraków grew wealthy from trade in the late 10th and early 11th centuries. Traders who passed through were required to stop here for a few days and sell their wares at a reduced cost. Local merchants turned around and sold those goods with big price hikes...and Kraków thrived. In 1038, it became Poland's capital.

Tatars invaded in 1241, leaving the city in ruins. Krakovians took this opportunity to rebuild their streets in a near-perfect grid, a striking contrast to the narrow, mazelike lanes of most medieval towns. The destruction also paved the way for the spectacular Main Market Square—still Kraków's best attraction.

King Kazimierz the Great sparked Kraków's Golden Age in the 14th century (see page 45). In 1364, he established the university that still defines the city (and counts Copernicus and St. John Paul II among its alumni).

But Kraków's power waned as Poland's political center shifted to Warsaw. In 1596, the capital officially moved north. At the end of the 18th century, three neighboring powers—Russia, Prussia, and Austria—partitioned Poland, annexing all of its territory and dividing it among themselves. Warsaw ended up as a satellite of oppressive Moscow, and Kraków became a poor provincial backwater of Vienna. After Napoleon briefly reshuffled the map of Europe in the early 19th century, Kraków was granted the status of a relatively independent city-state for about 30 years. The feisty Free City of Kraków, a tiny sliver wedged between three of Europe's mightiest empires, enjoyed an economic boom that saw the creation of the Planty park, the arrival of gas lighting and trams, and the construction of upscale suburbs outside the Old Town. Only after the unsuccessful Kraków Uprising of 1846 was the city forcefully brought back into the Austrian fold. But despite Kraków's reduced prominence, Austria's comparatively liberal climate allowed the city to become a haven for intellectuals and progressives (including a young revolutionary thinker from Russia named Vladimir Lenin).

day to fully appreciate (either as a round-trip from Kraków, or en route to or from another destination). Visiting Auschwitz requires a reservation, which can be hard to get. For all the details, see the next chapter.

If you have only two full days (the "express plan"), start off with my self-guided walk through the Old Town and a quick stroll up to Wawel Castle, then head over to the Schindler's Factory Museum and wind down your day in Kazimierz. Your second day is for a side-trip to Auschwitz. This plan gives you an enticing once-over-lightly, but leaves almost no time for entering the sights.

More time buys you the chance to relax, enjoy, and linger: Tackle the Old Town and Wawel Castle on the first day, Kazimi-

The Nazis overran Poland in September of 1939, installing a ruling body called the *Generalgouvernement,* headed by former attorney Hans Frank. Germany wanted to quickly develop "Krakau" (as they called it) into the German capital of the nation. They renamed the Main Market Square "Adolf-Hitler-Platz," tore down statues of Polish figures (including the Adam Mickiewicz statue that dominates the Main Market Square today), and invested heavily in construction and industrialization (opening the door for Oskar Schindler to come and take over a factory from its Jewish owners). The German overlords imposed a "New Order" that included seizing businesses, rationing, and a strict curfew for Poles and Jews alike. A special set of "Jewish laws" targeted, then decimated, Poland's huge Jewish population.

Kraków's cityscape—if not its people—emerged from World War II virtually unscathed. But when the communists took over, they decided to give intellectual (and potentially dissident) Kraków an injection of good Soviet values—in the form of heavy industry. They built Nowa Huta, an enormous steelworks and planned town for workers, on Kraków's outskirts, thereby dooming the city to decades of smog. Thankfully, Kraków is now much cleaner than it was 20 years ago.

St. John Paul II was born (as Karol Wojtyła) in nearby Wadowice and served as archbishop of Kraków before being called to Rome. Today, the hometown boy-turned-saint draws lots of pilgrims and is, for many, a big part of the city's attraction. Saintly ties aside, Kraków might be the most Catholic town in Europe's most Catholic country; be sure to visit a few of its many churches.

The story of Kraków continues to play out. In recent years, its Kazimierz district has come back to life—both with Jewish-themed cultural sights, and with some of Eastern Europe's best bars, food trucks, and restaurants. This mingling of the historic with the contemporary typifies a city that always has been, and continues to be, Poland's heartbeat.

erz and museums of your choice on the second day, and Auschwitz (and other side-trips) with additional days. If you have a special interest, you could side-trip to the St. John Paul II pilgrimage sights on the outskirts of town, or to the communist architecture of the Nowa Huta suburb. Wieliczka Salt Mine is another crowd-pleasing, half-day option.

Regardless of how long you stay, your evening choices are many and varied: Savor the Main Market Square over dinner or a drink, take in a jazz show, do a pub crawl through the city's many youthful bars and clubs (best in Kazimierz), or enjoy traditional Jewish music and cuisine (also in Kazimierz).

KRAKÓW

Kraków's Old Town Sights

OLD MARKET

WALK BEGINS

BARBICAN

FLORIAN GATE

CZARTORYSKI MUSEUM

OLD

SZOŁAYSKI HOUSE

Main Market Square

CLOTH HALL

ST. MARY'S

Small Market Square

COLLEGIUM MAIUS

MICKIEWICZ Statue

TOWN HALL TOWER

PASAŻ 13 MALL

ARCH-BISHOP'S MANSION

#8 plac Wszystkich Świętych

DOMINICAN CHURCH

WC

To Airport, Auschwitz & Kościuszko Mound

ST. FRANCIS

WYSPIAŃSKI PAVILION

TOWN

MILK BAR
MILK BAR

Mary Mag. Square

STS. PETER & PAUL

BISHOP ERAZM CIOŁEK PALACE

ARCHDIOCESAN MUSEUM

WALK ENDS

ST. ANDREW'S

JOHN PAUL II CENTER

CATHEDRAL

WAWEL HILL

INNER COURTYARD

LOST WAWEL MUSEUM

ST. BERNARDINO'S

Vistula River

DRAGON STATUE

#24 Teater Bagately

KRAKÓW

TRAIN STN.

Ⓑ BUS STATION

Ⓑ Kurniki

KURNIKI

GALERIA KRAKOWSKA MALL

#3 �"T" Dworzec Główny Zachód

Plac Matejki

#24 �"T" Basztowa

BASZTOWA

ZACISZE

PAWIA

Plac Jana Jerozioranskego

POST OFFICE

LUBICZ

To Nowa Huta

BOSACKA

PEDESTRIAN UNDERPASS
#3 & 24 �"T"
Dworzec Główny

SŁOWACKI THEATER

Planty

ŚW. KRZYŻA

WESTERPLATTE

RADZIWIŁŁOWSKA

MIKOŁAJSKA

KOPERNIKA

ZYBLIKIEWICZA

�"T" ⑫
#3 & 24
Poczta Główna

BLICH

MAIN POST OFFICE

WIELOPOLE

STAROWIŚLNA

DIETLA

GRZEGÓRZECKA

⑫
#3 & 24 �"T"
Dietla

⑧

200 Meters

200 Yards

ŚW. SEBASTIANA

See Kazimierz map

B. JOSELEWICZA

KAZIMIERZ

New Cemetery

⑫
#3 & 24 �"T"
Miodowa

POST

DIETLA

PODBRZEZIE

MIODOWA

Old Cemetery

STAROWIŚLNA

GALERIA KAZIMIERZ

REMU'H SYNAGOGUE

Plac Nowy

DAJWÓR

MARKET HALL

To Podgórze & Wieliczka Salt Mine

Sights

❶ John Paul II Wawel Cathedral Museum

❷ Sandomierska Tower

❸ Gallery of 19th-Century Polish Art (Entrance)

❹ Rynek Underground Museum

❺ Kraków City Museum Visitors Center

❻ Wieliczka Promotion Office

Services & Other

❼ Massolit Books

❽ Frania Café/Laundry

❾ Betty Clean Laundry

❿ Kraków Bike Tours & Rental

⓫ KRK Bike Rental

⓬ Trams #3 & #24 to/from Kazimierz (3)

Orientation to Kraków

Kraków (Poles say KROCK-oof, but you can say KRACK-cow; it's sometimes spelled "Cracow" in English) is mercifully compact, flat, and easy to navigate. While the urban sprawl is big (with 757,000 people), the tourist's Kraków feels small—from the main square, you can walk to just about everything of interest in less than 15 minutes. Just to the south is Poland's main river, the Vistula (Wisła, VEES-wah).

Most sights—and almost all recommended hotels and restaurants—are in the **Old Town** (Stare Miasto, STAH-reh mee-AH-stoh), which is surrounded by a greenbelt called the Planty (PLAHN-tee). In the center of the Old Town lies the Main Market Square (Rynek Główny, REE-nehk GWOHV-nee)—it's such an important landmark, I call it simply "the Square." At the Old Town's northeast corner, just outside the ring road, is the main train station. And at the southern end of the Old Town, on the riverbank, is the hill called **Wawel** (VAH-vehl)—with a historic castle, museums, and Poland's national church.

About a 20-minute walk (or quick tram/taxi ride) southeast of the Square is the neighborhood called **Kazimierz** (kah-ZHEE-mehzh)—with Jewish landmarks and Holocaust sites (including the Schindler's Factory Museum) and the city's best foodie and nightlife area.

A few more attractions are just beyond the core, including the St. John Paul II pilgrimage sights (in the Łagiewniki neighborhood), the communist-planned town of Nowa Huta, Wieliczka Salt Mine, and the Kościuszko Mound.

TOURIST INFORMATION

Kraków has many helpful TIs, called InfoKraków (www.infokrakow.pl). Five branches are in or near the Old Town (all open daily May-Sept 9:00-19:00, Oct-April 9:00-17:00, unless otherwise noted):

• In the **Planty** park, between the main train station and Main Market Square (in round kiosk at ulica Szpitalna 25, tel. 12-354-2720)

• On **ulica Św. Jana,** just north of the Main Market Square (specializes in concert tickets, daily year-round 9:00-19:00, at #2, tel. 12-354-2725)

• In the **Cloth Hall** right on the Main Market Square (tel. 12-354-2716)

• In the **Wyspiański Pavilion,** just south of the Square on ulica Grodzka (daily 9:00-17:00, plac Wszystkich Świętych 3, not at the window but inside the building, tel. 12-616-1886)

• Just west of **Wawel Hill** (also covers the entire region, Powiśle 11, tel. 12-354-2710)

Other TI branches are in **Kazimierz** (daily 9:00-17:00, ulica Józefa 7, tel. 12-354-2728) and the **airport** (daily 9:00-19:00, tel. 12-285-5341).

Note that the TIs sell tickets *only* for one walking-tour company, See Kraków; for additional options, see "Tours in Kraków," later, and look around online.

Sightseeing Pass: The TI's **Kraków Tourist Card** includes admission to 40 city museums (basically everything except the Wawel Hill sights and Wieliczka Salt Mine)—but admissions are so cheap, it's unlikely you'd save money with the card. Given how walkable Kraków is, the version that does not include public transit (70 zł/3 days) is a better value for most people than the one that does (100 zł/2 days, 120 zł/3 days).

Warning: Many private travel agencies, room-booking services, and tour operators masquerade as TIs, with deceptive blue-and-white *i* signs. If I haven't listed them in this section, they're not a real TI.

Kraków City History Museum's Visitor Center: Tucked in the Cloth Hall (on the quiet western side) is a little information office operated by the Kraków City History Museum, where you can book tickets, without a line, for the popular Schindler's Factory Museum. If you anticipate crowds at the Schindler museum, drop by this office to book an entry time (daily 10:00-19:00, until 20:00 in summer, at #1).

ARRIVAL IN KRAKÓW
By Train

Kraków's main train station (called "Kraków Główny," KROCK-oof GWOHV-nee) sits just northeast of the Old Town, adjoining the sprawling Galeria Krakowska shopping mall. The station and the mall face a broad plaza (plac Dworcowy) across the ring road from the Planty park and Old Town. My recommended Old Town hotels are within about a 15-minute walk, or a quick tram or taxi ride. (If you're staying in the Old Town, the tram doesn't save you much time, but could cut down on how far you have to haul your bags. If you're staying in Kazimierz—a 30-minute walk away—the tram is definitely worthwhile.)

Whether you're arriving or departing, get oriented to the station's layout. The main concourse has all of the amenities: ATMs, lockers (under the big schedule board between the ticket windows), WCs, takeaway coffee, a handy Biedronka minisupermarket, and a shopping mall. From this area, five numbered escalators lead up to the corresponding train platforms. Tucked under these escalators, find a long row of numbered ticket windows (some for domestic tickets only, others for domestic and international—check signs before you line up; a few are marked with UK flags to denote English-speaking staff). In the middle of the row of ticket windows (between #11 and #12) is the PKP Passenger Service Center, which may have a longer wait but is more likely to have staff who speak English (no extra fee).

Getting Between the Station and Downtown: The easiest option is to take a **taxi** (they wait in the parking lot on the station's rooftop—go up the stairs or elevator from your platform). The usual metered rate to downtown is a reasonable 10-15 zł; only take a taxi marked with a company name and telephone number. You can also summon an **Uber,** which is often cheaper (for more on Uber, see "Getting Around Kraków," later).

If you prefer to walk or take a tram, you first must navigate the Galeria Krakowska shopping mall. Begin by following *Exit to the City* signs. Once inside the mall, continue straight ahead. To **walk,** follow *Old Town* signs, which eventually route you to the left. You'll pop out at a big plaza where you'll continue straight, taking the broad ramp down into a pedestrian underpass beneath the ring road. Emerging at the other side, bear right up the ramp into the Planty. The Main Market Square is straight ahead (you'll see the twin spires of St. Mary's Church).

If you'd rather take a **tram,** continue straight ahead through the mall, following signs to *Pawia street.* Emerging here, you'll see the Dworzec Główny Zachód tram stop. Buy a ticket from the machine and hop on tram #3 in the direction of Nowy Bieżanów. This tram stops at the eastern edge of the Old Town (Poczta Główna stop) before continuing to Kazimierz (Miodowa stop). (Note: Avoid the tram stop you'll see signposted inside the station—this is served only by trams that don't go anywhere near the Old Town or Kazimierz.)

There is a **shortcut** to avoid going through the sprawling and sometimes congested mall: The modern train station is attached to the old station (the yellow building facing the big plaza, now hosting art exhibitions) by a sidewalk under a green canopy. This can save you a little walking (and a lot of shopping temptations). It's tricky to find from inside the station: Go behind the Biedronka supermarket, near track 1, and exit toward Lubicz street. Walk up the ramp and follow the green canopy to the plaza.

To get **from town to the station** (or to the bus station behind it), head to the northeast corner of the Planty, take the underpass beneath the ring road, walk across the plaza and into the Galeria Krakowska mall, and once inside, follow signs to *Railway Station* and *Station Hall.*

By Bus

The bus station is directly behind the main train station. When arriving by bus, it's easiest to get into town by first heading into the train station, then continuing through it, following the above directions.

To get *to* the bus station from the Old Town (such as to catch a bus to Auschwitz), follow the directions above, then walk all the way through to the far end of the train station area (past platform 5, exit marked for *bus station*). Exiting the train station, escalate up to the bus terminal (marked *MDA Dworzec Autobusowy*). Inside are the standard amenities (lockers and WCs), domestic and international ticket windows, and an electronic board showing the next several departures. Some bus departures, marked on the board with a *G*, leave from the upper *(gorna)* stalls, which you can see out the window. Other bus departures, marked with a *D*, leave from the lower *(dolna)* stalls; to find these, use the stairs or the elevator right in the middle of the bus terminal. Note that some minibuses, such as those to Auschwitz, also leave from, or near, this station (though the buses and minibuses that go to the Wieliczka Salt Mine leave from nearby streets—see page 105).

By Car

Centrum signs lead you into the Old Town—you'll know you're there when you hit the ring road that surrounds the Planty park. Parking garages surround the Old Town. Your hotelier can advise you on directions and parking.

By Plane

The modern **John Paul II Kraków-Balice Airport** is about 10 miles west of the center (airport code: KRK, airport info: tel. 12-295-5800, www.krakowairport.pl). The easiest way downtown is to hop on the slick and speedy **train** (follow signs to the platform across the street from the arrivals area, 8 zł, buy ticket from machine or from conductor on board, 2/hour, 18 minutes to Kraków's main train station—see arrival instructions earlier, under "By Train"). Alternatively, **public bus** #208 or (at night) #902 leaves from right in front of the arrivals area (*Kolej do Centrum* signs, 4 zł, goes to main bus station—see arrival instructions earlier, under "By Bus," 50-minute trip depending on traffic). There's also a **taxi** stand in front of the terminal (ask about the fare up front—rates vary, but official cabs should not exceed 90 zł, more expensive at night, about 30 minutes). You can also request an Uber, or arrange a taxi transfer in advance (such as with recommended driver Andrew Durman, listed later, under "Tours in Kraków").

Many budget flights—including those on Wizz Air and Ryanair—use the **International Airport Katowice in Pyrzowice**

(Międzynarodowy Port Lotniczy Katowice w Pyrzowicach, airport code: KTW, www.katowice-airport.com). This airport is about 18 miles from the city of Katowice, which is about 50 miles west of Kraków. Direct buses run sporadically between Katowice Airport and Kraków's main train station area (50 zł, trip takes 1.75 hours, generally scheduled to meet incoming flights). You can also take the bus from Katowice Airport to Katowice's train station (hourly, 50 minutes), then take the train to Kraków (hourly, 1.5 hours). Wizz Air's website is useful for figuring out your connection: www.wizzair.com.

HELPFUL HINTS

Exchange Rate: 1 złoty (zł, or PLN) = about 25 cents; 4 zł = about $1.

Country Calling Code: 48 (see page 302 for dialing instructions)

Sightseeing Schedules: Some sights are closed on Monday (including the Gallery of 19th-Century Polish Art, Szołayski House, and a few museums in Kazimierz), but many sights are open (including the churches and Jagiellonian University Museum, and in Kazimierz, all of the Jewish-themed sights). On Saturday, most of Kazimierz's Jewish-themed sights are closed. Before heading out, check the "Kraków at a Glance" sidebar on page 36. Also be aware of days that certain sights are free: On Sunday, the National Museum branches (including the Gallery of 19th-Century Polish Art in the Cloth Hall) are free, but some are open limited hours. And on Monday, Schindler's Factory Museum is free (and especially crowded), as are two of the sights at Wawel Castle (but open only in the morning April-Oct).

Post Office: The main post office (Poczta Główna) is at the intersection of Starowiślna and the Westerplatte ring road, a few blocks east of the Main Market Square (Mon-Fri 8:30-20:30, Sat 8:00-15:00, closed Sun). In summer, look for a kitschy postal wagon on the Main Market Square, where you can mail postcards.

Bookstore: For an impressive selection of new and used English books, try **Massolit Books,** just west of the Old Town. They also have a café with drinks and light snacks, and a good children's section (Sun-Thu 10:00-20:00, Fri-Sat 10:00-21:00, ulica Felicjanek 4, tel. 12-432-4150, www.massolit.com).

Laundry: Frania Café, halfway between the Old Town and Kazimierz, is an inviting café/pub with ample washers and dryers, relaxing ambience, free Wi-Fi, a full bar serving espresso drinks and laundry-themed hard drinks, long hours, and a friendly staff (21 zł/load self-service, 29 zł for them to do it for you in 2-3 hours—consider dropping it off on your way to

Kazimierz and picking it up on the way back, likely open daily 10:30-24:00, ulica Starowiślna 26, mobile 783-945-021).

Betty Clean is a full-service laundry that's slightly closer to the Old Town, but pricey (about 13 zł/shirt, 22 zł/pants, takes 24 hours, 50 percent more for express 3-hour service, Mon-Fri 7:30-19:30, Sat 8:00-15:30, closed Sun, just outside the Planty park at ulica Zwierzyniecka 6, tel. 12-423-0848).

GETTING AROUND KRAKÓW

Kraków's top sights and best hotels are easily accessible by foot. You'll need wheels only if you're going to outlying areas (Kazimierz, Nowa Huta, John Paul II pilgrimage sights, and so on).

By Public Transit

Trams and buses zip around Kraków's urban sprawl. The same tickets work system-wide and can be purchased at most kiosks, or at the machines you'll see at most stops (these accept coins and small bills). You can also buy tickets on board—most trams have machines (coins only); otherwise, you'll buy your ticket from the driver and pay a bit more. For a good route planner, see www.jakdojade.pl.

A *bilet jednoprzejazdowy*, which covers any single journey (including transfers), costs 3.80 zł. However, many journeys you're likely to take—such as between the Old Town and Kazimierz—are likely to be brief, so you'll save a bit by buying a 20-minute ticket *(20-minutowy)* for 2.80 zł. You can also get longer-term tickets for 24 hours (15 zł), 48 hours (24 zł), and 72 hours (36 zł)—though unless your accommodations are a tram ride away from the sights, you're unlikely to need these. These prices are for a "one-zone" ticket, which covers almost everything of interest in Kraków (including Nowa Huta, the St. John Paul II pilgrimage sights, and the Kościuszko Mound)—unless you're headed for the airport or Wieliczka Salt Mine, which are beyond the city limits and require a slightly more expensive *aglomeracyjny* ticket (4 zł for a single journey). Always validate your ticket when you board the bus or tram (24-, 48-, and 72-hour tickets must be validated only the first time you use them).

Tram #3 is particularly handy. It goes from the side of the train station (Dworzec Główny Zachód) to the ring road in front of the station (Dworzec Główny), then stops at the eastern edge of the Old Town (Poczta Główna, at the main post office) before continuing to Kazimierz (Miodowa is at the north end, near ulica Szeroka; Św. Wawrzyńca is at the south end, near the old tram depot) and Podgórze, near Schindler's Factory Museum (plac Bohaterow Getta). **Tram #24** is also handy: It stops at the western edge of the Old Town (Teatr Bagately), then loops around the northern edge to stop near the Barbican (Stary Kleparz) before meeting up with tram #3 in front of the train station (Dworzec Główny) and continuing on to Kazimierz and Podgórze (same stops as listed above).

By Taxi or Uber

Only take cabs that are clearly marked with a company logo and telephone number. Kraków taxis start at 7 zł and charge about 3 zł per kilometer. Rides generally cost less than 20 zł, but can take longer than you'd expect: Due to the Old Town's many traffic restrictions and pedestrian zones, a "short ride across town" may require looping all the way around the ring road. You're more likely to get the fair metered rate by calling or hailing a cab, rather than taking one waiting at tourist spots. To call a cab, try **Radio Taxi** (tel. 19191).

If you're comfortable using **Uber** back home, try it here. As in the US, Uber is typically cheaper than official taxis (though prices can spike during busy "surge" periods). In my experience, Polish Uber drivers (and their cars) are a bit less polished and professional than back home—but they're cheap. When requesting a ride on your app, you can choose between the basic UberPop and the more professional UberSelect for a few zlotys more.

By Bike

The riverfront bike path is enticing on a nice day; the Planty park, while inviting, can be a bit crowded for biking. **Kraków Bike Tours** rents a wide variety of new, good-quality bikes (10 zł/first hour, cheaper per hour for longer rentals, 50 zł/day, 60 zł/24 hours, daily 9:00-19:00, until 20:00 in summer, just off the Square at Grodzka 2; see listing later, under "Tours in Kraków"). Nearby, **KRK Bike Rental** rents basic, cheaper bikes (9 zł/hour, 50 zł/24 hours, April-Oct daily 9:00-21:00, less in bad weather, closed Nov-March, ulica Św. Anny 4, mobile 509-267-733, www.krkbikerental.pl).

Tours in Kraków

Local Guides

Hiring a guide in Kraków is fun and affordable, and makes a huge difference in your experience. I've enjoyed working with three in particular, any of whom can show you the sights in Kraków and also have cars for day-tripping into the countryside: **Tomasz Klimek** (350 zł/half-day, 500 zł/day, slightly more with a car, mobile 605-231-923, tomasz.klimek@interia.pl); **Marta Chmielowska** (350 zł/4 hours, 500 zł/day, same prices by foot or car, can be more for larger groups and for long-distance trips, mobile 603-668-008, martachm7@gmail.com); and **Anna Bakowska** (same prices as Marta, mobile 604-151-293, www.leadertour.eu, leadertour@wp.pl). I wouldn't bother hiring a guide for the trip to Auschwitz (which generally costs 600-700 zł)—only official Auschwitz guides can legally give tours onsite, so you'll wind up joining one of the tours once there; instead, it's a better value to hire a driver (like Andrew, listed next).

Drivers

Since Kraków is such a useful home base for day trips, it can be handy to splurge on a private driver for door-to-door service. **Andrew (Andrzej) Durman,** a Pole who lived in Chicago and speaks fluent English, is a gregarious driver, translator, miracle worker, and all-around great guy. While not an officially licensed tour guide, Andrew is an eager conversationalist and loves to provide lively commentary while you roll. Although you can hire Andrew for a simple airport transfer or an Auschwitz day trip, he also enjoys tackling more ambitious itineraries, from helping you track down your Polish roots to taking you on multiple-day journeys around Poland and beyond (prices are for up to 4 people if you book directly: 400 zł to Auschwitz, 250 zł to Wieliczka Salt Mine, 80 zł for transfer from Kraków-Balice Airport, 500 zł for transfer from Katowice Airport, 600 zł for an all-day trip into the countryside—such as into the High Tatras or to track down your Polish roots near Kraków, more to cover gas costs for trips longer than 100 km one-way; long-distance transfers for up to 4 people to Prague, Budapest, Vienna, or Berlin for 1,800 zł—or 200 zł extra if he picks you up there; also available for multiday trips—price negotiable, all prices higher for bigger van, tel. 12-411-5630, mobile 602-243-306, www.tour-service.pl, andrew@tour-service.pl). If he's busy, Andrew may send you with one of his English-speaking colleagues, Bartek or Matthew.

Local guide Marta Chmielowska's husband, **Czesław** (a.k.a. Chester), can also drive you to nearby locations (300 zł for all-day trip to Auschwitz for 1-2 people, 350 zł for 3-8 people; 220 zł to Wieliczka Salt Mine, including waiting time, or a very long day combining Wieliczka and Auschwitz for 550 zł; 1,700 zł for a transfer to Prague; to book, see Marta's contact information, earlier).

Walking Tours

Various companies run daily city walking tours in English in summer. Most do a three-hour tour of the Old Town as well as a three-hour tour of Kazimierz, the Jewish district (most charge about 50 zł per tour, depending on company). Three people can hire their own great local guide for about the same amount of money. Because the scene is continually evolving, it's best to pick up local fliers (the TI works exclusively with one company, See Kraków, but hotel reception desks generally have more options), then choose the one that fits your interests and schedule. You'll also see ads for

KRAKÓW

Kraków at a Glance

▲▲▲**Main Market Square** Stunning heart of Kraków and a people magnet any time of day. **Hours:** Always open. See page 45.

▲▲▲**Schindler's Factory Museum** Historic building where Oskar Schindler saved more than 1,000 Jewish workers, now filled with engaging exhibit about Kraków's WWII experience. **Hours:** April-Oct Mon 10:00-16:00 (closes at 14:00 first Mon of month), Tue-Sun 9:00-20:00; Nov-March Mon 10:00-14:00, Tue-Sun 10:00-18:00. See page 94.

▲▲**Planty** Once a moat, now a scenic park encircling the city. **Hours:** Always open. See page 40.

▲▲**St. Mary's Church** Landmark church with extraordinary wood-carved Gothic altarpiece. **Hours:** Mon-Sat 11:15-17:45, Sun 14:00-17:45. See page 43.

▲▲**Cloth Hall** Fourteenth-century market hall with 21st-century souvenirs. **Hours:** Summer Mon-Fri 9:00-18:00, Sat-Sun 9:00-15:00, sometimes later; winter Mon-Fri 9:00-16:00, Sat-Sun 9:00-15:00. See page 48.

▲▲**St. Francis Basilica** Lovely Gothic church with some of Poland's best Art Nouveau. **Hours:** Daily 6:00-19:45. See page 51.

▲▲**Wawel Cathedral** Poland's splendid national church, with tons of tombs, a crypt, and a climbable tower. **Hours:** April-Sept Mon-Sat 9:00-17:00, Sun 12:30-17:00; Oct-March daily until 16:00. See page 58.

▲▲**Wawel Castle Grounds** Historic hilltop with views, castle, cathedral, courtyard with chakras, and a passel of museums. **Hours:** Grounds open daily 6:00 until dusk, but many of the museums closed Mon, and Sun in winter. See page 62.

▲▲**Gallery of 19th-Century Polish Art** Worthwhile collection of paintings by should-be-famous artists, upstairs in the Cloth Hall. **Hours:** Tue-Sun 10:00-18:00, closed Mon. See page 69.

"free" tours—which are, of course, not really free (the guide gets paid only if you tip generously).

Food Tours

In this stealth-foodie city, you have multiple good options. **Eat Polska**—which does a marvelous job of connecting food to culture and history, making the experience equal parts informative and

▲▲**Rynek Underground Museum** Super-modern exhibit on medieval Kraków filling excavated cellars beneath the Main Market Square. **Hours:** Mon 10:00-20:00 (closed second Mon of each month), Tue 10:00-16:00, Wed-Sun 10:00-22:00, shorter hours in winter. See page 76.

▲▲**Old Jewish Cemetery** Poignant burial site in Kazimierz, with graves from 1552 to 1800. **Hours:** Sun-Fri 9:00-16:00, sometimes until 18:00 May-Sept, closes earlier in winter and by sundown on Fri, closed Sat. See page 83.

▲**Czartoryski Museum** Varied collection, with European paintings and Polish armor, handicrafts, and decorative arts. **Hours:** Likely closed for restoration, otherwise Tue-Sun 10:00-16:00, closed Mon. See page 74.

▲**Jagiellonian University Museum Collegium Maius** Proud collection of historic university, surrounding a tranquil courtyard where medieval professors lived. **Hours:** Entry by guided tour; 30-minute version—Mon-Fri 10:00-14:20, Sat 10:00-13:20, until 17:20 Tue and Thu in April-Oct, no tours Sun; one-hour version in English—usually Mon-Fri at 13:00, no tours Sat-Sun. See page 77.

▲**New Jewish Cemetery** Graveyard with tombs from after 1800, partly restored after Nazi desecration. **Hours:** Sun-Fri 8:00-18:00, winter until 16:00, closed Sat. See page 91.

▲**Ethnographic Museum** Traditional rural Polish life on display. **Hours:** Tue-Sun 10:00-19:00, closed Mon. See page 89.

▲**Pharmacy Under the Eagle** Small Podgórze exhibit about the Holocaust in Kraków, including three evocative historic films. **Hours:** Mon 10:00-14:00, Tue-Sun 9:00-17:00; closed the second Tue of each month. See page 93.

▲**Museum of Contemporary Art in Kraków** Today's thought-provoking art, displayed in renovated old warehouses behind Schindler's Factory Museum. **Hours:** Tue-Sun 11:00-19:00, closed Mon. See page 99.

delicious—does top-notch, insightful food tours (at 13:00, 290 zł, 4 hours) and vodka tours with food pairings (at 17:00, 260 zł, 3.5 hours; for details on either, see www.eatpolska.com). **Urban Adventures,** a bit more casual, does evening food walks that basically assemble a full meal with a little sightseeing thrown in (at 18:00, 310 zł, 3 hours, www.urbanadventures.com).

Crazy Guides

This irreverent company offers tours to the communist suburb of Nowa Huta and other outlying sights. For details, see page 107.

Bike and Segway Tours

Kraków Bike Tours is a well-established operation that runs daily four-hour bike tours in English, with 25 stops in the Old Town, Kazimierz, and Podgórze (90 zł, May-Sept daily at 10:00 and 15:00, spring and fall only 1/day at 12:00, confirm schedule and meet tour at their office down the passage at Grodzka 2—right at the bottom of the Square, mobile 510-394-657, www.krakowbiketour.com). They also offer Segway tours.

Bus Tours to Auschwitz or Wieliczka

As Kraków is so easily enjoyed on foot, taking a bus tour doesn't make much sense in town. But they can be handy for reaching outlying sights. Various tour companies run big-bus itineraries to Auschwitz (6 hours), Wieliczka Salt Mine (4 hours), and other regional side-trips (each itinerary around 120-180 zł).

Given the difficulty of reserving your own appointment at Auschwitz (explained in the next chapter), one of these bus tours—which include a guided tour of the camp—may be your most convenient option. **See Kraków** (which has a monopoly at the TI, www.seekrakow.com) and **Discover Cracow** (www.discovercracow.com) both use smaller 19-seat minibuses. They sometimes offer hotel pick-up, which seems convenient, but you'll waste a lot of time driving around the city to other hotels. **Cracow City Tours** (www.cracowcitytours.com) uses larger 50-seat buses with a central pick-up point (on plac Matejki, across the ring road from the Barbican, at the north end of the Old Town).

At any company, the on-bus guiding is hit-or-miss but largely irrelevant anyway—since you'll be handed off to an official Auschwitz guide once at the camp. Note that the many tour offices and faux-TIs you'll see around town simply sell tickets for these companies. If you waited too long to reserve at Auschwitz and are desperate to get in at short notice, try dropping in to various agencies around town to see if any of these outfits has space.

Buggy Tours

You'll see (and hear) horse-drawn buggies that trot around Kraków from the Main Market Square. The going rate is a hefty 100 zł for a 30-minute tour. After dark, they're all lit up like fanciful Cinderella coaches—a memorable scene, all lined up in front of St. Mary's Church.

Golf-Cart Tours

Several outfits around town (including on the Square) offer tours on a golf cart with recorded commentary. Given the limits on car traffic in the old center, this can be a handy way to connect the sights for those with limited mobility. Generally you'll pay about 160 zł for a 45-minute tour around the Old Town; to extend the trip to Kazimierz, it's 300 zł; and adding the Podgórze former Jewish ghetto and Schindler's Factory Museum costs a total of 380 zł (these prices are for the entire golf cart, up to 5 people). Some outfits also do point-to-point transfers within town for 50 zł.

Tour Packages for Students
Andy Steves (Rick's son) runs Weekend Student Adventures (WSA Europe), offering 3-day and 10-day budget travel packages across Europe including accommodations, skip-the-line sightseeing, and unique local experiences. Locally guided and DIY unguided options are available for student and budget travelers in 12 of Europe's most popular cities, including Kraków (guided trips from €199, see www.wsaeurope.com for details).

Kraków's Royal Way Walk

Most of Kraków's major sights are conveniently connected by this self-guided walk. This route is known as the "Royal Way" because the king used to follow this same path when he returned to Kraków after a journey. After the capital moved to Warsaw, most kings still used Wawel Cathedral for important events. In fact, from 1320 to 1795, nearly every Polish king traversed Kraków's Royal Way at least twice: on the day he was crowned and on the day he was buried. You could sprint through this walk in about an hour and a half (less than a mile altogether), but it's much more fun if you take it like the kings did...slowly.

• *Begin just outside the main gate (the Florian Gate) at the north end of the Old Town.*

▲Barbican (Barbakan) and City Walls

Tatars—those mysterious and terrifying invaders from Central

Asia—destroyed Kraków in 1241. To better defend their city, Krakovians built this wall. The original rampart had 47 watchtowers and eight gates. (You can see a bronze model of the wall just to the right of the tower.)

The big, round defensive fort standing outside the wall is the **Barbican**—built to provide extra fortification to weak sections—namely, the gates. Imagine how it looked in 1500, when the Barbican stood outside the town moat with a long bridge leading to the Florian Gate—the city's main entryway. Today you can pay to scramble along the passages and fortifications of the Barbican, though there's little to see inside, other than a small but good exhibit giving you a sense of how the walls were designed (8 zł, April-Oct daily 10:30-18:00, closed Nov-March). The same ticket also lets you climb up onto the surviving stretch of Old Town walls flanking the Florian Gate (entry from inside walls).

• *The greenbelt in which the Barbican sits is called the...*

▲▲Planty

By the 19th century, Kraków's no-longer-necessary city wall had fallen into disrepair. As the Austrian authorities were doing all over their empire, they decided to tear down what remained, fill in the moat, and plant trees. (The name comes not from the English "plant," but from the Polish *plantovac,* or "flat"—because they flattened out this area to create it.) Today, the Planty is a beautiful park that stretches 2.5 miles around the entire perimeter of

Kraków's Old Town. To give your Kraków visit an extra dimension, consider a quick bike ride around the Planty (best early in the morning, when it's less crowded) with a side-trip along the parklike riverbank near Wawel Castle; you'll see bike-rental places around the Old Town, including the two mentioned on page 34.

Circle around the left side of the Barbican. On your left, keep an eye out for a unique monument depicting an elderly, bearded man in the corner of a huge frame. This honors **Jan Matejko,** arguably Poland's most beloved painter, who specialized in giant-scale epic historical scenes that would easily fill this frame. We'll hear Matejko's name several more times on this walk.

As you continue around the Barbican, look down to see the much lower ground level around its base—making it easy to imagine that the Planty was once anything but flat.

• *Across the busy street from the Barbican, standing in the middle of the long park, is the...*

Grunwald Monument

This memorial honors one of the most important battles in the history of a nation that has seen more than its share: the Battle of Grunwald on July 15, 1410, when Polish and Lithuanian forces banded together to finally defeat the Teutonic Knights, who had been running roughshod over the lands along the Baltic. (For more on the battle and the knights, see page 290.) Lying dramatically slain at the base of this monument, like a toppled Goliath, is the defeated Grand Master of the Teutonic Knights—German crusaders who had originally been brought to Poland as mercenaries. It's easy to see this vanquished statue as a thinly veiled metaphor for one of Poland's powerful, often domineering neighbors that the Poles stood up to—and defeated. When the Nazis took power here, this statue was one of the first things they tore down. When they left, it was one of the first things the Poles put back up.

• *If you'd like to see a slice of Krakovian life, side-trip one block to the left of the monument, to the local farmers market.*

The Old Market (Stary Kleparz)

The colorful Old Market offers a refreshing dash of today's Kraków that has nothing to do with history or tourism. It's just lots of hardscrabble people selling what they grow or knit, and lots of others buying. Wander around as if on a cultural scavenger hunt. Find the freshest doughnuts *(pączki),* the most popular bakery, the villager selling slippers she knitted, and the old man with the smoked cheese (Mon-Sat 7:00-18:00—but busiest and most interesting in the morning, closed Sun).

• *Now retrace your steps to the Barbican, and enter the Old Town by walking through the...*

Florian Gate (Brama Floriańska)

As you approach the gate, look up at the **crowned white eagle**—representing courage and freedom—the historic symbol of the Polish people.

Inside the gate, notice the little chapel on the right with a replica of the famous **Black Madonna of Częstochowa,** probably the most important religious symbol among Polish Catholics. The original, located in Częstochowa (70 miles north of Kraków), is an

Eastern Orthodox-style icon of mysterious origin with several mystical legends attached to it. After the icon's believed role in protecting a monastery from Swedish invaders in the mid-17th century, it was named "Queen and Protector of Poland."

Once through the gate, look back at it. High above is **St. Florian,** patron of the fire brigade. As fire was a big concern for a wooden city of the 15th century, Florian gets a place of honor.

You'll often see traditionally clad **musicians** near the gate, performing their lilting folk melodies for tips.

• *You're standing at the head of Kraków's historic (and now touristic) gamut...*

▲Floriańska Street (Ulica Floriańska)

Hanging on the inside of the city wall in both directions is a make-shift **art gallery,** where—traditionally—starving students hawk

the works they've painted at the Academy of Fine Arts (across the busy street from the Barbican). These days, the art is so kitschy, this stretch of the town's fortification is nicknamed "The Wailing Wall." The entrance to get on top of the wall—covered by the Barbican ticket—is at the end of this starving artists' gallery. If you detoured even farther along the wall, soon you'd reach the eclectic Czartoryski Museum, home to a rare Leonardo da Vinci oil painting (see page 74).

Now begin strolling down **Floriańska street** (floh-ree-AHN-skah). Notice that all over town, storefronts advertising themselves as "tourist information" offices are actually tourist sales agencies (legitimate TIs are listed on page 28). And money-exchange counters can be thieves with an address. (Do the arithmetic—the buying and selling rates should be within 6 percent or so, and there should be no fee.) Along with the fast-food joints, also notice some uniquely Polish snacks: The various pizza and kebab windows also sell *zapiekanki*—a toasted baguette with toppings, similar to a French bread pizza. Or, for an even quicker bite, buy an *obwarzanek* (ring-shaped, bagel-like roll, typically fresh) from a street vendor; many still use their old-fashioned blue carts.

About halfway down the first block, on the left (at #45, round green sign), look for **Jama Michalika** ("Michael's Cave"). This

dark, atmospheric café, popular with locals for its coffee and pastries, began in 1895 as a simple bakery in a claustrophobic back room. Around the turn of the 20th century, this was a hangout of the Młoda Polska (Young Poland) movement—the Polish answer to Art Nouveau (explained on page 47). The walls are papered with sketches from poor

artists—local bohemians who couldn't pay their tabs. In 1915, this was home to the first Polish cabaret. Today that stage is used by a folk troupe that performs traditional music and dance with dinner many evenings (pick up the flier; also see listing under "Entertainment in Kraków," page 116). Poke around inside this circa-1900 time warp and appreciate this unique art gallery. Consider having coffee and dessert here, or a cigar in the charming smokers' bar in front.

About a block farther down, at #20 (on the right), **Staropolskie Trunki** ("Old Polish Drinks") offers an education in vodka—with as much tasting as you'd like. It's a friendly little place with a long bar and countless local vodkas and liquors—all open and ready to be tasted. Best of all, there's a cheery local barista to talk you through the experience (four tastes for 10 zł with a fun explanation that amounts to a private tour, buy a bottle and the tastes are free, daily 10:00-24:00).

• *Continue into the Main Market Square, where you'll run into...*

▲▲St. Mary's Church (Kościół Mariacki)

A church has stood on this spot for 800 years. The original church was destroyed by the first Tatar invasion in 1241, but all subsequent versions—including the current one—have been built on the same foundation. You can look down the sides to see how the Main Market Square has risen about seven feet over the centuries.

How many church towers does St. Mary's have? Technically, the answer is one. The shorter tower belongs to the church; the taller one is a municipal watchtower, from which you'll hear a bugler playing the hourly *hejnał* song. According to Kraków's favorite legend, during that first Tatar invasion, a town watchman saw the enemy approaching and sounded the alarm. Before he could finish the tune, an arrow pierced his throat—which is why, even today, the *hejnał* stops suddenly partway through. Today's buglers—12 in all—are firemen first, musicians second. Each one works a 24-hour shift up there, playing the *hejnał* four times on the hour—with one bugle call for each direction. (It's even broadcast on national Polish radio at noon.) While you're in Kraków, you'll certainly hear one of these tiny, hourly, broken performances.

To see one of the most finely crafted Gothic altarpieces anywhere, it's worth paying admission to enter the church. The front door is open 14 hours a day and is free to those who come to pray, but tourists use the door around the right side (buy your ticket across the little square from this door).

KRAKÓW

Cost and Hours: 10 zł, Mon-Sat 11:15-17:45, Sun 14:00-17:45 (these are last-entry times). The famous wooden altarpiece is open between noon and 18:00; try to be here by 11:50 for the ceremonial opening (Mon-Sat) or at 18:00 for the closing (except on Sat, when it's left open for the service on Sun).

Visiting the Church: Inside, you're struck by the lavish decor. This was the church of the everyday townspeople, built out of a spirit of competition with the royal high church at Wawel Castle. At the altar is one of the best medieval woodcarvings in existence—the exquisite, three-part **altarpiece** by German Veit Stoss (Wit Stwosz in Polish). Carved in 12 years and completed in 1489, it's packed with emotion rare in Gothic art. Get as close as you can and study the remarkable details. Stoss used oak for the structural parts and linden trunks for the figures. When the altar doors are closed, you see scenes from the lives of Mary and Jesus. The open altar depicts the Dormition (death—or, if splitting theological hairs, heavenly sleep) of the Virgin. The artist catches the apostles around Mary, reacting in the seconds after she collapses. Mary is depicted in three stages: life leaving her earthly body, being escorted to heaven by Jesus, and (at the very top) being crowned in heaven. The six scenes on the sides are the Annunciation, birth of Jesus, visit by the Three Magi, Jesus' Resurrection, his Ascension, and Mary becoming the mother of the apostles at Pentecost.

There's more to St. Mary's than the altar. While you're admiring this church's art, notice the flowery Neo-Gothic painting covering the choir walls. Stare up into the starry, starry blue ceiling. As you wander around, consider that the church was renovated a century ago by three Polish geniuses from two very different artistic generations: the venerable positivist Jan Matejko and his Art Nouveau students, Stanisław Wyspiański and Józef Mehoffer (we'll learn more about these two later on our walk). The huge silver bird under the organ loft in back is that symbol of Poland, the crowned white eagle.

Tower Climb: You may be able to climb up the 239 stairs to the top of the taller tower to visit the *hejnał* fireman. While it's a huff—with some claustrophobic stone stairs, followed by some steep, acrophobic wooden ones—the view up top is the best you'll find of the Square (15 zł, pay at the ticket office for the church, departs at :10 and :40 past each hour, April-Oct Mon-Sat 9:30-11:10 & 13:10-17:40, closed Sun, usually closed Nov-March).

Kazimierz the Great (1333-1370)

Out of the many centuries of Polish kings, only one earned the nickname "great," and he's the only one worth remembering: Kazimierz the Great.

K. the G., who ruled Poland from Kraków in the 14th century, was one of those larger-than-life medieval kings who left his mark on all fronts—from war to diplomacy, art patronage to womanizing. His scribes bragged that Kazimierz "found a Poland made of wood, and left one made of brick and stone." He put Kraków on the map as a major European capital. He founded many villages (some of which still bear his name—including one that's an important neighborhood of Kraków) and replaced wooden structures with stone ones (such as Kraków's Cloth Hall). Kazimierz also established the Kraków Academy (today's Jagiellonian University), the second-oldest university in Central Europe. And to protect all these new building projects, he heavily fortified Poland by building a series of imposing forts and walls around its perimeter. If you have a 50-zł note, take a look at it: That's Kazimierz the Great on the front, and on the back you'll see his capital, Cracovia, and the most important town he founded, Casmirus.

Most of all, Kazimierz is remembered as a progressive, tolerant king. In the 14th century, other nations were deporting—or even interning—their Jewish subjects, who were commonly scapegoated for anything that went wrong. But the enlightened Kazimierz created policies that granted Jews more opportunities (often related to banking and trade) and allowed them a chance for higher social standing—establishing the country as a safe haven for Jews in Europe.

Kazimierz the Great was the last of Poland's long-lived Piast dynasty. Although he left no male heir—at least, no legitimate one—Kazimierz's advances set the stage for Poland's Golden Age (14th-16th centuries). After his death, Poland united with Lithuania (against the common threat of the Teutonic Knights), the Jagiellonian dynasty was born, and Poland became one of Europe's mightiest medieval powers.

• *Leaving the church, notice the neck clamps dangling from the exterior walls near the side door. If you were leaving Mass in centuries past, there would be locals chained here for public humiliation. You'd spit on them before turning right and stepping into one of the biggest market squares anywhere.*

▲▲▲Main Market Square (Rynek Główny), a.k.a. "The Square"

Kraków's marvelous Square, one of Europe's most gasp-worthy public spaces, bustles with street musicians, colorful flower stalls, cotton-candy vendors, loitering teenagers, the local breakdancing troupe, businesspeople commuting by foot, gawking tourists, soap-balloon-blowers, and the lusty coos of pigeons. The Square is where Kraków lives. It's often filled with various special events, markets, and festivals. The biggest are the seasonal markets before Easter and Christmas, but you're likely to stumble on something special going on just about any time of year (especially June through Aug).

The Square was established in the 13th century, when the city had to be rebuilt after being flattened by the Tatars. At the time, it

was the biggest square in medieval Europe. It was illegal to sell anything on the street, so everything had to be sold here on the Main Market Square. It was divided into smaller markets, such as the butcher stalls, the ironworkers' tents, and the still-standing Cloth Hall (described later).

Notice the modern **fountain** with the glass pyramid at this end of the Square. A major excavation of the surrounding area created a museum of Kraków's medieval history that literally sprawls beneath the Square (for more on the recommended **Rynek Underground Museum,** see page 76).

The statue in the middle of the Square is a traditional meeting place for Krakovians. It depicts Romantic poet **Adam Mickiewicz** (1789-1855), who's considered the "Polish Shakespeare." His epic masterpiece, *Pan Tadeusz,* is still regarded as one of the greatest works in Polish literature. A wistful, nostalgic tale of Polish-Lithuanian nobility, *Pan Tadeusz* stirred patriotism in a Poland that had been dismantled by surrounding empires.

If you survey the Square from here, you'll notice that the Old Town was spared the bombs of World War II. The Nazis considered Kraków a city with Germanic roots and wanted it saved. But they were quick to destroy any symbols of Polish culture or pride. The statue of Adam Mickiewicz, for example, was pulled down immediately after occupation.

Near the end of the Square, you'll see the tiny, cubical, copper-domed **Church of St. Adalbert,** one of the oldest churches in Kraków (10th century). This Romanesque structure predates the Square. Like St. Mary's (described earlier), it seems to be at an angle because it's aligned east-west, as was the custom when it was built. (In other words, the churches aren't crooked—the Square is. Any other "crooked" building you see around town predates the 13th-century grid created during the rebuilding of Kraków.)

Drinks are reasonably priced at cafés on the Square (most around 10-15 zł). Find a spot where you like the view and the chairs, then sit and sip. Order a coffee, Polish *piwo* (beer, such

The Młoda Polska (Young Poland) Art Movement

Polish art in the late 19th century was ruled by positivism, a school with a very literal, straightforward focus on Polish his-

tory (Jan Matejko led the charge; see page 190). But when the new generation of Kraków's artists came into their own in the early 1900s, they decided that the old school was exactly that. Though moved by the same spirit and goals as the previous generation—evoking Polish patriotism at a time when their country was being occupied—these new artists used very different methods. They were inspired by a renewed appreciation of folklore and peasant life. Rather than being earnest and literal (an 18th-century Polish war hero on horseback), the new art was playful and highly symbolic (the artist frolicking in a magical garden in the idyllic Polish countryside). This movement became known as Młoda Polska (Young Poland)—Art Nouveau with a Polish accent.

Stanisław Wyspiański (vees-PAYN-skee, 1869-1907) was the leader of Młoda Polska. He produced beautiful artwork, from simple drawings to the stirring stained-glass images in Kraków's St. Francis Basilica. Wyspiański was an expert at capturing human faces with realistic detail, emotion, and personality. The versatile Wyspiański was also an accomplished stage designer and writer. His patriotic play *The Wedding*—about the nuptials of a big-city artist and a peasant girl—is regarded as one of Poland's finest dramas. You'll find excellent examples of Wyspiański's art in Kraków's St. Francis Basilica and Szołayski House, and in Warsaw's National Museum.

Józef Mehoffer (may-HOH-fehr), Wyspiański's good friend and rival, was another great Młoda Polska artist. Mehoffer's style is more expressionistic and abstract than Wyspiański's, often creating an otherworldly effect. See Mehoffer's work in Kraków's St. Francis Basilica and at the artist's former residence (see the Józef Mehoffer House, page 76); and in Warsaw, at the National Museum.

Other names to look for include Jacek Malczewski (mahl-CHEHV-skee), who specialized in self-portraits, and Olga Boznańska (bohz-NAHN-skah), the movement's only prominent female artist. Both are featured in Warsaw's National Museum; Malczewski's works also appear in Kraków's Gallery of 19th-Century Polish Art.

as Żywiec, Okocim, or Lech), or a shot of *wódka* (Żubrówka is a good brand; for more on Polish drinks, see page 17). For a higher vantage point, the Cloth Hall's **Café Szał terrace**—overlooking the Square and St. Mary's Church—offers one of the best views in town (open daily until 24:00, affordable drinks, some light meals, enter through Gallery of 19th-Century Polish Art entrance).

As the Square buzzes around you, imagine this place before 1989. There were no outdoor cafés, no touristy souvenir stands, and no salesmen hawking cotton candy or neon-lit whirligigs. The communist government shut down all but a handful of the businesses. They didn't want people to congregate here—they should be at home, resting, because "a rested worker is a productive worker." The buildings were covered with soot from the nearby Lenin Steelworks in Nowa Huta. The communists denied the pollution, and when the student "Green Brigades" staged a demonstration in this Square to raise awareness in the 1970s, they were immediately arrested. How things have changed.

• *The huge, yellow building right in the middle of the Square is the...*

▲▲Cloth Hall (Sukiennice)

In the Middle Ages, this was the place where cloth sellers had their market stalls. Kazimierz the Great turned the Cloth Hall into a permanent structure in the 14th century. In 1555, it burned down and was replaced by the current building. The crowned letter *S* (at the top of the gable above the entryway) stands for King Sigismund the Old, who com-

missioned this version of the hall. As Sigismund fancied all things Italian (including women—he married an Italian princess), this structure is in the Italianate Renaissance style. Sigismund kicked off a nationwide trend, and you'll still see Renaissance-style buildings like this one all over the country, making the style as typically Polish as it is typically Italian. We'll see more works by Sigismund's imported Italian architects at Wawel Castle.

The Cloth Hall is still a functioning market—selling mostly souvenirs, including wood carvings, chess sets, jewelry (especially amber), painted boxes, and trinkets (summer Mon-Fri 9:00-18:00, Sat-Sun 9:00-15:00, sometimes later; winter Mon-

Fri 9:00-16:00, Sat-Sun 9:00-15:00). Cloth Hall prices are slightly inflated, but still cheap by American standards. You're paying a little extra for the convenience and the atmosphere, but you'll see locals buying gifts here, too.

Pay WCs are at each end of the Cloth Hall. The upstairs of the Cloth Hall is home to the excellent **Gallery of 19th-Century Polish Art** (enter behind the statue of Adam; for a self-guided tour, see page 70).

• *Browse through the Cloth Hall passageway. As you emerge into the sleepier half of the Square, the big tower on your left is the...*

KRAKÓW

Town Hall Tower

This is all that remains of a town hall building from the 14th century—when Kraków was the powerful capital of Poland. After the 18th-century Partitions of Poland, Kraków's prominence took a nosedive. By the 19th century, Kraków was Nowheresville. As the town's importance crumbled, so did its town hall. It was cheaper to tear down the building than to repair it, and all that was left standing was this nearly 200-foot-tall tower. In summer, you can climb the tower, stopping along the way to poke around an exhibit on Kraków history, but the views from up top are disappointing. However, you can step into the entryway for a free look at a model of an earlier version of the building, with a fanciful, Prague-style, multispired tower.

Cost and Hours: 9 zł, free on Mon, open April-Oct daily 10:30-18:00, closed Nov-March.

Nearby: The **gigantic head** at the base of the Town Hall Tower is a sculpture by contemporary artist Igor Mitoraj, who studied here in Kraków. Typical of Mitoraj's works, the head is an empty shell that appears to be wrapped in cloth. While some locals enjoy having a work by their fellow Krakovian in such a prominent place, others disapprove of its sharp contrast with the Square's genteel Old World ambience. Tourists enjoy playing peek-a-boo with the head's eyes—a fun photo op.

• *When you're finished on the Square, we'll head toward Wawel Hill. The official Royal Way makes a beeline for the castle, but we'll take a scenic detour to see some less touristy back streets, visit Kraków's historic university and one of its best churches, and go for a quick walk through the Planty park.*

Exit the square at the corner nearest the Town Hall Tower, down ulica Św. Anny. After two short blocks, turn left onto Jagiellońska street. Enter the courtyard of the big, red-brick building on your right.

Jagiellonian University and the Collegium Maius

Kraków had the second university in Central Europe (founded in 1364, after Prague's). Over the centuries, Jagiellonian U. has

boasted such illustrious grads as Copernicus and St. John Paul II. And today, the city's character is still defined largely by its huge student population (numbering around 150,000). Many of the university buildings fill the area to the west of the Old Town, so you'll see more students (and fewer tourist traps) in this part of town than elsewhere.

This building—called the Collegium Maius—is the historic heart of Kraków's university culture. It dates from the 15th century. In the Middle Ages, professors were completely devoted to their scholarly pursuits. They were unmarried and lived, ate, and slept here in an almost monastic environment. They taught downstairs and lived upstairs. In many ways, this building feels more like a monastery than a university. While this courtyard is the most interesting part, you can also tour the interior (for details, see page 77).

The university also comes with some chilling history. On November 6, 1939, the occupying Nazis called all professors together for a meeting. With 183 gathered unknowingly in a hall, they were suddenly loaded into trucks and sent to their deaths in concentration camps. Hitler knew: If you want to decapitate a culture, you kill its intelligentsia.

Before you leave, if you're a fan of rich, thick hot chocolate, enjoy a cup at **Kawiarnia U Pęcherza** (down the stairs near the entrance)—widely regarded as the best in town.

Head down the *sgraffito*-lined passage on the side of the courtyard (it's the first door on your left as you entered the courtyard—just past the little security office). You'll emerge into the **Professors' Garden,** a tranquil space filled with red brick, ivy, stony statues, and inviting benches (open daily 9:00-18:30 or until dusk).

• *Exit the garden and turn right on Jagiellońska. Spot any students? You'll follow this for two more blocks, passing the much larger and newer, but still red-brick, **Collegium Novum** building—the modern administrative headquarters of Jag U., built in the late 19th century to commemorate the 500th anniversary of the building we just left.*

*Jagiellońska dead-ends at a dynamic statue on a pillar. Turn left into the inviting **Planty**—the ring park we saw at the start of this walk.*

You'll stroll about five minutes through the Planty, with the Old Town buildings on your left and the ring road through the park on your right. When you reach a street with tram tracks, cross it and turn left. Pause in the park just before the church, and take note of the light-yellow building on the left (across the street), with a picture of St. John Paul II smiling down from above the stone doorway.

Archbishop's Palace

This building was St. John Paul II's residence when he was the archbishop of Kraków. And even after he became Pope, it remained

his home-away-from-Rome for visits to his hometown. After a long day of saying formal Mass during his visits to Kraków, he'd wind up here. Weary as he was, before going to bed he'd stand in the window above the entrance for hours, chatting casually with the people assembled below—about religion, but also about sports, current events, and whatever was on their minds.

In 2005, when the Pope's health deteriorated, this street filled with his supporters, even though he was in Rome. For days, somber locals focused their vigil on this same window, their eyes fixed on a black crucifix that had been placed here. At 21:37 on the night of April 2, 2005, the Pope passed away in Rome. Ten thousand Krakovians were on this street, under this window, listening to a Mass broadcast on loudspeakers from the church. When the priest announced the Pope's death, every single person simultaneously fell to their knees in silence. For the next several days, thousands of the faithful continued to stand on this street, staring intently at the window where they last saw the man they considered to be the greatest Pole.

• *Now go through the back door of one of Kraków's finest churches…*

▲▲St. Francis Basilica (Bazylika Św. Franciszka)

This beautiful Gothic church, which was St. John Paul II's home church while he was archbishop of Kraków, features some of Po-

land's best Art Nouveau in situ (in the setting for which it was intended). After an 1850 fire, it was redecorated by the two leading members of the Młoda Polska (Young Poland) movement: Stanisław Wyspiański and Józef Mehoffer. The glorious decorations inside this church are the result of their great rivalry run amok.

Cost and Hours: Free, daily 6:00-19:45—but frequent services, so be discreet.

◑ Self-Guided Tour: Step through the door and let your eyes adjust to the low light. Take a few steps up the nave, pausing at the third pew on the left. Notice the **silver plate** labeled "Jan Paweł II"—marking JPII's favorite place to pray when he lived in the Archbishop's Palace across the street.

Now walk another 20 feet down the nave, and notice the painting on the right, with an orange-and-blue background. This depicts **St. Maksymilian Kolbe,** the Catholic priest who sacrificed his own life to save a fellow inmate at Auschwitz in 1941 (notice the *16670*—his concentration camp number—etched into the background; read his story on page 148). Kolbe is particularly beloved here, as he actually served at this church.

Now turn around and look up above the door you entered. There, in all its glory, is the stained-glass window titled *God the Father Let It Be*, created by the great Art Nouveau artist Stanisław Wyspiański—and regarded by some as his finest masterpiece. (For more on Wyspiański, see page 47.) The colors beneath the Creator change from yellows and oranges (fire) to soothing blues (water), depending on the light. Wyspiański was supposedly inspired by Michelangelo's vision of God in the Sistine Chapel, though he used a street beggar to model God's specific features. Wyspiański also painted the delightful floral stained-glass windows that line the nave, high up—fitting for a church dedicated to a saint so famous for his spiritual connection to nature.

Now turn back around to face the main altar, and head into the **chapel** on the left (marked *Całun Turyński*). This important chapel houses a replica of the Shroud of Turin—which, since it touched the original shroud, is also considered a holy relic. At the main altar in this chapel, notice the plaques honoring Michała Tomaszek and Zbigniew Strzałkowski. These two Polish priests traveled to Peru as missionaries. There, they (along with an Italian priest) were murdered by communist guerrillas calling themselves the Shining Path. Today they are considered martyrs. Nearby, look for photos of Pope Francis (who, like this church and these missionaries, is Franciscan) praying at this altar.

Before leaving this chapel, look high on the walls at the glorious Stations of the Cross. These are painted by **Józef Mehoffer**—a friend and rival of Wyspiański—as a response to Wyspiański's work.

Now head back into the nave, turn left, and walk toward the main altar. (If a service is going on, you may not be able to get very far—just look from here.) On the walls, notice Wyspiański's gorgeous Art Nouveau floral patterns.

Up in the apse, take a moment to appreciate the Wyspiański-designed **stained-glass windows** flanking the high altar. On the right is St. Francis, the church's namesake. On the left is the Blessed Salomea—a medieval Polish woman who became queen of Hungary, but later returned to Poland and entered a convent after her husband's death. Notice she's dropping a crown—repudiating the earthly world and giving herself over to the simple, stop-and-smell-God's-roses lifestyle of St. Francis. Salomea (who's buried in a side chapel) founded this church. Notice also the Mucha-like paintings by Wyspiański on the pilasters between the windows... yet one more sumptuous Art Nouveau detail in this church that's so rich with them.

• *Head back outside. If no services are going on, you can slip out the side door, to the left of the altar. Otherwise, head back out the way you came and hook right. Either way, you're heading to the right along Franciszkańska street. After passing a few monuments and a tram stop, turn right down busy...*

Grodzka Street

Now you're back on the Royal Way proper. At the corner of Grodzka street stands the modern, copper-colored **Wyspiański Pavilion.** Step inside (daily 9:00-17:00), past the little TI, to see three new stained-glass windows based on designs Wyspiański once submitted for a contest to redecorate Wawel Cathedral. Although these designs were rejected back then, they were finally realized on the hundredth anniversary of his death (in 2007). Visible from inside the building during the day, and gloriously illuminated to be seen outside the building at night, they represent three Polish historical figures: the gaunt St. Stanisław (Poland's first saint), the skeletal Kazimierz the Great (in the middle), and the swooning King Henry the Pious.

If you're not churched out, you can dip into the **Dominican Church**—just a block away, to your left (described on page 78).

Now continue down Grodzka street. This lively thoroughfare, connecting the Square with Wawel, is teeming with shops—and

KRAKÓW

Karol Wojtyła (1920-2005):
The Greatest Pole

The man who became St. John Paul II began his life as Karol Wojtyła, born to a humble family in the town of Wadowice near Kraków on May 18, 1920. Karol's mother died when he was a young boy. When he was a teenager, he moved with his father to Kraków to study philosophy and drama at Jagiellonian University. Young Karol was gregarious and athletic—an avid skier, hiker, swimmer, and soccer goalie. During the Nazi occupation in World War II, he was forced to work in a quarry. In defiance of the Nazis, he secretly studied theology and appeared in illegal underground theatrical productions. When the war ended, he resumed his studies, now at the theology faculty.

After graduating in 1947, Wojtyła swiftly rose through the ranks of the Catholic Church hierarchy. By 1964, he was archbishop of Kraków, and just three years later, he became the youngest cardinal ever. Throughout the 1960s, he fought an ongoing battle with the regime when they refused to allow the construction of a church in the Kraków suburb of Nowa Huta. After years of saying Mass for huge crowds in open fields, Wojtyła finally convinced the communists to allow the construction of the Lord's Ark Church in 1977. A year later, Karol Wojtyła was called to the papacy—the first non-Italian pope in more than four centuries. In 1979, he paid a visit to his native Poland. In a series of cautiously provocative speeches, he demonstrated to his countrymen the potential for mass opposition to communism.

Imagine you're Polish in the 1970s. Your country was devastated by World War II and has struggled under an oppressive regime ever since. Food shortages are epidemic. Lines stretch around the block even to buy a measly scrap of bread. Life is bleak, oppressive, and hopeless. Then someone who speaks your language—someone you've admired your entire life, and one of the only people you've seen successfully stand up to the regime—becomes one of the world's most influential people. A Pole like you is the leader of a billion Catholics. He makes you believe that the impossible can happen. He says to you again and again: "Nie

some of Kraków's best restaurants (see "Eating in Kraków," later). Survey your options now, and choose (and maybe reserve) your favorite for dinner tonight. This street is also characterized by its fine arcades over the sidewalks. While this might seem like a charming Renaissance feature, the arcades were actually added by the Nazis after they invaded in 1939; they wanted to convert Kraków into a city befitting its status as the capital of their Polish puppet state.

This is also a good street to find some of Kraków's **milk bars** (two are listed on page 132). The most traditional one is about two blocks down, on the right (at #45), with a simple *Bar Mleczny* sign.

lękajcie się"—"Have no fear." And you begin to believe it.

From his bully pulpit, the Pope had a knack for cleverly challenging the communists—just firmly enough to get his point across, but stopping short of jeopardizing the stature of the Church in Poland. Gentle but pointed wordplay was his specialty. The inspirational role he played in the lives of Lech Wałęsa and the other leaders of Solidarity emboldened them to rise up; it's no coincidence that the first successful trade-union strikes in the Soviet Bloc took place shortly after John Paul II became pope. Many people (including Mikhail Gorbachev) credit John Paul II for the collapse of Eastern European communism.

Even as John Paul II's easy charisma attracted new worshippers to the Church (especially young people), his conservatism on issues such as birth control, homosexuality, and female priests pushed away many Catholics. Under his watch, the Church struggled with pedophilia scandals. Many still fault him for turning a blind eye and not putting a stop to these abuses much earlier.

By the end of his papacy, John Paul II's failing health and conservatism had caused him to lose stature in worldwide public opinion.

And yet, approval of the Pope never waned in Poland. His countrymen—even the relatively few atheists and agnostics—saw John Paul II both as the greatest hero of their people...and as a member of the family, like a kindly grandfather. When Pope John Paul II died on April 2, 2005, the mourning in his homeland was particularly deep and sustained. Musical performances of all kinds were canceled, and the irreverent MTV-style music channel simply went off the air out of respect.

A speedy nine years after his death, Karol Wojtyła became St. John Paul II in April of 2014. Out of 265 popes, only two have been given the title "great." There's already talk in Rome of increasing that number to three. Someday soon we may speak of this man as "St. John Paul the Great." His countrymen already do.

These government-subsidized cafeterias are the locals' choice for a quick, cheap, filling, lowbrow lunch. Prices are deliriously cheap (soup costs about a dollar), and the food isn't bad. For more on milk bars, see page 16.

• *One more block ahead, the small square on your right is...*

Mary Magdalene Square
(Plac Św. Marii Magdaleny)

This square offers a great visual example of Kraków's deeply religious character. In the Middle Ages, Kraków was known as "Small

Rome" for its many churches. Today, there are 142 churches and monasteries within the city limits (32 in the Old Town alone)—more per square mile than anywhere outside of Rome. You can see several of them from this spot: The nearest, with the picturesque white facade and row of saints out front, is the **Church of Saints Peter and Paul** (Poland's first Baroque church, and a popular tourist concert venue). The statues lining this church's facade are the 11 apostles (minus Judas), plus Mary Magdalene, the square's namesake. The next church to the right, with the twin towers, is the Romanesque **St. Andrew's** (now with a Baroque interior). Dating from the rough-and-tumble 11th century, it was designed to double as a place of last refuge—notice the arrow slits around the impassable lower floor. According to legend, a spring inside this church provided water to citizens who holed up here during the Tatar invasions. The church was spared, but that didn't save the rest of Kraków from being overrun by marauding armies. Imagine this stone fortress of God being the only building standing amid a smoldering and flattened Kraków after the 13th-century destruction.

If you look farther down the street, you can see three more churches. And even the square next to you used to be a church, too—it burned in 1855, and only its footprint survives.

• *Go through the square and turn left down...*

Kanonicza Street (Ulica Kanonicza)

With so many churches around here, the clergy had to live somewhere. Many lived on this well-preserved street—supposedly the oldest street in Kraków. As you walk, look for the cardinal hats over three different doorways. The **Hotel Copernicus,** on the left at #16, is named for a famous guest who stayed here five centuries ago. Directly across the street at #17, the **Bishop Erazm Ciołek Palace** hosts a good exhibit of medieval art and Orthodox icons. Next door, the yellow house at #19 is where Karol Wojtyła lived for 10 years after World War II—long before he became St. John Paul II. Today this building houses the **Archdiocesan Museum,** which is the top spot in the Old Town to learn about Kraków's favorite son. Both of these sights are described later, under "Sights in Kraków."

• *This marks the end of Kanonicza street—and the end of our self-guided walk. But there's still much more to see. Across the busy street, a ramp leads up to the most important piece of ground in all of Poland: Wawel (described next).*

Sights in the Old Town

WAWEL HILL: THE HEART AND SOUL OF POLAND

Wawel (VAH-vehl), a symbol of Polish royalty and independence, is sacred territory to every Polish person. A castle has stood here

since the beginning of Poland's recorded history. Today, Wawel—awash in tourists—is the most visited sight in the country. Crowds and an overly complex admissions system for the hill's many historic sights can be exasperating. Thankfully, a stroll through the cathedral and around the castle grounds requires no tickets, and—with the help of the following commentary—is enough. I've described these sights in the order of a handy self-guided walk. The many museums on Wawel (all described in this section) are mildly interesting, but can be skipped (grounds open daily from 6:00 until dusk, inner courtyard closes 30 minutes earlier). In May and June, it's mobbed with students, as it's a required field trip for Polish school kids.

Wawel Sights: The sights you'll enter at Wawel are divided into two institutions: church and castle, each with separate tickets. Tickets for the castle sights are sold at two points (at the long line at the top of the ramp, or with no line at the top of the hill, across the central square). The most important church sight—the cathedral—is mostly free, but to enter the paid sights inside (or the museum), get a ticket at the office across from the cathedral entrance.

• *From Kanonicza street—where my self-guided walk ends—head up the long ramp to the castle entry.*

Entry Ramp

Huffing up this ramp, it's easy to imagine how this location—rising above the otherwise flat plains around Kraków—was both strategic and easy to defend. When Kraków was part of the Habsburg Empire in the 19th century, the Austrians turned this castle complex into a fortress, destroying much of its delicate beauty. When Poland regained its independence after World War I, the castle was returned to its former glory. The bricks you see on your left as you climb the ramp bear the names of Poles from around the world who donated to the cause.

The jaunty equestrian statue ahead is **Tadeusz Kościuszko** (1746-1817), a familiar name to many Americans. Kościuszko was a hero of the American Revolution and helped design West

Point. When he returned to his native Poland, he fought bravely but unsuccessfully against the Russians (during the Partitions that would divide Poland's territory among three neighboring powers). Kościuszko also gave his name to several American towns, a county in Indiana, a brand of mustard from Illinois, and the tallest mountain in Australia.

• *Hiking through the Heraldic Gate next to Kościuszko, you pass the ticket office (if you'll be going into the museums, use the other ticket office, with shorter lines, on the top of the hill—see "Tickets and Reservations," later). As you crest the hill and pass through the stone gate, on your left is...*

▲▲Wawel Cathedral

Poland's national church is its Westminster Abbey. While the history buried here is pretty murky to most Americans, to Poles, this

church is *the* national mausoleum. It holds the tombs of nearly all of Poland's most important rulers and greatest historical figures.

Cost and Hours: It's usually free to walk around the main part of the church. You must buy a 12-zł ticket to climb up the tallest tower; visit the crypt, the royal tombs, and some of the lesser chapels; and tour the John Paul II Wawel Cathedral Museum. Buy this ticket at the house across from the cathedral entry—marked *KASA*—where you can also rent an audioguide (7 zł). The cathedral is open April-Sept Mon-Sat 9:00-17:00, Sun 12:30-17:00, Oct-March daily until 16:00 (tel. 12-429-9516, www.katedra-wawelska.pl). Note that the cathedral's museum (described later) is closed on Sunday.

Cathedral Exterior

Before entering, go around to the far side of the cathedral to take in its profile. This uniquely eclectic church is the product of centuries of haphazard additions...yet somehow, it works. It began as a simple, stripped-down Romanesque church in the 12th century. (The white base of the nearest tower is original. Anything at Wawel that's made of white limestone like this was probably part of the earliest Romanesque structures.) Kazimierz the Great and his predecessors gradually surrounded the cathedral with some 20 chapels, which were further modified over the centuries, making this beautiful church a happy hodgepodge of styles. To give you a sense of the historical sweep, scan the chapels from left to right: 14th-century Gothic, 12th-century Romanesque (the base of the tower), 17th-century Baroque (the inside is Baroque, though the exterior is a copy of its Renaissance neighbor), 16th-century Renaissance, and 18th- and 19th-century Neoclassical. (This variety in styles is even more evident in the chapels' interiors, which we'll see soon.)

Pay attention to the two particularly interesting domed chapels to the right of the tall tower. The gold one is the Sigismund Chapel, housing memorials to the Jagiellonian kings—including Sigismund the Old, who was responsible for Kraków's Renaissance renovation in the 16th century. The Jagiellonian Dynasty was a high point in Polish history. During that golden 16th century, Poland was triple the size it is today, stretching all the way to the Ottoman Empire and the Black Sea. Poles consider the Sigismund Chapel, made with 80 pounds of gold, to be the finest Renaissance chapel north of the Alps. The copper-domed chapel next to it, home to the Swedish Vasa dynasty, resembles its neighbor (but it's a copy built 150 years later, and without all that gold).

Go back around and face the church's **front entry** for more architectonic extravagance. The tallest tower, called the Sigismund

Tower, has a clock with only an hour hand. Climbing a few steps into the entry, you see Gothic chapels (with pointy windows) flanking the door, a Renaissance ceiling, lavish Baroque decoration over the door, and some big bones (a simple whale rib). In the Middle Ages, these were thought to have been the bones of the mythic Wawel dragon, and put here as an oddity to be viewed by the public. (Back then, there were no museums, so notable items like these were used to lure people to the church.) It's said that as long as the bones hang here, the cathedral will stand. The door is the original from the 14th century, with fine wrought-iron work. The *K* with the crown stands for Kazimierz the Great. The black marble frame is made of Kraków stone from nearby quarries.

Cathedral Interior

The cathedral interior is slathered in Baroque memorials and tombs, decorated with tapestries, and soaked in Polish history. The ensemble was designed to help keep Polish identity strong through the ages. It has...and it still does.

Visiting the Cathedral: After you step inside, you'll follow the one-way, clockwise route that leads you through the choir, then around the back of the apse, then back to the entry.

At the entry, look straight ahead to see the silver tomb under a **canopy,** inspired by the one in St. Peter's Basilica at the Vatican. It contains the remains of the first Polish saint, Stanisław (from the 11th century). In front of the canopy, look for a metallic reliquary that's shaped like a book with its pages being ruffled by the wind (labeled, in Latin, *Sanctus Johannes Paulus II*). The glass capsule in the reliquary holds a drop of St. John Paul II's blood. It takes this shape because of what believers consider a highly significant moment during his memorial service: Before a crowd of thousands on St. Peter's Square in Rome, a book was placed on John Paul II's simple wooden coffin. As the service processed, its pages were ruffled back and forth by the wind, until they were finally slammed shut...as if the Holy Spirit were "closing the book" on his life.

Go behind this canopy into the ornately carved **choir** area. For 200 years, the colorful chair to the right of the high altar has been the seat of Kraków's archbishops, including Karol Wojtyła, who served here for 14 years before becoming pope. It's here that Polish royal coronations took place.

Now you'll continue into the left aisle. From here, if you have a ticket, you can enter two of the optional attractions: Seventy claustrophobic wooden stairs lead up to the 11-ton **Sigismund Bell** and pleasant views of the steeples and spires of Kraków. Then, to the left (closer to where you entered), descend into the little **crypt** (with a rare purely Romanesque interior), which houses the remains of Adam Mickiewicz, the Romantic poet whose statue dominates the Main Market Square, and another beloved Romantic poet and playwright, Juliusz Słowacki. You'll also find a white marble monument to Fryderyk Chopin (who's buried in Paris), put here on the 200th anniversary of his birth in 2010.

Now continue around the apse (behind the main altar). After curving around to the right, look for the red-marble tomb (on the right) of The Great One— **Kazimierz,** of course. Look for *Kazimierz Wielki*—at his feet you can see a little beaver. This is an allusion to a famous saying about Kazimierz, the nation-builder: He found a Poland made of wood, and left one made of brick and stone.

You may notice that there's one VIP (Very Important Pole) who's missing...Karol Wojtyła, a.k.a. John Paul II. Even so, a few more steps toward the entrance, on the left, is the **Chapel of St. John Paul II.** The late pontiff left no specific requests for his body, and the Vatican controversially (to Poles, at least) chose to entomb him in Vatican City, instead of sending him back home to Wawel. While Karol Wojtyła's rcmains are in St. Peter's Basilica, this chapel was recently converted to honor him—with a plaque in the floor and an altar with his picture. Someday, Poles hope, he may be moved here (but, the Vatican says, don't hold your breath).

Directly opposite the chapel, you'll see the rusty funeral regalia (orb and scepter) of **St. Jadwiga;** ten steps farther is her white sarcophagus (with a dog at her feet). This 14th-century "king" of Poland advanced the fortunes of her realm by partnering with the king of Lithuania. The resulting Jagiellonian dynasty fought off the Teutonic Knights, helped Christianize Lithuania, and oversaw a high-water mark in Polish history. (Despite the queen's many contributions, the sexism of the age meant that she was considered a "king" rather than a "queen.") All the flowers here demonstrate how popular she remains among Poles today; she was sainted by Pope John Paul II in 1997.

Across from Jadwiga, peek into the gorgeous 16th-century **Sigismund Chapel,** with its silver altar (this is the gold-roofed chapel you just saw from outside). Locals consider this the "Pearl of the Polish Renaissance" and the finest Renaissance building outside Italy.

Just beyond is a door leading back outside. If you don't have a ticket, your tour is finished—head out here. But those with a ticket can keep circling around.

Next, look into the **Vasa Chapel:** Remember that its exterior matches the restrained, Renaissance style of the Sigismund Chapel, but the interior is clearly Baroque, slathered with gold and silver—quite a contrast.

To the left of the main door, take a look at the Gothic **Holy Cross Chapel,** with its seemingly Orthodox-style 14th-century frescoes.

In the back corner of the church—on the other side of the main door—is the entrance to the **royal tombs.** (You'll exit outside the church, so be sure you're done in here first.) Once downstairs, the first big room, an original Romanesque space called St. Leonard's Crypt, houses Poland's greatest war heroes: Kościuszko (of American Revolution fame), Jan III Sobieski (who successfully defended Vienna from the Ottomans; he's in the simple black coffin with the gold inscription *J III S*), Sikorski, Poniatowski, and so on. Poles consider this room highly significant as the place where St. John Paul II celebrated his first Mass after becoming a priest (in November of 1946). Then you'll wander through several rooms of second-tier Polish kings, queens, and their kids. Head down more stairs to find the plaque honoring the Polish victims of the Katyń massacre in the USSR during World War II. Stepping into the next room, you'll see the cathedral's newest tomb: President Lech Kaczyński and his wife Helena, who were among the 96 Polish politicians killed in a tragic 2010 plane crash—which was delivering those diplomats to a ceremony memorializing the Katyń massacre. Up a few stairs is the final grave, belonging to Marshal Józef Piłsudski, the WWI hero who later seized power and was the de facto ruler of Poland from 1926 to 1935. His tomb was moved here so the rowdy soldiers who came to pay their respects wouldn't disturb the others.

• *Nearby (and covered by the same ticket as the tower and crypt) is the cathedral's museum.*

John Paul II Wawel Cathedral Museum

This small museum, up the little staircase across from the cathedral entry, was recently spiffed up and re-dedicated to Kraków's favorite archbishop. It fills four rooms with artifacts relating to both the cathedral and St. John Paul II.

Downstairs is the Royal Room, with vestments, swords, regalia, coronation robes, and items that were once buried with the kings, as well as early treasury items (from the 11th through 16th centuries). Upstairs is the "Papal Room" with items from St. John Paul II's life: his armchair, vestments, caps, shoes, and miter (pointy pope hat), plus souvenirs from his travels. (If you're into papal memorabilia, the collection at the nearby Archdiocesan Museum—described later—is better.) The adjoining room holds a later treasury collection (17th through 20th centuries).

Cost and Hours: Admission to this museum is included with your ticket to the cathedral's special options (Sigismund Bell tower, plus crypt and royal tombs); open April-Sept Mon-Sat 9:00-17:00, Oct-March until 16:00, closed Sun year-round; tel. 12-429-3321.

• *When you're finished with the cathedral sights, stroll around the...*

▲▲Wawel Castle Grounds

In the rest of the castle, you'll uncover more fragments of Kraków's history and have the opportunity to visit several museums. I consider the museums skippable, but if you want to visit them, buy tickets before you enter the inner courtyard. Read the descriptions on page 65 to decide which museums appeal to you.

➋ Self-Guided Tour: This guided stroll, which doesn't enter any of the admission-charging attractions, is plenty for most visitors.

• *For a historical orientation, stand with the cathedral to your back, and survey the empty field between here and the castle walls.*

Field of History: This hilltop has seen lots of changes over the years. Kazimierz the Great turned a small fortress into a mighty Gothic castle in the 14th century. But that original fortress burned to the ground in 1499, and ever since, Wawel has been in flux. For example, in the grassy field, notice the foundations of two Gothic churches that were destroyed when the Austrians took over Wawel in the 19th century and needed a parade ground for their troops. (They built the red-brick hospital building beyond the field, now used by the Wawel administration.)

• *Facing the cathedral, look right to find a grand green-and-pink entryway. Go through here and into the palace's dramatically Renaissance-style...*

Inner Courtyard: If this space seems to have echoes of Florence, that's because it was designed and built by young Florentines after Kazimierz's original castle burned down. Notice the three distinct levels: The ground floor housed the private apartments of the higher nobility (governors and castle administrators); the middle level held the private apartments of the king; and the top floor—much taller, to allow more light to fill its large spaces—were the public state rooms of the king. The ivy-covered wing to the right of where you entered is Fascist in style, built as the headquarters of the notorious Nazi governor of German-occupied Poland, Hans Frank. (He was tried and executed in Nürnberg after the war.) At the far end of the courtyard is a false wall, designed to create a pleasant Renaissance symmetry, and also to give the illusion that the castle is bigger than it is. Looking through the windows, notice that there's nothing but air on the other side. When foreign dignitaries visited, these windows could be covered to complete the illusion. The entrances to most Wawel museums are around this courtyard, and some believe that you'll find something even more special: chakra.

Adherents to the Hindu concept of **chakra** believe that a powerful energy field connects all living things. Some believe that, mirroring the seven chakra points on the body (from head to groin), there are seven points on the surface of the earth where this energy is most concentrated: Delhi, Delphi, Jerusalem, Mecca, Rome, Velehrad...and Wawel Hill—specifically over there in the corner (immediately to your left as you enter the courtyard—the stretches of wall flanking the door to the baggage-check room). Look for peaceful people (here or elsewhere on the castle grounds) with their eyes closed. One thing's for sure: They're not thinking of Kazimierz the Great. The smudge marks on the wall are from people pressing up against this corner, trying to absorb some good vibes from this chakra spot.

The Wawel administration seems creeped out by all this. They've done what they can to discourage this ritual (such as putting up information boards right where the power is supposedly most focused), but believers still gravitate from far and wide to hug the wall. Give it a try...and let the chakra be with you. (Just for fun, ask a Wawel tour guide about the chakra, and watch her squirm—they're forbidden to talk about it.)

• *If you want to visit some of the* **castle museums** *(you can enter four of the five from this courtyard), you'll first need to buy tickets elsewhere. Stick with me for a little longer to finish our tour of the grounds, and we'll wind up near a ticket office.*

Head downhill through the square, across to the gap in the buildings beyond the field, to the...

Viewpoint over the Vistula: Belly up to the wall and enjoy the panorama over the **Vistula River** and Kraków's outskirts. The "Polish Mississippi"—which runs its entire course in Polish lands—is the nation's artery for trade and cultural connection. It stretches 650 miles from the foothills of the Tatra Mountains in southern Poland, through most of the country's major cities (Kraków, Warsaw, Toruń), before emptying into the Baltic Sea in Gdańsk.

From this viewpoint, you can see some unusual landmarks, including the odd wavy-roofed building just across the river (which houses the Manggha Japanese art gallery) and the biggest conference center in Poland (opened in 2015, to the left of the wavy building). A bit farther to the left is an eyesore of a communist concrete department store, now used as a billboard. In the summer, you'll see a popular and very cool "beach bar" filling the field in front of the building (the Forum Przestrzenie, described on page 120). To the right, the suspiciously symmetrical little bulge that tops the highest hill on the horizon is the artificial Kościuszko Mound (see page 109). And on a particularly crisp day, far in the distance (beyond the wavy building), you can see the Tatra Mountains marking the border of Slovakia.

Now look directly below you, along the riverbank, to find a fire-belching monument to the **dragon** that was instrumental in the founding of Kraków. Once upon a time, a prince named Krak founded a town on Wawel Hill. It was the perfect location—except for the fire-breathing dragon who lived in the caves under the hill and terrorized the town. Prince Krak had to feed the dragon all of the town's livestock to keep the monster from going after the townspeople. But Krak, with the help of a clever shoemaker, came up with a plan. They stuffed a sheep's skin with sulfur and left it outside the dragon's cave. The dragon swallowed it, and before long, developed a terrible case of heartburn. To put the fire out, the dragon started drinking water from the Vistula. He kept drinking and drinking until he finally exploded. The town was saved, and Kraków thrived. Today visitors enjoy watching the dragon blow fire into the air (about every four minutes, but can vary from a big plume to a tiny puff).

If you want to head down to see the Vistula and the dragon close up, take a shortcut through the nearby **Dragon's Den** (Smocza Jama, enter at the little copper-roofed brick building, at the far right of this viewpoint plaza). It's just a 135-step spiral staircase and a few underground caverns—worthwhile only as a quick way to get from the top of Wawel down to the banks of the Vistula (3 zł, pay at machine—coins only, daily 10:00-17:00, July-Aug until 18:00, closed Nov-March).

If you'd like a higher viewpoint on the riverfront, you can pay 4 zł to climb 137 stairs to the top of **Sandomierska Tower**

(at the far end of the hill, past the visitors center, no elevator). But I'd skip it—disappointingly, the view from up top is only through small windows (daily 10:00-18:00, June-Aug until 19:00, Oct Sat-Sun only 10:00-17:00, closed Nov-April).

• *Our Wawel tour is finished. If you'd like to explore some of the museums, you can buy your tickets in the nearby visitors center (head back into the main Wawel complex—with the empty field—and turn right); here you'll also find WCs, a café, a gift shop, and other amenities. Or go down to the riverfront park: Walk downhill (through the Dragon's Den, or use the main ramp and circle around the base of the hill) to reach the park—one of the most delightful places in Kraków to simply relax, with beautiful views back on the castle complex.*

Wawel Castle Museums

There are five museums and exhibits in Wawel Castle (not including the cathedral and Cathedral Museum, the Dragon's Den, or Sandomierska Tower—all described above). A sixth exhibit, featuring Leonardo da Vinci's masterful painting *Lady with an Ermine,* may be on display here at the castle, or it could be at the Czartoryski Museum, if it's reopened (see page 74).

Remember: While the following sights are fascinating to Poles, casual visitors often find that the best visit is simply to enjoy the exteriors and the cathedral (following my self-guided tour, described earlier). Each sight has its own admission and slightly different hours (tel. 12-422-5155, ext. 219, www.wawel.krakow. pl). English descriptions are posted, and you can rent an audioguide for 20 zł that covers some of the sights. If you're visiting all of the sights, start with the Royal State Rooms and/or Royal Private Apartments (which share an entrance), then—on your way back down—see the Leonardo exhibit (if it's still here), the Oriental Art exhibit, and the Crown Treasury and Armory. Then head back out into the outer courtyard for the Lost Wawel exhibit.

Tickets and Reservations: Each sight has separate tickets (prices listed below), which you'll buy at one of two ticket windows. Most people line up at the top of the entry ramp, but it's faster to buy tickets at the visitors center at the far corner of the castle grounds (across the field from the cathedral, near the café). You generally can't buy tickets at the door of each sight, so decide in advance which ones you want to see and buy all your tickets at the start of your visit. A limited number of tickets are sold for each sight; boards count down the number of tickets available for each one on the day you're there. Tickets come with an assigned entry time (though you can usually sneak in before your scheduled appointment). In the summer, ticket lines can be long, and sights can sell out by midmorning. You can make a free reservation for some of the sights (tel. 12-422-1697, extra fee applies), but frankly, the sights aren't worth all the fuss—if they're sold out, you're not missing much.

Hours: Unless otherwise noted, the museums are open April-Oct Tue-Fri 9:30-17:00, Sat-Sun 10:00-17:00, closed Mon; Nov-March Tue-Sat 9:30-16:00, closed Sun-Mon. The last ticket is sold 1.25 hours before closing, and the last entry is one hour before closing.

Exceptions: In summer (April-Oct), Lost Wawel and the Crown Treasury and Armory are free and open on Mondays (9:30-13:00). Off-season (Nov-March), everything is closed on Monday and most are closed on Sunday except Lost Wawel, the Royal State Rooms, and the Leonardo exhibit (Jan-March only).

Eating: Various light eateries circle the castle courtyard, but if you just want a drink, it's hard to beat the affordable self-service café next to the Lost Wawel entrance, with fine views across to the cathedral.

▲Royal State Rooms (Komnaty Królewskie)

While precious to Poles, these rooms are mediocre by European standards. Still, this is the best of the Wawel museums. First, climb up to the top floor and wander through some ho-hum halls with paintings and antique furniture. Along the way, you'll walk along the outdoor gallery (enjoying views down into the courtyard). Finally, you'll reach the Throne Room, with 30 carved heads in the ceiling. According to legend, one of these heads got mouthy when the king was trying to pass judgment—so its mouth has been covered to keep it quiet. Continue into some of the palace's finest rooms, with 16th-century Brussels tapestries (140 of the original series of 300 survive), remarkably decorated wooden ceilings, and gorgeous leather-tooled walls. Wandering these halls (with their period furnishings), you get a feeling for the 16th- and 17th-century glory days of Poland, when it was a leading power in Eastern Europe. The Senate Room, with its throne and elaborate tapestries, is the climax.

Cost and Hours: 18 zł, see hours listed earlier, plus Nov-March also open—and free—Sun 10:00-16:00, enter through courtyard.

Royal Private Apartments
(Prywatne Apartamenty Królewskie)

The rooms, which look similar to the State Rooms, can only be visited with a guided (and included) 45-minute tour. As spaces are strictly limited, these tend to sell out the fastest (on busy days, they may already be booked up by around 10:00).

Cost and Hours: 25 zł, request English tour when buying your ticket—they depart 3/hour, see hours listed earlier, enter through courtyard.

Oriental Art (Sztuka Wschodu)

Though small, this exhibit displays swords, carpets, banners, vases, and other items dating from the 1683 Battle of Vienna, in which the Ottoman army attempted to capture the Austrian capital. These are trophies of Jan III Sobieski, the Polish king who led a pan-European army to victory in that battle.

Cost and Hours: 8 zł, see hours listed earlier, enter through courtyard; don't miss entry on your way back downstairs from Royal State Rooms.

Crown Treasury and Armory (Skarbiec i Zbrojownia)

This is a decent collection of swords, saddles, and shields; ornately decorated muskets, crossbows, and axes; and cannons in the basement. Off in a smaller side room are some of the most precious items. Look for the regalia given to Jan III Sobieski as thanks for his defeat of the Ottoman invaders in the Battle of Vienna: giant swords consecrated by the pope and the mantle (robe) of the Order of the Holy Ghost from France's King Louis XIV. Nearby is the

13th-century coronation sword of the Polish kings and some gorgeously inlaid rifles.

Cost and Hours: 18 zł, see hours listed earlier, plus April-Oct also open—and free—Mon 9:30-13:00, enter through courtyard.

▲▲Leonardo da Vinci's *Lady with an Ermine*

The single best and most famous painting in Kraków is normally displayed at the Czartoryski Museum. But while that space is closed for renovation (likely through 2017, and possibly longer), you'll most likely find the canvas at Wawel Castle. It's well worth the price of entry to view this rare, small (21 x 16 inches), but magnificently executed portrait of a teenage girl—a rare surviving work by one of history's greatest minds. (If you have your heart set on seeing this painting, make sure it's here before making the trip—it may be on loan or in storage.)

Cost and Hours: 10 zł, see hours listed earlier, plus Jan-March also open Sun 10:00-16:00, enter through courtyard.

Visiting the Museum: Spend some time lingering over the canvas (dating from 1489 or 1490). The girl is likely Cecilia Gallerani, the young mistress of Ludovico Sforza, the duke of Milan and Leonardo's employer. The ermine (white during winter) suggests chastity (thus bolstering Cecilia's questioned virtue), but is also a naughty reference to the duke's nickname, Ermellino—notice that his mistress is sensually, um, "stroking the ermine."

Painted before the *Mona Lisa*, the portrait was immediately recognized as revolutionary. Cecilia turns to look at someone, her gaze directed to the side. Leonardo catches this unguarded, informal moment, an unheard-of gesture in the days of the posed, front-facing formal portrait. Her simple body language and faraway gaze speak volumes about her inner thoughts and personality. Leonardo tweaks the generic Renaissance "pyramid" composition, turning it to a three-quarters angle, and softens it with curved lines that trace from Cecilia's eyes and down her cheek and sloping shoulders before doubling back across her folded arms. The background—once gray and blue—was painted black in the 19th century.

In a recent high-tech analysis using special lights and cameras, conservators were able to virtually peel back layers of paint to see earlier "drafts" of the painting (Leonardo was known to tinker with his works over time). They've revealed that the ermine was likely not included in the original version. Perhaps Leonardo added it later as a nod to the duke.

Lady with an Ermine is one of only three surviving oil paintings by Leonardo. It's better preserved than her famous cousin in Paris *(Mona Lisa)*, and—many think—simply more beautiful. Can we be sure it's really by the enigmatic Leonardo? Yep—the master's fingerprints were found literally pressed into the paint (he was known to work areas of paint directly with his fingertips).

▲Lost Wawel (Wawel Zaginiony)

This exhibit traces the history of the hill and its various churches and castles. Begin by viewing the model of the entire castle complex in the 18th century (pre-Austrian razing). From here, the one-way route leads through scarcely explained excavations of a 10th-century church. The collection includes models of the cathedral at various historical stages (originally Romanesque—much simpler, before all the colorful, bulbous domes, chapels, and towers were added—then Gothic, and so on). Circling back to the entrance, find the display of fascinating decorative tiles from 16th-century stoves that once heated the place.

Cost and Hours: 10 zł, see hours listed earlier, plus April-Oct also open—and free—Mon 9:30-13:00; Nov-March also open—and free—Sun 9:30-13:00; enter near snack bar across from side of cathedral.

NATIONAL MUSEUM BRANCHES

Kraków's National Museum (Muzeum Narodowe) is made up of a series of small but interesting collections scattered throughout the city (www.muzeum.krakow.pl). I've listed the best of the National Museum's branches below. A 35-zł **combo-ticket** covers the permanent collections in all of these museums (good for your entire stay)—worth considering if you'll be visiting more than three of them. National Museum branches are free to enter on Sunday (but some have reduced hours).

▲▲Gallery of 19th-Century Polish Art (Galeria Sztuki Polskiej XIX Wieku)

This small and surprisingly enjoyable collection of works by obscure Polish artists fills the upper level of the Cloth Hall. While you probably won't recognize any of the Polish names in here—and this collection isn't quite as impressive as Warsaw's National Gallery—many of these paintings are just plain delightful. It's worth a visit to see some Polish canvases in their native land, and to enjoy views over the Square from the hall's upper terraces.

Cost and Hours: 16 zł, free on Sun, Tue-Sun 10:00-18:00, closed Mon, dry 7-zł audioguide, entrance on side of Cloth Hall facing Adam Mickiewicz statue, tel. 12-424-4600.

Background: Keep in mind that during the 19th century—when every piece of art in this museum was created—there was no "Poland." The country had been split up among its powerful neighbors in a series of three Partitions, and would not appear again on the map of Europe until after World War I. Meanwhile, the 19th century was a period of national revival throughout Europe, when various previously marginalized ethnic groups began to take pride in what made them different from their neighbors. So the artists you see represented here were grappling with trying to forge a national identity at a time when they didn't even have a nation. You'll sense a pessimism that comes from a country that feels abused by foreign powers, mingled with a resolute spirit of national pride.

⊘ **Self-Guided Tour:** The collection fills just four rooms: Two small rooms in the center and two big halls on either side. On a quick visit, focus on the highlights in the big halls I mention here.

Entering the Cloth Hall, buy your ticket and head up the stairs—pausing on the first floor to peek out onto the inviting **café**

terrace for a fine view of the Square and St. Mary's. Then continue up to the main exhibit, on the second floor.

The first two small rooms don't feature much of interest. You enter **Room I** (Bacciarelli Room), with works from the Enlightenment; straight ahead is **Room II** (Michałowski Room), featuring Romantic works from 1822 to 1863. The larger, twin halls on either side merit a linger.

Siemiradzki Room (Room III, on the right): This features art of the Academy—that is, "conformist" art embraced by the art critics of the day. Entering the room, turn right and survey the canvases counterclockwise. The space is dominated by the works of Jan Matejko, a remarkably productive painter who specialized in epic historical scenes that also commented on his own era (for more on Matejko, see page 190).

• *Circling the room, look for these paintings.*

1. Jan Matejko—*Wenyhora:* The first big canvas is Matejko's depiction of Wenyhora, a late-18th-century Ukrainian soothsayer who, according to legend, foretold Poland's hardships—the three Partitions, Poland's pact with Napoleon, and its difficulties regaining nationhood. Like many Poles of the era, Matejko was preoccupied with Poland's tragic fate, imbuing this scene with an air of inevitable tragedy.

2. Jacek Malczewski—*Death of Ellenai:* A similar gloominess is reflected in this canvas. The main characters in a Polish Romantic poem, Ellenai and Anhelli, have been exiled to a remote cabin in Siberia (in Russia, one of the great powers occupying Poland). Just when they think things can't get worse...Ellenai dies. Anhelli sits immobilized by grief.

• *A few canvases down, dominating the right side of the hall, is...*

3. Jan Matejko—*Tadeusz Kościuszko at Racławice:* One of the heroes of the American Revolution, now back in his native

Poland fighting the Russians, doffs his hat after his unlikely victory at the Battle at Racławice. In this battle (which ultimately had little bearing on Russia's drive to overtake Poland), a ragtag army of Polish peasants defeated the Russian forces. Kościuszko is clad in an American uniform, symbolizing Matejko's respect for the American ideals of democracy and self-determination.

KRAKÓW

• *Dominating the far wall is...*

4. Henryk Siemiradzki—*Nero's Torches:* On the left, Roman

citizens eagerly gather to watch Christians being burned at the stake (on the right). The symbolism is clear: The meek and downtrodden (whether Christians in the time of Rome, or Poles in the heyday of Russia and Austria) may be persecuted now, but we have faith that their noble ideals will ultimately prevail.

• *On the next wall, find...*

5. Pantaleon Szyndler—*Bathing Girl:* This piece evokes the orientalism popular in 19th-century Europe, when romanticized European notions of the Orient (such as harem slave girls) were popular artistic themes. Already voyeuristic, the painting was originally downright lewd until Szyndler painted over a man leering at the woman from the left side of the canvas.

• *The huge canvas on this wall is...*

6. Jan Matejko—*The Prussian Homage:* The last Grand Master of the fearsome Teutonic Knights swears allegiance to the Polish king in 1525. This historic ceremony took place in the Main Market Square in Kraków, the capital at the time. Notice the Cloth Hall balustrade and the spires of St. Mary's Church in the background. Matejko has painted his own face on one of his favorite historical figures, the jester Stańczyk at the foot of the throne (for more on Stańczyk, see page 191).

• *Continue the rest of the way around the room. Keep an eye out for Tadeusz Ajdukiewicz's portrait of Helena Modrzejewska, a popular actress of the time, attending a party in this very building. Finally, backtrack through Room I and continue into the...*

Chełmoński Room (Room IV): Featuring works of the late 19th century, this section includes Realism and the first inklings of Symbolism and Impressionism. Just as elsewhere in Europe (including Paris, where many of these artists trained), artists were beginning to throw off the conventions of the Academy and embrace their own muse.

• *As you turn right and proceed counterclockwise through the room, the first stretch of canvases features landscapes and genre paintings. Among these, a particularly fine canvas is...*

1. Wladyslaw Malecki—*A Gathering of Storks:* The majestic birds stand under big willows in front of the setting sun. Even seemingly innocent wildlife paintings have a political message: Storks are particularly numerous in Poland, making them a subtle patriotic symbol.

• *A few canvases down, find...*

2. Józef Brandt—*A Meeting on a Bridge:* This dramatic painting shows soldiers and aristocrats pushing a farmer into a ditch—a comment on the state of the Polish people at that time. Just to the right, see Brandt's *Fight for a Turkish Standard.* This artist specialized in battle scenes, frequently involving a foe from the East—as was often the reality here along Europe's buffer zone with Asia.

• *Just to the left of Brandt's works is...*

3. Samuel Hirszenberg—*School of Talmudists:* Young Jewish students pore over the Talmud. One of them, deeply lost in thought, may be pondering more than ancient Jewish law. This canvas suggests the inclusion of Jews in Poland's cultural tapestry during this age. While still subject to pervasive bigotry here, many Jewish refugees found Poland to be a relatively welcoming, tolerant place to settle on a typically hostile continent.

• *Dominating the end of the room is...*

4. Józef Chełmoński—*Four-in-Hand:* In this intersection of worlds, a Ukrainian horseman gives a lift to a pipe-smoking nobleman. Feel the thrilling energy as the horses charge directly at you through splashing puddles.

• *Heading back toward the entrance, on the right wall, watch for...*

5. Witold Pruszkowski—*Water Nymphs:* Based on Slavic legends (and wearing traditional Ukrainian costumes), these mischievous, siren-like beings have just taken one victim (see his hand in the foreground) and are about to descend on another (seen faintly in the upper-right corner). Beyond this painting are some travel pictures from Italy and France (including some that are very Impressionistic, suggesting a Parisian influence).

• Flanking the entrance/exit door are two of this room's best works. First, on the right, is...

6. Władysław Podkowiński—*Frenzy:* This gripping painting's title *(Szał),* tellingly, has been translated as either *Ecstasy* or *Insanity.* A pale, sensuous woman—possibly based on a socialite for whom the artist fostered a desperate but unrequited love—clutches an all-fired-up black stallion, who's frothing at the mouth. This sexually charged painting caused a frenzy indeed at its 1894 unveiling, leading the unbalanced artist to attack his own creation with a knife (you can still see the slash marks in the canvas).

KRAKÓW

• And finally, on the other side of the door is...

7. Jacek Malczewski—*Introduction:* A young painter's apprentice on a bench contemplates his future. Surrounded by nature and with his painter's tools beside him, it's easy to imagine this as a self-portrait of the artist as a young man...wondering if he's choosing the correct path. Malczewski was an extremely talented Młoda Polska artist who tends to be overshadowed by his contemporary, Wyspiański. Viewing this canvas—and others by him—makes me feel grateful that he decided to stick with painting.

Szołayski House (Kamienica Szołayskich)

This restored mansion, just one block from the Main Market Square, features high-quality temporary exhibits, most often featuring artists from the early 20th century; one recent exhibit honored the French sculptor Auguste Rodin, and many others have showcased Art Nouveau works by the Młoda Polska movement (for more on this movement and its members, see page 47). In the past, the museum featured that movement's prodigiously talented headliner, Stanisław Wyspiański—and in the future, he may be back here. But in the meantime, find out what's on, and if the artist or theme interests you, check it out.

Cost and Hours: Price depends on exhibits, may be free on Sun, open Tue-Sat 10:00-18:00, Sun 10:00-16:00, closed Mon, one block northwest of the Square at plac Szczepański 9, tel. 12-433-5450.

Nearby: The charming and stately square that Szołayski House faces, **plac Szczepański,** is a hub for youthful, cutting-edge, artistic types. Tucked in a corner of the Old Town, just away from the Square, it's a strange and wonderful little oasis of urban sophistication holding out against the rising tide of tacky tourism. In addition to Szołayski House itself, the square has several bohemian cafés (including the recommended Charlotte). If you follow Szczepańska street one more block out to the Planty, then turn left, you'll find **Bunker Sztuki,** an art gallery that fills an unfortunate communist-era building that really does feel like a bunker. But this conformist architecture is filled with quite the opposite: changing exhibitions of contemporary art (12 zł, free on Tue, open Tue-Sun 11:00-19:00, closed Mon, http://bunkier.art.pl). The gallery's fine café, under a delightfully airy canopy facing the Planty, has a Parisian ambience—a great place to escape the crowds and/or rain (see "Eating in Kraków," later).

Bishop Erazm Ciołek Palace (Pałac Biskupa Erazma Ciołka)

This branch of the National Museum features two separate art collections. Upstairs, the extensive "Art of Old Poland" section shows off works from the 12th through the 18th centuries, with room after room of altarpieces, sculptures, paintings, and more. The "Orthodox Art of the Old Polish Republic" section on the ground floor offers a taste of the remote Eastern reaches of Poland, with icons and other ecclesiastical art from the Orthodox faith. You'll see a sizeable section of the iconostasis (wall of icons) from the town of Lipovec. Both collections are covered by the same ticket and are very well-presented in a modern facility. Items are labeled in English, but there's not much description.

Cost and Hours: 9 zł, free on Sun, Tue-Sat 10:00-18:00, Sun 10:00-16:00, closed Mon, audioguide-7 zł, Kanonicza 17, tel. 12-424-9371.

▲Czartoryski Museum (Muzeum Czartoryskich)

This eclectic collection, displaying armor, handicrafts, decorative arts, and paintings, is one of Kraków's best-known (and most overrated) museums. It's wrapping up a multiyear renovation; during your visit, some or all of its collection may already be open again. But the painting gallery—with its top pieces (a Leonardo and a Rembrandt)—may take longer to reopen. Likely through at least 2017, its undisputed highlight, Leonardo's *Lady with an Ermine,* will be displayed instead at Wawel Castle. Before visiting this museum, get the latest from a TI about how much is open.

Cost and Hours: If museum is open—around 12 zł, free on Sun, open Tue-Sun 10:00-16:00 or possibly until 18:00, closed

Mon, 2 blocks north of the Main Market Square at ulica Św. Jana 19, tel. 12-422-5566, www.czartoryski.org.

Background: The museum's collection came about, in part, thanks to Poland's 1791 constitution (Europe's first), which inspired Princess Izabela Czartoryska to begin gathering bits of Polish history and culture. She fled with the collection to Paris after the 1830 insurrection, and 45 years later, her grandson returned it to its present Kraków location. When he ran out of space, he bought part of the monastery across the street, joining the buildings with a fancy passageway. The Nazis took the collection to Germany, and although most of it has been returned, some pieces are still missing.

The museum owns two undisputed masterpieces, which are in varying states of accessibility. Art lovers will want to ask around for the scoop on their latest locations. While the museum is closed, its top painting—**Leonardo da Vinci's** *Lady with an Ermine*—can likely be found at Kraków's Wawel Castle (described on page 68). **Rembrandt van Rijn's** *Landscape with the Good Samaritan* (1638) may be on display in another city (or possibly in Kraków).

The museum technically owns a third masterpiece, **Raphael's** *Portrait of a Young Man,* but its whereabouts are unknown. Arguably one of the most famous and most valuable stolen paintings of all time, it's quite likely a self-portrait (but possibly a portrait of Raphael by another artist), depicting a Renaissance dandy, clad in a fur coat, with a self-satisfied smirk. Painted (perhaps) by the Renaissance master in 1513 or 1514, and purchased by a Czartoryski prince around the turn of the 19th century, the work was seized by the occupying Nazis during World War II. Along with the paintings by Leonardo and Rembrandt, this Raphael decorated the Wawel Castle residence of Nazi governor Hans Frank. But when Frank and the Nazis fled the invading Red Army at the end of the war, many of their pilfered artworks were lost—including the Raphael. For decades, this canvas was synonymous with art theft—the (literal) poster boy for Nazi crimes against culture. Then, dramatically, a Polish news site announced in 2012 that the priceless painting had been found, safe and sound (in a bank vault in an undisclosed location). Unfortunately, this was a misinterpretation of remarks made by government officials. But authorities are still hopeful the painting "will surface sooner or later" and that the "Czartoryski Raphael," as it's called, will be returned to this museum.

Visiting the Museum: If the museum is open, you'll wander through rooms of ornate armor (including a ceremonial Turkish tent from the 1683 siege of Vienna, plus feathered Hussar armor), tapestries, treasury items, majolica pottery, and Meissen porcelain figures. Rounding out the exhibits are painting galleries (including

Italian, French, and Dutch High Renaissance and Baroque, as well as Czartoryski family portraits) and ancient art (mostly sculptures and vases).

More National Museum Branches

While less interesting than the branches listed above, the National Museum's **Main Branch** (Gmach Główny) is worth a visit for museum completists. It features 20th-century Polish art and temporary exhibits (11 zł, a few blocks west of the Main Market Square at aleja 3 Maja 1). In 2017 (and beyond), they are planning a big retrospective exhibit on the works of Stanisław Wyspiański—the founder of the Młoda Polska (Art Nouveau) movement—which would easily be worth ▲, or more for art lovers. Check their website to see what's on (www.muzeum.krakow.pl).

The National Museum has yet more branches: The **Europeum** collection, housed in a restored granary, features works by European masters, including Breughel and Veneziano, along with a range of lesser-known artists (just west of the Old Town at plac Sikorskiego 6). You can also check out the museum of Wyspiański's friend and rival, the **Józef Mehoffer House** (Dom Józefa Mehoffera, 6 zł, ulica Krupnicza 26, tel. 12-421-1143), and the former residence of their mentor, the **Jan Matejko House** (Dom Jana Matejki, 8 zł, ulica Floriańska 41, tel. 12-422-5926).

OTHER OLD TOWN ATTRACTIONS

▲▲Rynek Underground Museum (Podziemia Rynku)

Recent work to renovate the Square's pavement unearthed a wealth of remains from previous structures. Now you can do some urban spelunking with a visit to this high-tech medieval-history museum, which is literally underground—beneath all the photo-snapping tourists on the Square above.

Cost and Hours: 19 zł, free on Tue, open Mon 10:00-20:00 (but closed second Mon of each month), Tue 10:00-16:00, Wed-Sun 10:00-22:00, shorter hours Nov-March; last entry 1.25 hours before closing, enter at north end of Cloth Hall near the fountain, Rynek Główny 1, tel. 12-426-5060, www.podziemiarynku.com.

Visiting the Museum: You'll enter through a door near the north end of the Cloth Hall (close to the fountain, facing St. Mary's). Climb down a flight of stairs, buy your ticket, then follow the numbered panels—1 to 70—through the exhibit (all in English). Cutting-edge museum technology illuminates life and times in medieval Kraków: Touchscreens let you delve into topics that intrigue you, 3-D virtual holograms resurrect old buildings, and video clips illustrate everyday life on unexpected surfaces (such as a curtain of fog).

All of this is wrapped around large chunks of early structures that still survive beneath the Square; several "witness columns" of rock and dirt are accompanied by diagrams helping you trace the layers of history. Interactive maps emphasize Kraków's Europe-wide importance as an intersection of major trade routes, and several models, maps, and digital reconstructions give you a good look at Kraków during the Middle Ages—when the Old Town looked barely different from today. You'll see a replica of a blacksmith's shop and learn how "vampire prevention burials" were used to ensure that the suspected undead wouldn't return from the grave. In the middle of the complex, look up through the glass of the Square's fountain to see the towers of St. Mary's above. Under the skylight is a model of medieval Kraków. While it looks much the same as today, notice a few key changes: the moat ringing the Old Town, where the Planty is today; and the several smaller market halls out on the Square.

Deeper in the exhibit, explore the long corridors of ruined buildings that once ran alongside the length of the Cloth Hall. There are many intriguing cases showing artifacts that shops would have sold (jewelry, tools, amber figurines, and so on). Also in this area, you'll find a corridor with images of the Square all torn up for the recent renovation, plus a series of five modern brick rooms, each showing a brief, excellent film outlining a different period of Kraków's history. These "Kraków Chronicles" provide a big-picture context to what otherwise seems like a loose collection of cool museum gizmos, and also help you better appreciate what you'll see outside the museum's doors.

▲Jagiellonian University Museum: Collegium Maius

Kraków's historic university building can be toured with a student guide. While the courtyard itself (described earlier in "Kraków's Royal Way Walk") is the best part, the musty interior is mildly interesting. You'll choose between two different guided tours: 30 minutes (very popular) or one hour. It's smart to call ahead to find out when the shorter tour is scheduled in English, and to reserve for either tour (tel. 12-663-1307 for advance reservations, or tel. 12-663-1521 for same day, www.maius.uj.edu.pl). The building is two short blocks west of the Main Market Square, at ulica Jagiellońska 15.

The **30-minute tour** covers the "main exhibition" route: the library, refectory (with a gorgeously carved Baroque staircase), treasury (including Polish filmmaker Andrzej Wajda's honorary Oscar), assembly hall, and some old scientific instruments (12 zł, a few tours per day in English, 20 people maximum, leaves every 20 minutes Mon-Fri 10:00-14:20, Tue and Thu until 17:20 in April-Oct, Sat 10:00-13:20, these are the last tour times, no tours Sun). On Tuesday afternoons, you can see the route on your own, for free (15:00-17:20, shorter hours in winter).

The **one-hour tour** adds some more interiors, room after room of more old scientific instruments, medieval art (mostly church sculptures), a Rubens, a small landscape from the shop of Rembrandt, and Chopin's piano (16 zł, usually in English Mon-Fri at 13:00, no tours Sat-Sun).

Dominican Church, a.k.a. Holy Trinity Church (Bazylika Trójcy Świętej)

In most towns, this would be something special. In church-crazy Kraków, it's an also-ran. Still, it's convenient (just a couple of blocks south of the Square) and worth a peek.

Cost and Hours: Free but donation requested, daily 6:30-13:00 & 16:00-20:00, facing plac Dominikański at Stolarska 12.

Visiting the Church: Inside, you'll find a Neo-Gothic space that was rebuilt after a devastating 1850 fire. You may be approached and offered an audioguide to tour the church, in exchange for a donation; it's a good little tour and worth doing, if you have the time. Or, for a quick visit, tune in to just a few details: The unique metal chandeliers are one of many modern flourishes added during the late-19th-century restoration of the church. Climb the staircase in the left aisle to reach the chapel of St. Hyacinth. Locally known as St. Jacek, this early Dominican leader—called the "Apostle of the North"—is also the patron saint of pierogi (stuffed dumplings, similar to ravioli). During a famine, St. Jacek supposedly invented pierogi and—in a loaves-and-fishes-type miracle—produced plateful after plateful, feeding the desperate locals. His image adorns Kraków's annual Pierogi Cup contest, and to this day, when old-fashioned Poles are surprised, they might exclaim, "*Święty Jacek* *z pierogami!*" ("St. Hyacinth and his pierogi!"). Back down in the main part of the church, stroll slowly past the gorgeously carved wooden seats of the choir area (behind the altar); then, at the main altar, identify the three parts of the Trinity: Jesus (short beard), God (long beard), and Holy Spirit (beardless dove).

Archdiocesan Museum (Muzeum Archidiecezjalne)

This museum, in a building where St. John Paul II lived both as a priest and as a bishop, is the best place in town to learn more about Kraków's favorite son (without making the trip to the St. John Paul II Sanctuary on the outskirts—described later). You'll head upstairs and tour the rooms where JPII actually lived, both as a priest and (later) as a bishop. You'll see John Paul II's personal effects, including clothes, handwritten notes, travel gear, bike, kayak, and skis—reminding visitors that he was one sporty pope. Then you'll tour the lavish private apartments where he lived from 1958 until 1967, as archbishop of Kraków. Throughout the collection are many portraits and photographs of the late pontiff—making his cult of personality almost palpable.

Cost and Hours: 5 zł, Tue-Fri 10:00-16:00, Sat-Sun 10:00-15:00, closed Mon, Kanonicza 19-21, tel. 12-421-8963, www.muzeumkra.diecezja.pl.

Sights in Kazimierz

The neighborhood of Kazimierz (kah-ZHEE-mehzh), 20 minutes by foot southeast of Kraków's Old Town, is the historic heart of

Kraków's once-thriving Jewish community. After years of neglect, the district began a rejuvenation in the early 2000s. Today, while not quite as slick and polished as Prague's Jewish Quarter, Kazimierz's assortment of synagogues, cemeteries, and museums helps visitors appreciate the neighborhood's rich Jewish history. At the same time, Kazimierz also happens to be the city's edgy, hipster culture center—jammed with colorful bars, creative eateries, and designer boutiques. This unlikely combination—where somber synagogues coexist with funky food trucks—makes Kazimierz a big draw for travelers both young and old.

When To Go: Try to visit any day except Saturday, when most Jewish-themed sights are closed (except the Old Synagogue, High Synagogue, and Galicia Jewish Museum). Monday comes with a few closures: the Ethnographic Museum, Museum of Contemporary Art in Kraków, and Museum of Municipal Engineering.

Kazimierz Walk

1 Kazimierz Monument
2 Old Jewish Cemetery & Jan Karski Statue
3 Old Shop Fronts
4 Hamsa Rest. & Jarden Bookshop
5 Klezmer-Hois Restaurant
6 New Jewish Cemetery
7 Rubinstein Birthplace
8 Popper Synagogue
9 Old Synagogue
10 Food Trucks
11 Isaac Synagogue
12 Plac Nowy
13 Meiselsa & Bożego Ciała Streets
14 "Schindler's List Passage"
15 Ulica Józefa
16 Plac Wolnica
17 Ethnographic Museum
18 Old Tram Depot
19 Museum of Municipal Engineering
20 Judah Square
21 Galicia Jewish Museum

On Monday, the Schindler's Factory Museum is free, but it's open shorter hours and is more crowded than usual. For more suggestions of what to do in Kazimierz, see the Shopping, Entertainment, Sleeping, and Eating sections.

Etiquette: To show respect, men cover their heads while visiting a Jewish cemetery or synagogue. Most sights offer loaner yarmulkes, or you can wear your own hat.

Getting to Kazimierz: From the Old Town, it's about a

20-minute **walk.** From the Main Market Square, head down ulica Sienna (near St. Mary's Church) and through the Planty park. When you hit the busy ring road, bear right and continue down Starowiślna for 15 more minutes. The **tram** shaves off a few minutes: Find the stop along the ring road, on the left-hand side of ulica Sienna (across the street from the Poczta Główna, or main post office). Catch tram #3 or #24, and ride two stops to Miodowa. Walking or by tram, at the intersection of Starowiślna and Miodowa, you'll see a small park across the street and to the right. To reach the heart of Kazimierz—ulica Szeroka—cut through this park. The same trams continue to the sights in Podgórze (including the Schindler's Factory Museum).

To return to the Old Town, catch tram #3 or #24 from the intersection of Starowiślna and Miodowa (kitty-corner from where you got off the tram).

Information: An official **TI** is just a few blocks off the bottom of ulica Szeroka, at ulica Józefa 7 (daily 9:00-17:00, tel. 12-422-0471).

▲KAZIMIERZ WALK

This self-guided walk is designed to help you get your bearings in Kazimierz, connecting both its Jewish sights (mostly in "Part 1") and its eclectic other attractions, from trendy bars to under-rated museums ("Part 2"). Allow about an hour for the entire walk, not counting museum visits along the way. From the end of the walk, you can easily cross the river to this area's biggest sight, the Schindler's Factory Museum.

Part 1: Jewish Heritage on Ulica Szeroka

• *We'll start on ulica Szeroka ("Broad Street")—the center of the neigh-borhood, which feels like more of an elongated square than a "street." Begin at the bottom (southern) edge of the small, grassy park, near the strip of restaurants. In the park, look for the low-profile, stone...*

Kazimierz Monument

You're standing in the historical heart of Kraków's Jewish com-munity. In the 14th century, King Kazimierz the Great enacted policies that encouraged Jews fleeing other kingdoms to settle in Poland—including in Kraków. He also founded this town, which still bears his name. Originally, Jews lived in the Old Town, but they were scapegoated after a 1495 fire and forced to relocate to Kazimierz. Back then, Kazimierz was still a separate town, divided by a wall into Christian (west) and Jewish (east) neighborhoods. Ulica Szeroka was the main square of the Jewish community. Over time, Jews were more or less accepted into the greater community, and Jewish culture flourished here.

All that would change in the mid-20th century. The **monu-ment** honors the "65 thousand Polish citizens of Jewish national-ity from Kraków and its environs"—more than a quarter of the city's pre-WWII population—who were murdered by the Nazis during the Holocaust. When the Nazis arrived, they immediately sent most of Kraków's Jews to the ghetto in the eastern Polish city of Lublin. Soon after, they forced Kraków's remaining 15,000 Jews into a walled ghetto at Podgórze, across the river. The Jews' cemeteries were defiled, and their buildings were ransacked and destroyed. In 1942, the Nazis began transporting Kraków's Jews to death camps (including Płaszów, just on Kraków's outskirts, and Auschwitz).

Only a few thousand Kraków Jews survived the war. During the communist era, this waning population was ignored or mistreated. After 1989, interest in Kazimierz's unique Jewish history was faintly rekindled. But it was only when Steven Spielberg chose to film *Schindler's List* here in 1993 that the world took renewed interest in Kazimierz. (A local once winked to me, "They ought to build a statue to Spielberg on that square.") Although the current Jewish population in Kraków numbers only 200, Kazimierz has become an internationally known destination for those with an interest in Jewish heritage.

KRAKÓW

• *Facing the park, look to the left. The arch with the Hebrew characters marks the entrance to the...*

▲▲Old Jewish Cemetery (Stary Cmentarz)

This small cemetery was used to bury members of the Jewish community from 1552 to 1800. With more than a hundred of the top Jewish intellectuals of that age buried here, this is considered one of the most important Jewish cemeteries in Europe.

Cost and Hours: 10 zł includes cemetery and attached Remu'h Synagogue; sporadic hours according to demand—especially outside peak season—but generally open Sun-Fri 9:00-16:00, can be open until 18:00 May-Sept, closes earlier off-season and by sundown on Fri, closed Sat year-round, ulica Szeroka 40.

Visiting the Cemetery: Walk under the arch, pay the admission fee, step into the cemetery, and survey the tidy rows of headstones. This early Jewish resting place (later replaced by the New Cemetery, described later) was desecrated by the Nazis during the Holocaust. In the 1950s, it was discovered, excavated, and put back together as you see here. Shattered gravestones form a mosaic wall around the perimeter. As in all Jewish cemeteries, you'll see many small stones stacked on the graves. The tradition comes from placing stones—representing prayers—over desert graves to cover the body and prevent animals from disturbing it. Behind the little synagogue to the left, the tallest tombstone next to the tree belonged to Moses Isserles (a.k.a. Remu'h), an important 16th-century rabbi. He is believed to have been a miracle worker, and his grave was one of the only ones that remained standing after World War II. Notice the written prayers crammed into the cracks and crevices of the tombstone.

Near the gate to the cemetery, step into the tiny **Remu'h Synagogue** (c. 1553, covered by cemetery ticket). Tight and cozy, this has been carefully renovated and is fully active. Notice the original 16th-century frescoed walls and ceilings, and the donation box at the door. For more on typical synagogue architecture, see the sidebar.

• *Back outside, turn left and continue up to the top of...*

Ulica Szeroka

Just above the cemetery gate, notice a bronze statue of a gentleman seated on a bench. This is a tribute to **Jan Karski** (1914-2000), a Catholic Pole and resistance fighter who published his eyewitness account *The Story of a Secret State* about the Holocaust in 1944. Karski—the ultimate whistleblower—was one of the first people who spoke out about Nazi atrocities, at a time when even many world leaders had only an inkling about what was happening in Hitler's realm. Karski's message, so shocking as to be literally unbelievable to many, went ignored by some key leaders—arguably extending the horrors of the Holocaust.

Just above that, at the top corner of the square, notice the side street with a row of rustic old Jewish **shop fronts,** which evoke the bustle of prewar Kazimierz. The Jewish names—Rattner, Weinberg, Nowak, Holcer—stand testament to the lively soul of this neighborhood in its heyday. This lane leads to Miodowa street, which you can follow left to reach two of Kazimierz's lesser-known synagogues (Tempel and Kupa, both described later).

The building at the top of the square houses the recommended **Hamsa** restaurant (with modern Israeli food) and **Jarden Bookshop,** which serves as an unofficial information point for the neighborhood and sells a wide variety of fairly priced books on Kazimierz and Jewish culture in the region (Mon-Fri 9:00-18:00, Sat-Sun 10:00-18:00, ulica Szeroka 2).

Kitty-corner from the bookshop, notice **Klezmer-Hois**—one of many restaurants offering live traditional Jewish klezmer music nightly in summer (for more on klezmer music, and details on your options, see page 119).

The **New Jewish Cemetery**—less touristed and a striking contrast to the Old Jewish Cemetery we just saw—is a worthwhile detour, about a five-minute walk away (see description on page 83).

The Synagogue

A synagogue is a place of public worship, where Jews gather to pray, sing, and read from the Torah. Most synagogues have similar features, though they vary depending on the congregation.

The synagogue generally faces toward Jerusalem (so in Kraków, worshippers face east). At the east end is an alcove called the ark, which holds the Torah. These scriptures (the first five books of the Old Testament) are written in Hebrew on scrolls wrapped in luxuriant cloth. The other main element of the synagogue is the bema, an elevated platform from which the Torah is read aloud (the equivalent of a pulpit in a Christian church). In traditional Orthodox synagogues, the bema is near the center of the hall, and the reader stands facing the same direction as the congregation. In other branches of Judaism, the bema is at the front, and the reader faces the worshippers. Orthodox synagogues have separate worship areas for men and women, usually with women in the balcony.

The synagogue walls might be decorated with elaborate patterns of vines or geometric designs, but never statues of people, which could be considered idol worship. A lamp above the ark is always kept lit, as it was in the ancient temple of Jerusalem, and candelabras called menorahs also recall the temple. Other common symbols are the two tablets of the Ten Commandments given to Moses, or a Star of David, representing the Jewish king's shield.

At a typical service, the congregation arrives at the start of Sabbath (Friday evening). As a sign of respect toward God, men don yarmulkes (small round caps). As the cantor leads songs and prayers, worshippers follow along in a book of weekly readings. At the heart of the service, everyone stands as the Torah is ceremoniously paraded, unwrapped, and placed on the bema. Someone—the rabbi, the cantor, or a congregant—reads the words aloud. The rabbi ("teacher") might give a commentary on the Torah passage.

KRAKÓW

To get there, cut through the grassy little lot between Jarden Bookshop and Klezmer-Hois, turn right, cross the busy street, then go through the railway underpass.

When you're ready to move on, do a 180 and head back downhill on ulica Szeroka. You'll pass the little park again, then come to a row of lively, mostly Jewish-themed **restaurants** with outdoor tables. Several places along here (especially Ester Hotel, at the bottom of the row) feature outdoor klezmer music in good weather—allowing you to get a taste of this unique musical form before committing to a full meal.

Halfway down this side of the square, the green house at #14 is where **Helena Rubinstein** was born in 1870. At age 31, she emigrated to Australia, where she parlayed her grandmother's traditional formula for hand cream into a cosmetics empire. Many cosmetics still used by people worldwide today were invented by Rubinstein, who died at age 92 in New York City as one of the most successful businesswomen of all time—just one of many illustrious Jewish residents of Kazimierz.

Two doors past the Rubinstein house, notice the round arch marking the courtyard of the **Popper Synagogue,** a popular venue for klezmer concerts.

Continue past the restaurants to the very bottom of ulica Szeroka, and pause at the steps before heading down into the sunken area around the Old Synagogue. To the synagogue's left, notice a short, reconstructed stretch of Kazimierz's 14th-century **town wall.** This is a reminder that medieval Kazimierz was a separate city from Kraków. It's easy to read some history into a map of Kazimierz (you'll find one on the big panel in front of the Old Synagogue): Today's Starowiślna and Dietla streets—which frame off Kazimierz in a triangle of land hemmed in by the riverbank—were once canals (Kazimierz was built on an island). When King Kazimierz the Great—who reportedly didn't care much for Krakovians—founded this district in 1335, he envisioned it as a separate town to rival Kraków. It wasn't until around 1800 that the two towns merged.

• *Turn your attention to the bottom of the square, with the...*

Old Synagogue
(Stara Synagoga)

The oldest surviving Jewish building in Poland (15th century) sits eight steps below street level. Jewish structures weren't allowed to be taller than Christian ones—and so, in order to have the proper proportions, the synagogue's "ground floor"

had to be underground. Today the synagogue houses a good three-room museum on local Jewish culture, with informative English descriptions and a well-preserved main prayer hall (9 zł, free on Mon; April-Oct Mon 10:00-14:00, Tue-Sun 9:00-17:00; shorter hours off-season; good 50-stop audioguide-10 zł; ulica Szeroka 24, tel. 12-422-0962).

• *A few more Jewish sights can be found in the surrounding streets; I'll point these out in "Part 2," though the rest of this walk focuses on a more recent chapter.*

Part 2: Contemporary Kazimierz

• *Stand with your back to the Old Synagogue and turn left, heading up the little alley next to Szeroka 28—called Lewkowa.*

Hipster Kazimierz

Follow Lewkowa between some old buildings. When you pop out into an open area, jog right, then continue straight along ulica Ciemna. Soon you'll hit an inviting little **pod of food trucks** (described on page 87). Pause here—perhaps while nursing an açaí smoothie, an artisanal kielbasa, or a taco—and ponder the explosion of youthful culture that's taken place in Kazimierz over the last generation.

At the end of World War II, Kazimierz was badly damaged and depopulated. And so it remained for generations, as the communist authorities brushed Jewish heritage under the rug. By the early 2000s, Kazimierz's artistically dilapidated buildings, low rents, and easy proximity to the Old Town became enticing to creative young people. A variety of artsy entrepreneurs took root here, beginning with a cluster of ramshackle, rustic bars (inspired partly by Budapest's "ruin pub" scene). Today the district has the city's (and probably Poland's) highest concentration of trendy food trucks, cafés, bars, restaurants, and design shops—several of which we'll see as we continue.

• *From the food trucks, continue straight ahead (on Izaaka street). This leads you around the left side of...*

Isaac Synagogue (Synagoga Izaaka)

One of Kraków's biggest synagogues, this was built in the 17th century. Inside, the walls in the prayer hall are decorated with giant paintings of prayers for worshippers who couldn't afford to buy books (with translations posted below). The synagogue also serves as the local center for the Hasidic Jewish group Chabad, with a kosher restaurant and a library (7 zł; April-Oct Sun-Thu 8:30-20:00, Fri 8:30-14:30, closed Sat year-round, shorter hours off-season; ulica Kupa 18, tel. 12-430-2222). In addition to its Sabbath services, this is Kraków's only synagogue that has daily prayers (at 8:30). They also host klezmer music concerts many evenings at 18:00 (60 zł).

• *Just past Isaac Synagogue is the heart of Kazimierz's nightlife zone (also bustling by day). Dive in, passing some characteristic cafés (on your left) and the chic Taawa nightclub (on your right). Then jog right at the glitzy Plac Nowy 1 beer hall to reach...*

Plac Nowy

Kazimierz's endearing "new" market square, plac Nowy (plats NOH-vee), retains much of the gritty flavor of the district before tourism and gentrification. The circular brick building in the center is a slaughterhouse where Jewish butchers would properly kill livestock, kosher-style. Today its windows are filled with little stand-up eateries ranging from burgers and ice cream to the traditional local pizza-like *zapiekanki*. Circle the market hall and browse for a snack (for more on the plac Nowy scene, see "Eating in Kraków," later). Good Lood has Kraków's best artisanal ice cream—if you don't mind the long line. This square is also ringed by several fun and funky bars—enjoyable by day, but hopping at night (see page 117).

• *Leave plac Nowy along Meiselsa street (to the left from where you entered, past the yellow Jewish Cultural Center). After one block, pause at the intersection of...*

Meiselsa and Bożego Ciała Streets

The Holocaust was a dark chapter that dominates Kazimierz's history. But this intersection is a reminder that, up until the Nazis arrived, Kazimierz was a place where Jews and Christians lived side-by-side, in relative harmony. Notice the street names, which mix Jewish and Catholic namesakes: ulica Meiselsa ("Meisels Street"—honoring a deeply respected 19th-century rabbi) and ulica Bożego Ciała ("Corpus Christi Street"—named for the towering brick church you can see just ahead). As if to celebrate the ecumenism of this intersection, a street artist has painted a graffiti Gene Kelly on the wall...very "happy again" indeed that Kazimierz is blossoming and full of life.

• *Backtrack a few steps up Meiselsa and duck into the courtyard on the right, under the dilapidated arch (labeled* Stajnia).

"*Schindler's List* Passage"

This courtyard is a popular tourist spot thanks to its brush with fame, as a location for some key scenes in *Schindler's List* (find the back-and-white stills from the movie partway down on the right, just before the arch). Spielberg connection aside, this is a particularly evocative setting to nurse a relaxing drink at one of the atmospheric cafés.

KRAKÓW

• *Carry on all the way through the passage. You'll pop out at...*

Ulica Józefa: Design Street

This street has Kazimierz's highest concentration of funky, one-off boutiques: jewelry, fashion, housewares, and more. For a rundown of the best options along here, see page 112. There's also a TI just across the street.

• *When you're ready to move along, take ulica Józefa a few steps to the intersection with ulica Bożego Ciała, turn left, and follow it a long block. You'll pass Corpus Christi Church on your left, then arrive at...*

Plac Wolnica

Remember that Kazimierz was originally a separate town from Kraków. This was its main market square, designed to one-up its crosstown rival—right down to the dramatic, red-brick Catholic church on the corner (Corpus Christi).

The former Kazimierz town hall at the far end of the square houses an unusually good **Ethnographic Museum** (Muzeum Etnograficzne)—worth ▲. If you're interested in Polish folk culture, it's worth a visit. On the ground floor, you'll find models of traditional rural Polish homes, as well as musty replicas of the interiors (like an open-air folk museum moved inside). The exhibit continues upstairs, where each in a long lineup of traditional Polish folk costumes is identified by specific region. Follow the one-way route through exhibits on village lifestyles, rustic tools, and musical instruments (including a Polish bagpipe). A highlight is the explanation of traditional holiday celebrations—from elaborate crèche scenes at Christmas, to a wall of remarkably painted Easter eggs. Some items are labeled in English, but it's mostly in Polish. The top floor features temporary exhibits (13 zł, free on Sun, open Tue-Sun 10:00-19:00, closed Mon, ulica Krakowska 46, tel. 12-430-6023, www.etnomuzeum.eu).

• *There's more to see in Kazimierz. But if you're pooped, you could catch tram #6, #8, #10, or #13 back to Wawel Castle, then on to the plac Wszystkich Świętych stop in the heart of the Old Town (catch tram from along Krakowska street, behind the Ethnographic Museum).*

To continue the walk from plac Wolnica, head up ulica Św. Wawrzyńca (at the corner where you entered the square, with the Corpus Christi Church on your left).

Ulica Św. Wawrzyńca: Industrial Kazimierz

By the late 19th century, Kazimierz was not just a Jewish cultural hotspot, but also a center of local industry. (It's no coincidence that Oskar Schindler had his factory near here.) After the church, on your left, look for the glass-and-steel arched roof of the Industrial Age **old tram depot,** which now houses a recommended brewpub. In sunny summer weather, the pebbly courtyard is filled with happy drinkers.

Across the street, notice the many tram tracks leading in to a courtyard with several more storage sheds for local trams. This gorgeously restored complex now houses the **Museum of Municipal Engineering** (Muzeum Inżynierii Miejskiej). Exhibits include a history of the town's public-transit system (including several antique trams), old Polish-made cars and motorcycles (among them the tiny commie-era Polski Fiat), typography and historical printing presses, and a hands-on area for kids called "Around the Wheel" (10 zł, family ticket-29 zł, includes English audioguide, free on Tue; open Tue-Sun 10:00-16:00; Tue, Thu, and Sun until 18:00 in June-Sept; closed Mon year-round; Św. Wawrzyńca 15, tel. 12-421-1242, www.mimk.com.pl).

Continue along ulica Św. Wawrzyńca a few more steps. At the intersection with Wąska, **Judah Square** (Skwer Judah) is a vacant lot with a gaggle of enticing food carts watched over by a giant mural. Commissioned for Kraków's Jewish Cultural Festival in 2013, the illustration was painted by Israeli street artist Pilpeled. It shows a young boy who feels small and scared, but lionhearted nevertheless—a poignant symbol for the Holocaust survivors of Kazimierz. If you're ready for a meal or snack, you'll find several good options here.

• *A half-block farther down ulica Św. Wawrzyńca is another place for refreshment, the recommended Craftownia (Polish microbrews on tap, on the left at #22). Next you'll reach the intersection with Dajwór street. Turn left here and walk a few steps up the street; on the right, you'll find the...*

Galicia Jewish Museum (Galicja Muzeum)

This museum, worth ▲ and housed in a restored Jewish furniture factory, focuses on the present rather than the past. The permanent "Traces of Memory" photographic exhibit shows today's remnants of yesterday's Judaism in the area around Kraków (a region known as "Galicia"). From abandoned synagogues to old Jewish gravestones flipped over and used as doorsteps, these giant postcards of Jewish artifacts (with good English descriptions) ensure that an important part of this region's heritage won't be forgotten. Good temporary exhibits complement this permanent collection (15 zł, daily 10:00-18:00, 1 block east of ulica Szeroka at ulica Dajwór 18, tel. 12-421-6842, www.galiciajewishmuseum.org). The museum also serves as a sort of cultural center, with a good bookstore and café.

• *Notice yet another cluster of food trucks across the street from the museum.*

*Our Kazimierz orientation walk is finished. From here, you have several options. To **return to ulica Szeroka**, where we began, walk up Dajwór street past the museum, then angle left through the park at the reconstructed chunk of town wall—you'll wind up at the Old Synagogue.*

*For the next two options, you'll first head back down to ulica Św. Wawrzyńca, turn left, and walk one more block to the intersection with Starowiślna street. Just to the left on Starowiślna, look for the tram stops. The tram stop on the far side of the street takes you **back to the Old Town** (tram #3 or #24). From the tram stop on the near side of the street, tram #3 or #24 zips you to the **sights in Podgórze**—including Ghetto Heroes' Square and the Schindler's Factory Museum (both described later). You can also reach the Podgórze sights on foot by turning right on Starowiślna and crossing the bridge (about a 10-minute walk).*

MORE JEWISH SIGHTS IN KAZIMIERZ

In addition to the sights connected by the walk above, here's another cemetery and a few more synagogues to round out your Jewish Kazimierz experience.

▲New Jewish Cemetery (Nowy Cmentarz)

This burial place—much larger than the Old Jewish Cemetery—has graves of those who died after 1800. It was vandalized by the

Nazis, who sold many of its gravestones to stonecutters and used others as pavement in their concentration camps. Many have since been cemented back in their original positions, while others—which could not be replaced—have been used to create the moving mosaic wall and Holocaust monument (on the right as you enter). Most gravestones are in one of four languages: Hebrew (generally the oldest, especially if there's no other language, though some are newer "retro" tombstones); Yiddish (sounds like a mix of German and Hebrew and uses the Hebrew alphabet); Polish (Jews who assimilated into the Polish community); and German (Jews who assimilated into the German community). The earliest graves are simple stones, while later ones imitate graves in Polish Catholic cemeteries—larger, more elaborate, and with a long stone jutting out to cover the body. Notice that some new-looking graves have old dates. These were most likely put here well after the Holocaust (or even after the communist era) by relatives of the dead.

Cost and Hours: Free, Sun-Fri 8:00-18:00, winter until 16:00, closed Sat. It's tricky to find: Go under the railway tunnel at the east end of ulica Miodowa, and jog left as you emerge. The cemetery is to your right (enter through gate with small *cmentarz żydowski* sign).

Synagogues

In addition to the three synagogues mentioned on the Kazimierz Walk (Old Synagogue, Isaac, and Remu'h), others also welcome visitors. Each of these charges a small admission fee and is closed Saturdays (unless noted). The **High Synagogue**—so called because its prayer room is upstairs—displays changing exhibits, most of which focus on the people who lived here before the Holocaust (daily, ulica Józefa 38). **Tempel Synagogue** (Synagoga Templu) has the grandest interior—big and dark, with elaborately decorated, gilded ceilings and balconies (corner of ulica Miodowa and ulica Podbrzezie). The **Jewish Community Centre** next door offers activities both for members of the local Jewish community and for tourists (lectures, genealogical research, Friday-night Shabbat meals, Hebrew and Yiddish classes, and so on; www.jcckrakow. org). Nearly across the street, the smaller **Kupa Synagogue** (Synagoga Kupa)—clean and brightly decorated—sometimes hosts temporary exhibits (Miodowa 27).

NEAR KAZIMIERZ: PODGÓRZE

The neighborhood called Podgórze (POD-goo-zheh), directly across the Vistula from Kazimierz, has one of Kraków's most famous sights: Schindler's Factory Museum. I've listed these sights in the order you'll reach them as you come from Kazimierz or the Old Town.

Background: This is the neighborhood where the Nazis forced Kraków's Jews into a ghetto in early 1941. (*Schindler's List* and the films in the Pharmacy Under the Eagle museum depict the sad scene of the Jews loading their belongings onto carts and trudging over the bridge into Podgórze.) Non-Jews who had lived here were displaced to make way for the new arrivals. The ghetto was surrounded by a wall with a fringe along the top that resembled

Jewish gravestones—a chilling premonition of what was to come. A short section of this wall still stands along Lwowska street. The tram continued to run through the middle of Podgórze, without stopping—giving Krakovians a chilling glimpse at the horrifying conditions inside the ghetto.

Getting There: To go directly to Ghetto Heroes' Square, continue through Kazimierz on tram #3 or #24 (described earlier, under "Getting to Kazimierz") to the stop called plac Bohaterow Getta. Or you can ride the tram or walk 10 minutes across the bridge from the end of my Kazimierz Walk.

Ghetto Heroes' Square (Plac Bohaterow Getta)

This unassuming square is the focal point of the visitor's Podgórze. Today the square is filled with a monument consisting of 68 empty

metal chairs—representing the 68,000 people deported from here. This is intended to remind viewers that the Jews of Kazimierz were forced to carry all of their belongings—including furniture— to the ghetto on this side of the river. It was also here that many Jews waited to be sent to extermination camps. The small, gray building at the river end of Ghetto Heroes' Square feels like a train car inside, evocative of the wagons that carried people from here to certain death.

▲Pharmacy Under the Eagle (Apteka pod Orłem)

This small but good museum, on Ghetto Heroes' Square, tells the story of Tadeusz Pankiewicz, a Polish Catholic pharmacist who chose to remain in Podgórze when it became a Jewish ghetto. During this time, the pharmacy was an important meeting point for the ghetto residents, and Pankiewicz and his staff heroically aided and hid Jewish victims of the Nazis. (Pankiewicz survived the war and was later acknowledged by Israel as one of the "Righteous Among the Nations"—non-Jews who risked their lives to help the Nazis' victims during World War II. You'll see his medal on display in the white memorial room at the end of the museum.) Today the pharmacy hosts an exhibit about the Jewish ghetto. You'll enter into the re-created pharmacy, where the "windows" are actually screens that show footage from the era. Push buttons, pull out drawers, answer the phone—it's full of interactive opportunities to better understand what ghetto life was like. You'll learn about people who worked in the pharmacy (including riveting interviews with eye-witnesses—some in English, others subtitled) and hear Pankiewicz telling stories about that tense time. You'll also learn a bit about the pharmacy business from that period.

Cost and Hours: 10 zł; if you're also going to the Schindler's Factory Museum, buy the 23-zł combo-ticket, free on Mon, open Mon 10:00-14:00, Tue-Sun 9:00-17:00, closed the second Tue of each month, plac Bohaterow Getta 18, tel. 12-656-5625, www.mhk.pl/branches/eagle-pharmacy.

▲▲▲Schindler's Factory Museum (Fabryka Emalia Oskara Schindlera)

One of Europe's best museums about the Nazi occupation fills some of the factory buildings where Oskar Schindler and his Jewish employees worked. While the museum tells the story of Schindler and his workers, it broadens its perspective to take in the full experience of all of Kraków during the painful era of Nazi rule—making it the top WWII museum in this country so profoundly affected by that war. It's loaded with in-depth

information (all in English), and touchscreens invite you to learn more and watch eyewitness interviews. Scattered randomly between the exhibits are replicas of everyday places from the age—a photographer's shop, a tram car, a hairdresser's salon—designed to give you a taste of 1940s Kraków. Throughout the museum are calendar pages outlining wartime events and giving a sense of chronology. Note that you'll see nothing of the actual factory or equipment, as the threat of the advancing Red Army forced Schindler to move his operation lock, stock, and barrel to Nazi-occupied Czechoslovakia in 1944.

Cost and Hours: 21 zł, 24-zł combo-ticket with next-door Museum of Contemporary Art, 23-zł "Memory Trail" combo-ticket with Pharmacy Under the Eagle; free on Mon; open April-Oct Mon 10:00-16:00 (except closes at 14:00 first Mon of month), Tue-Sun 9:00-20:00; Nov-March Mon 10:00-14:00, Tue-Sun 10:00-18:00; last entry 1.5 hours before closing, tel. 12-257-1017, www.mhk.pl/branches/oskar-schindlers-factory.

Crowd-Beating Tips: Crowds can be a real problem at this popular sight—especially on Mondays (when it's free, and many other museums are closed), during the summer holidays (June-Aug), and midday (usually worst 11:00-16:00). At busy times, you may have to wait in a long line—an hour or more—just to buy a ticket. And then, once inside, congestion can make it challenging to fully appreciate the place. If you anticipate crowds, you can book tickets for no extra fee up to three days before your visit (www.bilety.mhk.pl); or you can buy tickets anytime (even for later the same day) at the Kraków City Museum Visitors Center in the Cloth Hall on the Main Market Square (see "Tourist Information," page 28). But even if you avoid the ticket line, it could still be jammed inside. The best strategy is to arrive early (9:00 or soon after on most days) or late (in summer, arriving by 18:00 gives you two hours to tour the exhibits)—but be warned that if you're arriving late, it's possible on very busy days that all tickets could be sold out.

Getting There: It's in a gloomy industrial area a five-minute walk from Ghetto Heroes' Square (plac Bohaterow Getta): Go up Kącik street (use the pedestrian underpass, then head to the left of the big, glass skyscraper), go under the railroad underpass, and continue two blocks, past MOCAK (the Museum of Contemporary Art in Kraków, described later) to the second big building on the left (ulica Lipowa 4). Look for signs to *Emalia*.

Visiting the Museum: You'll begin on the ground floor, where you'll buy your ticket and have the chance to tour the special exhibits. There's also a "film café" (interesting for fans of the movie) with refreshments. Then head upstairs to the first floor.

First Floor: The 35-minute **film,** called *Lipowa 4* (this building's address), sets the stage with interviews of both Jews and

non-Jews describing their wartime experience (find it just off of the museum's first, circular room; subtitled in English, it runs continuously). From here, the one-way route winds through the permanent exhibit, called **"Kraków Under Nazi Occupation 1939-1945."** First, while idyllic music plays, "stereoscopic" (primitive 3-D) photos of prewar Kraków capture an idyllic age when culture flourished and the city's Jews (more than one-quarter of the population) blended more or less smoothly with their Catholic-Pole neighbors. But then, a video explains the Nazi invasion of Poland in early September of 1939: It took them only a few weeks to overrun the country (which desperately awaited the promised-for help of their British and French allies, who never arrived). Through the next several rooms, watch the film clip of SS soldiers marching through the Main Market Square—renamed "Adolf-Hitler-Platz"—and read stories about how the Nazis' *Generalgouvernement* attempted to reshape the life of its new capital, "Krakau." (Near the tram car, look for the decapitated head of the Grunwald monument—described on page 40—which had been a powerful symbol of a Polish military victory over German forces.)

Oskar Schindler (1908-1974) and His List

Steven Spielberg's instant-classic, Oscar-winning 1993 film, *Schindler's List,* brought the world's attention to the inspiring story of Oskar Schindler, the compassionate German business-man who did his creative best to save the lives of the Jewish work-ers at his factory in Kraków. Spielberg chose to film the story right here in Kazimierz, where the historical events actually unfolded. Today the Schindler's Factory Museum gives visitors the chance to learn not just about the man and his workers, but about the historical context of their story: the Nazi occupation of Poland.

Oskar Schindler was born in 1908 in the Sudetenland (cur-rently part of the Czech Republic, then predominantly German). Early on, he displayed an idiosyncratic interpretation of ethics that earned him both wealth and enemies. As Nazi aggressions escalated, Schindler (who was very much a Nazi) carried out es-pionage against Poland; when Germany invaded the country in 1939, Schindler smelled a business opportunity. Early in the Nazi occupation of Poland, Schindler came to Kraków and lived in an apartment at ulica Straszewskiego 7 (a block from Wawel Cas-tle, but unmarked and not available for tours). He took over the formerly Jewish-owned Emalia factory at ulica Lipowa 4, which produced metal pots and pans that were dipped into protec-tive enamel; later the factory also began producing armaments for the Nazi war effort. The factory was staffed by about 1,000 Jews from the nearby Płaszów Concentration Camp, which was managed by the ruthless SS officer Amon Göth (depicted in *Schindler's List*—based on real events—shooting at camp inmates for sport from his balcony).

At a certain point, Schindler began to sympathize with his Jewish workers, and gradually did what he could to protect them and offer them better lives. Schindler fed them far better than most concentration-camp inmates and allowed them to sell some of the pots and pans they made on the black market to make money. After he saw many of his employees and friends murdered

You'll see the story of a newly German-owned shop selling Nazi propaganda and learn how professors at Kraków's Jagiellonian University were arrested to prevent them from fomenting rebel-lion among their students. During this time, even Polish secondary schools were closed—effectively prohibiting learning among Poles, whom the Nazis considered inferior. But Polish students continued to meet clandestinely with their teachers. You'll also see images of Hans Frank—the hated puppet ruler of Poland—moving into the country's most important symbol of sovereignty, Wawel Castle. The exhibit also details how early Nazi policies targeted Jews with roundups, torture, and execution. (Down the staircase is an eerie simulation of a cellar prison.) As the Nazis ratcheted up their genoduring an SS raid in 1943, he ramped up these efforts. He would come up with bogus paperwork to classify those threatened with deportation as "essential" to the workings of the factory—even if they were unskilled. He sought and was granted permission to build a "concentration camp" barracks for his workers on the factory grounds, where they lived in far better conditions than those at Płaszów. These lucky few became known as Schindlerjuden— "Schindler's Jews."

As the Soviet army encroached on Kraków in October of 1944, word came that the factory would need to be relocated west, farther from the front line. While Schindler could easily have simply turned his workers over to the concentration-camp system and certain death—as most other industrialists did—he decided to bring them with him to his new factory at Brünnlitz (Brněnec, in today's Czech Republic). He assembled a list of 700 men and 300 women who worked with him, along with 200 other Jewish inmates, and at great personal expense, moved them to Brünnlitz. At the new factory, Schindler and the 1,200 people he had saved produced grenades and rocket parts—virtually all of them, the workers later claimed, mysteriously defective.

After the war, Schindler—who had spent much of his fortune protecting his Jewish workers—hopped around Germany and Argentina, repeatedly attempting but failing to break back into business (often with funding from Jewish donors). He died in poverty in 1974. In accordance with his final wishes, he was buried in Jerusalem, and today his grave is piled high with small stones left there by appreciative Jewish visitors. He has since been named one of the "Righteous Among the Nations" for his efforts to save Jews from the Holocaust. Thomas Keneally's 1982 book *Schindler's Ark* brought the industrialist's tale to a wide audience that included Steven Spielberg, who vaulted Schindler to the ranks of a pop-culture icon.

cidal activities, troops swept through Kraków on March 3, 1941, forcing all the remaining Jews in town to squeeze into the newly created Podgórze ghetto. At the bottom of the stairs, look for the huge pile of plunder—Jewish wealth stolen by the Nazis.

Second Floor: Climb upstairs using the long **staircase,** which was immortalized in a powerful scene in *Schindler's List*. At the top of the stairs on the right is a small room that served as "Schindler's office" for the film; more recently, it's been determined that his actual office was elsewhere (we'll see it soon).

You'll walk through a corridor lined by a replica of the wall that enclosed the **Podgórze ghetto** and see poignant exhibits about the horrific conditions there (including a replica of the cramped living quarters). The Nazis claimed that Jews had to be segregated here, away from the general population, because they "carried diseases."

Continue into the office of Schindler's secretary, with exhibits about Schindler's life and video touchscreens that play testimonial footage of Schindler's grateful

employees. Then proceed into the actual **Schindler's office.** The big map (with German names for cities) was uncovered only in recent years when the factory was being restored. Because Schindler's short tenure here was the only time in the factory's history that these Polish place names would appear in German, it's believed that this map was hung over his desk. Facing the map is a giant monument of enamel pots and pans, like those that were made in this factory. There are 1,200 pots—one for each Jewish worker that Schindler saved. Inside the monument, the walls are lined with the names on Schindler's famous list. The creaky floorboards are intentional: a reminder that the Nazis knew every step you took.

Proceeding through the exhibit, you'll learn more about everyday life—both for ghetto dwellers and for everyday non-Jewish Krakovians, including the Polish resistance (see the Home Army's underground print shop). More eyewitness accounts relate the terrifying days of March 13 and 14, 1943, when the Podgórze ghetto was liquidated, sending survivors to the nearby Płaszów Concentration Camp. The replica of the Płaszów quarry, where inmates were forced

to work in unimaginably difficult conditions, provides a poignant memorial for those who weren't fortunate enough to wind up on Schindler's list.

Now head all the way back down to the ground floor.

Ground Floor: Exhibits here capture the uncertain days near the end of the war in the summer of 1944, when Nazis arrested between 6,000 and 8,000 suspected saboteurs after the Warsaw Uprising, and sent them to Płaszów (see the replica of a basement hideout for 10 Jews who had escaped the ghetto); and later, when many Nazis had fled Kraków, leaving residents to await the Soviet Union's Red Army (see the replica air-raid shelters). The Red Army arrived here on January 18, 1945—at long last, the five years, four months, and twelve days of Nazi rule were over. The Soviets caused their own share of damage to the city before beginning a whole new occupation that would last for generations...but that's a different museum.

Finally, walk along the squishy floor—evoking how life for anyone was unstable and unpredictable during the Nazi occupation—into the **Hall of Choices.** The six rotating pillars tell the stories of people who chose to act—or not to act—when they witnessed atrocities. Think about the ramifications of the choices they made...and what you would have done in their shoes. The final room holds two books: a white book listing those who tried to help, and a black book listing Nazi collaborators. Exiting the museum, notice the portraits of Oscar Schindler's workers who lived long and happy lives after the war.

Nearby: Before heading back to downtown Kraków, consider paying a visit to the superb—and very different—**art museum** that fills the buildings on the factory grounds, behind this main building (described next). Or, for a glass of wine, head just a few doors down from the museum to find the delightful **Krakó Slow Wines** (marked *Lipowa 6F*). This mellow, inviting wine bar and shop is well-stocked with wines mostly from Central and Eastern Europe (daily 10:00-22:00, mobile 669-225-222, www. krakoslowwines.pl).

▲Museum of Contemporary Art in Kraków (Muzeum Sztuki Współczesnej w Krakowie)

Called "MOCAK" for short, this museum exhibits a changing array of innovative and thought-provoking works by contempo-

rary artists, often with heavy themes tied to the surrounding Holocaust sites. With the slogan *Kunst macht frei* ("Art will set you free"—a pointed spin on the Nazis' *Arbeit macht frei* concentration-camp motto), the museum occupies warehouse buildings once filled by Schindler's workers. Now converted to wide-open, bright-white halls, the buildings house many temporary exhibits as well as two permanent ones (the MOCAK Collection in the basement, and the library in the smaller side building). Pick up the floor plan as you enter. It's all well-described in English, and engaging even for those who don't usually like modern art.

Cost and Hours: 10 zł, 24-zł combo-ticket with next-door Schindler's Factory Museum, free on Tue, open Tue-Sun 11:00-

19:00, closed Mon, last entry one hour before closing, Lipowa 4, tel. 12-263-4001, www.mocak.pl.

Sights Outside of Kraków

Along with the St. John Paul II pilgrimage sights (best suited for believers), there are other interesting sights outside of town—an impressive salt mine, a purpose-built communist town, and an unusual earthwork. All require a bus or tram ride to reach.

ST. JOHN PAUL II AND PILGRIMAGE SIGHTS

Pilgrims coming to Kraków eager to walk in the footsteps of St. John Paul II are sometimes disappointed by the low number of actual museums relating to the man in the city center (though the churches affiliated with him are dazzling). However, there are worthwhile sights outside the city: the John Paul II Sanctuary on the outskirts of Kraków; and the John Paul II Family Home Museum in the town of Wadowice, an hour's drive away (and covered later).

Sanctuaries in Kraków

The two biggest, most impressive JPII destinations are about four miles south of Kraków's Old Town, in the Łagiewniki neighborhood. While the main attraction here for pilgrims is the John Paul II Sanctuary, historically and geographically you'll come first to the Divine Mercy Sanctuary—so I've covered that first. The sights aren't worth the trek for the merely curious, but they offer a glimpse of the powerful reverence and deep faith that characterizes the Polish people. If you're a pilgrim—or think you might be one—visiting these sights can be worthwhile; to make the most of your time, consider hiring a driver or a local guide with a car (see page 34).

Getting There: Public transportation from central Kraków is workable, but not ideal. (As these connections are still in flux, it's smart to ask about the best connection at the TI before making the trip.) The easiest public-transit route is to take **tram #8** (which loops around the Old Town, including stops next to St. Francis Basilica at plac Wszystkich Świętych, and near Wawel Castle) to the Divine Mercy Sanctuary (Sanktuarium Bożego Miłosierdzia stop)—about 30 minutes. From the tram stop, you'll huff a few minutes uphill along the wall to find the entrance to the complex. After touring the Divine Mercy sights, you can cross a footbridge to the St. John Paul II Sanctuary. A **taxi** or **Uber** from downtown costs around 30-40 zł one-way and takes 20-30 minutes.

Divine Mercy Sanctuary
(Sanktuarium Bożego Miłosierdzia)

This complex, built around a humble red-brick convent, honors the early-20th-century St. Faustina, who saw a miraculous vision of Jesus that became a powerful religious symbol for many Catholics. Today, pilgrims from around the world come here to revere the relics both of Faustina and of John Paul II (who advocated for her sainthood), and to learn more about her story from the convent's present-day sisters—many of whom speak English.

Background: One cold and blustery evening in 1931, Sister Faustina Kowalska (1905-1938) answered the convent doorbell to find a beggar asking for some food. Faustina brought some soup to the man, who revealed his true nature: a figure of Jesus Christ clad in a white robe, with one hand raised in blessing, and the other touching his chest. Emanating from his chest were twin beams of light: red (representing blood, the life of souls) and white (water, which through baptism washes souls righteously clean). Transformed by her experience, Faustina worked with an artist to create a painted version of the image—called the Divine Mercy—which has been embraced by Polish Catholics as one of the most important symbols of their faith.

Always frail in health, Faustina died at 33—the same age as Jesus. The story of Faustina deeply moved a young Karol Wojtyła. When he became pope, he dedicated the first Sunday after Easter as the day of Divine Mercy worldwide. In 2000, he made his fellow Krakovian the first Catholic saint of the third millennium. To properly revere the newly important St. Faustina, a bold, futuristic church and visitors center was built alongside her original convent.

Cost and Hours: All three parts of the complex—the smaller original chapel, a replica of Faustina's cell, and the huge, modern church, with its soaring bell tower—are free to enter, but donations are happily accepted. Each one has slightly different hours (listed later).

Visiting the Complex: Entering the complex through the side gate, you'll come up a **walkway** with flags from around the world, and plaques translating the Divine Mercy's message—"Jesus, I trust in you"—in dozens of languages.

Just before entering the **original chapel,** look up and to the right—the window with the flowers marks the cell where Faustina died. Inside the chapel (daily 6:00-21:15), the altar to the left of the main altar displays an early copy of Faustina's Divine Mercy painting. Her relics are in the white case just below; in the white kneeler just in front of the chapel, notice the little reliquary holding one of her bones (which worshippers can embrace as they pray).

Leaving the chapel, turn left and go to the far end of the accommodations building. Enter the door on the right (follow signs for *Cela Św. Siostry Faustyny*) to find the **replica of Faustina's cell.** While this is a newer building, here they've created Faustina's convent cell, including many of her personal effects. Drop a coin in the slot for an evocative headphone description of these items, and of the vision of Jesus that put her convent on the map (usually open daily 8:30-18:00).

Dominating the campus is the futuristic, glass-and-steel **main church.** Consecrated by Pope John Paul II on his final visit to Poland in 2002, this building has several parts (daily 7:00-20:00). The lower level has a variety of small chapels, each one donated by Catholic worshippers in a different country (Germany, Hungary, Slovakia, and so on)—and each with a dramatically different style. The central chapel on this level has a modern altar and another bone of St. Faustina. Upstairs, the main sanctuary is a sleek cylindrical space with wooden sunbeams sharply radiating from the altar area. That altar—framed by the gnarled limbs of windblown trees, representing the suffering of human existence—contains a replica of the Divine Mercy painting, flanked by the woman who saw the vision (Faustina, on the right) and the Polish pope who made it a worldwide phenomenon (John Paul II, on the left).

Head back out to the terrace surrounding the church. The bold **tower**—as tall as St. Mary's on Main Market Square, and with a statue of John Paul II at the bottom—has an elevator that you can ride up to a glassed-in viewpoint offering panoramas over the Divine Mercy campus, the adjacent John Paul II Sanctuary complex, and—on the distant horizon—the spires of Wawel Cathedral and Kraków's Old Town. Near the base of the tower is a **canopy** where Mass is said on Divine Mercy Sunday each year, before a crowd of 100,000 who fill the fields below.

From here, it's about a 15-minute walk to the next sight (you'll pay a small fee to cross the "Bridge of Mercy," which spans a scenic gorge).

John Paul II Sanctuary (Sanktuarium Jana Pawła II)

This new complex, funded entirely by private donors, celebrates the life and sainthood of Kraków's favorite son. Construction is ongoing, but for now there are at least two sections of the complex worth visiting: the sanctuary and museum.

Cost and Hours: Sanctuary—free, daily 7:30-19:00, until 18:00 in winter, www.sanktuariumjp2.pl; museum—7 zł, Wed-Sat 10:00-16:00, Sun 10:00-15:00, closed Mon-Tue.

Sanctuary of St. John Paul II: This hypermodern church is big and splendid. In the **downstairs** area, the central chapel features paintings of JPII's papal visits to various pilgrimage sites, both in Poland (Częstochowa) and abroad (Fátima, Lourdes). Most of the chapels ringing the outside have different depictions of the Virgin Mary. Find the chapel that's a replica of the St. Leonard's Crypt under Wawel Cathedral—where a young priest named Karol Wojtyła celebrated his first Mass. In this chapel, you'll see JPII's empty papal tomb from the crypt beneath St. Peter's Basilica at the Vatican. (When he became a saint, his remains—which, controversially, are kept in Rome rather than his homeland—were moved up into the main part of the church, and this simple grave marker was donated to this church.) You'll also see a reliquary in the shape of a book with fluttering pages, holding a small amount of John Paul II's blood (for the story of the book, see page 59). This blood was kept in secret by JPII's personal secretary, only revealed after his death, when it was divvied up among a select few churches. In another chapel, you'll find the tombs of a few recent cardinals; as they're running out of space below Wawel Cathedral, this chapel is poised to handle the overflow. And in yet another chapel, you'll see finely executed reliefs in rock salt, in the style of Wieliczka Salt Mine.

Head upstairs to the sleek, modern **main sanctuary.** The concrete structure supports large walls, providing a canvas for dynamic

mosaics of Bible stories. Above the main altar, in the middle, you'll see the Three Kings delivering their gifts to the Baby Jesus and the Virgin Mary—with St. John Paul II serenely overlooking the scene. In the back-left corner, a smaller chapel focuses on a painting of St. John Paul II; in the hazy background, you can see the dome of St. Peter's at the Vatican (left) and the twin spires of St. Mary's in Kraków (right)—driving home the point that although John Paul II belonged to the world, first and foremost he's considered a son of Kraków and of Poland.

The sanctuary anchors a sprawling complex of conference facilities and other attractions for pilgrims. Poke around. The museum, described next, is the sight most worth visiting.

St. John Paul II Museum: This collects the many gifts bestowed on the beloved pope (African carved masks and ivory tusks; Latin American tapestries; the key to the city of Long Branch, New Jersey; and a pair of glass doves of peace given to him—perhaps with a touch of irony—by US Vice President Dick Cheney); ornate worship aids (chalices, crosses, and so on); and modern art that celebrates the modern pope and his life's work. There are also personal items, from his papal ski gear to the place settings from his Vatican dinner table to his stylish red leather shoes. You'll also see the throne from his last visit to Poland in 2002, and a replica of the humble room across the street from St. Francis Basilica where he stayed on visits back to his homeland.

John Paul II Sights in Wadowice

Karol Wojtyła was born and lived up until age 18 in Wadowice (VAH-doh-veet-seh), about 30 miles (a one-hour drive) southwest of Kraków. As it's roughly in the same direction as Auschwitz, a local guide or driver can help you connect both places for one busy day of contrasts. Visiting by public bus or minibus is possible (about 1.25 hours one-way); ask the TI for details.

The lovely town of Wadowice (about 20,000 people) has a quaint and beautifully restored main square with a pretty Baroque steeple. John Paul II pilgrims find it worth a visit to see the **John Paul II Family Home Museum,** which fills four floors of the tenement building where his family lived through his adolescence. You'll explore a multimedia overview of the life and times of one of the newest Catholic saints, including rooms of the family home, a collection of clothing and other articles that belonged to JPII, photographs and video clips of his life and of the tumultuous period in which he lived, and plenty of interactive displays to bring the entire story to life. Admission is limited, and you'll be accompanied the entire time. Ideally, time your visit to go with an English guide (typically 2/day, likely at 11:00 and 14:00—but confirm online or by phone); otherwise, you'll join the Polish tour. Either way, the tour can be a bit rushed, with less time to linger over the exhibits than you might like (20 zł with a Polish guide, or 30 zł with English guide, free and crowded on Tue; open daily May-Sept 9:00-19:00, April and Oct 9:00-18:00, Nov-March 9:00-16:00, closed the last Tue of each month, last entrance 1.5 hours before closing, across the street from the town church at ulica Kościelna 7, tel. 33-823-2662, www.homejp2.com).

MORE SIGHTS OUTSIDE OF KRAKÓW
▲▲Wieliczka Salt Mine (Kopalnia Soli Wieliczka)

Wieliczka (veel-EECH-kah), a salt mine 10 miles southeast of Kraków, is beloved by Poles. Deep beneath the ground, the mine is filled with sculptures that miners have lovingly carved out of the salt. You'll explore this unique gallery—learning both about the art and about medieval mining tech-niques—on a required tour. Though the sight is a bit overrated, it's unique and practically obligatory if you're in Kraków for a few days. In my experi-ence with tour groups, about half the people love Wieliczka, while half feel it's a waste of time—but it can be hard to predict which half you're in. Read the description here carefully before you decide. And expect a lot of walk-ing.

Cost and Hours: The standard "tourist route" costs 84 zł and is by guided tour only. The mine is open April-Oct 7:30-18:00, Nov-March 9:00-17:00 (these are last tour times). English-language tours leave every 30 minutes in the morning (10:00-13:00) and all day in summer (June-Sept), and otherwise depart hourly. They also have other routes that are more in-depth (such as the interactive "Miner's Route," where visitors wear coveralls and helmets and actually operate some of the old equipment); for details on these, see the website. The mine is in the town of Wieliczka at ulica Daniłowicza 10 (tel. 12-278-7302, www.kopalnia.pl).

You'll pay an extra 10 zł for permission to use your camera—but be warned that flash photos often don't turn out, thanks to the irregular reflection of the salt crystals. Dress warmly—the mine is a constant 57 degrees Fahrenheit. Before entering, you'll have to check large bags and go through a security checkpoint.

Your ticket includes a dull **mine museum** at the end of the tour. It adds an hour to the mine tour and is discouraged by locals ("1.5 miles more walking, colder, more of the same"). Make it clear when you buy your ticket that you're not interested in the museum.

You can buy your tickets—and an appointed entry time—at the **Wieliczka Promotion Office,** in Kraków's Old Town (Mon-Fri 9:00-17:00, closed Sat-Sun, Wiślna 12a).

Getting There: The salt mine is 10 miles from Kraków. By far the easiest option is to hop on the **train** at Kraków's main train station (track 3, 2/hour, 3 zł, takes 20 minutes, get off at Wieliczka Rynek-Kopalnia and walk 5-10 minutes to the mine). In a pinch, you can take **bus #304** (at Kurniki stop across from church near Galeria Krakowska mall) or a **minibus,** but these take longer (40 minutes)—get details at the TI. **Private drivers** also make this trip (see page 35).

Background: Wieliczka Salt Mine has been producing salt since at least the 13th century. Under Kazimierz the Great, one-third of Poland's income came from these precious deposits. Wieliczka miners spent much of their lives underground, leaving for work before daybreak and returning after sundown, rarely emerging into daylight. To pass the time, and to immortalize their national pride and religiosity in art, 19th-century miners began to carve figures, chandeliers, and eventually even an elaborate chapel out of the salt. Until a few years ago, the mine still produced salt. Today's miners—about 400 of them—primarily work on maintaining the 200 miles of chambers. This entire network is supported by wooden beams (because metal would rust).

Visiting the Mine: From the lobby, your guide leads you 380 steps down a winding staircase. From this spot you begin a 1.5-mile stroll, generally downhill (more than 800 steps down altogether), past 20 of the mine's 2,000 chambers (with signs explaining when they were dug), finishing 443 feet below the surface. When you're done, an elevator beams you back up.

The tour shows how the miners lived and worked, using horses who spent their whole adult lives without ever seeing the light of day. It takes you through vast underground caverns, past subterranean lakes, and introduces you to some of the mine's many sculptures (including one of Copernicus—who actually visited here in the 15th century—as well as an army of salt elves, and this region's favorite son, St. John Paul II). Your jaw will drop as you enter the enormous **Chapel of St. Kinga,** carved over three decades in the early 20th century. Look for the salt-relief carving of

the Last Supper (its 3-D details are astonishing, considering it's just six inches deep). You'll end your visit with a five-minute multimedia show.

While advertised as two hours, your tour finishes in a deep-down shopping zone 1.5 hours after you started (they hope you'll hang out and shop). Note when the next elevator departs (just 3/hour), and you can be outta there on the next lift. Zip through the shopping zone in two minutes, or step over the rope and be immediately in line for the great escape (you'll be escorted quite some distance to the elevator, into which you'll be packed like mine workers).

Nearby: Near the parking lot, you'll see the **"Graduation Tower,"** a modern fort-like structure with a wooden walkway up top. The tower is designed to evaporate and then condense the supposedly very healthy brine from deep underground. The resulting moist, salty air is used to treat patients with lung problems. While locals are actually prescribed visits here, for most tourists it's not worth the extra money.

▲Nowa Huta

Nowa Huta (NOH-vah HOO-tah, "New Steel Works"), an enormous planned workers' town, offers a glimpse into the stark, grand-scale aesthetics of the communists. Because it's five miles east of central Kraków and a little tricky to see on your own, skip it unless you're determined—it can be tricky to appreciate. But architects and communist sympathizers may want to make a pilgrimage here.

Getting There: Tram #4 goes from near Kraków's Old Town (catch the tram on the ring road near Kraków's main train station, at the Dworzec Główny stop) along John Paul II Avenue (aleja Jana Pawła II) to Nowa Huta's main square, plac Centralny (about 30 minutes total), then continues a few minutes farther to the main gate of the Tadeusz Sendzimir Steelworks—the end of the line. From there it returns to plac Centralny and back to Kraków.

Tours: True to its name, Mike Ostrowski's **Crazy Guides** is a loosely run operation that takes tourists to Nowa Huta in genuine communist-era vehicles (mostly Trabants and Polski Fiats). If you've got an interest in the history—and would enjoy spending the day careening around the streets of Kraków in a car that feels like a cardboard box with a lawnmower engine—hire one of their laid-back hipster guides (139 zł/person for 2.5-hour "communism tour" of Nowa Huta; 179 zł/person for 4-hour "communism deluxe" tour

that also includes lunch at a milk bar and a visit to their period-decorated communist apartment; other options available—described on website, mobile 500-091-200, www.crazyguides.com, info@crazyguides.com). If you're already hiring a **local guide** in Kraków, consider paying a little extra to add a couple of hours for a short side-trip by car to Nowa Huta.

Background: Nowa Huta was the communists' idea of paradise. It's one of only three towns outside the Soviet Union that were custom-built to showcase socialist ideals. (The others are Dunáujváros—once called Sztálinváros—south of Budapest, Hungary; and Eisenhüttenstadt—once called Stalinstadt—near Brandenburg, Germany.) Completed in just 10 years (1949-1959), Nowa Huta was built primarily because the Soviets felt that smart and sassy Kraków needed a taste of heavy industry. Farmers and villagers were imported to live and work in Nowa Huta. Many of the new residents, who weren't accustomed to city living, brought along their livestock (which grazed in the fields around unfinished buildings). For commies, it was downright idyllic: Dad would cheerily ride the tram into the steel factory, mom would dutifully keep house, and the kids could splash around at the man-made beach and learn how to cut perfect red stars out of construction paper. But Krakovians had the last laugh: Nowa Huta, along with Lech Wałęsa's shipyard in Gdańsk, was one of the home bases of the Solidarity strikes that eventually brought down the regime. Now, with the communists long gone, Nowa Huta remains a major suburb of Poland's cultural capital, with a whopping 200,000 residents.

Touring Nowa Huta: Nowa Huta's focal point used to be known simply as **Central Square** (plac Centralny), but in a fit of poetic justice, it was recently renamed for the anticommunist Ronald Reagan. A map of Nowa Huta looks like a clamshell: a semicircular design radiating from Central/Reagan Square. Numbered streets fan out like spokes on a wheel, and trolleys zip workers directly to the immense factory.

Believe it or not, the inspiration for Nowa Huta was the Renaissance (which, thanks to the textbook Renaissance design of the Cloth Hall and other landmarks, Soviet architects considered typically Polish). Notice the elegantly predictable arches and galleries that would make Michelangelo proud. The settlement was loosely planned on the gardens of Versailles (comparing aerial views of those two very different sites—both with axes radiating from a central hub—this becomes clear). When first built (before it was layered with grime), Nowa Huta was delightfully orderly, primly painted, impeccably maintained, and downright beautiful... if a little boring. It was practical, too: Each of the huge apartment blocks is a self-contained unit, with its own grassy inner courtyard, school, and shops. Driveways (which appear to dead-end at underground garage doors) lead to vast fallout shelters.

Today's Nowa Huta—while gentrifying—is a far cry from its glory days. Wander around. Poke into the courtyards. Reflect on what it would be like to live here. It may not be as bad as you imagine. Ugly as they may seem from the outside, these buildings are packed with happy little apartments filled with color, light, and warmth.

The wide boulevard running northeast of Central/Reagan Square, now called Solidarity Avenue (aleja Solidarności, lined with tracks for tram #4), leads to the **Tadeusz Sendzimir Steel-works.** Originally named for Lenin, this factory was supposedly built using plans stolen from a Pittsburgh plant. It was designed to be a cog in the communist machine—reliant on iron ore from Ukraine, and therefore worthless unless Poland remained in the Soviet Bloc. Down from as many as 40,000 workers at its peak, the steelworks now employs only about 10,000. Today there's little to see other than the big sign, stern administration buildings, and smokestacks in the distance. Examine the twin offices flanking the sign—topped with turrets and a decorative frieze inspired by Italian palazzos, these continue the Renaissance theme of the housing districts.

KRAKÓW

Another worthwhile sight in Nowa Huta is the **Lord's Ark Church** (Arka Pana, several blocks northwest of Central/Reagan Square on ulica Obrońców Krzyża).

Back when he was archbishop of Kraków, Karol Wojtyła fought for years to build a church in this most communist of communist towns. When the regime refused, he insisted on conducting open-air Masses before crowds in fields—until the communists finally capitulated. Consecrated on May 15, 1977, the Lord's Ark Church has a Le Corbusier–esque design that looks like a fat, exhausted Noah's Ark resting on Mount Ararat—encouraging Poles to persevere through the floods of communism. While architecturally interesting, the church is mostly significant as a symbol of an early victory of Catholicism over communism.

▲Kościuszko Mound (Kopiec Kościuszki)

On a sunny day, the parklands west of the Old Town are a fine place to get out of the city and commune with Krakovians at play. On the outskirts of town is the Kościuszko Mound, a nearly perfectly conical hill erected in 1823 to honor Polish and American military hero Tadeusz Kościuszko. The mound incorporates soil that was brought here from battlefields where the famous general fought, both in Poland and in the American Revolution. Later, under Habsburg rule, a citadel with a chapel was built around the mound, which provided a fine lookout over this otherwise flat terrain. And more recently, the hill was reinforced with steel and cement to prevent it from eroding away. You'll pay to enter the walls and walk to the top—up a curlicue path that makes the mound resemble a giant soft-serve cone—and inside you'll find a modest Kościuszko museum. While not too exciting, this is a pleasant place for an excursion on a nice day.

Cost and Hours: 12 zł, includes museum, mound open daily 9:00-dusk, Fri-Sun until 23:00 in May-Sept, museum open daily 9:30-18:30—less off-season, café, tel. 12-425-1116, www.kopieckosciuszki.pl.

Getting There: Ride tram #1 or #6 (from in front of the Wyspiański Pavilion or the main post office) to the end of the line, called Salvator. From here, you can either follow the well-marked path uphill for 20 minutes, or hop on bus #100 to the top (runs at :10 past each hour).

Shopping in Kraków

Two of the most popular Polish souvenirs—amber and pottery—come from areas far from Kraków. You won't find any great bargains on those items here, but several shops specializing in them are listed below. Somewhat more local are the many wood carvings you'll see.

The **Cloth Hall,** smack-dab in the center of the Main Market Square, is the most convenient place to pick up any Polish souvenirs. It has a great selection at respectable prices (summer Mon-Fri 9:00-18:00, Sat-Sun 9:00-15:00, sometimes later; winter Mon-Fri 9:00-16:00, Sat-Sun 9:00-15:00).

Here are some other souvenir ideas, and neighborhoods or streets that are particularly enjoyable for browsing.

Jewelry

The popular **amber** *(bursztyn)* you'll see sold around town is found on northern Baltic shores; if you're also heading to Gdańsk, wait until you get there (for more on amber, see page 246). One unique alternative that's a bit more local is **"striped flint"** *(krzemień pasiasty),* a stratified stone that's polished to a high shine. It's mined in a very specific subregion near Kraków, and has become popular recently among Hollywood celebrities. Each piece has its own unique wavy, sandy patterns.

Jewelry shops abound in the Old Town. For a good selection of striped flint, amber, and other jewelry, try the no-name shop on **plac Mariacki,** the little square facing the side entrance of St. Mary's Church; they also have a selection of Polish folk costumes in the basement (at #9). A few more jewelry and design shops cluster along Sławkowska street, which runs north from the Main Market Square. **Galeria Skarbiec** ("Treasury"), two blocks south of the Main Market Square, is another good choice, with a stylish, upscale vibe (Grodzka 35).

Polish Pottery

"Polish pottery," with distinctive blue-and-white designs, is made in the region of Silesia, west of Kraków (mostly in the town of

Bolesławiec). But, assuming you won't be going there, you can browse one of the shops in Kraków. **Ceramika Bolesławiecka,** on a busy urban street between the Old Town and Kazimierz, has a tasteful, affordable selection of pottery that's oriented more for locals than tourists (closed Sun, Starowiślna 37). In the Old Town—and with inflated prices to match—two places face each other across Sławkowska street, just a block north of the Square: **Dekor Art** at #11 and **Mila** at #14.

Foods, Drinks, and Cosmetics

Krakowski Kredens is a handy, well-curated shop for overpriced but good-quality traditional foods from Kraków and the surrounding region, Galicia. While the deli case in the back is a pricey place to shop for a picnic (head for a supermarket instead), this is a good chance to stock up on souvenir-quality Polish foods for the folks back home. They have several locations around Kraków—and elsewhere in Poland—but one handy branch is just steps south of the Main Market Square down Grodzka, at #7 (www.krakowskikredens.pl).

    Szambelan, a block south of the Main Market Square, is a fun concept for vodka lovers: Peruse the giant casks of three dozen different flavored vodkas, buy an empty bottle, and they'll fill and seal it to take home (Gołębia 2 at the corner with Bracka).

    Mydlarnia u Franciszka, with a few locations around Kraków (including a handy one just south of the Main Market Square at Gołębia 2), sells a variety of fragrant local soaps, lotions, shampoos, and other cosmetics, some produced locally.

T-Shirts

Two creative shops in the Old Town sell souvenir T-shirts that are a step up in quality (and price) from the generic shops on the square. **Chrum** specializes in locally themed ironic T-shirts (closed Sun, across the street from the Barbican at plac Matejki 3, www.chrum.com), while **Red is Bad** sticks with tasteful, classic Polish eagles and flags on quality materials (just west of the Square at Szewska 25, www.redisbad.pl).

Stolarska Street

The relatively undiscovered, traffic-free Stolarska street—just a block off of the Main Market Square—is a fine place to stroll day or night, and to browse for gifts. (For more on this street, see page 130 in "Eating in Kraków.") Wander the street from north (Small Market Square) to south (Dominican Church) and window-shop. A few fun places are in the covered arcade on the left, after the Herring Embassy. One of the most interesting is **Galeria Plakatu Kraków,** a print, poster, and postcard shop with a wide variety of engaging images, from commie-retro to contemporary arts to unique Polish variations on American movie posters (closed Sun, Stolarska 8-10). Nearby are an antique bookstore and a pottery art gallery.

Designer Shops along Ulica Józefa, in Kazimierz

As the epicenter of Kraków's hipster scene, Kazimierz is the best place in town to browse one-off boutiques (both design and fashion). Several good options line up along ulica Józefa, mostly concentrated along a two-block stretch. Head just one block south from plac Nowy on Estery street, turn right, and keep an eye out for these options (mostly on the left side of the street): **Blazko,** at #11, has some modern, colorful jewelry, handmade right on the premises. A few doors down **Galerie d'Art Naïf** features fascinating works by untrained artists, and (next door) **Deccoria Galeria** feels like a junk shop, cluttered with handmade jewelry, art, accessories, and vintage clothes. Next are **Panon Nonchalant,** with Polish fashion, and a vintage shop. **Art Factory,** at #9, is worth a browse for colorful jewelry, accessories, and housewares by local designers. **Pracownia** ("Lab"), farther down and also at #9, sells handmade art, jewelry, and clothes. And more clothes by Polish designers are across the street at **Nuumi Boutique** (#14).

A couple of blocks away, just off plac Wolnica, is another great spot for local design, housewares, jewelry and casual fashion (i.e., creative T-shirts): **Idea Fix** and **The Hive Store,** which share a storefront at Bocheńska 7 (daily).

Shopping Malls

Two enormous shopping malls lie just beyond the tourist zone. The gigantic **Galeria Krakowska,** with 270 shops, shares a square with the train station (Mon-Sat 9:00-22:00, Sun 10:00-21:00, has a kids' play area upstairs from the main entry). Only slightly smaller is **Galeria Kazimierz** (Mon-Sat 10:00-21:00, Sun until 20:00, just a few blocks east of the Kazimierz sights, along the river at Podgórska 24). A small but swanky mall called **Pasaż 13** is a few steps off the southeast corner of the Main Market Square, where Grodzka street enters the Square. Enter the mall under the balcony marked *Pasaż 13.* You'll find a cool brick-industrial interior, with upscale international chains...and not much that's Polish (Mon-Sat 11:00-21:00, Sun until 17:00).

Entertainment in Kraków

As a town full of both students and tourists, Kraków has plenty of fun options, especially at night.

IN THE OLD TOWN

For locations of the following places, see the map on page 114.

Main Market Square

Intoxicating as the Square is by day, it's even better at night...pure enchantment. Have a meal or nurse a drink at an outdoor café, or just grab a bench and enjoy the scene. There's often live al fresco music coming from somewhere (either at restaurants, at a temporary stage set up near the Town Hall Tower, or from talented buskers). You could spend hours doing slow laps around the Square after dark, and never run out of diversions. For a great view over the Square at twilight, nurse a drink at **Café Szał**—on the Cloth Hall's upper terrace (long hours, enter through Gallery of 19th-Century Polish Art).

Concerts

You'll find a wide range of musical events, from tourist-oriented Chopin concerts and classical "greatest hits" selections in quaint old ballrooms and churches, to folk-dancing shows, to serious philharmonic performances. Several companies offer competing concerts; some of the best-established include www.cracowconcerts. com, www.newculture.pl, www.facebook.com/orkiestrasm, and www.orfeusz.eu. The free, monthly *Karnet* cultural-events book lists everything (also online at www.karnet.krakow.pl). Because the offerings change from week to week, inquire locally about what's on during your visit. Hotel lobbies are stocked with fliers, but to get all of your options, visit the TI north of the Square on ulica Św. Jana, which specializes in cultural events (they can book tickets for most concerts with no extra fee, and can tell you how to get tickets for the others).

Popular Classical Concerts: The three main choices are organ concerts in churches (usually at 17:00); orchestral or chamber music; or Chopin (either can happen anytime between 18:00 and 20:00). The going rate for any concert is 60 zł. Many are held in churches (such as **Sts. Peter and Paul** on ulica Grodzka, **St. Adalbert** on the Square, **St. Bernadino's/Bernardynów** near Wawel Castle, **St. Idziego/Giles** near Wawel Castle, or the **Piarist Church of the Transfiguration** at the northern end of the Old Town). You'll also find concerts in fancy mansions on or near the Main Market Square (including the **Polonia House/Dom Polonii** at #14, near ulica Grodzka; the **Chopin Gallery**—also billed as the **Royal Chamber Orchestra Hall**—just up Sławkowska street from the Square at #14; and the **Bonerowski Palace** near the top of the Square at ulica Św. Jana 1). Occasionally in summer, they're also held in various gardens around town (July-Aug only, as part of a festival).

Folk Music: Two different venues present dinner shows in the old center. At both, a small, hardworking ensemble of colorfully costumed Krakovian singers, dancers, and musicians put on a fun

Kraków's Old Town Shopping & Entertainment

Shopping
1. Cloth Hall
2. Plac Mariacki Jewelry
3. Galeria Skarbiec
4. Ceramika Bolesławiecka
5. Dekor Art
6. Mila & Chopin Gallery/Royal Chamber Orchestra Hall
7. Krakowski Kredens
8. Szambelan & Mydlarnia u Franciszka
9. Chrum
10. Red is Bad
11. Galeria Plakatu Kraków
12. To Ulica Józefa Shops
13. Galeria Krakowska
14. Galeria Kazimierz
15. Pasaż 13 Mall

Entertainment
16. Sts. Peter and Paul Church
17. St. Adalbert Church
18. St. Bernadino's/Bernardynów
19. St. Idziego/Giles Church
20. Piarist Church of the Transfiguration
21. Polonia House/Dom Polonii
22. Bonerowski Palace
23. Jama Michalika
24. Hotel Royal (bus to Skansen Smaków)
25. Jazz Club u Muniaka
26. Harris Piano Jazz Bar
27. Buddha Nightclub
28. Vodka Café Bar
29. Staropolskie Trunki (Vodka Tasting)
30. To Forum Przestrzenie

little folk show. While the food, the space, and the clientele are all quite tired, it's a nice taste of Polish folk traditions—and the performers try hard to involve members of the audience in the polkas and circle dances. One option is in the historic **Jama Michalika,** with its dusty old Art Nouveau interior right along Floriańska street (85 zł includes dinner; Wed, Fri, and Sun at 19:00; Floriańska 45, mobile 604-093-570, www.cracowconcerts.com). A similar option is in the more modern **Tradycyja Restaurant,** right on the Main Market Square (at #15; 60 zł for just the show, or 120 zł to add dinner; Sat at 19:00; mobile 602-850-900, www.newculture.pl).

For a more serious folk music performance—and to really make an evening of it—consider a show in a more rustic setting just outside of town. The restaurant **Skansen Smaków,** filling a log cabin-like building, has shows each Thursday night. You'll meet the bus at the Hotel Royal near Wawel Castle at 18:30, ride to the restaurant, have a traditional Polish feast during the show, then be brought back home to the Old Town at 22:00 (100 zł, book ahead, tel. 600-349-429, www.skansensmakow.pl).

Jazz

Kraków has a surprisingly thriving jazz scene. Several popular clubs hide on the streets surrounding the Main Market Square (open nightly, most shows start around 21:30, sometimes free or a cover of 10-25 zł for better shows). **Jazz Club u Muniaka** is the most famous and best for all-around jazz in a sophisticated cellar environment (ulica Floriańska 3, tel. 12-423-1205). **Harris Piano Jazz Bar,** right on the Square (at #28), is more casual and offers a mix of traditional and updated "fusion" jazz, plus blues (tel. 12-421-5741, www.harris.krakow.pl).

Nightlife in the Old Town

The entire Old Town is crammed with nightclubs and discos pumping loud music on weekends. On a Saturday, the pedestrian streets can be more crowded at midnight than at noon. However, with the exception of the jazz clubs mentioned earlier, most of the nightspots in the Old Town are garden-variety dance clubs, completely lacking the personality and creativity of the Kazimierz nightspots described next. Worse, to save money, young locals stand out in front of nightclubs to drink their own booze (BYOB), rather than pay high prices for the drinks inside—making the streets that much more crowded and noisy. For low-key hanging out, people choose a café on the Square; otherwise, they head for Kazimierz.

In addition to the Harris Piano Jazz Bar (listed earlier), two places on the Square worth checking out are near the southeast corner. At #6, head into the passage to find the **Buddha** nightclub, with comfy lounge sofas under awnings in an immaculately restored old courtyard. For something funkier and even more local, go down the passage at #12, which runs a surprisingly long distance through the block. Soon you'll start to see tables for the **Herring Embassy;** you'll eventually emerge at **Stolarska street,** a still-enjoyable but far less touristy scene (for more on the Herring Embassy and Stolarska, see page 131).

If you have (or would like to cultivate) an appreciation for vodka, stop by the **Vodka Café Bar,** serving more than 100 types of vodkas, liquors, and hard drinks. You can buy a tasting flight board with six small shots; they'll help you narrow down your options (usually around 30 zł for the flight, more for top-shelf vodkas). It's a mellow, uncluttered space that lets you focus on the vodka and the company (Mon-Thu 15:00-24:00, Fri-Sun 13:00-24:00, Mikołajska 5).

IN KAZIMIERZ
Aside from the Old Town's gorgeous Square, Kraków's best area to hang out after dark is Kazimierz. Although this is also the former Jewish quarter, the Jewish Sabbath has nothing to do with the bar scene here. You can, however, still hear traditional Jewish music called klezmer. For tips on enjoying a concert of klezmer music, see the sidebar.

Bars and Clubs
Squeezed between centuries-old synagogues and cemeteries are wonderful hangouts running the full gamut from sober and tasteful to wild and clubby. The classic recipe for a Kazimierz bar: Find a dilapidated old storefront, fill it with ramshackle furniture, turn the lights down low, pipe in old-timey jazz music from the 1920s, and sprinkle with alcohol. Serves one to two dozen hipsters. After a few clubs of this type caught on, a more diverse cross-section of nightspots began to move in, including some loud dance clubs. The whole area is bursting with life—it's the kind of place where people just spontaneously start dancing.

On and near Plac Nowy: The highest concentration of bars ring the plac Nowy market square. While most of these are nondescript, a few stand out. Fronting the square, **Kolory** has a pleasant Parisian brasserie ambience (Estery 10). Circling to the right, you'll spot **Plac Nowy 1,** which specializes in Polish microbrews and up-market pub grub in a bright, sleek (and arguably "un-Kazimierz") setting. Spinning about 90 more degrees to the right, look for a branch of the Poland-wide **Pijalnia Wódki i Piwa** chain—part of the trend for 4/8 bars (that's 4 zł for a shot of vodka, 8 zł for a bar snack such as herring). Tucked in the corner just to the right of that is the easy-to-miss entrance for **Atelier,** which hides a relaxed, minimalist, art-gallery interior with cushy sofas and a hidden garden (plac Nowy 7 1/2). **Le Scandale** is all black leather and serves

KRAKÓW

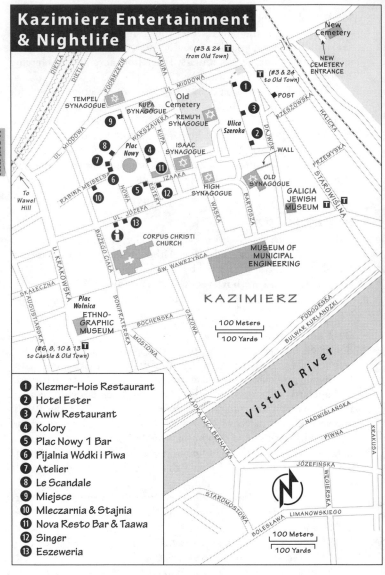

Kazimierz Entertainment & Nightlife

1 Klezmer-Hois Restaurant
2 Hotel Ester
3 Awiw Restaurant
4 Kolory
5 Plac Nowy 1 Bar
6 Pijalnia Wódki i Piwa
7 Atelier
8 Le Scandale
9 Miejsce
10 Mleczarnia & Stajnia
11 Nova Resto Bar & Taawa
12 Singer
13 Eszeweria

tapas, Italian fare, and cocktails; don't miss the big garden in the back (plac Nowy 9). And at the end of this block, **Alchemia,** one of the first—and still one of the best—bars in Kazimierz, is candlelit, cluttered, and claustrophobic, with cave-like rooms crowded with rickety old furniture, plus a cellar used for live performances (Estery 5, www.alchemia.com.pl).

Just around the corner, on Estery street, Alchemia has its

Klezmer Music in Kazimierz

On a balmy summer night, Kazimierz's main square, ulica Szeroka, is filled with the haunting strains of klezmer—traditional Jewish music from 19th-century Poland, generally with violin, string bass, clarinet, and accordion. Skilled klezmer musicians can make their instruments weep or laugh like human voices. There are two main ways to enjoy some klezmer music: at a restaurant or at a concert.

Restaurants: Several eateries on ulica Szeroka offer klezmer music, typically starting between 19:00 and 20:00. The musicians move from room to room, and the menus tend to be a mix of traditional Jewish and Polish cuisine (which are quite similar). But don't come here just for the food—it's an afterthought to the music. While most places claim to do concerts "nightly year-round," they can be canceled anytime it's slow (especially off-season)—confirm ahead.

Some old-school restaurants offer reasonably priced food, but charge 30 zł per person for the music. Probably your best choice is the well-established **$$$ Klezmer-Hois,** filling a venerable former Jewish ritual bathhouse and making you feel like you're dining in a rich grandparent's home (daily 8:00-22:00, at #6, tel. 12-411-1245, www.klezmer.pl).

A newer trend is for restaurants with outdoor seating on ulica Szeroka to offer "free" al fresco klezmer music for customers (though the food tends to be that much more expensive). Because the music is free, anybody (at neighboring restaurants, or simply strolling past) can enjoy a taste of klezmer. Just show up, comparison-shop music and menus, and—if you like what you hear—pick a place for dinner or a drink. Eateries offering this option include **$$ Hotel Ester** (at #20, with relatively reasonable prices, and live music that begins in the early afternoon rather than evening) and **$$$ Awiw** (at #13, overpriced food).

Concerts: To really focus on klezmer as an art form, pay a bit more to attend a concert. Popular options include the Jascha Lieberman Trio, which performs most summer nights at 20:00 in the Popper Synagogue (65 zł, ulica Szeroka 16, www.jaschalieberman.com); or a performance in arguably the most powerful space, the giant old prayer hall of Isaac Synagogue (60 zł, Sun-Mon and Wed-Thu at 18:00, Kupa 18, www.sibelia.pl). For the latest lineup, check for fliers around town, or ask at any TI.

Don't worry too much about seeking out a particular musician—they are equally good, and each brings a unique style to the music. Many venues share musicians, so on any given night it's hard to predict who's performing where. Bottom line: If you're interested in klezmer music, you can't go wrong in Kazimierz.

own restaurant (described later, under "Eating in Kazimierz"). Hiding just a half-block beyond that is **Miejsce** ("The Place"), which is bright and minimalist, with stripped-down walls and carefully chosen Scan-design old furniture—it's run by the owners of a design firm specializing in decor from the 50s, 60s, and 70s (Estery 1).

Late at night, the little windows in the plac Nowy **market hall** do a big business selling *zapiekanki* (baguette with toppings) to hungry bar-hoppers.

On Rabina Meiselsa street, just a half-block off plac Nowy, two places share a long courtyard: **Mleczarnia,** a top-notch beer garden with rickety tables squeezed under the trees and its cozy old-fashioned pub across the street (at #20); and **Stajnia,** at the far end of the courtyard, where scenes from *Schindler's List* were filmed (see photos on wall at inner arch). Its interior feels like a Polish village drenched in red light and turned into a dance hall.

Near Isaac Synagogue: A block east of plac Nowy, a few more places cluster on the wide street in front of Isaac Synagogue. The huge **Nova Resto Bar** dominates the scene with a long covered terrace, a vast interior, and seating in their courtyard—all with a cool-color-scheme Las Vegas polka-dot style. This feels upscale and a bit pretentious compared to many of the others, but it's *the* place to be seen (25-40-zł meals, Estery 18). Upstairs is the similarly trendy music club **Taawa** (http://taawa.pl). Facing this double-decker wall of style are some smaller, more accessible options: **Singer** is classy and mellow, with most of its tables made of old namesake sewing machines (Estery 20), while **Warsztat** has an exploding-instruments-factory ambience (Izaaka 3; also recommended later, under "Eating in Kraków").

On Józefa Street: More good bars are just a short block south. Along Józefa, you'll find a pair of classic Kazimierz joints: **Eszeweria,** which wins the "best atmosphere" award, feels like a Polish speakeasy that's been in mothballs for the last 90 years—a low-key, unpretentious, and inviting hangout (Józefa 9). A block up, look for **Kolanko No. 6,** with a cozy bar up front, a pleasant beer garden in the inner courtyard, and a fun events hall in back (Józefa 17, www.kolanko.net; also recommended later, under "Eating in Kraków").

In Podgórze: If you run out of diversions in the heart of Kazimierz, head south. With the construction of a new pedestrian bridge over the river just south of this area, Kazimierz's nightlife scene is spreading to Podgórze, just across the river. Here in this fast-evolving zone, prices are a bit lower.

Beach Bar on the Riverbank

South of the river, roughly between Kazimierz and Wawel Castle, **Forum Przestrzenie** fills a dilapidated concrete department store—a mostly abandoned dinosaur from communist times, today used primarily as an extra-large billboard. But in recent years, the ground floor has been taken over by a lively hipster bar—especially appealing in the balmy summer months, when comfy low-slung chairs sprawl across a tidy lawn and a pebbly "beach" with views across the Vistula to Wawel Castle. They serve coffee, wine, beer, summery cocktails, and cheap bar snacks. A few artists and designers also have boutiques here (open daily in good weather 10:00-late, skip the trip if it's not nice out, ulica Marii Konopnickiej 28, mobile 515-424-724, www.forumprzestrzenie.com).

Sleeping in Kraków

Kraków is popular, with lots of accommodations options. Healthy competition keeps Kraków's prices reasonable and makes choosing a hotel fun rather than frustrating. Splurge dollars go a long way here—accommodations are inexpensive, and moving up a price class buys you a lot more luxury. Rates are soft; hoteliers don't need much of an excuse to offer you 10 to 20 percent off, especially on weekends or off-season. I've focused my accommodations in two areas: in and near the Old Town; and in Kazimierz, a local-style, more affordable neighborhood that is home to both the old Jewish quarter and a thriving dining and nightlife zone.

The Old Town is jam-packed with discos that thump loud music on weekend nights to attract roving gangs of rowdy students, backpackers, and obnoxious "stag parties" of drunken louts from the UK in town for a weekend of carousing. The "quiet after 22:00" law is flagrantly ignored. Kazimierz is also home to various hip dance clubs. Because of all these clubs, virtually all of my accommodations come with some risk of noise; to help your odds, always ask for a quiet room when you reserve...and bring earplugs.

IN AND NEAR THE OLD TOWN
Most of my listings are inside (or within a block or two of) the Planty park that rings the Old Town. Sleeping inside the Old Town comes with pros (maximum atmosphere; handy location for sightseeing and dining) and cons (high prices; the potential for noise—especially on weekends—as noted earlier). Places just outside the Old Town are still handy, but quieter. If you need a room in a pinch, several slick, international chains (Ibis, Mercure, Puro) have branches near the train station.

Sleep Code

Hotels are classified based on the average price of a standard double room with breakfast in high season.

$$$$	**Splurge:** Most rooms over 550 zł
$$$	**Pricier:** 400-550 zł
$$	**Moderate:** 250-400 zł
$	**Budget:** 100-250 zł
¢	**Backpacker:** Under 100 zł
RS%	**Rick Steves discount**

Unless otherwise noted, credit cards are accepted, hotel staff speak basic English, and free Wi-Fi is available. Comparison-shop by checking prices at several hotels (on each hotel's own website, on a booking site, or by email). For the best deal, *book directly with the hotel.* Ask for a discount if paying in cash; if the listing includes **RS%,** request a Rick Steves discount.

Guest Houses

These good-value pensions come with lots of stairs (no elevators) and are located in the heart of the Old Town along busy pedestrian streets, many without air-conditioning—so they can be noisy with the windows open in the summer, especially on weekends. Don't expect a 24-hour reception desk; it's always smart to tell them your arrival time, especially if it's late in the day.

$$ Tango House, run by dance instructor Marcin Miszczak, is in a well-located building with an ancient-feeling stairwell decorated with faded Art Nouveau paintings. Its eight long, skinny, retro-stylish rooms have parquet floors (ask for quieter courtyard room to avoid rowdy street noise on weekends, ulica Szpitalna 4, tel. 12-429-3114, www.tangohouse.pl, info@tangohouse.pl).

$$ Globtroter Guest House offers 17 basic, somewhat stuffy, rustic-feeling rooms with high ceilings and big beams around a serene garden courtyard. Jacek (Jack), who really understands and respects travelers, conscientiously focuses on value—keeping prices reasonable by not offering needless extras (RS%, 2 people can cram into a single to save money, family rooms, breakfast at nearby café extra, pay laundry service, fun 700-year-old brick cellar lounge down below, go down passageway at #7 at the square called plac Szczepański, tel. 12-422-4123, www.globtroter-krakow.com, globtroter@globtroter-krakow.com).

$$ La Fontaine B&B, run by a French-Polish family, offers 11 rooms and 13 apartments just off the Main Market Square. Tastefully decorated with French flair, it's cute as a poodle. Each room has a little lounge with a microwave and fridge—most in the hall, some inside the room. If you don't mind huffing up lots of stairs, this is a fine value (air-con in some rooms, low slanted ceilings in some rooms, guest kitchen, pay laundry service, ulica Sławkowska 1, tel. 12-422-6564, www.bblafontaine.com, biuro@bblafontaine.com).

$ Golden Lion Guest House is cheap and basic but well-located, with 11 smallish, dated rooms on a bustling pedestrian street a block off the Main Market Square (ask for quieter room in back, air-con in some rooms, guest kitchen, no parking, ulica Szewska 19, mobile 501-066-958, tel. 12-422-9323, www.goldenlion.pl, reservation@goldenlion.pl, Łodziński family).

Outside of the Old Town: $$ Cracowdays is the farthest of my listings from the center of town, about a 15-minute walk away (a tram can cut a few minutes off the trek). But it's also a notch more refined than the guest houses listed previously. It sits in a pleasant residential neighborhood west of the Main Market Square, with six beautifully decorated and thoughtfully tended rooms, all sharing a central kitchen (stand-alone studio apartment in another building, breakfast extra, air-con, Grabowskiego 7, mobile 666-971-478, www.cracowdays.com, reservation@cracowdays.com).

Hotels

$$$$ Donimirski Boutique Hotels, with four different locations in or near Kraków's Old Town, set the bar for splurge hotels in Kraków (www.donimirski.com). All Donimirski hotels come with friendly staff, discounts for my readers, and classy little extras that add up to a memorable hotel experience. **Hotel Polski Pod Białym Orłem,** conveniently located near the Florian Gate just inside the Old Town walls, has 60 luxurious rooms (RS%, apartments available, air-con, elevator, ulica Pijarska 17, tel. 12-422-1144, hotel.polski@donimirski.com). **Hotel Gródek** offers 23 rooms a three-minute walk behind St. Mary's Church, on a quiet dead end street overlooking the Planty park (RS%, pay parking, Na Gródku 4, tel. 12-431-9030, grodek@donimirski.com). **Hotel Maltański** has 16 rooms in the beautifully renovated former royal stables, facing the Planty park just two blocks from Wawel Castle (RS%, no elevator but only 2 floors, pay parking, ulica Straszewskiego 14, tel. 12-431-0010, maltanski@donimirski.com). And **Hotel Pugetów,** with seven small but plush rooms, is in the workaday neighborhood between the Main Market Square and Kazimierz (RS%, air-con, pay parking, ulica Starowiślna 15A, tel. 12-432-4950, pugetow@donimirski.com).

$$$$ Hotel Senacki is a business-class place renting 20 comfortable rooms between Wawel Castle and the Main Market Square. The location is handy, but it can be noisy on weekends—ask for a quieter back room. The staff is warm, professional, and conscientious. Top-floor "attic" rooms have low beams, skylight windows, and a flight of stairs after the elevator (air-con, eleva-

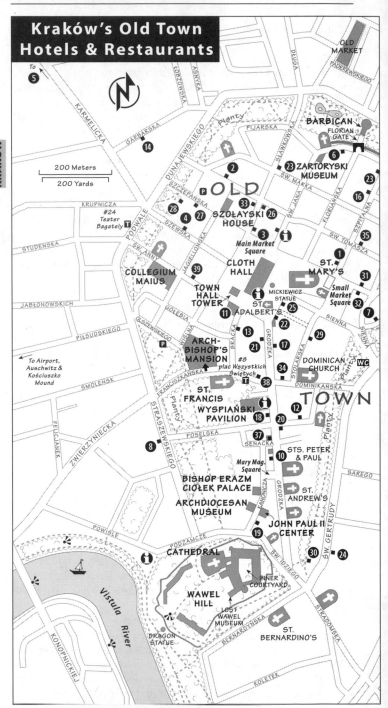

Kraków's Old Town Hotels & Restaurants

KRAKÓW

Accommodations

1 Tango House
2 Globtroter Guest House
3 La Fontaine B&B
4 Golden Lion Guest House
5 To Cracowdays
6 Hotel Polski Pod Białym Orłem
7 Hotel Gródek
8 Hotel Maltański
9 Hotel Pugetów
10 Hotel Senacki & Bar Grodzki
11 Wentzl Hotel
12 Hotel Wawel
13 Bracka 6
14 Hotel Amber
15 Hotel Wielopole
16 Kraków City Apartments
17 Kraków for You Apartments

Eateries

18 Restauracja pod Aniołami
19 Pod Nosem
20 Miód Malina
21 Marmolada
22 Wesele
23 U Babci Maliny (2)
24 Pod Baranem
25 Szara
26 Ed Red
27 Charlotte
28 Café Bunkier
29 Ambasada Śledzia
30 Pod Wawelem Beer Hall
31 Cyklop Pizza & Jadłodajnia "U Stasi"
32 Moa Burger
33 Krowarzywa
34 Lajkonik Sandwiches
35 Milkbar Tomasza
36 Academy of Music Café
37 Bar Mleczny
38 Restauracja Samoobsługowa Polakowski
39 Chimera Cafeteria

tor—but doesn't go to "attic" rooms, ask about nearby pay parking, ulica Grodzka 51, tel. 12-422-7686, www.hotelsenacki.pl, senacki@hotelsenacki.pl).

$$$$ Wentzl Hotel is your splurge-right-on-the-Square option, with 18 rooms. The decor is over-the-top-classy Old World with modern touches, like state-of-the-art TVs and bathrooms. When reserving, request either a room with a view on the Square—which can be noisy, especially on weekends—or one of the three quieter back rooms (air-con, elevator, Rynek Główny 19, tel. 12-430-2664, www.wentzl.pl, hotel@wentzl.pl).

$$$ Hotel Wawel has 39 rooms on a well-located street that's quieter than the Old Town norm. It's colorful and feels plush for the price; above the swanky marble lobby are hallways creatively painted with the history of the building and images from around Kraków. Out back, a fountain gurgles in a cute little courtyard (air-con, elevator—but doesn't go to top floor, steam room and whirlpool bath extra, ulica Poselska 22, tel. 12-424-1300, www.hotelwawel.pl, hotel@hotelwawel.pl).

$$$ Bracka 6, wonderfully located just one short block off the Main Market Square, is a sort of a hybrid between a hotel and an apartment house. The 16 stylish rooms—with sleek lines, lots of glass, and exposed brick—each have a kitchen, so breakfast is extra. It's on the second and third floors with no elevator, and the reception is open limited hours (daily 8:00-22:00 or so)—but the lack of full hotel amenities keeps the prices affordable for this level of modern elegance (air-con, Bracka 6, tel. 12-341-4011, www.bracka6.pl, info@bracka6.pl).

$$$ Hotel Amber sits on a dreary urban street just outside the Planty park, but still less than a 10-minute walk from the Square. The staff is proud of their attentive service (and circulates a handy little informative newsletter daily). The hotel has two parts: 18 perfectly fine, if smallish, rooms in the original building; and 20 slightly more upscale rooms in the newer "design" section. While a bit overpriced, both parts share a small gym, sauna, and garden in back (air-con, elevator, Garbarska 8-10, tel. 12-421-0606, www.hotel-amber.pl, office@hotel-amber.pl).

$$ Hotel Wielopole sits a block outside of the Planty, on the way to the lively Kazimierz district. Its 35 tight rooms are tucked down a (relatively) quiet side street just past the main post office, facing a big Holiday Inn. Run by the same company as Hotel Amber (described above), it has an equally pleasant emphasis on welcoming service (air-con, elevator, vegetarian restaurant in cellar, Wielopole 3, tel. 12-422-1475, www.wielopole.pl, office@wielopole.pl).

Apartments

Apartments aren't just for long stays—these places welcome even one-nighters. As reception times are limited, be sure to clearly communicate your arrival time. A wide variety of apartments are easy to find at online booking sites, but both of these places have a reception desk that manages several units, making them a bit more hotelesque than the norm. Still, you're on your own for breakfast, and don't expect your room to be cleaned during your stay.

$$ Kraków City Apartments, conscientiously run by Andrzej and Katarzyna, has 14 straightforward, modern apartments tucked away in a quiet courtyard at the corner of the Old Town (2-bedroom apartments available for up to 6 people, nonsmoking, elevator to all rooms except studios, reception open daily 9:00-20:00, ulica Szpitalna 34, reception mobile 507-203-050, Andrzej's mobile 504-235-925, www.krakowapartments.info, info@krakowapartments.info).

$$ Kraków for You Apartments offers 12 modern, well-decorated studios and one- and two-bedroom units around a courtyard along one of Kraków's most happening streets, just a few steps off the Main Market Square (reception open daily 10:00-20:00, request quieter courtyard room, lots of stairs with no elevator, go down the passage at Grodzka 4, tel. 12-421-4835, mobile 660-541-085, www.krakowforyou.com, info@krakowforyou.com, Mikołaj).

IN KAZIMIERZ

Kazimierz is both Kraków's Jewish heart and soul, and its trendiest eating and nightlife zone. Sleeping here puts you in close proximity to both synagogues and klezmer concerts, and to food trucks and hip nightclubs (expect some noise, especially on weekends). Keep in mind that, while pleasant in its own right, Kazimierz is a 20-minute walk or a 5-minute tram ride from Kraków's atmospheric old center (for details on getting to Kazimierz from the Old Town, see page 80). For locations, see the map on page 80.

$$$$ Metropolitan Boutique Hotel is an upscale refuge, just a block before the heart of Kazimierz (just off the busy road on the way to Kraków's Old Town). Its 39 rooms—with exposed brick and slick modern style—sit along a somewhat dreary but conveniently located side street (air-con, elevator, gym, Joselewicza 19, tel. 12-442-7500, www.hotelmetropolitan.pl).

$$$ Rubinstein Residence sits right in the middle of ulica Szeroka—surrounded by klezmer restaurants and synagogues, in the heart of the neighborhood. It fills a painstakingly restored old townhouse (parts of it dating to the 15th century) with heavy wood beams and 30 swanky rooms—some of them palatial suites that incorporate old features like frescoes and pillars. The rooftop terrace—with views over Kazimierz and to the Old Town—sets this

KRAKÓW

place above (air-con, elevator, Szeroka 12, tel. 12-384-0000, www. rubinstein.pl, recepcja@rubinstein.pl).

$$ Karmel Hotel, with 11 rooms above an Italian restaurant, sits on a pleasant side street near the heart of Kazimierz. It offers elegance at a reasonable price (some rooms have air-con, upstairs with no elevator, some night noise on weekends, ulica Kupa 15, tel. 12-430-6697, www.karmel.com.pl, hotel@karmel.com.pl).

$ Tournet Guest House, well-run by friendly Piotr and Sylwia Działowy, is your cheap-and-cheery option, offering 18 colorful, overly perfumed rooms near the edge of Kazimierz toward Wawel Castle (elevator plus a few stairs, reception open 7:00-22:00, ulica Miodowa 7, tel. 12-292-0088, www.nocleg.krakow.pl, tournet@nocleg.krakow.pl).

¢ Hostel Momotown is a smidge more institutional and less party-oriented than your average hostel, but it's still loose and friendly. Run by Paweł Momot, it has 77 dorm beds, some private rooms, and a fun garden for hanging out (ulica Miodowa 28, tel. 12-429-6929, www.momotownhostel.com, info@momotownhostel.com). Two blocks away, they also rent 14 basic but cheap **$ private rooms** that share a kitchenette, overlooking Kazimierz's main square, ulica Szeroka.

Eating in Kraków

Kraków has a wide array of great restaurants—for every one I've listed, there are two or three nearly as good. As the restaurant scene changes constantly, I've chosen places that are well-established and have a proven track record for reliably good food. In my listings, you'll find a mix of old-school Polish places and modern foodie alternatives (which are still rooted in the local tradition). You could also consider a **food tour** (described under "Tours in Krakow," page 36).

IN THE OLD TOWN

Kraków's Old Town is loaded with dining options. Prices are reasonable even on the Main Market Square. And a half-block away, they get even better. All of these eateries (except the milk bars) are likely to be booked up on weekends—always reserve ahead.

$$$ Restauracja pod Aniołami ("Under Angels") offers a dressy, candlelit atmosphere on a wonderful covered patio, or in a deep, steep, romantic cellar with rough wood and medieval vaults. Peruse the elaborately described menu of medieval noblemen's dishes. The cuisine is traditional Polish, with an emphasis on grilled meats and trout (on a wood-fired grill). Every meal begins with *smalec* (spread made with lard, fried onion, bacon, and apple). Don't go here if you're in a hurry—only if you want to really slow

Restaurant Price Code

I've assigned each eatery a price category, based on the average cost of a typical main course. Drinks, desserts, and splurge items (steak and seafood) can raise the price considerably.

$$$$ **Splurge:** Most main courses over 60 zł
$$$ **Pricier:** 45-60 zł
$$ **Moderate:** 25-45 zł
$ **Budget:** Under 25 zł

In Poland, a milk bar or takeout spot is **$**; a basic sit-down eatery is **$$**; a casual but more upscale restaurant is **$$$**; and a swanky splurge is **$$$$**.

down and enjoy your dinner. Reservations are smart (daily 13:00-24:00, ulica Grodzka 35, tel. 12-421-3999, www.podaniolami.pl).

$$$ Pod Nosem ("Under the Nose") is a smart choice for refined, updated Polish cuisine in a sophisticated, less touristy atmosphere. It's tucked at the far end of sleepy Kanonicza lane, just beyond the tourists and before Wawel Castle. In a tight dining room that skips the kitsch, they offer an extensive wine list and a short menu of artfully executed Polish dishes (daily 12:00-22:00, Kanonicza 22, tel. 12-376-0014, www.kanonicza22.com).

$$$ Miód Malina ("Honey Raspberry") is a delightful, acceptably kitschy Polish-Italian fusion restaurant filled with the comforting aroma of its wood-fired oven. The menu is mostly Polish, with a few Italian dishes thrown in. Sit in the cozy, warmly painted interior, or out in the courtyard (reservations smart, daily 12:00-23:00, ulica Grodzka 40, tel. 12-430-0411, www.miodmalina.pl). The same people run two other restaurants a bit closer to the Square, with similar atmosphere and equally good food, but are more focused on Polish fare: **$$ Marmolada** (Grodzka 5) and **$$$ Wesele,** with outdoor tables right on the Square (at #10).

$$ Pod Baranem ("Under the Ram") is a solid midrange bet for traditional Polish food without being tacky or pretentious. Well-respected by locals, it sits just outside of the tourist chaos, quietly facing the Planty near Wawel Castle. Several cozy rooms—tasteful but not stuffy—sprawl through a homey old building (daily 12:00-22:00, lighter meals before 19:00, Św. Gertrudy 21, tel. 12-429-4022, www.podbaranem.com).

Splurging on the Main Market Square: You'll find plenty of expensive, tourist-oriented restaurants on the Square. Though all of them have rich interiors, there's not much point in paying a premium to dine here unless you're sitting outside. It's difficult to recommend any specific places here, but options with good reputations and relatively decent value include **$$$ Szara** (at #6) and **$$$ Wesele** (at #10; related to Miód Malina, above). Even the best of these places is overpriced. To enjoy the same experience more affordably, have just a drink on the square and dine elsewhere.

Steak House: $$$ Ed Red, by acclaimed local chef Adam Chrząstowski, serves up the best steaks in Kraków. He carefully sources his beef from Poland, and dry-ages it himself (21 or 45 days). A short walk from the Main Market Square, the space is classy but not stuffy, with exposed brick, leather benches, and a busy open kitchen. While it's a splurge by local standards, you can get a top-quality steak for under $20—a bargain anywhere else—as well as a short menu of affordably priced alternatives. Reservations are smart (daily 12:00-23:00, Sławkowska 3, mobile 690-900-555, www.edred.pl).

Youthful Style at Plac Szczepański: While seemingly every corner of the Old Town is jammed with tourists, the pleasant square called plac Szczepański feels more like the terrain of university students—a carefully protected bastion of the local upscale art culture. While just two blocks from the Square, this small array of cafés and galleries has a vibe that's more Warsaw-urbane than ye olde Kraków. **$ Charlotte** is a winner—it's a classy, French-feeling bakery/café/wine bar. They make their own breads and pastries in the basement (with lots of seating—you can watch the bakers work if you come early enough in the morning), cultivate a stay-awhile coffee-house ambience upstairs, and throw in a few square-facing sidewalk tables to boot. And it's affordable, serving up sandwiches, pastries, and salads. While the food is light café fare rather than a filling dinner, after 18:00 they redecorate to give it a more sophisticated flair (Mon-Fri 7:00-24:00, Sat 9:00-24:00, Sun 9:00-22:00, plac Szczepański 2, tel. 12-431-5610). Just around the corner, facing the Planty park, is the delightful **$$ Café Bunkier.** It belongs to the hulking Bunker Sztuki contemporary art gallery, but—in contrast to that building's concrete vibe—the café sits under a glass canopy that faces the lush greenbelt, with well-worn wooden tables and an almost Parisian ambience. While it's not the place for a filling meal, it's worth coming here for some light food and drinks while enjoying Kraków's greenery. It's especially cozy on a rainy day (daily 9:00-24:00, food from 12:00, plac Szczepański 3a, tel. 12-431-0585).

On Stolarska Street: Stolarska street, a neatly pedestrianized, oddly untrammeled "embassy row" just a block away from the Main Market Square, is worth exploring for a meal or a drink. Stolarska has a fun variety of more locals-oriented bars and cafés. Begin at the Small Market Square (Maly Rynek) behind St. Mary's Church and head south. On the left, look for the ridiculously long sign that perfectly identifies the business: Pierwszy Lokal Na Stolarskiej Po Lewej Stronie Idąc Od Małego Rynku ("The first pub on the left side of Stolarska coming from the Small Market Square"). Notice that this once-sleepy street is lined with embassies and consulates—it's easy to spot the flags of Germany, the US, and France. On the left, in the stretch of cafés under canopies, you'll see the **$ Ambasada Śledzia** ("Herring Embassy"), with a divey, youthful atmosphere and a "Polish tapas" approach: A dozen different types of herring and other light meals, plus a variety of vodka to wash it down, are posted on the menu. You'll order at the bar, then find a table, or take it to go (open long hours daily, Stolarska 8). Nearly across the street, the Pasaż Bielaka (look for the low-profile stone doorway at #5) runs through the middle of the block all the way out to the Main Market Square (emerging at Rynek Główny #12); partway along is another sprawling branch of the Herring Embassy.

KRAKÓW

Beer Hall: $$ Pod Wawelem ("Under Wawel") is a rollicking Czech-style beer hall right on the Planty park near Wawel Castle. It's packed with locals seeking big, sloppy, greasy portions of meaty fare, with giant mugs of various beers on tap (including Polish and Bavarian). Choose between the bustling interior or the outdoor terrace right on the Planty. Locals come here not for a romantic dinner, but for a rowdy evening out with friends (different specials every day—such as giant schnitzel, pork ribs, or roasted chicken; daily 12:00-24:00, ulica Św. Gertrudy 26-29, tel. 12-421-2336).

Pizza: $ Cyklop, with 10 tables wrapped around the cook and his busy oven, has good wood-fired pizzas and a cozy, charming ambience (daily 11:00-23:00, near St. Mary's Church at Mikołajska 16, tel. 12-421-6603).

Burgers (and Vegan Burgers): Gourmet hamburgers are all the rage in Poland these days. One of the best options in the center is **$ Moa Burger,** with a dozen different types of big, sloppy, "New Zealand-style" hamburgers. Order at the counter, then find a seat at a shared table (daily 11:00-23:00, Mikołajska 3, tel. 12-421-2144). Another fad is vegan "burgers"; a handy place in the center is **$ Krowarzywa** (a pun roughly meaning both "Cow Alive" and "Cow Vegetable")—with a hip atmosphere and an enticing menu of meatless options (daily 12:00-23:00, Sławkowska 8, mobile 531-777-136).

Quick Sandwich: If you need a. break from milk bars (described next), but want to grab a sandwich on the go, stop by **$ Lajkonik,** a modern bakery/coffee shop *(piekarnia i kawiarnia)* that sells fresh takeout sandwiches (Mon-Fri 7:00-21:00, Sat 8:00-21:00, Sun 8:00-22:00, handy location right in front of the Dominican Church at Dominikański 2, others are just outside of the Old Town).

Milk Bars and other Quick, Cheap, Traditional Eats

Kraków is a good place to try the cheap cafeterias called "milk bars." For pointers on eating at a milk bar, review the sidebar on page 16.

$ Milkbar Tomasza is an updated, upgraded milk bar popular with local students. Modern and relatively untouristy, it has a hipster ambience and serves big, splittable portions of high-quality food—often with some international flourishes—plus breakfast dishes all day (cheap soup and salad deals, great big salads, Tue-Sun 8:00-20:00, closed Mon, ulica Tomasza 24, tel. 12-422-1706).

$ Jadłodajnia "U Stasi" is a throwback that makes you feel like you're in on Kraków's best-kept secret. Its hidden location—tucked at the far end of the passage with the recommended Cyklop pizzeria—attracts a wide range of loyal local clientele, from hard-scrabble seniors to politicians, artists, and actors. They're all here for well-executed, unpretentious, home-style Polish lunch grub. There can be a bit of a language barrier, so go with the flow: Pick up the English menu as you enter, find a table, wait for them to take your order, enjoy your meal, then pay as you leave. This is an excellent value and a real, untouristy Polish experience. The short menu changes every day—and when they're out, they're out (Mon-Fri 12:00-17:00, closed Sat-Sun, Mikołajskiej 16).

$ U Babci Maliny ("Granny Raspberry"), with a grinning Granny on the sign, is another well-established and popular milk bar. One location, frequented almost entirely by Krakovians, is designed for university students and staff and is tucked into an inner courtyard of the Science Academy. Find the door at Sławkowska 17, then make your way into the inner courtyard, with an entrance to a rustic cellar where it looks like a kitschy cottage bomb went off (Mon-Fri 11:00-21:00, Sat-Sun 12:00-21:00). Another location is across the street from the National Theater building at Szpitalna 38. The main floor, also done up in a kitschy cottage style, is self-service and budget-priced, while the cellar—with a drawing-room vibe—has table service and is about 20 percent more expensive (daily 11:00-23:00). Both locations have walls of photos of the owner posing with bodybuilders and ultimate fighters...not quite in keeping with the country theme.

The **$ Academy of Music Café** (a.k.a. Restauracja U Romana) is a no-frills student cafeteria that enjoys a restful, top-floor perch with views over the back of St. Mary's Church and the rooftops of Kraków. It has a short, basic menu of food and drinks; come here not for high cuisine, but for high-up cuisine. You'll enter the Academy of Music at Św. Tomasza 43—using the heavy metal door opposite Hotel Campanile—then angle left inside to find the elevator in the stairwell and ride it to floor 6. Order at the counter, get your food, then head out to the tranquil terrace (mid-Sept-June Mon-Fri 9:00-18:00, Sat 9:00-16:00, closed Sun and July-mid-Sept).

Throwback Milk Bars on Grodzka Street: Just a couple of

blocks south of the Main Market Square, on busy ulica Grodzka, two classic milk bars somehow survive the onslaught of the modern world. First, at the corner with Senacka, is the remarkably basic and traditional milk bar, with a sign reading simply **$ Bar Mleczny** ("Milk Bar"; a low-profile sign over the door gives the eatery's name, *Restauracja "pod Temidą"*). The next best thing to a time machine to the communist era, this place has grumpy monolingual service, a mostly local clientele, and cheap but good food (daily 9:00-21:00). A few more steps down, also on the right (just before the two churches), **$ Bar Grodzki** is a single tight little room with

shared tables. They specialize in tasty potato pancake dishes *(placki ziemniaczane)*. Order high on the menu and try the rich and hearty "Hunter's Delight"—potato pancake with sausage, beef, melted cheese, and spicy sauce. The English menu posted by the counter makes ordering easy. Order, sit, and wait to be called to fetch your food (daily 9:00-19:00).

$ Restauracja Samoobsługowa Polakowski is a glorified milk bar with country-kitchen decor and cheap, tasty Polish fare. The tongue-twisting *samoobsługowa* simply means "self-service"—as at other milk bars, you'll order at the counter and bus your dishes when done. Curt service...cute hats (daily 11:00-22:00, facing St. Francis Basilica and the Wyspiański Pavilion at plac Wszystkich Świętych 10).

$ Chimera Cafeteria, just off the Main Market Square, is a handy spot for a quick lunch in the center. It serves fast traditional meals to a steady stream of students. You'll order at the counter—choose a big plate (6 items) or medium plate (4 items), and select from an array of salads and main dishes by pointing to what looks good. Then eat outside on their quiet garden courtyard (good for vegetarians, daily 9:00-22:00, near university at ulica Św. Anny 3). I'd skip their expensive full-service restaurant (in the basement), which shares an entryway.

IN KAZIMIERZ

The entire district is bursting with lively cafés and bars—it's a happening night scene. And, beyond the Jewish-themed places along ulica Szeroka, Kazimierz's restaurants are less touristy and more diverse than the Old Town's. For locations, see the map on page 134.

Kazimierz Hotels & Restaurants

Accommodations
1 To Metropolitan Boutique Hotel
2 Rubinstein Residence
3 Karmel Hotel
4 Tournet Guest House
5 Hostel Momotown

Eateries
6 Judah Square Food Trucks
7 Isaac Synagogue Food Trucks
8 Dajwór 21 Food Trucks
9 Plac Nowy Eateries
10 Nova Krova
11 Good Lood

12 Pod Ursa Major
13 Bagelmama
14 Stara Zajezdnia
15 Craftownia
16 Studio Qulinarne
17 Bottiglieria 1881
18 Hamsa Restaurant
19 Alchemia & Alchemia od Kuchni
20 Kolanko No. 6
21 Satori Café/Bistro
22 Warsztat (3)
23 Lody Tradycyjna Receptura
24 Ciastkarnia Bakery

Fast and Cheap

Kazimierz has some great carry-out and street food—handy for a lunch break from daytime sightseeing here, or for an affordable dinner break from bar-hopping.

$ Food Trucks: Kazimierz has three vacant lots filled with fun-to-browse food trucks—most open daily for lunch and dinner. Each one comes with about a half-dozen entirely different options. The first and best is at **Judah Square.** Named for its big graffiti mural (by an Israeli street artist), it's tucked at the southern fringe of the tourists' Kazimierz, near the old tram depot (corner of Św. Wawrzyńca and Wąska). Mainstays here include the Big Red Bustaurant (fish-and-chips sold from a double-decker London bus); Belgian-style fries; Andrus (super-decadent and gooey roasted pork sandwiches); Boogie Truck burgers; Pan Kumpir baked potatoes; and the beloved Chimney Cake Bakery, which rotisserie-roasts dough and sugar into a sweet and crunchy cake, then fills it with ice cream and other toppings. Right in the heart of the tourist zone, another food truck pod fills a vacant lot **behind Isaac Synagogue,** just steps from ulica Szeroka. Here you'll find painted-wooden-palate furniture, hammocks, twinkle lights, and a mellow vibe. You'll see Walenty Kania, who does one thing and does it well: kielbasa (Polish sausage), with options made of sheep, deer, horse, goat, and, of course, ham. There's also a Mexican burrito truck, an açaí smoothie place, a Thai ice cream stand, and—of course—more chimney cakes. Finally, a third, newer, and less interesting pod of food trucks is at **Dajwór 21,** across the street from the Galicia Jewish Museum. Note that any and all of these could reshuffle their carts—or be gone entirely, replaced by a ritzy new building—at any moment. But it's clear that, in general, Kazimierz's food-truck scene is here to stay.

Polish Fast Food on Plac Nowy: The centerpiece of the plac Nowy market is a circular brick slaughterhouse, which has recently been taken over by Kazimierz foodies. Each of the shop windows—which once housed butchers and basic Polish grub—is now operated by a different pop-up eatery, from burgers to kebabs to Belgian fries to sushi hand rolls. But the real specialty here is the Poles' beloved *zapiekanki*—a toasted baguette with cheese, ketchup, and a bewildering array of other toppings. You can take a spin around the building to survey your options—noting where the lines are longest (locals know which *zapiekanki* is best). For dessert, line up at Good Lood, top-quality ice cream that's made fresh each morning and available until it's sold out (this is an outpost of the main branch a few blocks away on plac Wolnica—see next).

Foodie Favorites on Plac Wolnica: The big main square of Kazimierz (a couple of blocks south of plac Nowy) has a few locally beloved eateries. **$ Nova Krova** ("New Cow") sells entirely vegan and organic "burgers" and other sandwiches in a hip, woody atmosphere (Mon-Thu 12:00-21:00, Fri-Sat 12:00-23:00, Sun 10:00-21:00, at #12). And just kitty-corner, on hot days you'll see a long line at **Good Lood** (a pun on *lody*—ice cream), with scoops of fresh and flavorful homemade ice cream (daily 11:00-22:00 or until the flavors run out—since it's made fresh daily, at #11). **Pod Ursa Major**—highly respected by local beer lovers—is a microbrew pub serving the six types of beer they brew in the mountains southeast of Kraków (long hours daily, at #10).

Creative Bagels: $ Bagelmama, run by an American named Nava (who has worked as a private chef for tennis star John McEnroe), is a casual bagel shop that's popular with expats and locals. The bagels come dressed with a wide variety of spreads, and they also sell sandwiches, soups, salads, desserts, and fresh juices. You can eat in or get it to go (daily 9:00-17:00, ulica Dajwór 10, tel. 12-346-1646).

Beer: Beer lovers find two different experiences along Św. Wawrzyńca. **$$ Stara Zajezdnia** ("Old Tram Depot") fills exactly that—a cavernous old industrial hall—with tables and happy drinkers, draining huge mugs of the five different types of beer brewed on the premises. (You can also order a sampler.) In good weather, the vast courtyard out front becomes an idyllic beer garden filled with relaxing lounge chairs. Both zones have table service and basic pub grub (Św. Wawrzyńca 12, mobile 664-323-988). For craft beer lovers, **Craftownia** has 18 Polish microbrews on tap (and many more by the bottle) in a nondescript setting (Mon-Thu 14:00-late, Fri-Sun 12:00-late, Św. Wawrzyńca 22, mobile 515-010-565).

Dining in Kazimierz

For a good-quality sit-down meal, consider these options.

$$$$ Studio Qulinarne is a big, glassy, industrial-mod space with a trendy vibe and a fine-dining menu. With artfully prepared, seasonal cuisine and a long wine list, it's a good choice for an upscale splurge—still affordable by international standards—that feels removed from the rollicking Kazimierz bustle (Mon-Fri 12:00-14:30 & 18:00-22:00, Sat 18:00-22:00 only, closed Sun, Gazowa 4, tel. 12-430-6914, www.studioqulinarne.com).

$$$ Bottiglieria 1881 is a chic, sophisticated wine bar tucked unassumingly just off plac Wolnica. The cellar is stocked with wines from all over the world (with an emphasis on Italian), all complemented by the short, seasonal, thoughtfully designed menu with modern Polish and international dishes. Come for a glass or for a full meal (Tue-Sat 12:00-23:00, Sun 12:00-20:00, closed Mon, Bochenska 5, mobile 660-661-756).

$$ Hamsa, with a prime location at the top of ulica Szeroka, offers "hummus and happiness," with an updated take on Israeli food (that's Middle Eastern, not traditional Jewish fare). Don't come here for matzo balls and klezmer music, but for an enticing menu of *mezes* (small plates, like hummus and various dips) and grilled meat dishes in a modern, hip atmosphere (daily 9:00-24:00, ulica Szeroka 2, mobile 515-150-145).

Kazimierz Bars and Cafés with Food

Some of my favorite atmospheric Kazimierz bars also serve food. It's not high cuisine—the food is an afterthought to the busy bar.

$$ Alchemia od Kuchni is an inviting little subway-tiled street-food restaurant—a sleek space around the corner from the ramshackle main branch. You can order at the counter for a bite to go, or opt for table service (daily 8:00-23:00, Estery 5).

$$ Kolanko No. 6 is a great spot for classic Kazimierz atmosphere. The bar up front is filled with old secondhand furniture. Walking toward the back, you discover an inviting garden with tables and, beyond that, a hall where they host events. They serve light meals, specializing in crêpes, toasted sandwiches, salads, and international dishes (daily 10:00-24:00, Józefa 17, tel. 12-292-0320).

$ Satori is a relaxing eddy of a café/bistro, which rests just outside of the Kazimierz tourist chaos. With an artfully mismatched-furniture atmosphere that encourages lingering, this is a good choice either for a coffee or an affordable full meal (homemade pastas and salads, daily 11:00-22:00, Sun until 21:00, Józefa 25, mobile 660-508-840).

$$ Warsztat ("Workshop") is littered with musical instruments: The bar is a piano, and the tight interior is crammed with other instruments and rakishly crooked lampshades. The menu is an odd hybrid of Italian, Middle Eastern, and Polish cuisine, and the portions are big (salads, pizzas, pastas, and meats; daily 9:00-24:00, Izaaka 3, tel. 12-430-1451). They also have two other locations: a small one (focusing on Polish dishes) by the front door of the Tempel Synagogue, and a bigger one on Bożego Ciała street.

Kazimierz Desserts

Ice Cream: Lody Tradycyjna Receptura has, true to its name, some of the best "ice cream from a traditional recipe" in Kraków—if not in Poland. The straightforward, seasonal flavors—just a few varieties—are made fresh each morning and sold until they run out. Locals line up here—and if you have a sweet tooth, you should, too (daily 9:00-19:00, Starowiślna 83). **Good Lood,** a newer version offering essentially the same concept, has an equally loyal following at its two locations—one on plac Wolnica, and the other in the plac Nowy market hall (both described earlier).

Cakes: Ciastkarnia ("Confectionery") is a cute little bakery with top-quality but still affordable cakes from traditional recipes, and a few pleasant tables facing a little park (daily 9:00-20:00, shorter hours off-season, Brzozowa 13, mobile 602-790-988).

Kraków Connections

For getting between Kraków and **Auschwitz,** see page 140 in the next chapter. To confirm rail journeys, check specific times online (www.rozklad-pkp.pl) or at the main train station.

From Kraków by Train to: Warsaw (hourly, about 2.5 hours, slick EIC express train, requires seat reservation), **Gdańsk** (6/day direct, 5.5 hours on EIC express, plus night train, 10 hours), **Toruń** (7/day, 5.5 hours, transfer at Warsaw's Zachodnia station), **Prague** (4/day with 1-2 changes, 7.5-8.5 hours; plus night train, 9 hours), **Berlin** (2/day, 7.5 hours with change at Warsaw's Zachodnia station, more options with multiple changes; plus 1 direct and handy Deutsche Bahn IC bus, 8 hours, www.bahn.com), **Budapest** (2/day, 10-11 hours, change in Katowice, Poland, and Břeclav, Czech Republic; plus night train, 11 hours; faster by infrequent Orange Ways bus: 4/week, 7 hours, www.orangeways.com), **Vienna** (2/day, 7 hours, change in Katowice; plus night train, 9 hours).

By Bus: Though train connections are typically faster, buses can be less expensive and make sense for some trips. Polski Bus prides itself on offering buses with Wi-Fi and electrical outlets (www.polskibus.com). However, some of my readers have reported hot, crowded, uncomfortable rides on these buses—you get what you pay for.

AUSCHWITZ-BIRKENAU

The unassuming regional capital of Oświęcim (ohsh-VEENCH-im) was the site of one of humanity's most unspeakably horrifying tragedies: the systematic murder of at least 1.1 million innocent people. From 1941 until 1945, Oświęcim was the home of Auschwitz, the biggest, most notorious concentration camp in the Nazi system. Today, Auschwitz is the most poignant memorial anywhere to the victims of the Holocaust.

"Auschwitz" (OWSH-vits) actually refers to a series of several camps in Poland—most importantly Auschwitz I, in the village of Oświęcim (50 miles west of Kraków), and Auschwitz II, a.k.a. Birkenau (about 1.5 miles west of Oświęcim). Those visiting Auschwitz generally see both parts, starting with Auschwitz I, then riding a shuttle bus to Birkenau. **Auschwitz I,** where public transportation from Kraków arrives, has the main museum building, the *Arbeit Macht Frei* gate, and indoor museum exhibits in former prison buildings. **Birkenau** (BEER-keh-now) is on a much bigger scale and mostly outdoors, with the infamous guard tower, a vast field with ruins of barracks, a few tourable rough barracks, the notorious "dividing platform," a giant monument flanked by remains of destroyed crematoria, and a prisoner processing facility called "the Sauna."

A visit here is obligatory for Polish 14-year-olds; students usually come again during their last year of school, as well. You may see Israeli high school groups walking through the grounds wearing Star of David emblems. Many visitors leave flowers and messages. One of the messages—from a German visitor—reads, "Nations who forget their own history are sentenced to live it again."

GETTING THERE

To reach Auschwitz from Kraków, it's easiest to join a package tour or hire a private guide or driver (75-minute drive each way). But the trip is also doable by public transportation (1.75-2.5 hours, depending on the type of transit). For details, see "Auschwitz Connections," at the end of this chapter.

Orientation to Auschwitz

Cost: Entrance to the grounds is free (though donations are gladly accepted). However, during busy times (April-Oct 10:00-15:00), you'll need to pay 45 zł to join a required organized tour at Auschwitz I. (Alternatively, you could opt to join a more in-depth, six-hour "study tour" for 70 zł, or you could hire your own guide—see sidebar.) At other times, you're allowed to visit Auschwitz I on your own—though the tour is still well worth considering. Any time of year, the grounds at Birkenau can be toured without a guide, though you'll likely need to be accompanied by a guide if you want to climb the guard tower.

Mandatory Reservations: With a million and a half visitors each year, Auschwitz struggles with crowd control. Reservations are required—whether visiting on your own or with a tour. It's free to reserve, but spaces book up very early. As soon as your dates are set—ideally weeks, or even months, in advance—visit http://visit.auschwitz.org. Select "Visit for individuals," then select a date, and choose between "General Tour 3,5 h" (for the 45-zł, 3.5-hour guided tour—be sure to select one

Why Visit Auschwitz?

Why visit a notorious concentration camp on your vacation?

Auschwitz-Birkenau is one of the most moving sights in Europe, and certainly the most important of all the Holocaust memorials. Seeing the camp can be difficult: Many visitors are overwhelmed by a combination of sadness and anger over the tragedy, as well as inspiration at the remarkable stories of survival. Auschwitz survivors and victims' families want tourists to come here and experience the scale and the monstrosity of the place. In their minds, a steady flow of visitors will ensure that the Holocaust is always remembered—so nothing like it will ever happen again.

Auschwitz isn't for everyone. But I've never met anyone who toured Auschwitz and regretted it. For many, it's a profoundly life-altering experience—at the very least, it will forever affect the way you think about the Holocaust.

in English) or "Tour for individuals without an educator" (to visit on your own, for free—not possible between 10:00 and 15:00 in summer). After you fill out the form, you'll receive an eticket. Print this out and bring it along when you visit the memorial. If you hire a local guide or driver to bring you here from Kraków, they can usually handle making a reservation for you—but be very clear on the details, as this can take some coordination.

Available time slots can fill up quickly—particularly at popular times, such as May and June, when school groups flood the site. If an English tour isn't available for your dates, consider booking one in a **foreign language,** then splitting off and using this chapter's self-guided tour. If you arrive in Poland without reservations, there are a couple of last-minute options: **Book a day tour** through a private company in Kraków, which includes both transportation and a tour of the camp (see sidebar); or consider taking your chances and **just showing up.** A white booth in front of the main building (facing the parking lot, opens at 8:00) lists spaces available on upcoming tours that day. You may luck out and get a tour right away...or, on busy days, you could wait hours. (You can pass any wait time by first going to Birkenau, which has less strict timing requirements.) If you anticipate crowds, try to arrive early (get there at 9:00 or 9:30); the later you arrive, the longer you may have to wait.

Hours: The museum opens every day at 8:00, and closes June-Aug at 19:00, April-May and Sept at 18:00, March and Oct at 17:00, Feb at 16:00, Jan and Nov at 15:00, and Dec at 14:00. These are "last entry" times; the grounds at Auschwitz I stay open 1.5 hours later (though many buildings—including the national memorials—close promptly at these times). The grounds at Birkenau, where many groups end their visits, may stay open even later.

Information: Tel. 33-844-8100, www.auschwitz.org.

Getting from Auschwitz I to Birkenau: Buses shuttle visitors two miles between the camps (free, about 4/hour in peak season, less off-season, times posted at the bus stop outside the main building of each site, timed to correspond with tours). Taxis are also standing by (about 15 zł). Many visitors, rather than wait for the next bus, decide to walk the 30 minutes between the camps, offering a much-needed chance for reflection. Along the way, you'll pass the Judenrampe, an old train car like the ones used to transport prisoners, explained by an informational sign.

Services: Auschwitz I's main building has a helpful information desk, bookshops, exchange offices, baggage storage (large bags aren't allowed on site), WCs, and basic eateries. You'll also find maps of the camp (posted on the walls) and a theater that shows the film described below. The guard tower at Birkenau has another bookshop and more WCs.

Film: The 17-minute movie (too graphic for children) was shot by Ukrainian troops days after the Red Army liberated the camp (4 zł, schedule for showings in English varies—ask when you arrive).

Photography: Because the philosophy of the camp is to spread the story of Auschwitz, taking photographs of anything outdoors is encouraged. However, to ease the movement of visitors, photography is not allowed inside certain museum buildings (when it *is* allowed, don't use a flash or tripod).

Eating: A café and decent cafeteria are at the main Auschwitz building. More options are in the commercial complex across the street.

Expect Changes: Various parts of the Auschwitz museum are continually maintained and updated. Some things may be different than described here, but everything is always well-signposted.

Etiquette: The camp encourages visitors to remember that Auschwitz is the place where more than a million people lost their lives. Behave and dress here as you would at a cemetery.

Guided Tours at Auschwitz

Visiting Auschwitz on your own works well, given the abundance of English descriptions (and this chapter's self-guided tour). However, due to crowd-control issues, from May through October individual visitors are not allowed to enter the Auschwitz I part of the complex on their own between the peak times of 10:00 and 15:00. Instead, you're required to either join one of the museum's organized tours or reserve your own private museum guide. Note that even during these busy times, individuals may enter Birkenau without a guide.

Organized Museum Tours: The Auschwitz Museum's excellent guides are serious and frank historians, who feel a strong sense of responsibility about sharing the story of the camp. The regularly scheduled 3.5-hour English tour covers Auschwitz, Birkenau, and the film (45 zł). These tours must be pre-booked at http://visit.auschwitz.org. There are usually several English tours each day—check availability on the website. Due to crowd concerns, arrive for your scheduled tour 30 minutes early.

Private Official Museum Guides: If you have a special interest, a small group, or just want a more personalized visit, it's affordable and worthwhile to hire one of the museum's guides for a private tour. Choose between the basic 3.5-hour tour of the camp (300 zł) or a longer "study tour" (480 zł/6 hours, 570 zł/8 hours—possible all in one day, or spread over two days; all rates are higher for more than 10 people). Because English-speaking guides are limited, try to reserve as far ahead as possible (ideally several months) at http://visit.auschwitz.org.

Tours from Kraków: Various Kraków-based companies sell round-trip tours from Kraków to Auschwitz, which include a guided tour of the camp (typically around 150 zł). I wouldn't normally recommend these, but they can be handy if you're trying to book a time slot on your own and everything is sold out. The main outfits are **See Kraków** (www.seekrakow.com), **Discover Cracow** (www.discovercracow.com), and **Cracow City Tours** (www.cracowcitytours.com)—for details, see page 38.

Local Guides and Drivers from Kraków: For hassle-free transportation to the camp, you can hire a Kraków-based guide or driver to bring you to Auschwitz; I've listed my favorites on page 35 (drivers) and 34 (guides). However, since they're not officially registered museum guides, they technically aren't allowed to show you around the site. Instead, they'll help you book a slot on an organized English tour (which can be handy, as it saves you having to deal with the website). While it's pricey, some travelers consider hiring a driver/guide to be a worthwhile splurge, since you'll have door-to-door service to the camp and three hours in the car with a local expert.

Auschwitz Tour

AUSCHWITZ I

• *From the entrance building, step out and look over the grassy field to get oriented.*

Before World War II, this camp was a base for the Polish army. When Hitler occupied Poland, he took over these barracks and turned it into a concentration camp for his Polish political enemies. The location was ideal, with a nearby rail junction and rivers providing natural protective boundaries. An average of 14,000 prisoners were kept at this camp at one time. (Birkenau could hold up to 100,000.) In 1942, Auschwitz became a death camp for the extermination of European Jews

and others whom Hitler considered "undesirable." By the time the camp was liberated in 1945, at least 1.1 million people had been murdered here—approximately 960,000 of them Jewish.

• *Go closer to the camp entrance, approaching the notorious...*

"Arbeit Macht Frei" Gate

Although this gate imparts the message "Work Sets You Free," the only way out of the camp for the prisoners was through the crematorium chimneys. Note that the "B" was welded on upside down by belligerent inmates, who were forced to make this sign (and much of the camp). This is actually a replica; the original was stolen one night in December of 2009, then recovered two days later, cut up into several pieces. The original is now safely in the museum's possession, but no longer displayed in public.

Just inside the gate and to the right, the camp orchestra (made up of prisoners) used to play marches; having the prisoners march made them easier to count.

• *From the gate, proceed straight up the "main street" of the camp.*

You'll pass two rows of barracks. The first one holds a variety of national memorials. We'll circle back here later, if you'd like to enter some of them. But these are of less general interest than the second row of barracks, which hold the main museum exhibitions. Blocks 4 and 5 focus on how Auschwitz prisoners were killed. Blocks 6, 7, and 11 explore the conditions for prisoners who survived here a little longer than most. In each block, arrows send you on a one-way route from numbered room to numbered room; in many cases, there are also exhibits downstairs and upstairs—don't miss these.

• *Start with...*

Auschwitz I

To Oświęcim Town →

LEGIONÓW

To Bielsko-Biała →

WALL

MUSEUM EXHIBITS

② ③ ④ ⑤ ⑥ ⑦

NATIONAL MEMORIALS

⑯ ⑮ ⑭ ⑬ ⑫ ⑪ ⑩ ⑨

⑱

ARBEIT MACHT FREI GATE

⑰ ⑧

TOUR BEGINS

① ⑳

To Bielsko-Biała

⑲ Camp Commander's Home

TOUR ENDS

100 Meters
100 Yards

ⓘ

ENTRY BUILDING

To Bus Stop at Edge of Camp

ENTRANCE

㉑

To Oświęcim Train Station & Auschwitz II - Birkenau

P

AUSCHWITZ-BIRKENAU

① Arbeit Macht Frei Gate
② Extermination (Block 4)
③ Material Evidence (Block 5)
④ Everyday Life (Block 6)
⑤ Camp Conditions (Block 7)
⑥ Execution Courtyard
⑦ "Death Block" (Block 11)
⑧ All Jews (Block 27)
⑨ Netherlands (Block 21)
⑩ Belgium & France (Block 20)
⑪ Hungary (Block 18)
⑫ Austria & Former Yugoslavia (Block 17)
⑬ Czech & Slovak (Block 16)
⑭ Poland (Block 15)
⑮ Russia (Block 14)
⑯ Roma/Gypsy (Block 13)
⑰ Crematorium
⑱ Gallows
⑲ Camp Commander's Home
⑳ Theater (Graphic Film)
㉑ Shuttle Bus to Birkenau

Block 4: Extermination

In Room 1, a map identifies the countries from which Auschwitz prisoners were brought—as far away as Norwegian fjords and Greek isles. In an alcove along the side of the room is an urn filled with ashes, a symbolic memorial to all of the camp's victims.

Room 2 shows photographs of Jewish ghettos from all over Europe being "liquidated"—that is, its residents assembled and deported to various concentration camps. Thanks to its massive occupancy, Auschwitz was a common destination for many.

Room 3 displays rare photos of scenes inside the camp, taken by arrogant SS men. To prevent a riot, the Nazis claimed at first that this was only a transition camp for resettlement in Eastern Europe. At the far end of Room 3, a helpful orientation map for visitors shows the town of Oświęcim, Auschwitz I, Auschwitz II (Birkenau), and other parts of the camp network.

Upstairs in Room 4 is a model of a Birkenau crematorium. People entered on the left, then got undressed in the underground rooms (hanging their belongings on numbered hooks and encouraged to remember their numbers to retrieve their clothes later). They then moved into the "showers" and were killed by Zyklon-B gas (hydrogen cyanide), a German-produced cleaning agent that is lethal in high doses. This efficient factory of murder took about 20 minutes to kill 8,000 people in four gas chambers. Elevators brought the bodies up to the crematorium. Members of the *Sonderkommand*—Jewish inmates who were kept isolated and forced by the Nazis to work here—removed the corpses' gold teeth and shaved off their hair (to be sold) before putting the bodies in the ovens. It wasn't unusual for a *Sonderkommand* worker to discover a wife, child, or parent among the dead. A few of these workers committed suicide by throwing themselves at electric fences; those who didn't were systematically executed by the Nazis after a two-month shift. Across from the model of the crematorium are canisters of Zyklon-B.

Across the hall in the dimly lit Room 5 is one of the camp's most powerful exhibits: a wall of actual victims' hair—4,400 pounds of it. Also displayed is cloth made of the hair, used to make Nazi uniforms. The Nazis were nothing if not efficient...nothing, not even human body parts, could be wasted.

Back downstairs in Room 6 is an exhibit on the plunder of victims' personal belongings. People being transported here were encouraged to bring luggage—and some victims had even paid in advance for houses in their new homeland. After they were killed, everything of value was sorted and stored in warehouses that prisoners named "Canada" (after a country they associated with great wealth). Although the Canada warehouses were destroyed, you can see a few of these items in the next building.

• *Head next door.*

Chilling Statistics: The Holocaust in Poland

The majority of people murdered by the Nazis during the Holocaust were killed right here in Poland. For centuries, Poland was known for its relative tolerance of Jews, and right up until the beginning of World War II, Poland had Europe's largest concentration of Jews: 3,500,000. Throughout the Holocaust, the Nazis murdered 4,500,000 Jews in Poland (many of them brought in from other countries) at camps, including Auschwitz, and in ghettos such as Warsaw's.

By the end of the war, only 300,000 Polish Jews had survived—less than 10 percent of the original population. Many of these survivors were granted "one-way passports" (read: deported) to Israel, Western Europe, and the US by the communist government in 1968 (following a big student demonstration with a strong Jewish presence). Today, only about 10,000 Jews live in all of Poland.

Block 5: Material Evidence of the Nazis' Crimes

The exhibits in this block consist mostly of piles of the victims' goods, a tiny fraction of everything the Nazis stole. As you wander through the rooms, you'll see eyeglasses; fine Jewish prayer shawls; crutches and prosthetic limbs (the first people the Nazis exterminated were mentally and physically ill German citizens); and a pile of pots and pans. Then, upstairs, you'll witness a seemingly endless mountain of shoes; children's clothing; and suitcases with names of victims—many marked *Kind,* or "child." Visitors often wonder if the suitcase with the name "Frank" belonged to Anne, one of the Holocaust's most famous victims. After being discovered in Amsterdam by the Nazis, the Frank family was transported here to Auschwitz, where they were split up. Still, it's unlikely this suitcase was theirs. Anne Frank and her sister Margot were sent to the Bergen-Belsen camp in northern Germany, where they died of typhus shortly before the war ended. Their father, Otto Frank, survived Auschwitz and was found barely alive by the Russians, who liberated the camp in January of 1945.

• *Proceed to the next block.*

Block 6: Everyday Life

Although the purpose of Auschwitz was to murder its inmates, not all of them were killed immediately. After an initial evaluation, some prisoners were registered and forced to work. (This did not mean they were chosen to live—just to die later.) This block shows various aspects of daily existence at the camp.

The halls are lined with photographs of victims, each one

St. Maksymilian Kolbe (1894-1941)

Among the many inspirational stories of Auschwitz is that of a Polish priest named Maksymilian Kolbe. Before the war, Kolbe traveled as a missionary to Japan, then worked in Poland for a Catholic newspaper. While he was highly regarded for his devotion to the Church, some of his writings had an unsettling anti-Semitic sentiment. But during the Nazi occupation, Kolbe briefly ran an institution that cared for refugees—including Jews.

In 1941, Kolbe was arrested and interned at Auschwitz. When a prisoner from Kolbe's block escaped in July of that year, the Nazis punished the remaining inmates by selecting 10 of them to be put in the Starvation Cell until they died—based on the Nazi "doctrine of collective responsibility." After the selection had been made, Kolbe offered to replace a man who expressed concern about who would care for his family. The Nazis agreed. (The man Kolbe saved is said to have survived the Holocaust.)

All 10 of the men—including Kolbe—were put into Starvation Cell 18. Two weeks later, when the door was opened, only Kolbe had survived. The story spread throughout the camp, and Kolbe became an inspiration to the inmates. To squelch the hope he had given the others, Kolbe was executed by lethal injection.

In 1982, Kolbe was canonized by the Catholic Church. Some critics—mindful of his earlier anti-Semitic rhetoric—still consider Kolbe's sainthood controversial. But most Poles feel he redeemed himself for his earlier missteps through this noble act at the end of his life.

identified with a name, birthdate, occupation, date of arrival at Auschwitz, date of death, and camp registration number. Examining these dates, it's clear that those registered survived here an average of two to three months. (Flowers are poignant reminders that these victims are survived by loved ones.) Similar photographs hang in several other museum buildings, as well; as with the plundered items in the last block, keep in mind that these represent only a tiny fraction of the masses of people murdered at Auschwitz.

19472
DĄBROWSKI JAN
ur. 8.2.1920 r., robotnik
przybył: 30.7.1941, zginął: wrzesień 1942.

Room 1 (on the left as you enter the front door) displays drawings of the arrival process. After the initial selection, those chosen to work were showered, shaved, and photographed. After a while, photographing each prisoner got to be too expensive, so prisoners were tattooed instead (see photographs): on the chest, on the arm, or—for children—on the leg. A display shows the symbols that prisoners had to wear to show their reason for internment—Jew, Roma (Gypsy), homosexual, political prisoner, and so on. At the end of the room, a display case holds actual camp uniforms.

Across the hall, Room 4 shows the starvation that took place here. The 7,500 survivors that the Red Army found when the camp was liberated were essentially living skeletons (the "healthier" inmates had been forced to march to Germany). Of those liberated, 20 percent died soon after of disease and starvation.

In Room 5, you can see scenes from the prisoner's workday (sketched by survivors after liberation). Prisoners worked as long as the sun shone—eight hours in winter, up to twelve hours in summer—mostly on farms or in factories.

Room 6 is about Auschwitz's child inmates, 20 percent of the camp's victims. Blond, blue-eyed children were either "Germanized" in special schools or, if younger, adopted by German families. Dr. Josef Mengele conducted gruesome experiments here on children, especially twins and triplets, ostensibly to find ways to increase fertility for German mothers. Also in this room, look for a display of the prisoners' daily ration (in the glass case): a pan of tea or coffee in the morning; thin vegetable soup in the afternoon; and a piece of bread (often made with sawdust or chestnuts) for dinner. This makes it clear that Auschwitz was never intended to be a "work camp," where people were kept alive, healthy, and efficient to do work. Rather, people were meant to die here—if not in the gas chambers, then through malnutrition and overwork.

• *Block 7 shows living and sanitary conditions at the camp, which you'll see in more detail later at Birkenau. Blocks 8-10 are vacant (medical experiments were carried out in Block 10). And Block 11 was the most notorious of all.*

Block 11: The Death Block

Step into the walled-in **courtyard** between Blocks 10 and 11. The wall at the far end is where the Nazis shot several thousand political prisoners, leaders of camp resistance, and religious leaders. Notice that the windows are covered, so that nobody could witness the executions. Also take a close look at the memorial—the back of it is made of a material designed by Nazis to catch the bullets without a ricochet. Inmates were shot at short range—about three feet. The pebbles represent prayers from Jewish visitors.

Now head into the **"Death Block"** (#11), from which nobody ever left alive. Death here required a "trial"—but it was never a fair trial. Room 2 (on the left as you enter) is where these sham trials were held, lasting about two minutes each. In Room 5, you can see how prisoners lived in these barracks—three-level bunks, with three prisoners sleeping in each bed (they had to sleep on their sides so they could fit). In Room 6, people undressed before they were executed.

In the **basement,** you'll see several different types of cells. The Starvation Cell (#18) held prisoners selected to starve to death when a fellow prisoner escaped; Maksymilian Kolbe spent two weeks here to save another man's life (see sidebar on Kolbe). In the Dark Cell (#20), which held up to 30, people had only a small window for ventilation—and if it became covered with snow, the prisoners suffocated. In the Standing Cells (#22), four people would be forced to stand together for hours at a time (the bricks went all the way to the ceiling then).

Upstairs, you'll find gallows and a bench used for administering lashes. Filling this floor are exhibits on various forms of punishment, mostly focusing on resistance within the camp, escapees, and local Poles who were executed—either for trying to assist the prisoners, or for fighting with Nazi officers.

• *Leaving Block 11, proceed straight ahead, between the buildings, to the other row of barracks. Several of these blocks house...*

National Memorials

These exhibits were created not by museum authorities, but by representatives of the home countries of the camps' victims. As these memorials overlap with the general exhibits, and are designed for Europeans to learn more about the victims from their own home countries, most visitors skip this part of the site. On the other hand, while the main museum exhibits await renovation and modernization, the displays in these national memorials tend to be slicker and better-presented than the ones we just saw. (Some of these may be works in progress, as old exhibits are routinely upgraded.) As you walk along this street toward our next stop (the crematorium), consider stepping into the ones that interest you.

The first one you see is the memorial to **Jewish** victims (Block 27). It's compelling and thoughtfully presented, relying heavily on video clips, evocative music, and sound effects.

Most of the other national memorials are on the right side of the street. Across from the Jewish memorial, Block 21 honors **Dutch Jews;** it begins with a quote by perhaps the most famous

Dutch victim of the concentration camps, Anne Frank (whose story is also told—among many others'—throughout the exhibit).

Block 20, a former hospital block, is shared by **Belgium** and **France.** A room near the entrance explains how some prisoners were killed by lethal injection, with portraits and biographical sketches of victims. Upstairs is the powerful Belgium exhibit, with a room featuring victims' portraits. Block 18 holds a very modern, conceptual exhibit about **Hungary**'s victims, with an eerie heart-beat sound pervading the space. Block 17, which is likely a work in progress, is intended to memorialize victims from **Austria** and the **former Yugoslavia.** Across from this block, notice the long gallows used for mass hangings. Block 16 contains a new and well-presented exhibit about **Czech** and **Slovak** victims.

Block 15 honors victims from **Poland,** focusing on the 1939 Nazi invasion of the country, which resulted in the immediate internment of Polish political prisoners. Exhibits explain the process of "Germanization"—such as renaming Polish streets with German names—and (upstairs) the underground resistance that fought to get back some control over Poland.

Block 14 is the **Russian** national memorial. However, this one's a bit controversial: While Russia claims to have lost "Russian" Jews to the Holocaust, virtually all of them were technically Polish Jews who had been living within Russia. (They spoke Polish, not Russian.) To sidestep the hot topic of how to identify these victims, this memorial focuses not on victims, but on the Russian liberation of the camp.

Block 13 houses the **Roma (Gypsy)** exhibit. You'll learn that the Roma, along with the Jews, were considered no better than "rats, bedbugs, and fleas," and explore elements of the so-called *Zigeunerfrage*—the "Gypsy question" about what to do with this "troublesome" population.

• *At the end of this row of barracks, you reach a guard tower and a barbed-wire fence. Jog a few steps to the right, through the hole in the fence, then angle left toward the earthen mound with the giant, ominous brick chimney. The entrance is at the far end of the building.*

Crematorium

Up to 700 people at a time could be gassed here. People undressed outside, or just inside the door. As you enter, bear right and find your way into the big "shower room." Look for the vents in the ceiling—this is where the SS men dropped the Zyklon-B. In the adjacent room is a replica of the furnace. This facility could burn 340 bodies a day—so it took two days to burn all of the bodies from one round of executions. (The Nazis didn't like this inefficiency, so they built four more huge crematoria at Birkenau.)

• *Turning left as you exit the crematorium takes you back to the entrance building. But first, circle around to the opposite side of the crematorium for the closest thing this story has to a happy ending.*

Shortly after the war, camp commander Rudolf Höss was tried, convicted, and sentenced to death. Survivors requested that he be executed at Auschwitz, and in 1947, he was hanged here. The **gallows** are preserved behind the crematorium (about a hundred yards from his home where his wife—who is said to have loved her years here—raised their children in a villa maintained by slaves and furnished with possessions of the dead).

• *Take your time with Auschwitz I. When you're ready, continue to the second stage of the camp—Birkenau (see "Getting from Auschwitz I to Birkenau" on page 142).*

AUSCHWITZ II—BIRKENAU

In 1941, realizing that the original Auschwitz camp was too small to meet their needs, the Nazis began a second camp in some nearby farm fields. The original plan was for a camp that could hold 200,000 people, but at its peak, Birkenau (Brzezinka) held only about 100,000. They were still adding onto it when the camp was liberated in 1945.

• *Train tracks lead past the main building and into the camp. The first sight that greeted prisoners was the...*

Guard Tower

If you've seen *Schindler's List*, the sight of this icon of the Holocaust—shown in stirring scenes from the movie—may make you queasy.

Climb to the top of the entry building (also houses WCs and bookstore) for an overview of the massive camp. As you look over the camp, you'll see a vast field of chimneys and a few intact wooden and brick barracks. Some of the barracks were destroyed by Germans. Most were dismantled to be used for fuel and building materials shortly after the war. But the first row has been reconstructed (using components from the original structures). The train tracks lead straight back to the dividing platform, and then dead-end at the ruins of the crematorium and camp monument at the far side.

• *Descend the tower, enter the camp, turn right, and walk through the barbed-wire fence to reach the...*

Wooden Barracks

The first of these barrack buildings was the **latrine:** The front half

Auschwitz II – Birkenau

MONUMENT

Creek

CREMATORIA

FORMER RAIL LINE

FORMER

BARRACKS

GUARD
TOWER

TOUR
ENDS

CREMATORIA

TOUR
BEGINS

To Auschwitz I
& Oświęcim Town

MIESZKANCÓW NARODÓW

P

200 Meters
200 Yards

☐ Foundations
▬ Existing Buildings

❶ Guard Tower, Viewpoint, WC & Bookstore
❷ Latrine & Restored Barracks
❸ Dividing Platform
❹ Brick Barracks
❺ Crematoria Ruins (4)

❻ Monument
❼ "The Sauna"
❽ "Canada" Foundations
❾ Shuttle Bus to Auschwitz I

of the building contained washrooms, and the back was a row of toilets. There was no running water, and prisoners were in charge

of keeping the latrine clean. Because of the resulting unsanitary conditions and risk of disease, the Nazis were afraid to come in here—so the latrine became the heart of the black market and the inmates' resistance movement.

The third barrack was a **bunkhouse.** Each inmate had a personal number, a barrack number, and a bed number. Inside, you can see the beds (angled so that more could fit). An average of 400 prisoners—but up to 1,000—would be housed in each of these buildings. These wooden structures, designed as stables by a German company (look for the horse-tying rings on the wall), came in prefab pieces that made them cheap and convenient. Two chimneys connected by a brick duct provided a little heat. The bricks were smoothed by inmates who sat here to catch a bit of warmth.

• *Return to the train tracks, and follow them toward the monument about a half-mile away, at the back end of Birkenau. At the intersection of these tracks and the perpendicular gravel road (halfway to the monument)— now marked by a lonely train car—was the gravel pitch known as the...*

Dividing Platform

A Nazi doctor would stand facing the guard tower and evaluate each prisoner. If he pointed to the right, the prisoner was sentenced to death, and trudged—unknowingly—to the gas chamber. If he pointed to the left, the person would be registered and live a little longer. It was here that families from all over Europe were torn apart forever.

• *Photographs near the wooden building—on the left-hand side as you face the back of the camp complex—show the sad scene. Just beyond that building is a field with some...*

Brick Barracks

Enter one of these buildings. The supervisors lived in the two smaller rooms near the door. Farther in, most barracks still have the wooden bunks that held about 700 people per building. Four or five people slept on each bunk, including the floor—reserved for new arrivals. There were chamber pots at either end of the building. After a Nazi doctor died of typhus, sanitation improved, and these barracks got running water.

Now head back to the train tracks. As you walk along the camp's only road, which leads along the tracks to the crematorium, imagine the horror of this place—no grass, only mud, and all the barracks packed with people, with smoke blowing in from the busy crematoria. This was an even worse place to die than Auschwitz I.

• *The train tracks lead to the camp memorial and crematorium. At the end of the tracks, go 50 yards to the left and climb the three concrete steps to view the ruin of the...*

Crematorium

This is one of four crematoria here at Birkenau, each with a capacity to cremate more than 4,400 people per day. At the far-right end of the ruins, see the stairs where people entered the rooms to undress.

They were given numbered lockers, conning them into thinking they were coming back. (The Nazis didn't want a panic.) Then they piled into the "shower room"—the underground passage branching away from the memorial—and were killed. Their bodies were burned in the crematorium (on the left), giving off a scent of sweet almonds (from the Zyklon-B). Beyond the remains of the crematorium is a hole—once a gray lake where tons of ashes were dumped. This efficient factory of death was destroyed by the Nazis as the Red Army approached, leaving the haunting ruins you see today.

When the Soviets arrived on January 27, 1945, the nightmare of Auschwitz-Birkenau was over. The Polish parliament voted to turn these grounds into a museum, so that the world would understand, and never forget, the horror of what happened here.

• *At the back of the camp stands the...*

Monument

Built in 1967 by the communist government in its heavy "Socialist Realism" style, this monument represents gravestones and the chimney of a crematorium. The plaques, written in each of the languages spoken by camp victims (including English, far right), explain that the memorial is "a cry of despair and a warning to humanity."

• *With more time, you could continue deeper into...*

The Rest of the Camp

There's much more to see for those who are interested—Birkenau sprawls for a frightening distance. One place worth seeing is the

reception and disinfection building that prisoners called **"the Sauna"** (the long building with four tall chimneys). It was here that prisoners would be forced to strip and be deloused; their belongings were seized and taken to the "Canada" warehouses (described earlier) to be sorted. Walking through here (on glass floors designed to protect the original structure below), you'll see artifacts of the grim efficiency with which prisoners were "processed"—their heads were shaved, they were tattooed with a serial number, and they were assigned uniforms and wooden clogs to wear. Portraits at the end of the building humanize those who passed through here. Look for the cart, which was used to dispose of ashes. In front of the Sauna is a field of foundations of the **"Canada" warehouses.** Nearby are the other two destroyed **crematoria.**

AUSCHWITZ-BIRKENAU

Auschwitz Connections

The Auschwitz Museum is in the town of Oświęcim, about 50 miles west of Kraków. By bus or minibus, the journey takes 1.75 hours each way (longer by train); driving shaves off about 10-20 minutes.

FROM KRAKÓW TO AUSCHWITZ

The easiest way to reach Auschwitz is with a **package tour** (figure around 150 zł per person) or **private guide or driver** (300-500 zł for the carload); both of these options are described on page 143. While the package tours are more convenient than going on your own, three people can hire their own driver for less and have a more intimate experience.

If you're using public transportation, here are your choices (each one of these costs around 10-15 zł):

The most comfortable public-transit option is to take one of the frequent **buses,** mostly run by PKS Oświęcim (at least hourly, 1.75 hours, get the most recent schedule at any Kraków TI, buses depart from Kraków's main bus station behind the train station). Buy a one-way ticket from the bus-station ticket office or from the driver to leave your options open for getting home. Look for buses to "Oświęcim" (not necessarily "Auschwitz"). Note that these buses can be full, and because most come from other towns, there's no way to reserve a seat—so line up early (generally about 15 minutes ahead). If you don't get on a bus, you'll have to wait for the next one (or, if there's a minibus leaving sooner, you can take one of those instead—described next). Once in the town of Oświęcim, buses from Kraków stop first at the train station, then continue on to one of two stops near the museum: About half of the buses go directly into the parking lot at the museum itself, while the rest use a low-profile bus stop on the edge of the Auschwitz camp grounds (you'll see a small *Muzeum Auschwitz* sign on the right just before the stop, and a blue *Oświęcim Muzeum PKS* sign at the stop itself). From this bus stop, follow the sign down the road and into the parking lot; the main museum building is across the lot on your left. Note that since some buses don't actually go into the museum's parking lot, the Auschwitz stop can be easy to miss—don't be shy about letting your driver know where you want to go: *"Muzeum?"*

Several **minibuses** from Kraków head for Auschwitz (sporadic departures—generally 1-2/hour, 1.75 hours). Like the buses, some go directly to the museum, while others use the bus stop at the edge of camp. These generally depart from the lower platform of the main bus station (but confirm the departure point at the TI). Some of my readers report that the minibuses are a bit more cramped

On the Way to Auschwitz: The Polish Countryside

You'll spend about an hour gazing out the window as you drive or ride to Auschwitz. This may be your only real look at the Polish countryside. Ponder these thoughts about what you're passing...

The small houses you see are traditionally inhabited by three generations at the same time. Nineteenth-century houses (the few that survive) often sport blue stripes. Back then, parents announced that their daughters were now eligible by getting out the blue paint. Once they saw these blue lines, local boys were welcome to come a-courtin'.

Big churches mark small villages. Like in the US, tiny roadside memorials and crosses indicate places where fatal accidents have occurred.

Polish farmers traditionally had small lots that were notorious for not being very productive. These farmers somewhat miraculously survived the communist era without having to merge their farms. For years, they were Poland's sacred cows: producing little, paying almost no tax, and draining government resources. But since Poland joined the European Union in 2004, they're being forced to get up to snuff...and, in many cases, collectivize their farms after all.

Since most people don't own cars, bikes are common and public transit is excellent. There are lots of bus stops, as well as minibuses that you can flag down anywhere for a 2-zł ride. The bad roads are a legacy of communist construction, exacerbated by heavy truck use and brutal winters.

Poland has more than 2,000 counties, or districts, each with its own coat of arms; you'll pass several along the way. The forests are state-owned, and locals enjoy the right to pick berries in the summer and mushrooms in the autumn (you may see people—often young kids—selling their day's harvest by the side of the road). The mushrooms are dried and then boiled to make tasty soups in the winter.

than the buses and, while intended for local commuters, can be crammed with tourists. But they work fine in a pinch.

You could ride the **train** to Oświęcim, but it's less convenient than the bus because it leaves you at the train station, farther from the museum (nearly hourly, fewer Sat-Sun, 2-2.5 hours). If you do wind up at the Oświęcim train station, it's about a 20-minute walk to the camp (turn right out of station, go straight, then turn left at roundabout, camp is several blocks ahead on left). Or you can take a taxi (around 15 zł).

RETURNING FROM AUSCHWITZ TO KRAKÓW

Upon arrival at Auschwitz I, plan your departure by visiting the information window inside the main building. They can give you a schedule of departures and explain where the bus or minibus leaves from. (If you'll be staying late into the afternoon, make a point of figuring out the last possible bus or train back to Kraków, and plan accordingly.) Remember to allow enough time to make it from Birkenau back to Auschwitz I to catch your bus.

Although most minibuses and a few buses back to Kraków leave from the camp parking lot itself, if you're taking the bus, you'll most likely catch it from the stop on the edge of the Auschwitz I grounds. To reach this bus stop, leave the Auschwitz I building through the main entry and walk straight along the parking lot, then turn right on the road near the end of the lot. At the T-intersection, cross the street to the little bus stop with the blue *Oświęcim Muzeum PKS* sign. Don't be distracted by the ads for a nearby travel agency—you can buy tickets on board.

There's no public transportation back to Kraków from Birkenau, where most people end their tours; you'll have to take the shuttle bus back to Auschwitz I first.

WARSAW

Warszawa

Warsaw (Warszawa, vah-SHAH-vah in Polish) is Poland's capital and biggest city. It's huge, famous, and important...but not particularly romantic. If you're looking for Old World quaintness, head for Kraków. If you're tickled by spires and domes, get to Prague. But if you want to experience a truly 21st-century city, Warsaw's your place.

Not that long ago, the city was dreary and uninviting, but things have changed here—fast. Today, Warsaw's residents—Varsovians—are chic and sophisticated. Young professionals dress and dine as well as Parisians or Milanese do, and they have mastered the art of navigating an urban jungle in heels or a man bun. And from an infrastructure perspective, you can almost feel Warsaw peeling back the layers of communist grime as it replaces potholed highways with pedestrian-friendly parks. Today's Warsaw has gleaming new office towers and street signs, cutting-edge shopping malls, swarms of international businesspeople, hipster culture as vivid as anything in Brooklyn, and a gourmet coffee shop or designer pastry store on every corner.

Stroll down revitalized boulevards that evoke the city's glory days, pausing at an outdoor café to sip coffee and nibble at a *pączek* (the classic Polish jelly doughnut). Drop by a leafy park for an al fresco Chopin concert, packed with pensive Poles. Commune with the soul of Poland at the city's many

Warsaw History: Ebbs and Flows

Warsaw has good reason to be a city of the future: The past hasn't been very kind. Since becoming Poland's capital in 1596, Warsaw has seen wave after wave of foreign rulers and invasions—especially during the last hundred years. But in this horrific crucible, the enduring spirit of the Polish people was forged. As one proud Varsovian told me, "Warsaw is ugly because its history is so beautiful."

The city's Golden Age was between the World Wars, when Poland—newly reconstituted after a century and a half of foreign rule under the Partitions—was proudly independent and looking to the future. Interwar Warsaw saw a flourishing of commerce, construction, and the arts almost unmatched in Europe at that time.

Sadly, this age of unbridled optimism was cut brutally short by the city's darkest days, as the Nazis occupied the city (and all of Poland) at the outbreak of World War II. First, its Jewish residents were forced into a tiny ghetto. They rose up... and were slaughtered (the Ghetto Uprising—see page 200). Then, in the war's waning days, its Polish residents rose up... and were slaughtered (the Warsaw Uprising—see page 207). Fed up with the troublesome Varsovians, Hitler sent word to systematically demolish the entire city, block by block. At the war's end, Warsaw was virtually gone. An estimated 800,000 residents were dead—nearly two out of every three.

The Poles almost gave up on what was then a pile of rubble, planning to build a brand-new capital city elsewhere. But ultimately they decided to rebuild, creating a city of contrasts: painstakingly restored medieval lanes, retrofitted communist apartment blocks (bloki in Polish), and sleek skyscrapers. Between the buildings, you'll find fragments of a complex, sometimes tragic, and often inspiring history.

state-of-the-art museums focusing on Poland's artists (at the National Museum), its favorite composer (at the Chopin Museum), its dramatic history (at the Warsaw Historical Museum and Warsaw Uprising Museum), its dedication to the sciences (at the Copernicus Science Center), and its Jewish story (at the Museum of the History of Polish Jews). You can also dig into one of Europe's most affordable—and most interesting—foodie scenes, where a world of wildly creative chefs open new restaurants all the time. If you picture a dreary metropolis, think again. Warsaw is full of surprises.

PLANNING YOUR TIME

One day is the absolute minimum to get a quick taste of Warsaw. The city can easily fill two or three days, and even then you'll need to be selective. No matter how long you're staying, get your bearings by taking a stroll through Polish history on the Royal Way, using my self-guided walk from Palm Tree Circle to the Old Town. Then visit other sights according to your interests and time: Jewish history, the Warsaw Uprising, Polish artists, royalty, hands-on science gizmos, hipster hangouts, or Chopin. To slow down and take a break from the city, relax in Łazienki Park. For dinner, buck the tourist trend by leaving the overpriced Old Town and riding a tram, taxi, or Uber to the hip Śródmieście district, which has the highest concentration of quality eateries.

Orientation to Warsaw

Warsaw sprawls with 1.7 million residents. Everything is on a big scale—it seems to take forever to walk just a few "short" blocks. Get

comfortable with public transportation (or taxis or Uber), and plan your sightseeing to avoid backtracking.

The tourist's Warsaw blankets a mild hill on the west bank of the Vistula River (in Polish: Wisła, VEES-wah). To break things into manageable chunks, I think of the city as three major zones (from north to south):

The **Old Town and Royal Way,** at Warsaw's northern edge, is the most touristy area. Here you'll find the Old Town (Stare Miasto, STAH-reh mee-AH-stoh), the adjacent and nearly-as-old New Town (Nowe Miasto, NOH-vay mee-AH-stoh), the Royal Castle on Castle Square (Plac Zamkowy, plahts zahm-KOH-vee), and the historical artery called the Royal Way (Szłak Królewski, shwock kroh-LEHV-skee). This bustling strip has fine boulevards, genteel cafés, expansive squares and parks, and lots of stately landmarks both historic and faux-historic (much of this area was rebuilt after World War II).

"Palm Tree Circle" is my nickname for the center of the city, near the traffic circle with a fake palm tree—where busy Jerusalem Avenue (aleja Jerozolimskie, ah-LAY-uh yeh-ro-zoh-LIM-skyeh) crosses the shopping street called Nowy Świat (NOH-vee SHVEE-aht). Nearby are some good accommodations, trendy upscale eateries, pedestrianized shopping streets and glitzy malls, the National Museum (Polish art), the Palace of Culture and Science (communist-era landmark skyscraper), and the central train station (Warszawa Centralna).

The **Śródmieście** (SHROD-myesh-cheh, "Downtown") district, to the south, is a mostly-residential zone with the city's best restaurant and nightlife scene and some good accommodations.

The only real sight here is lush Łazienki Park, with its summertime al fresco Chopin concerts.

In sprawling Warsaw, many more sights—including some major ones—lie outside these three areas, but all are within a long walk or a short ride on public transit. These include the Museum of the History of Polish Jews and Warsaw Uprising Museum (to the west) and the Copernicus Science Center (to the east, along the river).

TOURIST INFORMATION

Warsaw's helpful, youthful TI has three branches: on the **Old Town Market Square** (daily May-Sept 9:00-20:00, Oct-April until 18:00), at the **Palace of Culture and Science** (enter on the side facing the train station, on Emilii Plater; daily May-Sept 8:00-19:00, Oct-April until 18:00), and at **Chopin Airport** (daily 9:00-19:00). The general information number for all TIs is 22-19115. All branches offer advice on live music and have piles of free, useful brochures ("city breaks," Jewish heritage, Chopin, mermaids, St. John Paul II, and so on). Everything is also available online (www.warsawtour.pl).

Busy sightseers might consider the **Warsaw Pass,** which covers public transportation, admission to several major sights, and free passage on the best hop-on, hop-off bus tour (119 zł/24 hours, 159 zł/48 hours, 189 zł/72 hours, sold at the TI). If your museum-going plans are ambitious, do the math.

ARRIVAL IN WARSAW
By Train

Most trains arrive at the **central train station** (Warszawa Centralna, vah-SHAH-vah tsehn-TRAHL-nah), a renovated communist-era monstrosity. (Don't get off at Warszawa Zachodnia, which is far from the tourist area.) Arriving at Warszawa Centralna, it can be tricky to get your bearings: Three parallel concourses run across the tracks, accessed by three different sets of escalators from each platform, creating a subterranean maze (with well-signed lockers, ticket windows, and lots of shops and eateries). Be patient: To get your bearings, ride up on your platform's middle escalator, then look for signs to the vast, open **main hall** (follow signs for *main hall/hala główna*). Here you'll find a row of ticket windows, a railroad service center, a supermarket, eateries, waiting areas (upstairs), and (from outside, near the taxi stand) views of the adjacent Palace of Culture

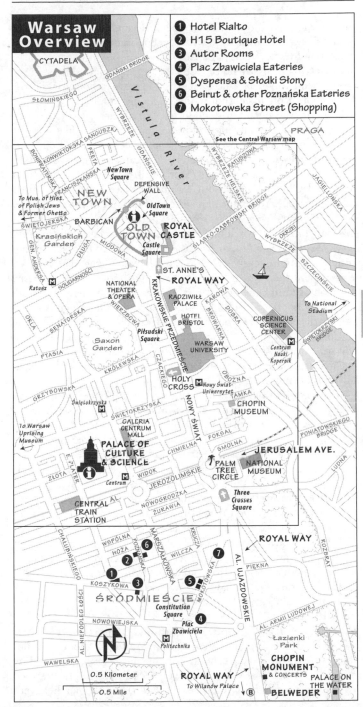

Warsaw Overview

CYTADELA

1 Hotel Rialto
2 H15 Boutique Hotel
3 Autor Rooms
4 Plac Zbawiciela Eateries
5 Dyspensa & Słodki Słony
6 Beirut & other Poznańska Eateries
7 Mokotowska Street (Shopping)

WARSAW

SŁOMINSKIEGO

Vistula River

PRAGA

GDAŃSKI BRIDGE

WYBRZEŻE

See the Central Warsaw map

BONIFRATERSKA   KONWIKTORSKA   SANGUSZKI

FRANCISZKAŃSKA

FRETA

GDAŃSKIE

WYBRZEŻE GDYŃSKIE

WYBRZEŻE HELSKIE

JAGIELLOŃSKA

New Town
Square

DEFENSIVE
WALL

NEW
TOWN

Old Town
Square

ROYAL
CASTLE

ŚLĄSKO-DĄBROWSKI BRIDGE

WYBRZEŻE

OKRZEI

SZCZECIŃSKIE

To Mus. of Hist.
of Polish Jews
& Former Ghetto

ŚWIĘTOJERSKA

BARBICAN

OLD
TOWN

Castle
Square

Krasińskich
Garden

GEN. ANDERSA

PŁUGA

MIODOWA

ST. ANNE'S

ROYAL WAY

To National
Stadium

Ratusz

SOLIDARNOŚCI

NATIONAL
THEATER
& OPERA

WIERZBOWA

RADZIWIŁŁ
PALACE

KAROWA

DOBRA

BROWARNA

COPERNICUS
SCIENCE
CENTER

ŚWIĘTOKRZYSKI
BRIDGE

OKLA

SENATORSKA

Saxon
Garden

Piłsudski
Square

HOTEL
BRISTOL

WARSAW
UNIVERSITY

Centrum
Nauki
Kopernik

PTASIA

KRÓLEWSKA

CZACKIEGO

KRAKOWSKIE PRZEDMIEŚCIE

HOLY
CROSS

OBOŻNA

Nowy Świat-
Uniwersytet

GRZYBOWSKA

ŚWIĘTOKRZYSKA

TAMKA

CHOPIN
MUSEUM

PONIATOWSKIEGO
BRIDGE

To Warsaw
Uprising
Museum

Świętokrzyska

GALERIA
CENTRUM
MALL

PALACE OF
CULTURE
& SCIENCE

NOWY ŚWIAT

FOKSAL

CHMIELNA

SMOLNA

JERUSALEM AVE.

LUDNA

ZŁOTA

E. PLATER

Centrum

WIDOK

JEROZOLIMSKIE

PALM
TREE
CIRCLE

NATIONAL
MUSEUM

CENTRAL
TRAIN
STATION

AL.

NOWOGRODZKA

ŻURAWIA

Three
Crosses
Square

CHAŁUBIŃSKIEGO

WSPÓLNA

MARSZAŁKOWSKA

POZNAŃSKA

HOŻA

6

WILCZA

KRUCZA

7

ROYAL WAY

AL. PIĘKNA

ROŻBRAT

2

KOSZYKOWA

1

3

AL. NIEPODLEGŁOŚCI

ŚRÓDMIEŚCIE

5

MOKOTOWSKA

AL. UJAZDOWSKIE

Constitution
Square

4

Plac
Zbawiciela

NOWOWIEJSKA

Politechnika

AL. ARMII LUDOWEJ

Łazienki
Park

N

CHOPIN
MONUMENT

& CONCERTS

PALACE ON
THE WATER

WAWELSKA

0.5 Kilometer

0.5 Mile

ROYAL WAY

To Wilanów Palace

B

BELWEDER

and Science and Złota 44 skyscrapers. If you have a little time to kill, walk across the street to the super-modern Złote Tarasy Shopping Mall (described on page 197).

Getting into Town: To reach the tourist zone and most of my recommended hotels, a taxi/Uber is the easiest choice, while the bus is more economical (but more challenging to find).

Taxis wait outside the main hall. Many are dishonest—look for one with a company logo and telephone number, and ask for an estimate up front (the fare should be no more than about 20-30 zł for most of my recommended hotels). You can also request an **Uber.**

From the station, **bus #175** or **#128** takes you to the Royal Way and Old Town in about 10 minutes (see "Getting Around Warsaw," later). You can catch either bus in front of the skyscraper with the Hotel Marriott (across busy Jerusalem Avenue from the station). From the corridors under the main hall, carefully track *Aleje Jerozolimskie* signs to find the pedestrian underpass. Several different exits are marked this way, but look for signs to *Śródmieście Station,* and then—near the end of that corridor—*Hotel Marriott.* Both buses terminate just off Piłsudski Square, a five-minute walk from the Old Town. **Bus #160** also goes to the Old Town (though not via the Royal Way), but it departs from the opposite side of the station: To find its stop from the main hall, go out the side door toward *ul. Emilii Plater.* Before boarding any bus, buy a ticket from the machine near the stop—or get one in the underground zone, at any kiosk marked *RUCH.*

Buying Train Tickets: Lining one wall of the main arrival hall *(hala główna)* are 16 **ticket windows.** A more user-friendly **passenger service center** is in the opposite corner (daily 9:10-20:30). While it can be slower to buy tickets or make reservations here (take a number as you enter), staff members are more likely to speak English and have patience for clueless tourists. Additional ticket windows are in the maze of corridors under the station. Allow yourself plenty of time to wait in line to buy tickets. Remember: Even if you have a rail pass, a reservation is still required on many express trains (including EIC trains to Kraków or Gdańsk). If you're not sure, ask. To get to your train, first find your way to the right platform *(peron,* as noted on schedules), then keep an eye on both tracks *(tor)* for your train. Train info: Tel. 19436 (22-19436 from outside Warsaw), www.rozklad-pkp.pl.

By Plane

Warsaw's **Fryderyk Chopin International Airport** (Port Lotniczy im. Fryderyk Chopina, airport code: WAW) is about six miles southwest of the center. The airport has just one terminal (Terminal A), which is divided into five check-in areas split between two zones: the southern hall (areas A and B) and the northern hall (areas C, D, and E). The airport is small and manageable; outside the arrivals area, you'll find a TI, ATMs, car-rental offices, and exchange desks *(kantor).* Airport info: tel. 22-650-4220, www. lotnisko-chopina.pl.

You can take the train or bus into town (similar prices, around 5 zł). The train is faster, but the bus makes more stops in the city center and may get you closer to your hotel. From the arrivals area, just follow signs to either option, and buy your ticket at the red machine before you board.

The **train** departs about every 15 minutes and takes 20-30 minutes. The route is operated by two different companies (SKM and KM)—take the one that's departing first. Be ready for your stop: Half the trains make fewer stops and take you to Centralna station; the others make a few more stops and use the Warszawa Śródmieście station—which feeds into the same underground passages as Centralna (these trains also continue one more stop to the Warszawa Powiśle station, which is a bit closer to Nowy Świat and can be more convenient to some hotels). Whether arriving at Centralna station or Warszawa Śródmieście, see the "By Train" arrival instructions, earlier.

Bus #175 departs every 15-20 minutes and runs into the city center (Centralna station, the Royal Way, and Piłsudski Square near the Old Town, 30-45 minutes depending on traffic).

For a **taxi,** head to the official taxi stand (avoid random hucksters offering you a ride out front). The trip to most hotels shouldn't cost more than 40-50 zł. It takes about 30 minutes, but potentially much longer during rush hour. You can also request an **Uber,** which is typically less expensive (except at very busy times).

Modlin Airport (airport code: WMI), about 21 miles northwest of the city center, primarily serves budget airlines (especially Ryanair). The most direct option for getting to downtown Warsaw is by shuttle bus—**ModlinBus** and **OKbus** both connect the airport to downtown (33 zł, 2/hour, 1-hour trip, cheaper if you book ahead online—www.modlinbus.com or www.okbus.pl). An alternative is the well-coordinated **bus-plus-train connection:** Take a shuttle bus to Modlin's main train station, then hop on a train to Warszawa Centralna station (17 zł, hourly, 1-1.5 hours total, www. mazowieckie.com.pl). If you want to ride a **taxi** all the way into Warsaw, the maximum legitimate fare is 200 zł (or 250 zł at night). Airport info: www.modlinairport.pl.

GETTING AROUND WARSAW

By Public Transit: In this big city, it's essential to get a handle on public transportation. You'll rely mostly on buses and trams, but the Metro can be useful for reaching a few sights. Everything is covered by the same ticket. A single ticket costs 4.40 zł (called *bilet*

Warsaw at a Glance

▲▲▲**Museum of the History of Polish Jews** Exceptional, expansive exhibit on the full Jewish experience through Polish history. **Hours:** Mon and Thu-Fri 10:00-18:00, Wed and Sat-Sun 10:00-20:00, closed Tue. See page 199.

▲▲**Royal Castle** Warsaw's best palace, rebuilt after World War II, but retaining its former opulence and many original furnishings. **Hours:** May-Sept Mon-Sat 10:00-18:00, Thu until 20:00, Sun 11:00-18:00; Oct-April Tue-Sat 10:00-16:00, Sun 11:00-16:00, closed Mon. See page 182.

▲▲**Old Town Market Square** Re-creation of Warsaw's glory days, with lots of colorful architecture. **Hours:** Always open. See page 186.

▲▲**National Museum** Collection of mostly Polish art, with unknown but worth-discovering works by Jan Matejko and the Młoda Polska (Art Nouveau) crew. **Hours:** Tue-Sun 10:00-18:00, Thu until 21:00, closed Mon. See page 189.

▲▲**Warsaw Uprising Museum** State-of-the-art space tracing the history of the Uprising and celebrating its heroes. **Hours:** Mon and Wed-Fri 8:00-18:00, Thu until 20:00, Sat-Sun 10:00-18:00, closed Tue. See page 205.

▲▲**Copernicus Science Center** Spiffy new science museum with well-explained, hands-on exhibits in English; Warsaw's best family activity. **Hours:** Tue-Fri 9:00-18:00, Sat-Sun 10:00-19:00, closed Mon. See page 194.

WARSAW

jednorazowy, good for one trip up to 75 minutes). But most trips should last no longer than 20 minutes, so you can save a zloty by buying a 3.40-zł "20-minute city travelcard" *(bilet 20-minutowy).* A 24-hour travelcard *(bilet dobowy)*—which pays for itself if you take at least five trips—costs 15 zł. Ticket machines, which are at most major stops and on board some trams, are easy to use. Or you can buy tickets at any kiosk with a *RUCH* sign. Be sure to validate your ticket as you board by inserting it in the little yellow box. Transit info: www.ztm.waw.pl.

Most of the city's major attractions line up on a single axis, the Royal Way, which is served by several different buses (but no trams). **Bus #175**—particularly useful on arrival—links Chopin Airport, the central train station, the Royal Way, and Old Town (it terminates at Piłsudski Square, about a five-minute walk from Castle Square). Once you're in town, the designed-for-tourists **bus**

▲**Castle Square** Colorful spot with whiffs of old Warsaw—Royal Castle, monuments, and a chunk of the city wall—and cafés just off the square. **Hours:** Always open. See page 181.

▲**Łazienki Park** Lovely, sprawling green space with Chopin statue, peacocks, and Neoclassical buildings. **Hours:** Always open; wonderful outdoor Chopin concerts mid-May-late Sept Sun at 12:00 and 16:00. See page 208.

Chopin Museum Elegant old mansion featuring slick exhibits but not much substance about Chopin; occasional piano concerts worthwhile. **Hours:** Tue-Sun 11:00-20:00, closed Mon. See page 193.

Warsaw Museum Glimpse of the city before and after World War II, with excellent movie in English. **Hours:** Closed until at least mid-2017; when open: Museum—likely Tue-Sun 10:00-20:00, off-season until 18:00, closed Mon year-round; Movie—likely Tue-Fri at 10:00 and 12:00; Sat-Sun at 12:00 and 14:00. See page 187.

Palace of Culture and Science Huge "Stalin Gothic" skyscraper with a more impressive exterior than interior, housing theaters, multiplex cinema, observation deck, and more. **Hours:** Observation deck—daily 10:00-20:00, may be open later in summer. See page 196.

Jewish Ghetto: Path of Remembrance Pilgrimage from Ghetto Heroes Square to the infamous Nazi "transfer spot" where Jews were sent to death camps. **Hours:** Always open. See page 204.

#180 conveniently connects virtually all the significant sights and neighborhoods: the former Jewish Ghetto and Museum of the History of Polish Jews, Castle Square/Old Town, the Royal Way, Łazienki Park, and Wilanów Palace (south of the center). This particularly user-friendly bus lists sights in English on the posted schedule inside (other buses don't). Buses #175 and #180, as well as buses **#116, #128,** and **#222,** go along the most interesting stretch of the Royal Way (between Jerusalem Avenue and the Old Town area). **Bus #178** conveniently connects Castle Square to the Warsaw Uprising Museum. Bus routes beginning with "E" (marked in red on schedules) are express, so they go long distances without stopping (these don't run July-Aug).

Note that on Saturdays and Sundays in summer (June-Sept), the Nowy Świat section of the Royal Way is closed to traffic, so the above routes detour along a parallel street.

Trams can be particularly useful for reaching the trendy Śródmieście district in the south. Several trams (including #4, #15, #18, and #35) run along the north-south Marszałkowska corridor, with stops at plac Konstytucji (Constitution Square, the heart of the Śródmieście) and at plac Zbawiciela (with the highest concentration of eateries).

Warsaw's two-line **Metro** system is handy for commuters, but less so for visitors. Still, it can be useful for some trips. Line 1 runs roughly parallel to the river and Royal Way, several blocks to the west; the most useful stops for tourists are Centrum (near the Palace of Culture and Science) and Świętokrzyska (where it crosses line 2). Line 2—which runs east to west, crossing deep under the river—is more practical; handy stops are Rondo Daszyńskiego (near the Warsaw Uprising Museum); Świętokrzyska (a transfer station between the two lines); Nowy Świat-Uniwersytet (in the middle of the Royal Way, near the Copernicus Monument); Centrum Nauki Kopernik (on the riverbank, near the Copernicus Science Center); and Stadion Narodowy (National Stadium).

By Taxi: As in most big Eastern European cities, it's wise to use only cabs that are clearly marked with a company logo and telephone number (or call your own: Locals like City Taxi, tel. 19459; MPT Radio Taxi, tel. 19191; or Ele taxi, tel. 22-811-1111). All official taxis have similar rates: 8 zł to start, then 3 zł per kilometer (4.50 zł after 22:00 or in the suburbs). The drop fee may be higher if you catch the cab in front of a fancy hotel. Note that **Uber** is active in Warsaw—if you're comfortable using it back home, it works the same way here, and is often cheaper.

Tours in Warsaw

Walking Tours

Each year, new companies crop up offering walking tours in Warsaw. These tend to have one of two approaches: A "free" tour of the main sights (with generous tipping expected); or communism-themed tours, often with a ride to a gloomy apartment-block area for a taste of the Red old days. The options change often, so survey the latest ones, do some homework (check online reviews), and pick a tour that suits your interests. The TI and most hotels have brochures.

Private Guides

Having a talented local historian as your guide in this city, with such a complex and powerful story to tell, greatly enhances your experience. I've worked with two excellent young guides: the smart and charming **Monika Oleśko** (320 zł/3 hours, 480 zł/5.5 hours, more for larger groups; by bike or by car; mobile 784-832-718, warsawteller.wordpress.com, olesko.monika@gmail.com) and the professorial **Hubert Pawlik** (660 zł for 5 hours on foot or with his car, or 115 zł per person for a walking tour, mobile 502-298-105, www.warsaw-citytours.com). Hubert's big, comfy SUV can fit a small group. Both Monika and Hubert can do theme tours or tailor the time to your interests.

Food Tours

Eat Polska does excellent food and vodka tours around this fast-emerging foodie mecca. A top-quality guide will take your small group (maximum 6 people for the food tours, 12 for the vodka tours) to a variety of restaurants and bars around the city, with tasting samples at each one. The guides do an exceptional job of providing insightful context about what you're tasting, making this educational about both Polish cuisine and Polish culture in general. If you have a serious interest in food, this is the most worthwhile tour in town (food tours typically daily at 13:00, 290 zł, 4 hours; vodka tours with food pairings daily at 17:00, 260 zł, 3.5 hours; contact to arrange details, www.eatpolska.com).

Bus Tours

Warsaw's spread-out landscape makes it a natural for a hop-on, hop-off bus—although heavy traffic may make you wish you'd taken a tram or the Metro instead. Two competing companies offer tours around Warsaw (60 zł/24 hours, 80 zł/48 hours): City-Sightseeing, with red buses, has two routes and generally better frequency; I'd skip City-Tour (with yellow buses), which runs only once hourly.

Warsaw's Royal Way Walk

The Royal Way (Szlak Królewski) is the six-mile route that the kings of Poland used to travel from their main residence (at Castle Square in the Old Town) to their summer home (Wilanów Palace, south of the center and not worth visiting). This self-guided walk covers a one-mile section of the Royal Way in the heart of the city—from Palm Tree Circle to the castle. This is a busy, mostly-pedestrian boulevard with two different names: At the south end, vibrant **Nowy Świat** offers shops, restaurants, and a good glimpse of urban Warsaw; to the north, and ending at the Old Town, **Krakowskie Przedmieście** is lined with historic landmarks and is better for sightseeing. Not counting sightseeing stops, figure about 30 minutes to walk along Nowy Świat ("Part 1"), then another 30 minutes along Krakowskie Przedmieście to the Old Town ("Part 2").

PART 1: PALM TREE CIRCLE AND NOWY ŚWIAT

• *Start this walk at the traffic circle officially named for Charles de Gaulle, but colloquially known as...*

Palm Tree Circle

This is one of the city's main intersections, marked by the quirky and now iconic palm tree. Stand near the communist-era monument under the spruce trees (on the curb, kitty-corner from the biggest building) and get oriented.

You're standing at the intersection of two major boulevards: **Nowy Świat** (where we're heading next) and **Jerusalem Avenue** (aleja Jerozolimskie, which heads from Warszawa Centralna station across the river). This street once led to a Jewish settlement called New Jerusalem. Like so much else in Warsaw, it's changed names many times. Between the World Wars, it became "May 3rd Avenue," celebrating Poland's 1791 constitution (Europe's first). But this was too nationalistic for the occupying Nazis, who called it simply Bahnhofstrasse ("Train Station Street"). Then the communists switched it back to "Jerusalem," strangely disregarding the religious connotations of that name. (Come on, guys—what about a good, old-fashioned "Stalin Avenue"?) The strikingly wide boulevards were part of the city's post-WWII Soviet rebuilding. Communist urban planners felt that eight- to twelve-lane roads were ideal for worker pageantry like big May Day parades...and, when the workers aren't happy, for Soviet tanks to thunder around, maintaining order.

You can't miss the giant **palm tree** in the middle of Jerusalem Avenue. When a local artist went to the real Jerusalem, she was struck by the many palm trees—and wanted to erect one along Warsaw's own little stretch of "Jerusalem." This artificial palm tree went up in 2002 as a temporary installation. It was highly controversial, dividing the neighborhood. One snowy winter day, the pro-palm tree faction—who appreciated the way the tree spiced up this otherwise dreary metropolis—camped out here in bikinis and beachwear to show their support. They prevailed, and the tree is now a permanent fixture.

The big, blocky building across the street (behind statue of de Gaulle) was the **headquarters of the Communist Party,** built in 1948. *Nowy Świat* translates as "New World," inspiring a popular communist-era joke: What do you see when you turn your back on the Communist Party? A "New World." Ironically, when the economy was privatized in 1991, this building became home to Poland's stock exchange. And then the country's only dealership for

Ferraris—certainly not an automobile for the proletariat—moved in downstairs.

On the corner in front of the former Communist Party HQ, a statue of **Charles de Gaulle** strides confidently up the street. A gift from the government of France, this celebrates the military tactician who came to Warsaw's rescue when the Red Army invaded from the USSR after World War I.

To the left of the Communist Party building is the vast **National Museum**—a good place for a fascinating lesson in Polish art (see the self-guided tour on page 70).

Before walking down Nowy Świat, notice the small but powerful **monument** near you. In 1956, this was dedicated to the "Poles who fought for People's Poland"—with a strong communist connotation. In a classic example of Socialist Realism, the communists appropriated a religious theme that Poles were inclined to embrace (this *pietà* composition)...and politicized it. But in 2014, the statue was rededicated to the "*partyzantom* who fought for free Poland in World War II." "Partisan" was a bad word in the 1950s, when it was used to describe the soldiers of the Polish Home Army—which fought against both the Nazis and the Soviets.

• *From here, turn your back to the Communist Party building and head into a new world—down Nowy Świat—to the first intersection. As you stroll, notice how massive and intense Warsaw suddenly becomes more intimate and accessible.*

Nowy Świat

This charming shopping boulevard is lined with boutiques, cafés, and restaurants—it's the most upscale, elegant-feeling part of the city. Before World War II, Nowy Świat was Warsaw's most popular neighborhood. And today, once again, rents are higher here than anywhere else in town. While most tourists flock into the Old Town, Varsovians and visiting businesspeople prefer this zone and farther south. The city has worked hard to revitalize this strip with broader, pedestrian-friendly sidewalks, flower boxes, and old-time lampposts.

Look down the street and notice the consistent architecture. In the 1920s, this was anything but cohesive: an eclectic and decadent strip of Art Deco facades, full of individualism. Rather than rebuild in that "trouble-causing" style, the communists used an idealized, more conservative, Neoclassical style, which feels more like the 1820s than the 1920s.

Ulica Chmielna, the first street to the left, is an appealing pedestrian boutique street leading to Emil Wedel's chocolate heaven (a five-minute walk away; described later, under "Eating in Warsaw"). Between here and the Palace of Culture and Science stretches one of Warsaw's top shopping neighborhoods (culminat-

WARSAW

Central Warsaw

Rondo Babka

PARKING LOT WITH FORMER GHETTO WALL

STAWKI

MIĘDZYPARKOWA

KONWIKTORSKA SANGUSZKI

Z. SŁOMIŃSKIEGO

UMSCHLAGPLATZ MONUMENT

MURANÓW
(Former Jewish Ghetto)

FORMER SS HQ BUNKER

NISKA DUBOIS

STAWKI

AL. JANA PAWŁA II

OKOPOWA

MUSEUM OF THE HISTORY OF POLISH JEWS

MILA

ZAMENHOFA

M. ANIELEWICZA

FRANCISZKAŃSKA

GHETTO HEROES SQUARE

Muranów

Plac Krasińskich

KARMELICKA

GEN. WŁ. ANDERSA

Krasińskich Garden

Nalewki

Ratusz

Plac Bankowy

SOLIDARNOŚCI

ELEKTORALNA

PTASIA

PL. MIROWSKI

AL. JANA PAWŁA II

WALICÓW

CHŁODNA

GRZYBOWSKA

Plac Grzybowski

TWARDA

CIEPŁA

ŚWIĘTOKRZYSKA

Muzeum Powstania Warszawskiego

TOWAROWA

PRZYOKOPOWA

WARSAW UPRISING MUSEUM

PROSTA

ŁUCKA

Rondo Daszyńskiego

Rondo Daszyńskiego

WRONIA

ŻELAZNA

ZELAZNA

PROSTA

PAŃSKA

SIENNA

MIEDZIANA

ZŁOTA

CHMIELNA

ZŁOTE TARASY MALL

Dworzec Centralny Bus #160

CENTRAL TRAIN STATION

Dw. Centralny

Dworzec Centralny Bus #175

400 Meters
400 Yards

Accommodations

1. Chopin Boutique B&B
2. Between Us B&B
3. Zgoda Apartment Hotel
4. Apple Inn
5. Oki Doki Hostel
6. Hotel Bristol
7. Hotel Le Régina
8. Castle Inn
9. Duval Apartments

Eateries

10. Opasły Tom
11. Kamanda Lwowska
12. Butchery & Wine
13. Bibenda
14. Tamka 43
15. A. Blikle Bakery
16. E. Wedel Pijalnia Czekolady (Chocolate)
17. Odette
18. To Solec 44
19. Warszawa Powiśle Café/Bar
20. Kawiarnia Kafka Café & Bookstore
21. Restauracja pod Samsonem
22. Freta 33
23. Zapiecek (4)

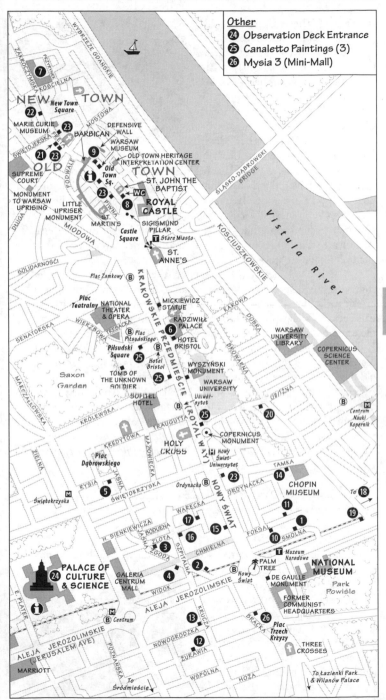

WARSAW

Other
- 24 Observation Deck Entrance
- 25 Canaletto Paintings (3)
- 26 Mysia 3 (Mini-Mall)

ing at the Galleria Centrum mall, just across from the Palace).

Across the street from Chmielna (on the right) is the restaurant street called **Foksal.** On a balmy summer evening, this street is filled with chatty al fresco diners.

A few steps farther down Nowy Świat, on the left, don't miss the recommended **A. Blikle** pastry shop and café—*the* place in Poland to buy sweets, especially *pączki* (rose-flavored jelly doughnuts; see page 18). Step inside for a dose of the 1920s: good-life Art Deco decor and historical photos. Or, if you're homesick for Starbucks, drop in to one of the many gourmet coffee shops that line this stretch of Nowy Świat—with American-style lattes "to go" (one of many American customs that the Poles have embraced).

A half-block down the street (on the left, at #39) is a rare surviving bit of preglitz Nowy Świat: Bar Mleczny Familijny, a classic **milk bar**—a government-subsidized cafeteria filled with locals seeking a cheap meal (an interesting cultural artifact, but not recommended for a meal; for more about milk bars, see page 16). Don't be surprised if it's gone by the time you visit; in this high-rent district, it's unlikely that these few remaining holdovers from the old days will survive for much longer.

Eat and shop your way along Nowy Świat. About one more block down, **Ordynacka street** (on the right) leads downhill to the Chopin Museum, worth considering for musical pilgrims.

• *Continuing along Nowy Świat through a duller stretch, you'll walk alongside a hulking, gloomy building before popping out in a pleasant square with a big statue of Copernicus.*

PART 2: KRAKOWSKIE PRZEDMIEŚCIE
• *The street name changes to Krakowskie Przedmieście at the big...*

Copernicus Statue
This statue, by the great Danish sculptor Bertel Thorvaldsen, stands in front of the Polish Academy of Science. **Mikołaj Kopernik** (1473-1543) was born in Toruń and went to college in Kraków. The Nazis stole his statue and took it to Germany (which, like Poland, claims Copernicus as its own). Now it's back where it belongs. The concentric circles radiating from the

front of the statue represent the course of the planets' orbits, from Mercury to Saturn.

Just to Copernicus' left is a low-profile, black-marble **Chopin bench**—one of many scattered around the center. These benches mark points related to his life (in this case, his sister lived across the street). Each of these benches plays Chopin's music with the push of a button (though because of passing traffic, this one is tough to hear).

Directly in front of the statue, in the glass case, find a replica of a **Canaletto painting** of this same street scene in 1778, and compare it to today's reality. As the national archives were destroyed, city builders referred to historic paintings like these for guidance after WWII. You'll see other Canaletto replicas like this one scattered around the city.

• *Across from Copernicus, the Church of the Holy Cross is worth a look.*

Church of the Holy Cross (Kościół Św. Krzyża)

We'll pass many churches along this route, but the **Church of the Holy Cross** is unique (free entry). Composer Fryderyk Chopin's

heart is inside one of the pillars of the nave (first big pillar on the left, look for the marker). After two decades of exile in France, Chopin's final wish was to have his heart brought back to his native Poland after his death. During World War II, the heart was hidden away in the countryside for safety. Check out the bright gold chapel, located on the left as you face the altar, near the front of the church. It's dedicated to a saint whom Polish Catholics believe helps them with "desperate and hopeless causes." People praying here are likely dealing with some tough issues. The beads draped from the altarpieces help power their prayers, and the many little brass plaques are messages of thanks for prayers answered.

In the back-left corner (as you face the altar) is a chapel dedicated to Poland's favorite son, St. John Paul II. His ghostly image appears out of the wall; beneath him is a rock inscribed with the words *Tu es Petrus* (Latin for "You are Peter"—what Jesus said when he made St. Peter the first-ever pope), embedded with a capsule containing JPII's actual blood. Just opposite, in the back-right corner, behind the giant barbed wire, is a memorial to the 22,000 Polish POWs—mostly officers and prominent civilians—massacred by Soviet soldiers in 1940 near Katyń, a village in today's Russia. Stalin was determined to decapitate Poland's military intelligentsia in a ruthless mass killing, which Poles have never forgotten.

WARSAW

• *Leaving the church, imagine how locals would relate to the 19th-century, bronze-and-granite...*

Statue of Christ Bearing the Cross

In front, a placard reads, "Lift up your hearts." Even as Warsaw bore the burden of Russian occupation, this statue inspired them to be strong and not lose hope. It was one of many crosses they bore: a Catholic nation pinched between Orthodox Russians and Protestant Germans.

• *Cross the street (appreciating how pedestrian-friendly it is—crossing here used to be a game of Frogger), and continue left.*

Warsaw University

A long block up the street on the right, you'll see the gates (marked *Uniwersytet*) to the main campus of **Warsaw University,** founded in 1816. This lively student district has plenty of bookstores and cafeterias.

The 18th century was a time of great political decline for Poland, as a series of incompetent foreign kings mishandled crises and squandered funds. But ironically, it was also Warsaw's biggest economic boom time. Along this boulevard, aristocratic families of the period built **mansions**—most of them destroyed during World War II and rebuilt since. Some have curious flourishes (just past the university on the right, look for the doorway supported by four bearded brutes admiring their overly defined abs). Over time, many of these families donated their mansions to the university.

• *The bright-yellow church a block up from the university, on the right, is the...*

Church of the Nuns of the Visitation (Kośicół Sióstr Wizytek)

This Rococo confection from 1761 is the only church on this walk that survived World War II, and is notable because Chopin was briefly the organist here.

The monument in front of the church commemorates **Cardinal Stefan Wyszyński,** who was the Polish primate (the head of the Polish Catholic Church) from 1948 to 1981. He took this post soon after the arrival of the communists, who opposed the Church, but also realized it would be risky for them to shut down the churches in such an ardently religious country. The Communist Party and the Catholic Church coexisted tensely in Poland, and when Wyszyński protested a Stalinist crackdown in 1953, he was arrested and imprisoned. Three years later, in a major victory for the Church, Wyszyński was released. He continued to fight the communists, becoming a great hero of the Polish people in their struggle against the regime.

Across the street is another then-and-now Canaletto illustration.

• *Farther up (on the right, past the park) is the elegant, venerable...*

Hotel Bristol

A striking building with a round turret on its corner, the Hotel Bristol was used by the Nazis as a VIP hotel and bordello, and survived World War II. If you wander

through any fancy Warsaw lobby... make it this one. Step in like you're staying here and explore its fine public spaces, with fresh Art Deco and Art Nouveau flourishes. The café in front retains its Viennese atmosphere, but the *pièce de résistance* is the stunning Column Bar deeper in, past the dramatically chandeliered lounge.

• *Leave the Royal Way briefly here to reach Piłsudski Square (a block away, up the street opposite Hotel Bristol).*

Piłsudski Square
(Plac Marszałka Józefa Piłsudskiego)

The vast, empty-feeling **Piłsudski Square** (pew-SOOD-skee) has been important Warsaw real estate for centuries, constantly changing with the times. In the 1890s, the Russians who controlled this part of Poland began construction of a huge and magnificent Orthodox cathedral on this spot. But soon after it was completed, Poland regained its independence, and anti-Russian sentiments ran hot. So in the 1920s, just over a decade after the cathedral went up, it was torn down. During the Nazi occupation, this square took the name "Adolf-Hitler-Platz." Under the communists, it was Zwycięstwa, meaning "Victory" (of the Soviets over Hitler's fascism). When the regime imposed martial law in 1981, the people of Warsaw silently protested by filling the square with a giant cross made of flowers. The huge **plaque** in the ground near the road (usually marked by flowers) commemorates two monumental communist-era Catholic events on this square: John Paul II's first visit as pope to his homeland on June 2, 1979; and the May 31, 1981 funeral of Cardinal Stefan Wyszyński, whom we met across the street. The cross nearby also honors the 1979 papal visit, with one of his most famous and inspiring quotes to his countrymen: "Let thy spirit descend, let thy spirit descend, and renew the face of the earth—of *this* earth" (meaning Poland, in a just-barely-subtle-enough dig against the communist regime that was tolerating his visit). More recently, on April 17, 2010, more than 100,000 Poles convened on this square for a more solemn occasion: a memorial service for President Lech Kaczyński, who had died in a tragic plane crash in Russia.

Stand in the center, near the giant plaque, with the Royal Way at your back, for this quick spin-tour orientation: Ahead are the Tomb of the Unknown Soldier and Saxon Garden (explained later); 90 degrees to the right is the old National Theater, eclipsed by a modern business center/parking garage; another 90 degrees to the right is a statue of Piłsudski (which you passed to get here—described later); and 90 more degrees to the right is the Sofitel—formerly the Victoria Hotel, the ultimate plush, top-of-the-top hotel where all communist-era VIPs stayed. To the right of the hotel, on the horizon, you can see Warsaw's newly emerging skyline. The imposing Palace of Culture and Science, which once stood alone over the city, is now joined by a cluster of brand-new skyscrapers, giving Warsaw a Berlin-esque vibe befitting its important role as a business center of Eastern Europe.

Walk to the fragment of colonnade by the park that marks the **Tomb of the Unknown Soldier** (Grób Nieznanego Żołnierza). The colonnade was once part of a much larger palace built by the Saxon prince electors (Dresden's Augustus the Strong and his son), who became kings of Poland in the 18th century. After the palace was destroyed in World War II, this fragment was kept to memorialize Polish soldiers. The names of key battles over 1,000 years are etched into the columns, the urns contain dirt from major Polish battlefields, and the two soldiers are pretty stiff. Every hour on the hour, they do a crisp Changing of the Guard—which, poignantly, honors those who have perished in this country, so shaped by wars against foreign invaders.

Just behind the Tomb is the stately **Saxon Garden** (Ogród Saski), inhabited by genteel statues, gorgeous flowers, and a spurting fountain. This park was also built by the Saxon kings of Poland. Like most foreign kings, Augustus the Strong and his son cared little for their Polish territory, building gardens like these for themselves instead of investing in more pressing needs. Poles say that foreign kings such as Augustus did nothing but "eat, drink, and loosen their belts" (it rhymes in Polish). According to Poles, these selfish absentee kings were the culprits in Poland's eventual decline. But they do appreciate having such a fine venue for a Sunday stroll.

Walk back out toward the Royal Way, stopping at the statue you passed earlier. In 1995, the square was again renamed—this time for **Józef Piłsudski** (1867-1935), the guy with the big walrus moustache. With the help of a French captain named Charles de Gaulle (whom we met earlier), Piłsudski forced the Russian Bolsheviks out of Poland in 1920 in the so-called Miracle on the Vistula. Piłsudski is credited with creating a once-again-independent Poland after more than a century of foreign oppression, and he essentially ran Poland as a virtual dictator after World War I. Of course, under the communists, Piłsudski was swept under the rug. But since 1989, he has enjoyed a renaissance as many Poles' favorite prototype anticommunist hero. His name adorns streets, squares, and bushy-mustachioed monuments all over the country.

• *Return to Hotel Bristol, turn left, and continue your Royal Way walk.*

Radziwiłł Palace

Next door to the hotel, you'll see the huge **Radziwiłł Palace.** The

Warsaw Pact was signed here in 1955, officially uniting the Soviet satellite states in a military alliance against NATO. This building has also, from time to time, served as the Polish "White House."

• *Beyond Radziwiłł Palace, on the right, you'll reach a park with a...*

Statue of Adam Mickiewicz

Poland's national poet, Adam Mickiewicz spearheaded Poland's cultural survival during more than a century when the country disappeared from maps—absorbed by Austria, Prussia, and Russia. This was an age when underdog nations (and peoples without nations) all over Europe had their own national revival movements. The statue was erected in 1898 with permission from the Russian czar, as long as the people paid for it themselves. It's still an important part of community life: Polish high school students have a big formal ball (like a prom) 100 days before graduation. After the ball, if students come here and hop around the statue on one leg, it's supposed to bring them good luck on their finals. Mickiewicz, for his part, looks like he's suffering from a heart attack—perhaps in response to the impressively ugly National Theater and Opera a block in front of him.

• *Continue to the end of the Royal Way, marked by the big pink palace. Just before the castle, on your right, is...*

St. Anne's Church
This church is Rococo, with playful capitals inside and out and a fine pulpit shaped like the prow of a ship—complete with a big anchor. The richly ornamented apse, behind the altar, survived World War II. This church offers organ concerts nearly daily in summer (see "Entertainment in Warsaw," later).

For a scenic finale to your Royal Way stroll, climb the 150 steps of the **view tower** by the church (5 zł, generally open daily 10:00-18:00, later in summer, closed in bad winter weather). You'll be rewarded with excellent views—particularly of Castle Square and the Old Town. From up top, visually retrace your steps along the Royal Way, and notice the emerging skyline surrounding the Palace of Culture and Science. The tower also affords a good look at the Praga district across the river, where the Red Army waited for the Nazis to level Warsaw during the uprising. Help was so close at hand...but stayed right where it was.

• *Just across from the view tower entrance, look for another Chopin bench. From St. Anne's Church, it's just another block to Castle Square, the TI, and the start of the Old Town.*

Sights in Warsaw

THE OLD TOWN
In 1945, not a building remained standing in Warsaw's "Old" Town (Stare Miasto). Everything you see is rebuilt, mostly finished by 1956. Some think the Old Town seems artificial and phony, in a Disney World kind of way. For others, the painstaking postwar reconstruction feels just right, with Old World squares and lanes charming enough to give Kraków a run for its money. Before 1989, stifled by communist repression and choking on smog, the Old Town was an empty husk of its historic self. But now, the outdoor restaurants and market stalls have returned, and tourists (and a few Varsovians) are out strolling.

These sights are listed in order from south to north, and linked with walking directions, beginning at Castle Square and ending at the New Town.

▲Castle Square (Plac Zamkowy)

This lively square is dominated by the big, pink Royal Castle that is the historic heart of Warsaw's political power.

After the second great Polish dynasty—the Jagiellonians—died out in 1572, it was replaced by the Republic of Nobles (about 10 percent of the population), which elected various foreign kings to their throne. The guy on the 72-foot-tall **pillar** is Sigismund III, the first Polish king from the Swedish Vasa family (Waza in Polish). In 1596, he relocated the capital from Kraków to Warsaw. This move made sense, since Warsaw was closer to the center of 16th-century Poland (which had expanded to the east), and because the city had gained political importance over the past 30 years as the meeting point of the Sejm, or parliament of nobles.

Along the right side of the castle, notice the two previous versions of this pillar lying on a lawn. The first one, from 1644, was falling apart and had to be replaced in 1887 by a new one made of granite. In 1944, a Nazi tank broke this second pillar—a symbolic piece of Polish heritage—into the four pieces (still pockmarked with bullet holes) that you see here today. As Poland rebuilt, its citizens put Sigismund III back on his pillar. Past the pillars are views of Warsaw's red-and-white National Stadium across the river—built for the Euro Cup soccer tournament in 2012.

Across the square from the castle, you'll see the partially reconstructed **defensive wall.** This rampart once enclosed the entire Old Town. Like all of Poland, Warsaw has seen invasion from all sides.

Explore the café-lined lanes that branch off Castle Square. Street signs indicate the year that each lane was originally built.

The first street is **ulica Piwna** ("Beer Street"), where you'll find **St. Martin's Church** (Kościół Św. Martina, on the left). Run by Franciscan nuns, this church has a simple, modern interior. Walk up the aisle and find the second pillar on the right. Notice the partly destroyed crucifix—it's the only church artifact that survived World War II. Across the street and closer to Castle Square, admire the carefully carved doorway of the house called *pod Gołębiami* ("Under Doves")—dedicated to the memory of an old woman who fed birds amidst the Old Town rubble after World War II.

Back on Castle Square, find the white **plaque** on the wall (at plac Zamkowy 15). It explains that 50 Poles were executed by Nazis on this spot on September 2, 1944. You'll see plaques like this all over the Old Town, each one commemorating victims or opponents of the Nazis. The brick planter under the plaque is often filled with fresh flowers to honor the victims.

• *Turn your attention to the...*

▲▲Royal Castle (Zamek Królewski)

A castle has stood here since the Mazovian dukes built a wooden version in the 14th century. It has grown through the ages, being

rebuilt and remodeled by many different kings. When Warsaw became the capital in 1596, this massive building served a dual purpose: It was both the king's residence and the meeting place of the parliament (Sejm). It reached its peak under Stanisław August Poniatowski— the final Polish king—who imported artists and architects to spiff up the interior, leaving his mark all over the place. Luftwaffe bombs destroyed it in World War II (only one wall remained standing). Rebuilding stalled because Stalin considered it a palace for the high-class elites. It was finally rebuilt in the more moderate 1970s, funded by local donations.

Warsaw's Royal Castle has a gorgeous interior—the most opulent I've seen in Poland. Many of the furnishings are original (hidden away when it became clear the city would be demolished in World War II). A visit to the castle is like perusing a great Polish history textbook. In fact, you'll likely see grade-school classes sitting cross-legged on the floors. Watching the teachers quizzing eager young history buffs, try to imagine what it's like to be a young Pole growing up in a country with such a tumultuous history.

Cost and Hours: 23 zł, free on Sun; open May-Sept Mon-Sat 10:00-18:00, Thu until 20:00, Sun 11:00-18:00; Oct-April Tue-Sat 10:00-16:00, Sun 11:00-16:00, closed Mon; last entry one hour before closing; plac Zamkowy 4, tel. 22-355-5170, www.zamek-krolewski.pl. A public WC is on the courtyard just around the corner of the castle.

Tours: The castle has a well-produced audioguide (17 zł, worth the extra cost) and good English information posted throughout. For the basics, use my commentary to follow the one-way route through the castle.

Visiting the Castle: Because the castle visitor route often changes, it's possible you won't see these rooms in this order; if that happens, match the labels in each room to the corresponding text below.

Entering the courtyard, go to the right to buy tickets, then cross to the opposite side to tour the interior. (If you want an audioguide, go downstairs to rent it first.) Head up the stairs and follow *Castle Route* signs.

Start in the Oval Gallery, then head into the **Council Chamber,** where a "Permanent Council" consisting of the king, 18 senators, and 18 representatives met to chart Poland's course. Next is the **Great Assembly Hall,** heavy with marble and chandeliers. The statues of Apollo and Minerva flanking the main door are modeled after King Stanisław August Poniatowski and Catherine the Great of Russia, respectively. (The king enjoyed a youthful romantic dalliance with Catherine on a trip to Russia, and never quite seemed to get over her...much to his wife's consternation, I'm sure.)

The **Knights' Hall** features the Polish Hall of Fame, with paintings of great events and busts and portraits of VIPs—Very Important Poles. The statue of Chronos—god of time, with the globe on his shoulders—is actually a functioning clock, though now it's stopped at 11:15 to commemorate the exact time in 1944 when the Nazis bombed this palace to bits. Just off this hall is the **Marble Room,** with more portraits of Polish greats ringing the top of the room. Above the fireplace is a portrait of Stanisław August Poniatowski.

Continuing through the Knights' Hall, you'll wind up in the remarkable **Throne Room.** Notice the crowned white eagles, the

symbol of Poland, decorating the banner behind the throne. The Soviets didn't allow anything royal or aristocratic, so postwar restorations came with crownless eagles. Only after 1989 were these eagles crowned again. Peek into the **European Monarchs' Portrait Rooms,** where you'll meet the likes of Russia's Catherine the Great, England's George III, and France's Louis XVI—in whose esteemed royal league Stanisław August Poniatowski liked to consider himself.

After four more grand rooms (including the King's Bedroom, with a gorgeous silk canopy over the bed), you'll enter the **Canaletto Room,** filled with canvases of late-18th-century Warsaw painted in exquisite detail by this talented artist. (This Canaletto, also known for his panoramas of Dresden, was the nephew of another more famous artist with the same nickname, known for painting Venice's canals.) Paintings like these helped post-WWII restorers resurrect the city from its rubble. To the left, on the lower wall, the biggest canvas features the view of Warsaw from the Praga district across the river; pick out the few landmarks that are still standing (or, more precisely, have been resurrected). The castle you're standing in dominates the center of the painting, overlooking the river. Notice the artist's self-portrait in the lower left. Opposite, on the right side of the room, is Canaletto's depiction of the election of Stanisław August Ponia-towski as king, in a field outside Warsaw (notice the empty throne in the middle of the group). Among the assembled crowd, each flag represents a different Polish province.

From here, head left of the big "view of Warsaw" painting into the **side chapel,** reserved for the king. In the box to the left of the altar is the heart of Tadeusz Kościuszko, a hero of both the Ameri-can Revolution and the Polish struggle against the Partitions (for more about the Partitions, see page 8).

As you cross over to the other part of the castle, you'll pass through the **Four Seasons Gallery** (with some fine but faded Gobelin tapestries) before entering a few rooms occupied by the houses of parliament—a reminder that this "castle" wasn't just the king's house, but also the meeting place of the legislature. In the **New Deputies' Chambers,** notice the maps showing Poland's constantly in-flux borders—a handy visual aid for the many school groups that visit here.

After several rooms, you'll reach the grand **Senators' Cham-ber,** with the king's throne, surrounded by different coats of arms. Each one represents a region that was part of Poland during its Golden Age, back when it was united with Lithuania and its ter-ritory stretched from the Baltic to the Black Sea (see the map on the wall). In this room, Poland adopt-ed its 1791 constitution (notice the replica in the display case to the left of the throne). It was the first in Europe, written soon after America's and just months before France's. And, like the Constitution of the United States, it was very progressive, based on the ideals of the Enlightenment. But when the final Partitions followed in 1793 and 1795, Poland was divided between neighboring powers and ceased to exist as a coun-try until 1918—so the constitution was never fully put into action.

Next, the **Crown Prince's Room** features paintings by Jan Matejko that capture the excitement surrounding the adoption of this ill-fated constitution (for more on Matejko, see page 190). The next room has another Matejko painting: King Stefan Batory ne-gotiating with Ivan the Terrible's envoys to break their siege of a Russian town. Notice the hussars—fearsome Polish soldiers wear-ing winged armor. Finally, you'll wind through more rooms with yet more paintings of great historical events and portraits of famous Poles.

Other Castle Sights: Sharing an entrance lobby with the main castle interiors, the **Gallery of Paintings, Sculpture, and Decorative Arts** isn't worth the 21-zł extra admission fee for most visitors; save your time and money for the National Museum instead. But art lovers may be interested to see the 36 paintings of the gallery's Landkronoski Collection. These originally belonged to Stanisław August Poniatowski, who sold them to an aristocratic family that eventually presented them to Poland as a gift. The prize of the gallery are two canvases by Rembrandt (both from 1641). *Girl in a Picture Frame* is exactly that—except that she's "breaking the frame" by resting her hands on a faux frame that Rembrandt has painted inside the real one...shattering the fourth wall in a way that was unusual for the time. The other, *A Scholar at His Writing Table,* shows the hirsute academic glancing up from his notes. Circle around behind the canvases to see X-rays of the paintings, which have helped experts better understand the master's techniques. The rest of the gallery consists of roomfuls of portraits and a fine cabinet of silver and crystal.

Consider a detour to the **Kubicki Arcades** (Arkady Kubiciego), the impressively excavated arcades deep beneath the castle.

From the entrance lobby, head downstairs to the area with the cloakroom, bathrooms, and bookshop, then find the long escalator that takes you down to the arcades. It's free to wander the long, cavernous, and newly clean and gleaming space, made elegant by grand drapes.

The castle has a vast collection, which it organizes into various exhibitions—some permanent and some temporary. The extensive **oriental carpet collection** in the "Tin-Roofed Palace" (Pałac pod Blachą) is sparsely described and skippable for most; the same building also features seven unimpressive apartments of Prince Józef Poniatowski, the king's brother (15 zł for both, free on Sun, same hours as castle, around the right side of the castle as you face it—past the two fallen columns, buy ticket at main ticket desk).

• *When you're ready to resume exploring the Old Town, leave the square at the far end, on* **St. John's Street** *(Świętojańska). On the plaque under the street name sign, you can guess what the dates mean, even if you don't know Polish: This building was constructed from 1433 to 1478, destroyed in 1944, and rebuilt from 1950 to 1953.*

Partway down the street on the right, you'll come to the big brick...

Cathedral of St. John the Baptist
(Katedra Św. Jana Chrzciciela)

This cathedral-basilica is the oldest (1370) and most important church in Warsaw. Superficially unimpressive, the church's own archbishop admitted that it was "modest and poor"—but "the historical events that took place here make it magnificent" (much like Warsaw itself). Poland's constitution was consecrated here on May 3, 1791. Much later, this church became the final battleground of the 1944 Warsaw Uprising—when a Nazi "tracked mine" (a huge bomb on tank tracks—this one appropriately named *Goliath*) drove into the church and exploded, massacring the rebels. You can still see part of that tank's tread hanging on the outside wall of the church (through the passage on the right side, between the buttresses near the end of the church).

Cost and Hours: Free, crypt-5 zł, good guidebook-5 zł, open to tourists daily 10:00-13:00 & 15:00-17:30, closed during services and organ concerts. The cathedral hosts organ concerts in summer (see "Entertainment in Warsaw," later).

Visiting the Cathedral: Head inside. Typical of brick churches, it has a "hall church" design, with three naves of equal height. Look for the crucifix ornamented with real human hair (chapel left of high altar). The high altar holds a copy of the Black Madonna—proclaimed "everlasting queen of Poland" after a victory over the Swedes in the 17th century. The original Black Madonna is in Częstochowa (125 miles south of Warsaw)—a mecca for Slavic Catholics, who visit in droves in hopes of a miracle. In the back-left corner, find the chapel with the tomb of Cardinal Stefan Wyszyński—the great Polish leader who, as Warsaw's archbishop, morally steered the country through much of the Cold War. (Notice the request to pray for his beatification, as Poles would love to see him become a saint.) The crypt holds graves of several important Poles, including Stanisław August Poniatowski (the last Polish king) and Nobel Prize-winning author Henryk Sienkiewicz.

• *Continue up the street and enter Warsaw's grand...*

▲▲Old Town Market Square (Rynek Starego Miasta)

For two centuries, this was a gritty market square. Sixty-five years ago, it was a pile of bombed-out rubble. And today, like a phoenix from the ashes, it's risen to remind residents and tourists alike of the prewar glory of the Polish capital.

Head to the **mermaid fountain** in the middle of the square.

The mermaid is an important symbol in Warsaw—you'll see her everywhere. Legend has it that a mermaid *(syrenka)* lived in the Vistula River and protected the townspeople. While this siren supposedly serenaded the town, she's most appreciated for her strength (hence the sword). This square seems to declare that life goes on in Warsaw, as it always has. Children frolic here, oblivious to the turmoil their forebears withstood. When the fountain gurgles, the kids giggle.

Each of the square's four sides is named for a prominent 18th-century Varsovian: Kołłątaj, Dekert, Barss, and Zakrzewski. These men served as "Presidents" of Warsaw (mayors, more or less), and Kołłątaj was also a framer of Poland's 1791 constitution. Take some time to explore the square. Enjoy the colorful architecture. Notice that many of the buildings were intentionally built to lean out into the square—to simulate the higgledy-piggledy wear and tear of the original buildings.

History Museums near the Square

If you'd like to learn more about Warsaw's history, two good museums are located nearby.

• *First, on the Dekert (north) side of the square is the...*

Warsaw Museum (Muzeum Warszawy): When this museum's lengthy and long-delayed restoration is complete (possibly as early as mid-2017), it promises to provide an insightful look at the turbulent history of this city—particularly the Old Town. The exhibits are an afterthought to the museum's best feature: a poignant 20-minute film (in English) tracing the tragic WWII experience of this city—from a thriving interwar metropolis, to a bombed-out wasteland, to the focus of a massive rebuilding effort (may be covered by a separate ticket). For the latest, see www.muzeumwarszawy.pl.

• *The other museum—focusing on the Old Town's history and reconstruction—is behind the buildings on the river side of the square (behind the mermaid's back). Walk one block, and turn left to find the...*

Old Town Heritage Interpretation Center: This fine little visitors center displays lots of before-and-after photos and videos of the Old Town—there are even glass floors looking down onto original fragments of the neighborhood (5 zł, Tue-Sun 10:00-19:00, closed Mon, ulica Brzozowa 11, www.muzeumwarszawy.pl).

• *When you're ready to move on, exit the square on Nowomiejska (at the mermaid's 2 o'clock, by the second-story niche sculpture of St. Anne). After a block, you'll reach the...*

Barbican (Barbakan)

This defensive gate of the Old Town, similar to Kraków's, protected the medieval city from invaders.

• *Once you've crossed through the barbican, you're officially in Warsaw's...*

New Town (Nowe Miasto)

This 15th-century neighborhood is "new" in name only: It was the first part of Warsaw to spring up outside the city walls (and is therefore slightly newer than the Old Town).

The New Town is a fun place to wander: only a little less charming than the Old Town, but with a more real-life feel—people live and work here. Its centerpiece is the **New Town Square** (Rynek Nowego Miasta), watched over by the distinctive green dome of St. Kazimierz Church.

Scientists might want to pay homage at the museum (and birthplace) of Warsaw native **Marie Skłodowska-Curie,** a.k.a. Madame Curie (1867-1934); it's along the street between the New Town Square and the barbican. This Nobel Prize winner was the world's first radiologist—discovering both radium and polonium (named for her native land) with her husband, Pierre Curie. Since she lived at a time when Warsaw was controlled by oppressive Russia, she conducted her studies in France. The museum—with photos, furniture, artifacts, and a paucity of English information—is a bit of a snoozer, best left to true fans (overpriced at 11 zł, Tue-Sun 9:00-16:30, closed Mon, ulica Freta 16, tel. 22-831-8092, www. muzeum-msc.pl).

From the New Town to Castle Square

You can backtrack the way you came, or, to get a look at the Old Town's back streets, consider this route from the big, round barbican gate (where the New Town meets the Old): Go back through the barbican and over the little bridge, turn right, and walk along the houses that line the inside of the wall. You'll pass a leafy garden courtyard on the left—a reminder that people actually live in the tourist zone within the Old Town walls. Just beyond the garden on the right, look for the carpet-beating rack, used to clean rugs (these are common fixtures in people's backyards). Go left into the square called Szeroki Dunaj ("Wide Danube") and look for another mermaid (over the Thai restaurant). Continue through the square and turn right at Wąski Dunaj ("Narrow Danube"). After about 100 yards, you'll pass the city wall. Just to the right (outside the wall), you'll see the monument to the **Little Upriser** of 1944, a child wearing a grown-up's helmet and too-big boots, and carrying a machine gun. Children—especially Scouts (Harcerze)—played a key role in the resistance against the Nazis. Their job was mainly carrying messages and propaganda.

Now continue around the wall (the upper, inner part is more pleasant). Admire more public art as you head back to Castle Square.

NEAR PALM TREE CIRCLE

These sights are in the city center, near Palm Tree Circle—where Jerusalem Avenue crosses Nowy Świat.

East of the Royal Way (Toward the River)

▲▲National Museum (Muzeum Narodowe)

A celebration of underrated Polish artists, this museum offers a surprisingly engaging and—if you follow my tour—concise overview of this country's impressive painters (many of whom are unknown outside their home country). A modern, state-of-the-art exhibition space allows these unsung canvases to really belt it out. Polish and other European artists are displayed side by side, as if to assert Poland's worthiness on the world artistic stage. After seeing a few of the masterpieces here, you won't disagree.

Cost and Hours: 15 zł, includes audioguide, more for temporary exhibits, permanent collection free on Tue; open Tue-Sun 10:00-18:00, Thu until 21:00, closed Mon, last entry 45 minutes before closing; one block east of Nowy Świat at aleja Jerozolimskie 3, tel. 22-629-3093, www.mnw.art.pl.

◆ Self-Guided Tour: The collection fills several separate galleries. The museum's strongest point—and the bulk of this tour—is its 19th-century Polish art. But before diving in, consider some of the other collections.

Overview: To get your bearings, pick up a floor plan as you enter. On the ground floor are Ancient Art (from Greek pieces to artifacts left by early Polish tribes); Gallery Faras (highlighting the museum's fine collection of archaeological findings from that ancient Egyptian city); and a good collection of Medieval Art, which gathers altarpieces from churches around Poland—organized both chronologically and geographically—and displays some of the most graphic crucifixes and *pietàs* I've seen.

Upstairs is the excellent Gallery of 19th-Century Art (described next), which flows into the Old Polish and European Portrait Gallery (as interesting as somebody else's yearbook). Nearby, through the gift shop, is the worthwhile 20th- and 21st-Century Art collection, with an impressive array of Modern and Postmodern Polish artists, including photographers and filmmakers. The underwhelming Old European Painting collection—pre-19th-century canvases arranged by theme and juxtaposed to highlight

Jan Matejko (1838-1893)

Jan Matejko (yawn mah-TAY-koh) is Poland's most important painter, period. In the mid- to late-19th century, the nation of Poland had been dissolved by foreign powers, and Polish artists struggled to make sense of their people's place in the world. Rabble-rousing Romanticism seemed to have failed (inspiring many brutally suppressed uprisings), so Polish artists and writers turned their attention to educating the people about their history, with the goal of keeping their traditions alive.

Matejko was at the forefront of this so-called positivist movement. Matejko saw what the tides of history had done to Poland and was determined to make sure his countrymen learned from it. He painted two types of works: huge, grand-scale epics depicting monumental events in Polish history; and small, intimate portraits of prominent Poles. Polish schoolchildren study history from books with paintings of virtually every single Polish king—all painted by the incredibly prolific Matejko.

Matejko is admired not for his technical mastery (he's an unexceptional painter) or for the literal truth of his works—he was notorious for fudging historical details to give his canvases a bit more propagandistic punch. But he is revered for the emotion behind—and inspired by—his works. His paintings are utilitarian, straightforward, and dramatic enough to stir the patriot in any Pole. The intense focus on history by Matejko and other positivists is one big reason why today's Poles are still so in touch with their heritage.

You'll see Matejko's works in Warsaw's National Museum and Royal Castle, as well as in Kraków's Gallery of 19th-Century Polish Art (above the Cloth Hall). You can also visit his former residence in Kraków.

the differences between southern and northern European art—is split up among all three floors.

To cut to the chase, focus on the **Gallery of 19th-Century Art.** We'll start with the granddaddy of Polish art, Jan Matejko.

• *From the entrance lobby, head up the left staircase, then turn left across the mezzanine and enter the collection. Matejko is hiding at the far end of this wing: Entering the collection, angle right, then head all the way to the room at the far end, which is dominated by a gigantic battlefield canvas. (If you get lost, ask the attendants, "mah-TAY-koh?")*

Jan Matejko: While not the most talented of artists—he's a fairly conventional painter, lacking a distinctive, recognizable style—Matejko more than made up for it with vision and productivity. His works—often on oversized canvases—are steeped in proud Polish history. Matejko's biggest work here—in fact, the biggest canvas in the whole building—is the enormous **Battle**

of Grunwald. This epic painting commemorates one of Poland's high-water marks: the dramatic victory of a Polish-Lithuanian army over the Teutonic Knights, who had been terrorizing northern Poland for decades (for more on the Teutonic Knights, see page 290). On July 15, 1410, some 40,000 Poles and Lithuanians (led by the sword-waving Lithuanian in red, Grand Duke Vytautas) faced off against 27,000 Teutonic Knights (under their Grand Master, in white) in one of the medieval world's bloodiest battles. Matejko plops us right in the thick of the battle's climax, painting life-size figures and framing off a 32-foot-long slice of the actual two-mile battle line.

In the center of the painting, the Teutonic Grand Master is about to become a shish kebab. Duke Vytautas, in red, leads the final charge. And waaaay up on a hill (in the upper-right corner, on horseback, wearing a silver knight's suit) is Władysław Jagiełło, the first king of the Jagiellonian dynasty...ensuring his bloodline will survive another 150 years.

Matejko spent three years covering this 450-square-foot canvas in paint. The canvas was specially made in a single seamless piece. This was such a popular work that almost as many fans turned out for its unveiling as there are figures in the painting. On the TV nearby, you can see how the vast painting was recently restored.

From Poland's high point in the *Battle of Grunwald,* look on the right wall for another, much smaller Matejko canvas, **Stańczyk,** to see how Poland's fortunes shifted drastically a century later. This more intimate portrait depicts a popular Polish figure: the court jester Stańczyk, who's smarter than the king, but not allowed to say so. This complex character, representing the national conscience, is a favorite symbol of Matejko's. Stańczyk slumps in gloom. He's just read the news (on the table beside him) that the city of Smolensk has fallen to the Russians after a three-year siege (1512-1514). The jester had tried to warn the king to send more troops, but the king was too busy partying (behind the curtain). The painter Matejko—who may have used his own features for Stańczyk's face—also blamed the nobles of his own day for fiddling while Poland was partitioned.

More Matejkos fill this room. Just to the right of *Stańczyk* is a self-portrait of the gray-bearded artist (compare their features), then a painting of the hoisting of the Sigismund Bell to the cathedral tower in Kraków (it's still there). Farther right, you'll see Matejko's portraits of his children and his wife.

On the final wall is a smaller but very dramatic scene, ***The Sermon of Piotr Skarga.*** In the upper-right corner, this charismatic, early-17th-century Jesuit priest waves his arms to punctuate his message: Poland's political system is broken. Skarga is addressing fat-cat nobles and the portly King Sigismund II Vasa (seated and wearing a ruffled collar), who were acting in their own self-interests instead of prioritizing what was best for Poland. Notice that Skarga's audience isn't hearing his ravings—they seem bored, bugged, or both. The king is even taking a nap. They should have listened: Poland's eventual decline is often considered the fault of its unworkable political system. After the Partitions, the ahead-of-his-time Skarga was rehabilitated as a visionary who should have been heeded. Notice that, like Stańczyk, Skarga is a self-portrait of Matejko.

• *Leaving Matejko, we'll pass through several more rooms of lesser-known Polish painters to the opposite wing, where we'll meet several of Matejko's students—each of whom developed his own style and left his mark on the Polish art world. But on the way, I'll point out a few canvases that may be worth pausing at.*

Other Polish Painters: First, head back down the long corridor the way you came (passing some Matejko copycats), cutting through a corner of the Portrait Gallery. When you reach the door you came in, bear right to stay inside the gallery. At the end of that first, large room, you'll find some battle scenes by **Józef Brandt**—the only painter who rivaled Matejko in capturing epic warfare on canvas. Many of Brandt's scenes focus on confronting an enemy from the east, which was Poland's lot for much of its history. His biggest work here, *Rescue of Tatar Captives,* is typical of his scenes.

Continue straight into the next room, with some fine landscape scenes. This room (the partition in the middle) also has works by the talented **Józef Chełmoński:** *Indian Summer* and (around back) *Storks*—a young boy and his grandfather look to the sky, as a formation of storks flies overhead.

Turn right and go through one more long room (watching, on the left wall, for **Aleksander Gierymski**'s small, evocative, personality-filled *Jewish Woman Selling Oranges*).

• *You'll emerge into a big room that kicks off the collection of...*

Młoda Polska: Matejko's pupils took what he taught them and incorporated the Art Nouveau styles that were emerging around Europe to create a new movement called "Young Poland" (see page 47). This room features works by two of the movement's big names. On the left wall are paintings by **Jacek Malczewski,** some of them depicting the goateed, close-cropped artist in a semisurrealistic, Polish countryside context. Malczewski painted more or less realistically, but enjoyed incorporating one or two subtle, symbolic elements evocative of Polish folkloric tradition—like magical realism on canvas. *The Death of Ellenai* (1907) shows the pivotal scene in Juliusz Słowacki's epic 1838 poem, *Anhelli,* in which a young nobleman exiled from Poland during the Partitions is forced to make his way through the wastelands of Siberia. When his young and idealistic travel companion, Ellenai, perishes, Anhelli kisses her feet and abandons all hope.

Most of the works on the opposite wall are by **Józef Mehoffer,** who paints with brighter colors in a more stylized form, with more abstraction. This creates dreamlike scenes that are, consequently, somehow less poignant than Malczewski's. Mehoffer's hypnotic *Strange Garden* is a bucolic vision of blue-clad Mary Poppinses, nude cherubs, lots of flowers...and a gigantic, hovering, golden dragonfly that places the otherwise plausible scene in the realm of pure fantasy. In the middle of the room, the small version of Auguste Rodin's *The Kiss* reminds us how this emotion-conveying style, called Symbolism, was also finding expression elsewhere in Europe.

The next room, at the end of the hall, features some lesser-known painters from the age. Among these, **Olga Boznańska**'s works are worth lingering over: gauzy, almost Impressionistic portraits that skillfully capture the humanity of each subject.

Head back into the Malczewski/Mehoffer room and find the small, darkened adjoining rooms. The first one features additional Malczewski paintings; the second is a treasure trove of works by the founder and biggest talent of Młoda Polska, **Stanisław Wyspiański.** The specific items in this room are subject to change—as Kraków, which owns the best collection of hometown boy Wyspiański, is shuffling its works in and out of special exhibitions—but you'll likely see both paintings and pastel works by this Art Nouveau juggernaut. Wyspiański also designed stage sets and redecorated some important churches; some of the large pastel-on-paper works you may see here were used as studies for those projects. And you'll likely see some self-portraits and portraits of his wife and children. Pondering the works here—and throughout the museum—think about how such a talented artist from a small country can be left out of textbooks across the ocean.

Chopin Museum (Muzeum Fryderyka Chopina)

The reconstructed Ostrogski Castle houses this slick museum honoring Poland's most famous composer. You'll see manuscripts, letters, and original handwritten compositions by the composer. Unfortunately, the museum's high tech gadgetry does more to distract from this rich collection of historic artifacts than to bring it to life. While Chopin devotees may find it riveting, those with only a passing familiarity with the composer may leave feeling like they still don't know much about this Polish cultural giant.

Cost and Hours: 22 zł, free on Sun, open Tue-Sun 11:00-20:00, closed Mon, last entry 45 minutes before closing, 3 blocks east of Nowy Świat at ulica Okólnik 1, tel. 22-441-6251, www.chopin.museum. Because the museum is highly interactive, only 70 visitors are allowed per hour. But, except for rare occasions, just dropping in should be no problem.

Visiting the Museum: Buy your ticket at the adjacent building, then enter the mansion that houses the exhibit. You'll be given an electronic card; tap it against glowing red dots to access additional information. You'll proceed more or less chronologically through the composer's life, with various opportunities to hear his compositions. You'll see a replica of Chopin's drawing room in Paris, and his last piano, which he used for composing during the final two years of his life (1848-1849). Exhibits here trace themes of the composer's life, such as the women he knew (including his older sister Ludwika, his mother, and George Sand—the French author who took a male pseudonym in order to be published, and who was romantically linked with Chopin). The exhibit ends in the basement, where you can nurture your appreciation of Chopin by listening to his music.

Concerts: Under the palace is a new **concert hall,** which hosts performances by students (call museum to ask for concert schedule and to reserve a space—only 70 seats available; usually Oct-July Thu at 18:00, and typically free).

Eating: The recommended **Tamka 43**—with affordable lunch deals downstairs and top-end fine dining (with a menu inspired by dishes Chopin enjoyed) upstairs—is in the glassy building that faces the museum.

Other Chopin Sight: The composer's tourable **birth house** is in a park in Żelazowa Wola, 34 miles from Warsaw. While interesting to Chopin devotees, it's not worth the trek for most. On summer weekends, the Chopin Museum sometimes runs a handy bus to the house—ask at the museum (departs from Marszałkowska street, 30 minutes each way; 7 zł for the bus, 7 zł for the park, 23 zł for the park and birth house, 39 zł also includes museum in Warsaw; birth house open Tue-Sun 9:00-19:00, Oct-March until 17:00, closed Mon year-round, tel. 46-863-3300).

▲▲Copernicus Science Center (Centrum Nauki Kopernik)

This facility, a wonderland of completely hands-on scientific doo-dads that thrill kids and adults alike, is a futuristic romper room. Filling two floors of an industrial-mod, purpose-built space, this is Warsaw's best family activity. Exhibits are grouped more or less thematically and described in both Polish and English.

Cost and Hours: 27 zł, 18 zł for kids 19 and under, 72-zł family ticket for up to 4 people; open Tue-Fri 9:00-18:00, Sat-Sun 10:00-19:00, closed Mon, last entry one hour before closing; Wybrzeże Kościuszkowskie 20, tel. 22-596-4100, www.kopernik.org.pl.

Crowd-Beating Tips: This popular attraction can get crowded—especially on weekends and school holidays, when the line can be long. (A webcam on their website shows the current line; you can also book tickets in advance online, but the center's website is in Polish only.) On weekdays, it's generally no problem to walk right in.

Getting There: It's an easy downhill walk from Warsaw's Royal Way, but the hike back up is fairly steep. Near the modern bridge, you'll find a Metro stop and a bus stop (both called Centrum Nauki Kopernik). From here, bus #102 goes to Nowy Świat, then up the Royal Way (Uniwersytet and Zachęta stops) before heading west to the Warsaw Uprising Museum. Metro line 2 connects the science center to the National Stadium, the Royal Way (near the Copernicus statue), and the Warsaw Uprising Museum.

Visiting the Center: Your ticket is a plastic card that you can insert into certain interactive exhibits. On the ground floor, the

"Roots of Civilization" features working models of various tools and machines, demonstrating how humanity has mastered the mechanics of physics. You can play archaeologist in a sandbox, listen to *Ode to Joy* while tuning into different instruments, and see a small "fire tornado" (every bit as cool as it sounds). A playroom for toddlers, called **"Buzzz!,"** has a nature theme. Meanwhile, **"RE: Generation"** targets teens and adults with computer touchscreens that investigate the biological underpinnings of emotion—from what makes you laugh to what grosses you out—and examines how cultures around the world are both similar and different.

The **"Heavens of Copernicus" planetarium** requires a separate ticket (19 zł, 14 zł for kids 19 and under, in Polish with English headset, show starts at the top of each hour—ask for schedule at ticket desk).

The fun continues upstairs, where **"Humans and the Environment"** illuminates the human body (find out just how long your intestines are, identify and place the organs, and see how various joints work like hinges). In the exercise arena, you can compete against various virtual animals (can you jump as high as a kangaroo or hang like a chimp?). The **"Lightzone"** illustrates how light trav-

WARSAW

els in waves, lets you try out an old-fashioned (but still impressive) camera obscura, and use prisms and lenses to play a game of "light billiards." **"On the Move"** features fascinating hands-on physics demos, including an earthquake simulator, an air cannon, and a tube that lets you harness sound waves to make water vibrate. New exhibits are added (and old ones refreshed) all the time—be sure to pick up the brochure at the entry to understand your options.

Nearby: The **Discovery Park** surrounding the museum was created when the busy riverfront highway was rerouted into an underground tunnel, creating this delightful people zone. From here you have good views of the modern Holy Cross Bridge (Most Świętokrzyski, from 2000) and the National Stadium, proudly wrapped in the patriotic red and white of the Polish flag. These riverbanks are a popular hangout by day and after dark; in the summer, a stroll along here reveals a world of picnics, family outings, and impromptu parties.

Two short blocks inland from the science center is the architecturally innovative **Warsaw University Library** (Biblioteka Uniwersytecka w Warszawie, or BUW), with its distinctive oxidized-copper-colored facade decorated with open books from various cultures. The facade is fun to ogle, and the rooftop holds a huge and inviting garden.

West of the Royal Way (near Centralna Station)
Palace of Culture and Science
(Pałac Kultury i Nauki, or PKiN)

This massive skyscraper, dating from the early 1950s, is the tallest building between Frankfurt and Moscow (760 feet with the spire, though several new buildings are threatening to eclipse that peak). While you can ride the lift to its top for a commanding view, the highlight is simply viewing it up close from ground level.

Viewing the Skyscraper: This building was a "gift" from Stalin that the people of Warsaw couldn't refuse. Varsovians call it "Stalin's Penis"...using cruder terminology than that. (There are seven such "Stalin Gothic" erections in Moscow.) If it feels like an Art Deco Chicago skyscraper, that's because the architect was inspired by the years he spent studying and working in Chicago in the 1930s. Because it was to be "Soviet in substance, Polish in style," Soviet architects toured Poland to absorb local culture before starting the project. Notice the frilly decorative friezes that top each level—evocative of Poland's many Renaissance buildings (such as Kraków's Cloth Hall). The clock was added in 1999 as part of the millennium celebrations. Since the end of communism, the younger generation doesn't mind the structure so much—and some even admit to liking it for the way it enlivens the predictable glass-and-steel skyline springing up around it.

Everything about the Pałac is big. Approach it from the east side (facing the busy Marszałkowska street and the slick Galeria Centrum shopping mall). Stand in front of the granite tribune where communist VIPs surveyed massive May Day parades and pageantry on the once-imposing square, which today is a sloppy parking lot. From there, size up the skyscraper—its grand entry flanked by massive statues of Copernicus on the right (science) and the great poet Mickiewicz on the left (culture). It's designed to show off the strong, grand-scale Soviet aesthetic and architectural skill. The Pałac contains various theaters (the culture), museums of evolution and technology (the science), a congress hall, a multiplex (showing current movies), an observation deck, and lots of office space. With all this Culture and Science under one Roof, it's a shame that only the ground-floor lobby (which feels like stepping into 1950s Moscow and is free to enter) and the 30th-floor observatory deck are open to the public.

Observation Deck: You can zip up to the "XXX Floor" in 20 seconds on the retrofitted Soviet elevators—but the trip is overpriced and the view's a letdown (20 zł, daily 10:00-20:00, may be open later in summer, enter through main door on east side of Pałac—opposite from Centralna station, tel. 22-656-7600, www.pkin.pl).

Złote Tarasy Shopping Mall

Tucked behind Centralna station, "Golden Terraces" is a super-modern shopping mall with a funky, undulating glass-and-steel roof. Yes, you didn't come all the way to Poland to visit a shopping mall. But if you're at the station, crossing the street to peek in here offers a taste of Poland's race into the future.

Hours: Mon-Sat 9:00-22:00, Sun 9:00-21:00, lots of designer shops, food court on top level, www.zlotetarasy.pl.

Złota 44

This skyscraper, with its dramatic swooping lines rising high from the Złote Tarasy shopping mall, was designed by world-renowned architect Daniel Libeskind (who also redeveloped the 9/11 site in New York City). Born in Poland, at a very young age Libeskind emigrated with his family to the US, returning only recently to em-

WARSAW

bark on this project. Its shape evokes an eagle (a symbol for Poland) just beginning to take flight. Of all the shiny new towers popping up in Warsaw's skyline, this is the most architecturally interesting—and offers a striking counterpoint to the Stalinist Palace of Culture and Science nearby. (For more on the building, visit www. zlota44.com/en.)

JEWISH WARSAW

In the early 1600s, an estimated 80 percent of all Jews lived in Poland—then the largest country in Europe. But after centuries of dwelling in relative peace in tolerant and pragmatic Poland, Warsaw's Jews suffered terribly at the hands of the Nazis. Several sights in Warsaw commemorate those who were murdered, and those who fought back. Because the Nazis leveled the ghetto, there is literally nothing left except the street plan, some monuments, and the heroic spirit of its former residents. However, the top-notch Museum of the History of Polish Jews—which opened in 2014—has rejuvenated the area, making it even more of a magnet for those interested in this chapter of Polish history.

Getting There: To reach Ghetto Heroes Square and the museum from the Old Town, you can hop a **taxi** or **Uber** (10 zł) or take a **bus** (to the Nalewki-Muzeum stop; bus #180 is particularly useful; bus #111 reaches this stop from farther south—Piłsudski Square, the university, and the National Museum). You can also **walk** there in about 15 minutes: Go through the barbican gate two blocks into the New Town, turn left on Świętojerska, and walk straight 10 minutes—passing the green-glass Supreme Court building. En route, at the corner of Świętojerska and Nowiniarska, watch for the pattern of bricks in the sidewalk, marking *Ghetto Wall 1940-1943*.

▲Ghetto Heroes Square (Plac Bohaterow Getta)

The square is in the heart of what was the Jewish ghetto—now surrounded by bland Soviet-style apartment blocks. After the uprising, the entire ghetto was reduced to dust by the Nazis, leaving the communists to rebuild to their own specifications. The district is called Muranów ("Rebuilt") today.

The **monument** in the middle of the square commemorates those who fought and died "for the dignity and freedom of the Jewish Nation, for a free Poland, and for the liberation of humankind." The statue features heroic Jewish men who knew that an inglorious death at the hands of the Nazis awaited them. Flames in the background show Nazis burning the ghetto. The opposite side features a sad procession of Jews trudging to concentration camps, with subtle Nazi bayonets and helmets moving things along.

As you face the monument, look through the trees to the right to see a seated statue. **Jan Karski** (1914-2000) was a Catholic Pole and resistance fighter who traveled extensively through Poland during the Nazi occupation, collected evidence, and then reported on the Warsaw Ghetto and the Holocaust to the leaders of the Western Allies (including a personal meeting with FDR). In 1944, while the Holocaust was still going on, Karski published his eye-witness account, *The Story of a Secret State* (which you can see on this statue's armrest). After the war he became a US citizen, and in 2012 President Barack Obama awarded him a posthumous Presidential Medal of Freedom.

• *The huge, glassy building facing the monument from across the square is the...*

▲▲▲Museum of the History of Polish Jews (Muzeum Historii Żydów Polskich, a.k.a. POLIN)

This world-class attraction thoughtfully traces the epic, millennium-long story of Jews in Poland. This is not a "Holocaust mu-

seum;" it provides stirring documentation of the full and very rich Polish Jewish experience across the centuries. In-depth, engaging, vividly illustrated, and eloquently presented, the exhibits present a powerful context for the many Jewish cultural sites around Poland—offering insights both for people familiar with the story and for beginners. The museum is at once expansive and intimate, with ample descriptions, videos, and touchscreens; you could spend all day here, but two hours is the absolute minimum. It wins my vote for the best museum in Poland, and it's easily Europe's best Jewish museum—and a strong contender for the best European historical museum, period. The building also hosts cultural events and temporary exhibits.

Cost and Hours: Core exhibition-25 zł, Mon and Thu-Fri 10:00-18:00, Wed and Sat-Sun 10:00-20:00, closed Tue, essential audioguide-10 zł, last entry 2 hours before closing, Anielewicza 6, cafeteria, tel. 22-471-0300, www.jewishmuseum.org.pl.

Visiting the Museum: Before entering, view the building's striking **exterior** (designed by Finnish architect Rainer Mahlamä-ki). You'll enter (and go through a security checkpoint) at the large,

Warsaw's Jews and the Ghetto Uprising

From the Middle Ages until World War II, Poland was a relatively safe haven for Europe's Jews. While other kings were imprisoning and deporting Jews in the 14th century, the progressive king Kazimierz the Great welcomed Jews into Poland, even granting them special privileges (see page 45).

By the 1930s, there were more than 380,000 Jews in Warsaw—nearly a third of the population (and the largest concentration of Jews in any European city). The Nazis arrived in 1939. Within a year, they had pushed all of Warsaw's Jews into one neighborhood and surrounded it with a wall, creating a miserably overcrowded ghetto (crammed with an estimated 460,000 people, including many from nearby towns). There were nearly 600 such ghettos in cities and towns all over Poland.

By the summer of 1942, more than a quarter of the Jews in the ghetto had either died of disease, committed suicide, or been murdered. The Nazis started moving Warsaw's Jews (at the rate of 5,000 a day) into what they claimed were "resettlement camps." Most of these people—300,000 in all—were actually murdered at Treblinka or Auschwitz. Finally the waning population—now about 60,000—began to get word from concentration camp escapees about what was actually going on there. Spurred by this knowledge, Warsaw's surviving Jews staged a dramatic uprising.

On April 19, 1943, the Jews attacked Nazi strongholds and had some initial success. The overwhelming Nazi war machine—which had rolled over much of Europe—imagined they'd be able to put down the rebellion easily. Instead, they struggled for a month to finally crush the Ghetto Uprising. The ghetto's residents and structures were "liquidated." About 300 of Warsaw's Jews survived, thanks in part to a sort of "underground railroad" of courageous Varsovians.

Warsaw's Jewish sights are emotionally moving, but even more so if you know some of their stories. You may have heard of **Władysław Szpilman,** a Jewish concert pianist who survived the war with the help of Jews, Poles, and even a Nazi officer. Szpilman's life story was turned into the highly acclaimed, Oscar-winning film *The Pianist,* which powerfully depicts events in Warsaw during World War II.

Less familiar to non-Poles—but equally affecting—is the story of Henryk Goldszmit, better known by his pen name, **Janusz Korczak.** Korczak wrote imaginative children's books that are still enormously popular among Poles. He worked at an orphanage in the Warsaw ghetto. When his orphans were sent off to concentration camps, the Nazis offered the famous author a chance at freedom. Korczak turned them down, choosing to die at Treblinka with his children.

WARSAW

asymmetrical hole in the side of the building. Once you're inside, the symbolism becomes clear: This represents Moses parting the Red Sea. (While the main exhibit covers the thousand years of Jews in Poland, this sets the stage by going back even further—to the Jewish origin story.)

Buy your tickets for the core exhibition and rent the invaluable 60-stop audioguide, which helps provide a concise structure for your exploration of the sprawling exhibitions. Then head downstairs and follow the one-way route. In this high-tech, interactive space, exhibits in eight galleries mingle with actual artifacts to bring history to life.

You'll begin by passing through a simulated forest—evocative of legends about the Jews' arrival in Poland—to reach the **First Encounters** exhibit. Here you'll learn how Jewish merchants made their way to Poland in the 10th century (with maps of their trade routes and samples of what they sold). The story is told partly from the perspective of Ibrahim ibn Jakub, a Sephardic Jew who penned early travelogues about Europe. In 1264, Duke Bolesław the Pious—the first of many tolerant Polish rulers—gave Jews rights, including minting coins; you'll see an example dating from the 13th century and marked with a Hebrew character. In the next room (on the left wall) are illustrations of the leading Polish cities of the time and (on the right wall) Polish medieval monarchs, with in-depth explanations of each one's policies toward their Jewish subjects.

Next, the **Paradisus Iudaeorum** explains how, as Jews became more established in Polish society in the 15th and 16th centuries, they enjoyed better and better living conditions. (Meanwhile, anti-Semites bitterly complained that Poland was becoming a "Jewish Paradise"—the name of this exhibit.) The centerpiece here is a gigantic, interactive model of Kraków and its Jewish quarter, Kazimierz. In the library section, you can flip through virtual pages of books from the era.

Continuing into the next area, you'll enter a dark hallway that explains the Khmelnytsky Uprising—a mid-17th-century Cossack rebellion against the Polish lords and the Jews who served them. This brought a new wave of pogroms and 10,000 Jewish deaths.

After the uprising, Polish lords invited Jews to privately owned market towns—called *shtetls*—to help re-establish the economy. **The Jewish Town** offers a fascinating look at different walks of life in a typical Jewish community: the market, where Jews and Christians could mingle at the tavern; the home, where a family would live, work, eat, and sleep in a single room; the cemetery (touchscreens invite you to learn about the symbolism of Jewish tombstones); and the synagogue, with a gloriously colorful replica of a ceiling and bema (prayer platform) from a wooden synagogue from the village of Gwoździec—dripping with symbolism that's explained on nearby touchscreens. An exhibit also traces the mid-18th-century rise of Hasidism—a mystical branch of Judaism—in the eastern Polish lands (today's Ukraine).

With the Partitions of the late 18th century (when Polish territory was divided among neighboring powers), Polish Jews found themselves split among three different empires—symbolized by a room with giant portraits of the rulers of Prussia, Russia, and Austria, all facing the Polish throne. **Encounters with Modernity** examines how Jews in different parts of the Polish lands had very different experiences. You'll see a replica salon of a wealthy Jewish family who mingled with elites, and learn about the debate at that time of what the role of Jews in society should be (illustrated by a fine collection of items from Jewish ceremonies commemorating rites of passage). You'll also learn about the competing movements within Judaism that emerged during this era: Hasidism, led by charismatic Tzadiks who promised a closer spiritual connection to God, and the more reform-minded Haskalah, an intellectual approach inspired by the Enlightenment. A riveting, painterly film follows a day in the life of a young student at a *yeshiva* (school). A railway station represents the Industrial Revolution, when the world got smaller and brought a new world of opportunities...and of threats. You'll learn how some Jews worked hard to integrate with their dominant cultures (such as the painter Maurycy Gottlieb). This period also saw the emergence of modern anti-Semitism, including a brutal pogrom in Warsaw in 1881. As Jews sought to define a modern Jewish identity in the late 19th century, many emigrated—some to North or South America, and still others to the Holy Land (the beginnings of Zionism).

All of this sets the stage for World War I, when Jews were drafted into various armies—and often forced to fight one another. But at war's end, Poland was reconstituted as an independent nation. You'll step out onto **The Street,** which re-creates an interwar shopping street from a Jewish community. ("The Jewish Street" was also slang for the Jewish world in general.) It was between the World Wars—when a newly independent Poland extended full citizenship and voting rights to its Jewish citizens—that Jewish cultural life flourished as never before. One-third of Poland's population was Jewish—that's three million people. You'll see re-created Warsaw sites relating to newspapers, cinema, writers, and artists; you'll learn about Jewish tourism of the era (when middle-class Jews would travel around Poland and Europe to visit Jewish cultural sites); and you'll see exhibits about education and reform—including bilingual schooling (Yiddish and Polish), the beloved educator and author Janusz Korczak, and the debate over "ghetto benches" (segregated seating areas in schools). However, this was also a time of rising anti-Semitism, segregation, boycotts, and anti-Jewish quotas; during this period, some 140,000 Jews emigrated to the Holy Land.

After one more nostalgic stroll down "The Street," you come to September 1, 1939, when the Nazis invaded Poland. They stripped Jews of their rights and possessions; humiliated, tortured, and executed them; and eventually implemented the **Holocaust.** The exhibit traces, step by step, the escalation of the Nazis' "Final Solution," with a focus on events here in Warsaw: Forcing Jews into a ghetto (you'll walk across a platform representing the bridge that connected the two parts of the ghetto, offering Jewish people fleeting glimpses of "normal" life going on outside their walls); the liquidation of the ghetto and the movement of Warsaw's Jews to the death camp at Treblinka; and the Ghetto Uprising, a desperate last stand in which the dwindling number of Warsaw's Jews put up a valiant, but ultimately failed, fight. Making these stories personal are contemporaneous diaries, documents, and photographs. The exhibit poses difficult questions about how Poles helped—or did not help—the Jews who were gradually disappearing from their cities. And it explains how a sort of "underground railroad" worked hard and at great peril to save as many Jews as possible—as depicted in the movie *The Pianist*. (Look for the chess set carved by a Jew in hiding.) All told, 9 out of every 10 Polish Jews were murdered in the Holocaust. Only about 300,000 survived.

Finally, **The Postwar Years** follows Holocaust survivors in the years just after the war, when, astonishingly, they were scapegoated for war crimes. About 150,000 more (half the total survivors) fled to the newly-created state of Israel, and those who remained had to navigate an unfriendly, anti-Semitic communist regime. In 1968, the communists launched an "anti-Zionist" campaign; eventually around 15,000 Polish Jews lost their citizenship and left for Israel, Western Europe, and the US. Not until the fall of communism could the rest finally enter a world of new possibilities. The creation of this museum—the first time that the full story of the Jews of Poland has ever been told in such a mainstream way, and in all its epic scope—represents a critical milestone in celebrating a culture that has survived a harrowing history.

Ghetto Walking Tour

For a poignant stroll through what was the ghetto, with faint echoes of a tragic history, take this brief, lightly guided walk for a few blocks. Facing the monument with the museum behind you, head left (with the park on your left) and walk along Zamenhofa—which, like many streets in this neighborhood, is named for a hero of the Ghetto Uprising. From the monument, you'll follow a series of three-foot-tall, black stone memorials to uprising heroes—the **Path of Remembrance.** Like Stations of the Cross, each recounts an event of the uprising. Every April 19th (the day the uprising began), huge crowds follow this path.

In a block, just beyond the corner of Miła (partly obscured by some bushes), you'll find a **bunker** where about 100 organizers of the uprising hid (and where they committed suicide when the Nazis discovered them on May 8, 1943).

Continue following the black stone monuments up Zamenhofa (which becomes Dubois), then turn left at the corner, onto broad and busy Stawki. The ugly gray building on your left (a half-block down at #5, near the tram stop) was the **headquarters of the SS** within the ghetto. This is where the transportation of Warsaw's Jews to concentration camps was organized.

Using the crosswalk at the tram stop, cross Stawki and proceed straight ahead into the gap between the two buildings. At the back of this parking lot is a surviving part of the red-brick **ghetto wall,** with a few remaining scraps of 1940s barbed wire.

Farther up Stawki street, on the right, you can stop at the **Umschlagplatz** monument—shaped like a cattle car. That's German for "transfer place," and it marks the spot where the Nazis brought Jewish families to prepare them to be loaded onto trains bound for Treblinka or Auschwitz. This was the actual site of the touching scene in the film *The Pianist* where the grandfather shares bits of chocolate with his family before being forever separated. In the walls of the monument are inscribed the first names of some of the victims.

WARSAW UPRISING SIGHTS

While the 1944 Warsaw Uprising is a recurring theme in virtually all Warsaw sightseeing, two sights in particular—one a monument, the other a museum—are worth a visit for anyone with a special interest. Neither is right on the main tourist trail; the monument is closer to the sightseeing action, while the museum is a subway, tram, or taxi ride away.

Warsaw Uprising Monument

The most central sight related to the Warsaw Uprising is the monument at plac Krasińskich (intersection of ulica Długa and Miodowa,

one long block and about a five-minute walk northwest of the New Town). Larger-than-life soldiers and civilians race for the sewers in a desperate attempt to flee the Nazis. Just behind the monument is the oxidized-copper facade of Poland's Supreme Court.

▲▲Warsaw Uprising Museum
(Muzeum Powstania Warszawskiego)

Thorough, modern, and packed with Polish field-trip groups, the museum celebrates the heroes of the uprising. It's a bit cramped, and finding your way through the exhibits can be confusing, but it helps illuminate this complicated chapter of Warsaw's history. The location is inconvenient (a 10-minute tram or bus ride west of Centralna station) and, because it eats up several hours to visit, may not be worth the trek for those with a casual interest. But history buffs find it worthwhile.

Cost and Hours: 18 zł, free on Sun (but you'll pay 2 zł for the good *City of Ruins* movie—buy ticket at cashier before entering museum), Mon and Wed-Fri 8:00-18:00, Thu until 20:00, Sat-Sun 10:00-18:00, closed Tue, tel. 22-539-7947, www.1944.pl.

Audioguide: The informative, two-hour audioguide is ideal if you really want to delve into the whole story (10 zł, rent it in the gift shop). But the museum is so well-described, you can just wander aimlessly and be immersed in the hellish events.

Eating: The museum's café is oddly pleasant, serving drinks and light snacks amidst genteel ambience from interwar Warsaw. In summer you can dine on a peaceful terrace.

Getting There: The museum is on the western edge of downtown—a long, dull walk through urban gloom—at ulica Przyokopowa 28. While it's easiest to reach by taxi or Uber (figure about 20 zł from the Royal Way), you can get close on public transit. The nearest tram/bus stop is called Muzeum Powstania Warszawskiego, which you can reach on tram #22 or #24 (from Centralna station, or the street in front of the National Museum), bus #178 (from Castle Square), bus #105 (from the Uniwersytet stop on the Royal Way), or bus #109 (from in front of Centralna station). From the stop, you'll see the back of the museum (with its tower); circle around to find the entrance. Only a little farther from the museum is the Metro stop called Rondo Daszyńskiego.

⊘ Self-Guided Tour: Buy your ticket at the little house on the left (marked *kasa*), then head into the main hall. The high-tech **main exhibit** sprawls across three floors. It tells the story of the uprising chronologically, with a keen focus on military history. The exhibit covers several topics, but doesn't provide a big-picture narrative; to fully understand the context of what you're seeing, read the sidebar before your visit.

The **children's area** (to the right as you enter) reminds visitors that Varsovian kids played a role in the Warsaw Uprising, too.

The **ground floor** sets the stage with Germany's invasion and occupation of Poland. The Generalgouvernement (Nazi puppet government of occupied Poland, ruled by Hans Frank in Kraków) wasted no time in asserting its control over the Poles; you'll learn how they imprisoned and executed priests, professors, and students. You'll also hear the story of the earlier, smaller uprisings that preceded the Warsaw Uprising, including the Poland-wide Operation Tempest (Burza) in 1943. During those earliest rebellions, Warsaw was intentionally left out of the fray...but only for the time being.

To keep with the chronological flow, skip the middle floor for now, and ride the elevator to the **top floor** (#2), which covers the main part of the uprising. You'll meet some of the uprising's heroes and learn about their uniforms, weapons, and methods. The "Kino Palladium" movie screen shows fascinating Home Army newsreel footage from the period (with English subtitles). To the right of the screen, you'll walk through a simulated sewer, reminiscent of the one that many Home Army soldiers and civilians used to evade the Germans. Imagine terrified troops quietly traversing a sewer line like this one more than a mile long (but with lower ceilings)—and doing it while knee-deep in liquid sewage. At the end of the "sewer," stairs lead down to the middle floor.

The **middle floor** focuses on the grueling aftermath of the uprising. The later days of the uprising are outlined, battle by battle. A chilling section describes how Warsaw became a "city of graves," with burial mounds and makeshift crosses scattered everywhere. One room honors the Field Postal Service, which, at great personal risk, continued mail delivery of both military communiqués and civilian correspondences. Many of these brave "mailmen" were actually Scouts who were too young to fight. Nearby, another room re-creates a clandestine radio broadcast station set up in a living room.

If you need a break, look for the red corridor leading through the USSR section to the **café** and WC.

End your visit by walking down the stairs into the **main hall,** which is dominated by two large-scale exhibits: a replica of an RAF Liberator B-24 J, used for airborne surveillance of wartime Warsaw; and a giant movie screen showing more newsreels assembled by the Home Army's own propaganda unit during the uprising.

The Warsaw Uprising

By the summer of 1944, it was becoming clear that the Nazis' days in Warsaw were numbered. The Red Army drew near, and by late July, Soviet tanks were within 25 miles of downtown Warsaw.

The Varsovians could simply have waited for the Soviets to cross the river and force the Nazis out. But they knew that Soviet "liberation" would also mean an end to Polish independence. The Polish Home Army numbered 400,000—30,000 of them in Warsaw alone—and was the biggest underground army in military history. The uprisers wanted Poland to control its own fate, and they took matters into their own hands. The resistance's symbol was an anchor made up of a P atop a W (which stands for Polska Walcząca, or "Poland Fighting"— you'll see this icon all around town). Over time, the Home Army had established an extensive network of underground tunnels and sewers, which allowed them to deliver messages and move around the city without drawing the Nazis' attention. These tunnels gave the Home Army the element of surprise.

On August 1, 30,000 Polish resistance fighters launched an attack on their Nazi oppressors. They poured out of the sewers and caught the Nazis off guard. The ferocity of the Polish fighters stunned the Nazis, who thought they'd put down the uprising within hours. But the Nazis regrouped, and within a few days, they had retaken several areas of the city murdering tens of thousands of innocent civilians as they went. In one notorious incident, some 5,500 Polish soldiers and 6,000 civilians who were surrounded by Nazis in the Old Town were forced to flee through the sewers; many drowned or were shot. (This scene is depicted in the Warsaw Uprising Monument on plac Krasińskich.)

Two months after it had started, the Warsaw Uprising was over. The Home Army called a cease-fire. About 18,000 Polish uprisers had been killed, along with nearly 200,000 innocent civilians. An infuriated Hitler ordered that the city be destroyed—which it was, systematically, block by block, until virtually nothing remained.

Through all this, the Soviets stood still, watched, and waited. When the smoke cleared and the Nazis left, the Red Army marched in and claimed the wasteland that was once called Warsaw. After the war, General Dwight D. Eisenhower said that the scale of destruction here was the worst he'd ever seen. The communists later tracked down the surviving Home Army leaders, killing or imprisoning them.

Depending on whom you talk to, the desperate uprising of Warsaw was incredibly brave, stupid, or both. As for the Poles, they remain fiercely proud of their struggle for freedom. The city of Warsaw has recently commemorated this act of bravery with the new Warsaw Uprising Museum.

Under the screen, behind the black curtains, an exhibit tells the story of Germans in Warsaw, along with another, more claustrophobic walk-through sewer.

Also in the main hall, look for the entrance to the seven-minute 3-D film *City of Ruins,* with virtual aerial footage of the postwar devastation. This gives you a look at the reality of the thousand people (nicknamed "Robinson Crusoes") who lived in bombed-out Warsaw immediately after the war. It's worth waiting in line to see this powerful film.

The **park** surrounding the building features several thought-provoking sights. A Chevy truck armored by the Home Army is both a people's tank and an example of how outgunned they were. Along the back is the Wall of Memory, a Vietnam War Memorial-type monument to soldiers of the Polish Home Army who were killed in action. You'll see their rank and name, followed by their code name, in quotes. The Home Army observed a strict policy of anonymity, forbidding members from calling each other by anything but their code names. The bell in the middle is dedicated to the commander of the uprising, Antoni Chruściel (code name "Monter").

SOUTH OF THE CENTER
▲Łazienki Park (Park Łazienkowski)
The huge, idyllic Łazienki Park (wah-ZHYEN-kee) is where Varsovians go to play. The park is sprinkled with fun Neoclassical buildings, strutting peacocks, and young Poles in love. It was built by Poland's very last king (before the final Partition), Stanisław August Poniatowski, to serve as his summer residence and provide a place for his citizens to relax.

On the edge of the park (along Belwederska) is a **monument to Fryderyk Chopin.** The monument, in a rose garden, is flanked by platforms, where free summer piano **concerts** of Chopin's music

are given weekly (mid-May-late Sept only, generally Sun at 12:00 and 16:00—confirm at TI). The statue shows Chopin sitting under a wind-blown willow tree. Although he spent his last 20 years and wrote most of his best-known music in France, his inspiration came from wind blowing through the willow trees of his native land, Poland. The Nazis were quick to destroy this statue, which symbolizes Polish culture. They melted the original (from 1926) down for its metal. Today's copy was recast after World War II. Savor this spot; it's great in summer, with roses wildly in bloom, and in autumn, when the trees provide a golden backdrop for the black, romantic statue.

Venture down into the ravine and to the center of the park, where (after a 10-minute hike) you'll find King Poniatowski's strik-

ing **Palace on the Water** (Pałac na Wodzie)—literally built in the middle of a river. Nearby, you'll spot a clever amphitheater with seating on the riverbank and the stage on an island. The king was a real man of the Enlightenment, hosting weekly Thursday dinners here for artists and intellectuals. But Poland's kings are long gone, and proud peacocks now rule this roost.

Łazienki Park is also slated to be the future home of the state-of-the-art **Museum of Polish History,** which is being built along the Łazienkowska highway (near Ujazdów Castle, at the northeastern edge of the park). While it likely won't open until at least 2018, this museum will be yet another big draw for visitors (to check on the progress, see www.en.muzhp.pl).

Getting There: The park is just south of the city center on the Royal Way. Buses #116 and #180 run from Castle Square in the Old Town along the Royal Way directly to the park (get off at the stop called Łazienki Królewskie, by Belweder Palace—you'll see Chopin squinting through the trees on your left). Maps at park entrances locate the Chopin monument, Palace on the Water, and other park attractions.

Shopping in Warsaw

You'll notice that many Varsovians are chic, sophisticated, and very well-dressed. To see where they outfit themselves, go shopping. **Mysia 3** is a super-hip mini mall with three concise floors dedicated to mostly Polish fashion designers, but also has cutting-edge housewares and decor (Mon-Sat 10:00-20:00, Sun 12:00-18:00, across Jerusalem Avenue from Nowy Świat, inside the former communist propaganda office at Mysia 3, www.mysia3.pl). Warsaw's main "fashion row" is a bit farther south, in the Śródmieście district. **Mokotowska street,** which angles northeast from trendy plac Zbawiciela, is lined with literally dozens of chichi boutiques, jewelry shops, shoe stores, designer pastry shops, hair salons, and hipster barbers. The highest concentration is a few short blocks north of plac Zbawiciela, north of Piękna. Along here, Mokotowska 48 is a small shopping complex of local fashionistas. If you enjoy this zone, the area immediately to the west—along Wilcza and Poznańska streets—has more of the same.

Entertainment in Warsaw

Warsaw fills the summer with live music options. In addition to more serious options (opera, symphony, etc.), consider these crowd-pleasing choices.

CHOPIN

My favorite Warsaw music option is to enjoy a Chopin performance. There's nothing like hearing Chopin's compositions passionately played by a teary-eyed Pole who really feels the music. The best option is the outdoor concert in front of the big Chopin statue in **Łazienki Park,** but it is held only one day a week in summer (free, mid-May–late-Sept Sun at 12:00 and 16:00, www.lazienki-krolewskie.pl; for more on this option, see the Łazienki Park listing on page 208).

If you're not in town on a Sunday, the next best thing is the **Chopin Salon.** Jarek Chołodecki, who runs the recommended Chopin Boutique B&B, hosts an intimate piano concert in his delightful salon nightly at 19:30. The performance can cover a range of musical styles and composers—but generally there are piano pieces featuring Chopin. The concert lasts from 45 minutes to more than an hour and is followed by wine, homemade cakes, and social time. A small group of locals and travelers gathers around Jarek's big shiny Steinway grand to hear great music by talented young artists in a great city (50 zł, ulica Smolna 14, reservations required, tel. 22-829-4801, www.bedandbreakfast.pl). Jarek is also involved in the **Warsaw House of Music**—described later—which also presents Chopin concerts and other music.

The **Chopin Museum** has a concert series where music academy students recommended by their professors perform an hour-long concert. These are free and typically take place October through July each Thursday at 18:00—but they can be cancelled, so it's smart to confirm (tel. 22-441-6100, www.en.chopin.nifc.pl; no concerts Aug-Sept).

Additionally, various **touristy Chopin concerts** are popping up all over the city; figure 60 zł for a piano performance set in a drawing room or small theater. This is a fast-changing scene; options include Time for Chopin (in the Old Town, www.timeforchopin. com) or Warsaw Classical Experience (in the House of Literature, facing Castle Square, www.waclaex.eu). Ask your hotel or the TI for the latest fliers.

OTHER MUSIC
Warsaw House of Music (also called Nowy Świat Muzyki—"New World of Music")—in a refurbished town house along the Royal Way—hosts an even wider range of musical events, both for locals and for out-of-towners. The lineup does include some Chopin, but goes beyond touristy cliches to delve into other historical musical forms from Warsaw, including Jewish klezmer music, interwar Polish cabaret songs, Slavic folk songs, and traditional and contemporary jazz (Nowy Świat 63, tel. 22-692-4824, www.warsawhouseofmusic.pl).

Two big, opulent churches in and near the Old Town put on 30-minute **organ concerts** most days through the summer. Choose between the Cathedral of St. John the Baptist, with lots of history and a pretty, plain brick interior, right in the heart of the Old Town (10 zł, Aug-late Oct Mon-Sat at 14:00, no concerts Sun); or the frilly, Rococo St. Anne's Church, with a more sumptuous interior, just outside the Old Town (10 zł, May-early Oct Mon-Sat at 12:00, no concerts Sun). Both are run by the same company (mobile 501-158-477, www.kapitula.org).

Free outdoor **jazz concerts** take place each Saturday in summer right on the Old Town Square (July-Aug at 19:00).

LIVELY HANGOUT ZONES
The Old Town and New Town are totally for tourists. To find some more interesting areas to explore and hang out after dark, your first stop should be **plac Zbawiciela** in the Śródmieście and the surrounding streets (see page 218). Locals also enjoy spending a balmy afternoon or evening on the **Vistula riverbanks.** Long ignored by Varsovians, the left (west) bank has undergone a dramatic renovation, with beautiful parklike embankments ideal for strolling. Meanwhile, the right (east) bank is still rugged and undeveloped, with forests and natural beaches—the biggest being around the eastern base of the Poniatowski Bridge (where Jerusalem Avenue crosses the river, just past Palm Tree Circle).

Sleeping in Warsaw

Because Warsaw is a major business destination, its hotel rates fluctuate from day to day. I've categorized them based on estimated prices during busy times, but you may find them much higher or much lower depending on what's happening in town. Regardless, you'll find Warsaw affordable for a European capital—for what you'd spend on a basic room in Rome or Amsterdam, you can get a palatial room in a top-end hotel here. That said, two of my Warsaw favorites—Chopin Boutique B&B and Duval Apartments—are both affordable and characteristic, making them excellent choices.

I've arranged my listings by neighborhood. Keep in mind that in the Old Town, you'll rarely see a local, while in Śródmieście, you'll rarely see a tourist. Choose your Warsaw experience.

NEAR PALM TREE CIRCLE (NOWY ŚWIAT AND JERUSALEM AVENUE)

Considering how spread out Warsaw is, this is a convenient location for reaching various sights around the city. While comfortable inside, these hotels are in big buildings on uninspiring urban streets.

$$ Chopin Boutique B&B offers more comfort and class than a hotel twice its price, in a beautifully renovated and well-located old building near the National Museum. Jarek Chołodecki, who lived near Chicago for many years, returned to Warsaw and converted apartments into this wonderful bed-and-breakfast with 24 rooms. It's a friendly, casual, stylish place, creatively decorated and impeccably maintained. You'll feel like you're staying with your Warsaw so-

phisticate cousin—quirky, charismatic Jarek loves to chat with his guests, many of whom return and become his good friends. Each morning, conversation percolates at the big, family-style breakfast table over a morning meal made mostly from organic and locally-sourced foods. The garden courtyard is a nice escape from the city, and the drawing room plays host to nightly music concerts—see "Entertainment in Warsaw," earlier (RS%, breakfast extra, elevator, ulica Smolna 14, tel. 22-829-4801, www.bedandbreakfast.pl, office@bedandbreakfast.pl).

$$ Between Us B&B is an ideal home-away-from-home for hipsters in Warsaw. Beata rents three trendy rooms above a youthful café centrally located in downtown Warsaw. As this place books up early, reserve far ahead (on second floor, no elevator, check in at Między Nami café downstairs, Bracka 20, tel. 22-828-5417, mobile 603-096-701, www.between-us.eu, info@between-us.eu).

$$ Zgoda Apartment Hotel, impersonal but comfortable, has 51 apartments designed for business travelers on a tight budget (breakfast extra or use the kitchenette, air-con, elevator, Zgoda 6, tel. 22-553-6200, www.desilva.pl, zgoda@desilva.pl).

$$ Apple Inn, with seven tight rooms in the attic of a hulking, central building, is your cheap-and-cheery option in the center

Sleep Code

Hotels are classified based on the average price of a standard double room with breakfast in high season.

$$$$	**Splurge:** Most rooms over 550 zł
$$$	**Pricier:** 400-550 zł
$$	**Moderate:** 250-400 zł
$	**Budget:** 100-250 zł
¢	**Backpacker:** Under 100 zł
RS%	**Rick Steves discount**

Unless otherwise noted, credit cards are accepted, hotel staff speak basic English, and free Wi-Fi is available. Comparison-shop by checking prices at several hotels (on each hotel's own website, on a booking site, or by email). For the best deal, *book directly with the hotel.* Ask for a discount if paying in cash; if the listing includes **RS%,** request a Rick Steves discount.

(breakfast extra, shared kitchen and library, sometimes unstaffed—clearly communicate your arrival time, Chmielna 21, unit 22B—ride elevator to fourth floor, mobile 601-746-006, www.appleinn.pl, Miki).

¢ Oki Doki Hostel, on a pleasant square a few blocks in front of the Palace of Culture and Science, is colorful, creative, and easy-going. Each of its 37 rooms was designed by a different artist with a special theme—such as Van Gogh, Celtic spirals, heads of state, or Lenin. It's run by Ernest—a Pole whose parents loved Hemingway—and his wife Łucja, with help from their sometimes jaded staff (private rooms available, plac Dąbrowskiego 3, tel. 22-826-5112, 22-828-0122, www.okidoki.pl, okidoki@okidoki.pl).

IN ŚRÓDMIEŚCIE ("DOWNTOWN")

Foodies, people who hate tourists, and travelers who really want to disappear into Warsaw choose to sleep in Śródmieście. A 10- to 15-minute walk (or quick tram ride) south of Jerusalem Avenue, it feels urban-residential and very local. And if trendy restaurants are on your agenda, sleeping near the culinary hotspots in Śródmieście is an efficient strategy. Compared to most of my other Warsaw listings, these feel a bit chic and trendy...just right for the neighborhood.

$$$ Hotel Rialto is a professional-feeling boutique hotel with Art Deco flair—both inside (in the lobby, respected restaurant, and 44 rooms) and out. It feels sophisticated, but without pretense (air-con, elevator, Wilcza 73, nearest tram/bus stop at Koszykowa, tel. 22-584-8700, www.rialto.pl, info@rialto.pl).

$$$ H15 Boutique Hotel feels posh for its price range, with a show-off lobby, a sleek black-and-white color scheme, and 46

WARSAW

rooms—ranging from simple doubles to expansive apartments. It tries very hard to be stylish—to the point of being a bit pretentious—but its handy location (surrounded by great restaurants) and reasonable rates make it worth considering (air-con, elevator, pay on-site parking, Poznańska 15, nearest tram/bus stop at Hoża, tel. 22-553-8700, www.h15boutiqueapartments.com, reservations@h15ab.com).

$$$ Autor Rooms is classy and intimate—a third-floor apartment with four rooms (each one different) and a shared breakfast table. It's off a busy street in an urban jungle just off Constitution Square, but once you're settled in, it's a handy home base (air-con, elevator, Lwowska 17, nearest tram/bus stop at plac Konstytucji, mobile 797-992-737, www.autorrooms.pl, hello@autorrooms.pl, Kaja).

IN OR NEAR THE OLD TOWN

The Old Town area has some fine splurges and easy access to the romantic, rebuilt historic core. But it's less handy to Warsaw's trendier side.

$$$$ Hotel Bristol is Warsaw's top splurge—as much a landmark as a hotel (see description on page 177), this classic address on the Royal Way is where you're likely to spot visiting dignitaries and celebrities. (Just inside the round entrance on the corner, find the wall of brass knobs identifying past VIP guests—from Pablo Picasso to Kelly Osborne.) The public spaces are palatial, with sumptuous Art Deco lounges, bars, and coffee shops that make you want to dress up just to hang out. And the 206 rooms are fresh, elegant, and well-equipped. If you like a posh home base, check the rates here first—you may be surprised at how affordable opulence can be (air-con, classy old vintage elevator, gym, swimming pool, sauna, Krakowskie Przedmieście 42, tel. 22-551-1000, www.hotelbristolwarsaw.pl, bristol@luxurycollection.com).

$$$$ Hotel Le Régina is another tempting splurge, buried in the quiet and charming New Town (just beyond the Old Town). From its elegant public spaces to its 61 top-notch rooms, everything here is done with class (pricey breakfast, elevator, exercise room, pool, Kościelna 12, tel. 22-531-6000, www.leregina.com, reception.leregina@mamaison.com).

$$$ Castle Inn, sitting on Castle Square at the entrance to the Old Town, is the next rung up the ladder for youth hostelers who've outgrown the grungy backpacker scene. Run by the owners of Oki Doki Hostel (described earlier), it has 22 creative and colorful rooms, each with different decor (breakfast extra, lots of stairs and no elevator, can be noisy—request quiet room, Świętojańska 2, tel. 22-425-0100, www.castleinn.pl, castleinn@castleinn.pl).

$$ Duval Apartments, named for a French woman who supposedly had an affair with the Polish king in this building, offers four beautifully appointed rooms above a restaurant and teahouse (called Same Fusy) a few steps off the square in the Old Town. Each spacious room has a different theme: traditional Polish, Japanese, glass, or retro. Offering B&B comfort with hotel anonymity, this is an excellent value and one of my Warsaw favorites (lots of stairs with no elevator, breakfast extra, some restaurant noise—light sleepers should request a quiet room, Nowomiejska 10, mobile 608-679-346, www.duval.net.pl, duval@duval.net.pl). Arrange a meeting time with Agnieszka or Marcin when you reserve.

Eating in Warsaw

Tourists are drawn to the Old Town, where prices are sky-high and quality is rock-bottom. But once you get outside that zone, Warsaw

is one of Eastern Europe's best foodie cities. For a memorable experience, don't be shy about exploring some more local neighborhoods. Prices are low, so even a "splurge" restaurant lets you experience high-end experimental cuisine for a fraction of the cost of a similar place in a Western European capital. For this reason—and to take full advantage of the city's exciting food scene—my recommendations here skew to fancier foodie options. Eat "ye olde" in Kraków and Prague, if you must—but in Warsaw, be adventurous.

Wherever you dine, most restaurants are open until the "last guest," which usually means about 23:00 (sometimes later in summer)—but can be earlier than expected on slow nights. If dining late, call ahead.

NEAR PALM TREE CIRCLE (NOWY ŚWIAT AND JERUSALEM AVENUE)

These practical options are right in the middle of your sightseeing plans—handy for lunch on the go, or worth going out of your way for to enjoy a memorable dinner. The clientele is a mix of local yuppies, savvy business travelers, and casual tourists smart enough to steer clear of Old Town restaurants.

$$$ Opasły Tom ("Bursting Tome"), a tidy, literary-themed restaurant by respected chef Agata Wojda, serves reasonably priced, modern cuisine inspired by Polish roots and ingredients. Reserve ahead at this dressy place (daily 12:00-22:00, Foksal 17, tel. 22-621-1881, http://kregliccy.pl/opaslytom). The area near Opasły Tom, along **Foksal street,** is lined with several lively, contemporary eateries where diners enjoy the al fresco tables.

Restaurant Price Code

I've assigned each eatery a price category, based on the average cost of a typical main course. Drinks, desserts, and splurge items (steak and seafood) can raise the price considerably.

$$$$	**Splurge:** Most main courses over 60 zł
$$$	**Pricier:** 45-60 zł
$$	**Moderate:** 25-45 zł
$	**Budget:** Under 25 zł

In Poland, a milk bar or takeout spot is **$**; a basic sit-down eatery is **$$**; a casual but more upscale restaurant is **$$$**; and a swanky splurge is **$$$$**.

$$$ Kamanda Lwowska is the best spot in Warsaw for traditional Polish cooking. It's named for the former Polish city that's now in Ukraine (Lwow, a.k.a. Lviv). It has a few outdoor seats and a charming, cluttered old cellar with just a touch of kitsch. The friendly and fun staff serves up well-executed Polish classics (daily 10:00-24:00, Foksal 10, tel. 22-828-1031).

$$$$ Butchery & Wine, in an unassuming location on a drab urban street, is a pocket of chic international cuisine in the heart of Warsaw. The waiters, smartly dressed in pinstripe aprons, serve upscale comfort food (specializing in steaks) to a small, lively room of business travelers. The wine list is extensive, and reservations are smart (Mon-Sat 12:00-22:00, Sun until 20:00, Żurawia 22, tel. 22-502-3118, www.butcheryandwine.pl).

$$ Bibenda is a super-trendy bar with cocktails and an enticing seasonal menu of Polish fusion dishes—using Polish classics as a starting point, then jazzing them up with elements borrowed from corresponding dishes in other cultures. For example, you might see fried chicken (a Polish staple), marinated in buttermilk (from the American south), with a raspberry/chipotle glaze (from Mexico). Or perhaps a *gołąbki* (Polish cabbage roll) done in the style of a Turkish *dolma* (stuffed grape leaves). It's trendy and affordable, and the food is delicious. Reservations are wise at dinnertime (Tue-Sun 12:00-late, closed Mon, Nowogrodzka 10, mobile 502-770-303, www.bibenda.pl.

Tamka 43, in a sleek but unpretentious modern space facing the Chopin Museum, has two parts: The main floor is an affordable **$$ café/wine bar,** handy for a quick lunch or glass of wine near the museum. Upstairs is a fine-dining **$$$$ restaurant,** with a menu based on historical research of Chopin's favorite dishes and a prizewinning wine list (reservations are smart). Both areas have lunch specials—which are a particularly good deal if you want to try the nice restaurant (daily 12:00-22:00, Tamka 43, tel. 22-441-6234, www.tamka43.pl).

Uniquely Polish Treats

These places are on or close to the busy Nowy Świat boulevard.

A. Blikle, Poland's most famous pastry shop, serves a wide variety of delicious treats. This is where locals shop for cakes when they're having someone special over for coffee. The specialty is *pączki* (PONCH-kee), the quintessential Polish doughnut, filled with rose-flavored jam. You can get your goodies "to go" in the shop, or pay double to enjoy them with coffee in the swanky, classic café with indoor or outdoor seating (daily 9:00-21:00, Nowy Świat 35, tel. 22-828-6601). They also have a sit-down restaurant, but I come here only for the *pączki*.

E. Wedel Pijalnia Czekolady thrills chocoholics. Emil Wedel made Poland's favorite chocolate, and today, his former residence houses this chocolate shop and genteel café. This is the spot for delicious pastries and a *real* hot chocolate—*czekolada do picia* ("drinking chocolate"), a cup of actual melted chocolate, not just hot chocolate milk. The staff describes it as, "True Wedel ecstasy for your mouth that will take you to a world of dreams and desires." Or, if you fancy chocolate mousse, try *pokusa* ("Wedel Temptation"). Wedel's was *the* Christmas treat for locals under communism. Cadbury bought the company when Poland privatized, but they kept the E. Wedel name, which is close to all Poles' hearts...and taste buds (Mon-Fri 8:00-22:00, Sat 9:00-22:00, Sun 9:00-21:00, between Palace of Culture and Science and Nowy Świat at ulica Szpitalna 8, tel. 22-827-2916, www.wedelpijalnie.pl/en).

Odette, tucked in a sleek, new, mixed-use complex a short walk from the main tourist zone and from Wedel, is a good choice for updated treats: pristinely executed designer cakes at reasonable prices. Look through the glass door to the kitchen (Tue-Sun 10:00-20:00, Mon 13:00-20:00, Wojciecha Górskiego 6, unit 7, mobile 604-745-444). These upscale dessert shops are all the rage—keep an eye out for them all over the city (such as Słodki Słony, described later).

In Powiśle, near the Riverbank

The low-lying Powiśle neighborhood—squeezed in the little canyon between the Royal Way and the river—is newly trendy, thanks partly to its proximity to the inviting riverbank parks. Solec 44 is worth going out of your way for to enjoy a memorable dinner, while the others are simply fun hangout cafés if you're in the area. To reach this area by foot, you can walk through the steep Beyera Park (behind the Chopin Museum), or go down Jerusalem Avenue toward the bridge, enter the rail station, go down the stairs, walk all the way along *peron* (platform) 1 to the end, then go down the stairs at the far end. You'll pop out right at Warszawa Powiśle, a short walk from Solec 44. Alternatively, you can walk partway across the bridge at Jerusalem Avenue, then go down the stairs at the first tower.

$$$ Solec 44 epitomizes Warsaw's foodie melding of old and new. They are deeply engaged with Polish culinary roots: They source traditionally-made, artisanal sausages and cheeses, and have a big wall of shelves (which looks like a bizarre culinary experiment) where they ferment various vegetables in the traditional manner. And yet, the food itself is modern, creative, and daring. It fills a once-deteriorating, communist-era cultural center, tucked unassumingly behind a kebab stand on an overgrown embankment. The rustic-chic interior and the outdoor deck (rich with the aroma of their busy smoker) are both inviting and unpretentious. A meal here gives you a good understanding of where Polish food has come from, and where it's heading in the next generation...and the cocktails are great, too. Reserve ahead (Tue-Sun 12:00-late, Mon 16:00-late, Solec 44, mobile 798-363-996, www.solec.waw.pl).

$ Warszawa Powiśle is a café/bar occupying the old, communist-style ticket office for the suburban train station of the same name. Tucked along a picturesque bike lane beneath the towering legs of a bridge, its sidewalk is jammed with cool Varsovians and in-the-know visitors (light sandwiches, daily 9:00 until late, Kruczkowskiego 3B, tel. 22-474-4084).

$ Kawiarnia Kafka combines a used bookstore (with books sold by weight) with a hip, creative café. Inside you'll find comfy chairs, stay-awhile tables, and checkerboard tiles; outside, on the lawn across from the café, guests lounge in slingback chairs (Mon-Fri 9:00-22:00, Sat-Sun 10:00-22:00, Oboźna 3, tel. 22-826-0822).

IN ŚRÓDMIEŚCIE ("DOWNTOWN")

Warsaw's Śródmieście district is the epicenter of Polish hipster/foodie culture—where you'll find young Varsovian foodies digging into affordable dishes at the trendiest new places. This area is a 15-minute walk south of Jerusalem Avenue, and also well-served by public transportation (for example, trams #4, #15, #18, and #35 run frequently along the main north-south Marszałkowska corridor to plac Zbawiciela; of these, tram #4 stops in the middle of the road below Castle Square, where the Royal Way meets the Old Town). Listed next are a few different restaurant-hunting zones, with some specific recommendations for each one. For locations, see the map on page 163.

On Plac Zbawiciela

Named "Holiest Savior Square" for the looming church, this is a dizzying six-way intersection with a big traffic circle ringed by el-

egant old colonnades. To get a quick taste of the Śródmieście scene, come here first and just do a slow loop around the circle, surveying your options. Starting to the right of the steeple and moving clockwise, here are a few options you'll see: **$$ Izumi Sushi,** **$ Karma** coffee shop, and **$$ Tuk Tuk** Thai street food are all popular, with great seating out on the square. Continuing two crosswalks around the circle, the Italian-themed **Pini Café & Vino** has nice outdoor tables across from the church. Farther around, just down Mokotowska from the circle, look for the line of people at **Sucré,** an unpretentious hole-in-the-wall serving all-natural, homemade ice cream. In the next section, **$$ Charlotte** designer bakery and wine bar is another popular choice, with homemade treats and tables spilling out all over the square. Up above, **Plan B** is a hipster dive bar with drinks, snacks, and views down over the square; this is where revelers head at 2 in the morning, after the restaurants are closed (find the graffiti-slathered staircase up, just past Charlotte).

Nearby, on Mokotowska ulica: This street, stretching north from plac Zbawiciela (past Sucré ice-cream shop), has more options. **$$$$ Dyspensa** is a good place for a serious sit-down meal in a dressy but not stuffy environment. They serve a thoughtfully selected menu of updated Polish cuisine, plus a few international options, as well as a handwritten list of daily specials. Reservations are smart (daily 12:00-23:00, Mokotowska 39, tel. 22-629-9989, www.dyspensa.pl). A half-block up the street is the mellower **$$ Słodki Słony** ("Sweet Salty"), at the casual end of the scale of Polish celebrity chef Magda Gessler's restaurant empire. Up front is a big, tempting display case bursting with over-the-top decadent desserts; farther in is a cozy dining area where you can dig into sandwiches, salads, and other light fare (daily, Mokotowska 45, tel. 22-622-4934, www.slodkislony.pl).

On and near Poznańska Street

A few short blocks west of plac Zbawiciela, this street is also lined with trendy and youthful eateries (especially around the intersection with Wilcza street; the nearest tram/bus stop is Hoża, and it's also not far from plac Konstytucji). Strolling this strip, you'll find several enticing options: **$$ Kaskrut** (a pun on *casse-croûte*) has a variety of well-executed minimalist dishes, including vegan options, a tight interior, and casual sidewalk tables (closed Mon, Poznańska 5). **$$$$ Nolita** is one of Warsaw's top splurges—top-end, white-tablecloth fine dining, but still affordable on a European scale (closed Sat lunch and all day Sun, Wilcza 46, www.nolita. pl). **$$$ Wilcza 50** is a big, glitzy, crank-'em-out place offering international fare in a modern and spacious setting (daily, Wilcza 50). And **$$ Tel Aviv** has gluten-free and vegan Middle Eastern food (daily, Poznańska 11). A favorite in this area is **$$ Beirut,** a gregariously crowded bar serving up excellent Middle Eastern food. The hummus bar, on the left, has a wide variety of *mezes* (small plates) and grilled meats, while the "Kraken Rum Bar" on the right has fish dishes (portions are modest—plan to share a few, order at the counter then find a table, Poznańska 12).

IN OR NEAR THE OLD TOWN

The restaurants in the Old Town and surrounding streets are 100 percent for tourists. Dining right on the Old Town Market Square is exorbitantly expensive, but could be worth it for those who treasure a romantic memory. Still, I'd rather walk a block or two to one of these options, which are as good as it gets in this area. For locations, see the map on page 172.

$$ Restauracja pod Samsonem ("Under Samson") is a quirky throwback and a sentimental favorite. The menu is affordable, well-executed, unfussy Jewish and Polish comfort food. The outdoor seating, on the New Town's main drag just outside the barbican, is enjoyable in good weather. And the staff is old-school: gruff, playfully opinionated, and stingy (you'll have to pay to check your coat or use the bathroom—yes, even if you're dining here). But nostalgic locals appreciate this as a stubborn remnant of the old days—a time before service with a smile, fine dining for business travelers, and hipster fusion restaurants (daily 10:00-23:00, Freta 3, tel. 22-831-1788).

$$ Freta 33—a block deeper into the New Town, facing the serene New Town Square—has decent international fare (such as pastas), fine outdoor seating, and a contemporary subway-tile interior (daily 12:00-23:00, Freta 33, tel. 22-635-0931).

$$ Zapiecek, with a half-dozen locations in and near the Old Town, is a kitschy chain serving up cheap and cheery traditional Polish dishes. But the prices are reasonable, and the food (especially the pierogi) is better and more authentic than it ought to be, given its tourist-trap vibe (handiest location faces the Cathedral of St. John the Baptist at Świętojańska 13, others are on the main drag through the New Town at Freta 1 and Freta 18, yet another on the Royal Way at Nowy Świat 64, all open long hours daily).

Warsaw Connections

Almost all trains into and out of Warsaw go through hulking Warszawa Centralna station (described earlier, under "Arrival in Warsaw," including ticket-buying tips). If you're heading to Gdańsk, note that the red-brick Gothic city of Toruń and the impressive Malbork Castle are on the way, but are on separate train lines, making it difficult to do both en route (see the Gdańsk and Pomerania chapters). Also be aware that EIC and IC express trains to many destinations—including Kraków and Gdańsk—require seat reservations, even if you have a rail pass.

To confirm rail journeys, check specific times online (www. rozklad-pkp.pl) or at Centralna station.

From Warszawa Centralna Station by Train to: Kraków (hourly, about 2.5 hours), **Gdańsk** (hourly, 3 hours), **Malbork** (hourly, 2.5 hours), **Toruń** (every 2 hours direct, 2.5 hours on express IC train), **Prague** (2/day direct, including 1 night train, more with change in Ostrava, 8-9.5 hours), **Berlin** (4/day direct, 6 hours, no direct night train), **Budapest** (1/day direct, 10 hours; 1/day overnight, 11.5 hours; also 2/day with change in Břeclav, Czech Republic, 10 hours), **Vienna** (2/day direct, 7 hours; plus 1 night train, 10 hours).

By Bus: PolskiBus—described on page 138—runs bus routes throughout Poland (www.polskibus.com).

WARSAW

GDAŃSK & THE TRI-CITY

Gdańsk (guh-DAYNSK) is a true find on the Baltic Coast of Poland. You may associate Gdańsk with dreary images of striking dock-workers from the nightly news in the 1980s—but there's so much more to this city than shipyards, Solidarity, and smog. It's surprisingly easy to look past the urban sprawl to find one of northern Europe's most historic and picturesque cities. Gdańsk is second only to Kraków as Poland's most appealing destination.

Exploring Gdańsk is a delight. The gem of a Main Town boasts block after block of red-brick churches and narrow, colorful, ornately decorated Hanseatic burghers' mansions. The riverfront embankment, with its trademark medieval crane, oozes salty maritime charm. Gdańsk's history is also fascinating—from its 17th-century Golden Age to the headlines of our own generation, big things happen here. You might even see ol' Lech Wałęsa still wandering the streets. And yet Gdańsk is also looking to its future, steadily repairing some of its WWII damage after a long communist hibernation. Over the past decade, whole swaths of the city have been remade with a bold new modernity...but always with a respect for the past.

Gdańsk and two nearby towns (Sopot and Gdynia) together form an area known as the "Tri-City," offering several day-trip opportunities north along the coast (see page 275). The once-faded, now-revitalized elegance of the seaside resort of Sopot beckons to tourists, while the modern burg of Gdynia sets the pace for today's Poland. Beyond the Tri-City, the sandy Hel Peninsula is a popular spot for summer sunbathing.

PLANNING YOUR TIME

This region merits two days to make the trip here worthwhile. Gdańsk's major sights can be seen in a day, but a second day allows you to see everything in town at a more relaxing pace, and take your pick from among several possible side-trips.

Gdańsk sightseeing has two major components: the Royal Way (historic main drag with good museums) and the modern shipyard where Solidarity was born (with a fascinating museum). With just one day, do one of these activities in the morning, and the other in the afternoon. With two days, do one each day, and round out your time with other attractions: Art lovers enjoy the National Museum (with a stunning altar painting by Hans Memling), history buffs make the pilgrimage to Westerplatte (where World War II began), and church and pipe-organ fans might visit Oliwa Cathedral in Gdańsk's northern suburbs (on the way to Sopot).

If you have more time, consider the wide variety of side-trips. The most popular option is the half-day round-trip to Malbork Castle (30-45 minutes each way by train, plus two or three hours to tour the castle—see next chapter). It only takes a quick visit to enjoy the resort town of Sopot (25 minutes each way by train), but on a sunny day, the town's beaches may tempt you to laze around longer. Consider a sprint through Gdynia to round out your take on the Tri-City. If you have a full day and great weather, and you don't mind fighting the crowds for a patch of sandy beach, go to Hel.

Gdańsk gets busy in late June, when school holidays begin, and it's crowded with (mostly German, Norwegian, and Swedish) tourists from July to mid-September—especially during St. Dominic's Fair (Jarmark Św. Dominika, three weeks from late July to mid-Aug), with market stalls, concerts, and other celebrations.

Several Gdańsk museums are closed Monday—especially outside summer. Monday is a good day to visit churches or the European Solidarity Center, or to take a side-trip to Sopot (but not to Malbork Castle, which is also closed Mon).

Orientation to Gdańsk

With 460,000 residents, Gdańsk is part of the larger urban area known as the Tri-City (Trójmiasto, total population of 1 million). But the tourist's Gdańsk is compact, welcoming, and walkable—virtually anything you'll want to see is within a 20-minute stroll of everything else.

Focus on the Main Town (Główne Miasto), home to most of

the sights described, including the spectacular Royal Way main drag, ulica Długa. The Old Town (Stare Miasto) has a handful of old brick buildings and faded, tall, skinny houses—but the area is mostly drab and residential, and not worth much time. Just beyond the northern end of the Old Town (about a 20-minute walk from the heart of the Main Town) is the entrance to the Gdańsk Shipyard, with the excellent European Solidarity Center and its topnotch museum. From here, shipyards sprawl for miles.

The second language in this part of Poland is German, not English. As this was a predominantly German city until the end of World War II, German tourists flock here in droves. But you'll win no Polish friends if you call the city by its more familiar German name, Danzig. You'll also find that Gdańsk is becoming an increasingly popular cruise destination, with about 100 ships calling here each year (most dock at the nearby city of Gdynia, and passengers take a bus or train in). During summer daytime hours, the town is filled with little tour groups.

TOURIST INFORMATION

Gdańsk has two different TI organizations: The regional TI occupies the **Upland Gate,** facing the busy road that hems in the Main Town, at the start of my self-guided walk (May-Sept Mon-Fri 9:00-20:00, Sat-Sun 9:00-18:00; Oct-April daily 9:00-18:00; tel. 58-732-7041, www.pomorskie.travel). The city TI has three branches—one conveniently located at the bottom end of the main drag, at **Długi Targ 28** (just to the left as you face the river gate; daily 9:00-19:00, Oct-April until 17:00; tel. 58-301-4355, www.gdansk4u.pl), with satellite TIs at the **main train station** (in the underpass, tel. 58-721-3277) and at the **airport** (open 24/7, tel. 58-348-1368). Yet another handy tourist website is www.visitgdansk.com.

Sightseeing Card: Busy sightseers should consider the **Tourist Card,** which includes entry to several sights in Gdańsk, Gdynia, and Sopot, and discounts at others (such as 20 percent off the European Solidarity Center). Check the list of what's covered, and do the arithmetic (60 zł/24 hours, 90 zł/72 hours, pay more to add local transit, sold only at TIs).

ARRIVAL IN GDAŃSK

By Train: Gdańsk's main train station (Gdańsk Główny) is a pretty brick palace on the western edge of the old center. (To save money, architects in Colmar, France copied this exact design to build their city's station.)

Trains to other parts of Poland (marked *PKP*) use platforms 1-3; regional trains with connections to the Tri-City (marked *SKM*) use the shorter platforms 3-5 (for instructions on riding these regional SKM trains, see page 275).

Inside the terminal building, you'll find lockers, ATMs, and ticket windows. Outside, the pedestrian underpass by the McDonald's has a TI and leads you beneath the busy road (first set of exits: tram stop; end of corridor: shopping mall at the edge of the Old Town).

The easiest choice for reaching your hotel is to hop in a **taxi** or request an **Uber** (which shouldn't cost more than 15 zł to any of my recommended hotels). Or it's a 15-minute walk to the heart of the Main Town and many recommended hotels: Go through the underpass, exit to the right, circle around the right side of Cinema City, and follow the busy road until you see the brick towers on your left. Riding the **tram** can shave a few minutes off this walk (buy tickets in underpass, then head up to find stop in the middle of the road; ride tram #2, #3, #6, #8, or #11 just one stop to Brama Wyżynna).

By Plane: Gdańsk's airport, named for Lech Wałęsa, is about five miles west of the city center (airport code: GDN, tel. 58-348-1163, www.airport.gdansk.pl). The **train** zips you to the main train station in just 30 minutes (6 zł, direct trains run hourly; additional trains run 4/hour but require a transfer at the Gdańsk Wrzeszcz station, where you can switch to the regional SKM train line). Public **bus** #210 stops near the main train station and at Brama Wyżynna, near the heart of the Main Town (3.20 zł, buy ticket at machine at stop or buy on board for a bit more; 2/hour on weekdays, 1/hour on weekends, 40 minutes). The 25-minute **taxi** or **Uber** ride into town should cost no more than 60 zł.

GETTING AROUND GDAŃSK

Nearly everything is within easy walking distance of my recommended hotels, but public transportation can be useful for reaching outlying sights such as Oliwa Cathedral, Westerplatte, Sopot, Gdynia, and Hel (specific transportation options for these places are described in each listing).

By Public Transportation: Gdańsk's trams and buses work on the same tickets: Choose between a single-ride ticket (3.20 zł), one-hour ticket (3.80 zł), and 24-hour ticket (13 zł). Major stops have user-friendly ticket machines. Otherwise, buy tickets *(bilety)* at kiosks marked *RUCH* or *Bilety ZKM*, or pay a little more to buy tickets on board. In the city center, the stops worth knowing about are Plac Solidarności (near the European Solidarity Center), Gdańsk Główny (in front of the main train station), and Brama Wyżynna (near the Upland Gate and the new Gdańsk Śródmieście

Gdańsk at a Gdlance

▲▲▲**Royal Way/Ulica Długa Walk** Gdańsk's colorful show-piece main drag, cutting a picturesque swath through the heart of the wealthy burghers' neighborhood. See page 230.

▲▲▲**Solidarity Sights and Gdańsk Shipyard** Home to the beginning of the end of Eastern European communism, with a towering monument and excellent museum. **Hours:** Memorial and shipyard gate—always open. European Solidarity Center exhibit—daily 10:00-20:00, Oct-April until 18:00. See page 251.

▲▲**Main Town Hall** Ornate meeting rooms, town artifacts, and tower with sweeping views. **Hours:** Mid-June-mid-Sept Mon-Thu 9:00-16:00, Fri-Sat 10:00-18:00, Sun 10:00-16:00; mid-Sept-mid-June Tue 10:00-13:00, Wed-Sat 10:00-16:00, Thu until 18:00, Sun 11:00-16:00, closed Mon. See page 247.

▲▲**Artus Court** Grand meeting hall for guilds of Golden Age Gdańsk, boasting an over-the-top tiled stove. **Hours:** Same as Main Town Hall. See page 248.

▲▲**St. Mary's Church** Giant red-brick church crammed full of Gdańsk history. **Hours:** Mon-Sat 8:30-18:30, Sun 11:00-12:00 & 13:00-18:30; Oct-April daily until 17:00. See page 238.

▲**Amber Museum** High-tech exhibit of valuable golden globs of petrified tree sap. **Hours:** Same as Main Town Hall, above. See page 245.

▲**Uphagen House** Tourable 18th-century interior, typical of the pretty houses that line ulica Długa. **Hours:** Same as Main Town Hall. See page 247.

▲**National Maritime Museum** Sprawling exhibit on all aspects of the nautical life, housed in several venues connected by a ferry boat. **Hours:** July-Aug daily 10:00-18:00; Sept-Oct and March-June Tue-Sun 10:00-16:00, closed Mon; Nov-Feb Tue-Sun 10:00-15:00, closed Mon. See page 250.

Historical Zone of the Free City of Gdańsk Tiny museum examining Gdańsk's unique status as a "Free City" between the World Wars. **Hours:** Tue-Sun 12:00-18:00, Sept-April until 17:00, closed Mon year-round. See page 249.

Archaeological Museum Decent collection of artifacts from this region's past. **Hours:** July-Aug Tue-Fri 9:00-17:00, Sat-Sun 10:00-17:00; Sept-June Tue and Thu-Fri 8:00-16:00, Wed 9:00-17:00, Sat-Sun 10:00-16:00; closed Mon year-round. See page 250.

National Museum in Gdańsk Ho-hum art collection with a single blockbuster highlight: Hans Memling's remarkable Last Judgment altarpiece. **Hours:** May-Sept Tue-Sun 10:00-17:00 (Thu 12:00-19:00 in June-Aug); Oct-April Tue-Fri 9:00-16:00, Sat-Sun 10:00-17:00, closed Mon year-round. See page 262.

commuter train station). When buying tickets, don't confuse *ZKM* (Gdańsk city transit) with *SKM* (commuter trains).

One public bus worth knowing about is Gdańsk's **bus #100.** Every 20 minutes, this made-for-tourists minibus (designed to navigate the twisty streets of the town center) makes a loop through the Old Town and Main Town, with stops strategic for sightseeing (covered by regular transit ticket).

By Taxi: Taxis cost about 8 zł to start, then 2-3 zł per kilometer (a bit more at night). Find a taxi stand, or call a cab (try Neptun, tel. 19686 or 585-111-555; or Dajan, tel. 58-19628).

Tours in Gdańsk

Private Guides

Hiring a local guide is an exceptional value. **Agnieszka Syroka**— youthful, bubbly, and personable—is a wonderful guide (400 zł for up to 4 hours, more for all day, mobile 502-554-584, www. tourguidegdansk.com, asyroka@interia.pl or syroka.agnieszka@ gmail.com).

Gdańsk Walk

In the 16th and 17th centuries, Gdańsk was Poland's wealthiest city, with gorgeous architecture (much of it in the Flemish Mannerist style) rivaling that in
the two historic capitals,
Kraków and Warsaw. During this Golden Age, Polish kings would visit this
city of well-to-do Hanseatic
League merchants and gawk
along the same route trod by
tourists today.

The following self-guided walk (rated ▲▲▲) introduces you to the best of Gdańsk. It bridges the two historic centers (the Main Town and the Old Town), dips into St. Mary's Church (the city's most important church), and ends at the famous shipyards and Solidarity Square (where Poland began what ultimately brought down the USSR). I've divided the walk into two parts (making it easier to split up, if you like): The first half focuses on a loop through the Main Town (with most of the high-profile sights), while the second part carries on northward, through the less-touristy Old Town to the shipyards.

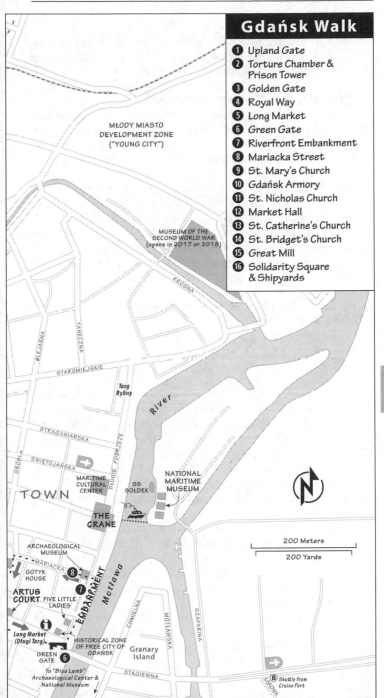

Gdańsk Walk

1. Upland Gate
2. Torture Chamber & Prison Tower
3. Golden Gate
4. Royal Way
5. Long Market
6. Green Gate
7. Riverfront Embankment
8. Mariacka Street
9. St. Mary's Church
10. Gdańsk Armory
11. St. Nicholas Church
12. Market Hall
13. St. Catherine's Church
14. St. Bridget's Church
15. Great Mill
16. Solidarity Square & Shipyards

MŁODY MIASTO DEVELOPMENT ZONE ("YOUNG CITY")

MUSEUM OF THE SECOND WORLD WAR (opens in 2017 or 2018)

KROSNA

PIEJARNA

TANECZNA

STAROMIEJSKIE

Targ Rybny

River

STRAGANIARSKA

ŚWIĘTOJAŃSKA

GROBLA

MARITIME CULTURAL CENTER

SS SOŁDEK

NATIONAL MARITIME MUSEUM

TOWN

THE CRANE

ARCHAEOLOGICAL MUSEUM

MARIACKA

GOTYK HOUSE

ARTUS COURT

FIVE LITTLE LADIES

Long Market (Długi Targ)

GREEN GATE

To "Blue Lamb" Archaeological Center & National Museum

HISTORICAL ZONE OF FREE CITY OF GDAŃSK

Granary Island

STAGIEWNA

DŁUGIE POBRZEŻE

EMBANKMENT

Motława

CHMIELNA

MOTŁAWSKA

SZAFARINA

ŁASOŃA

B Shuttle from Cruise Port

200 Meters

200 Yards

N

PART 1: THE MAIN TOWN

• *Begin at the west end of the Main Town, just beyond the last gate at the edge of the busy road (at a road sign that says* Sztokholm...*a reminder that the car ferry to Sweden leaves from near here).*

❶ Upland Gate (Brama Wyżynna)

The Main Town's fortifications were expanded with a Renaissance wall bound by the Upland Gate (built in 1588). "Upland" refers to the hills you see beyond—considered high country in this flat region. Standing with your back to the busy arterial (which traces the old moat), study the gate. Find its three coats of arms (the black eagle for Royal Prussia, the crowned white eagle for Poland, and the two crosses for Gdańsk). Recall that this city has, for almost the entirety of its history before the mid-20th century, been bicultural: German and Polish, coexisting more or less peacefully. Also notice the little wheels that once hoisted a drawbridge.

• *It's a straight line from here to the river. Walk through the arch (which houses a TI) to the next arch, just a few steps ahead.*

❷ Torture Chamber (Katownia) and Prison Tower (Wieża Więzienna)

The tall, Gothic brick gate before you was part of an earlier protective wall made useless after the Renaissance walls were built in 1588. While today these structures house the Amber Museum (described later), it's free to walk through the evocative passage. Inside, find gargoyles (on the left, a town specialty) and the shackles from which prisoners were hung (on the right). Look up at the inside of the high gable to the headless man, identifying this as the torture chamber. This old jail—with its 15-foot-thick walls—was used as a prison even in modern times, under Nazi occupation.

As you leave the Torture Chamber and Prison Tower, look to your left (100 yards away) to see a long, brick building with four fancy, uniform gables. This is the **Armory** (Zbrojownia), one of the finest examples of Dutch Renaissance architecture anywhere. Though this part of the building appears to have the facades of four separate houses, it's an urban camouflage to hide its real purpose from potential attackers. But there's at least one clue to what the building is really for: Notice the exploding cannonballs at the tops of the turrets. (We'll get a better look at the Armory from the other side, later in this walk.)

The round, pointy-topped tower next to the Armory is the **Straw Tower** (Baszta Słomiana). Gunpowder was stored here, and the roof was straw—so if it exploded, it could easily blow its top without destroying the walls.

• *Straight ahead, the final and fanciest gate between you and the Main Town is the...*

❸ Golden Gate (Złota Brama)

While the other gates were defensive, this one's purely ornamental. The four women up top represent virtues that the people of

Gdańsk should exhibit toward outsiders (left to right): Peace, Freedom, Prosperity, and Fame. The gold-lettered inscription, a psalm in medieval German, compares Gdańsk to Jerusalem: famous and important. Directly above the arch is the Gdańsk coat of arms: two white crosses under a crown on a red shield. We'll see this symbol all over town. Photographers love the view of the Main Town framed in this arch. Inside the arch, study the old photos showing the 1945 bomb damage. On the left is the glorious view you just enjoyed...ravaged by war. And on the right is a heartbreaking aerial view of the city in 1945, when 80 percent of its buildings were in ruins.

• *Passing through the Golden Gate, you reach the Main Town's main drag.*

❹ The Royal Way

Before you stretches ulica Długa (cleverly called the "Long Street") the main promenade of what, 600 years ago, was the biggest and richest city in Poland, thanks to its profitable ties to the Hanseatic League of merchant cities. This promenade is nicknamed the "Royal Way" because (just as in Warsaw and Kraków) the king would follow this route when visiting town.

Walk half a block, and then look back at the Golden Gate. The women on top of this side represent virtues the people of Gdańsk should cultivate in themselves (left to right): Wisdom, Piety, Justice, and Concord (if an arrow's broken, let's take it out of the quiver and fix it). The inscription—sharing a bit of wisdom as apropos today as it was in 1612—reads, "Concord makes small countries develop, and discord makes big countries fall." Gdańsk was cosmopolitan and exceptionally tolerant in the Middle Ages, attracting a wide range of people, including many who were persecuted elsewhere: Jews, Scots, Dutch, Flemish, Italians, Germans, and more. Members of each group brought with them strands of their culture, which they wove into the tapestry of this city—demonstrated by the eclectic homes along this street. Each facade and each gable were different, as nobles and aristocrats wanted to display their wealth. On my last visit, a traveler seeing this street for the first time gasped to me, "It's like stepping into a Fabergé egg."

During Gdańsk's Golden Age, these houses were taxed based on frontage (like the homes lining Amsterdam's canals)—so they were built skinny and deep. The widest houses belonged to the super-elite. Different as they are from the outside, every house had the same general plan inside. Each had three parts, starting with the front and moving back: First was a fancy drawing room, to show off for visitors. Then came a narrow corridor to the back rooms—often along the side of an inner courtyard. Because the houses had only a few windows facing the outer street, this court-yard provided much-needed sunlight to the rest of the house. The residential quarters were in the back, where the family actually lived: bedroom, kitchen, office. To see the interior of one of these homes, pay a visit to the interesting **Uphagen House** (at #12, on the right, a block and a half in front of the Golden Gate; described later).

This lovely street wasn't always so lively and carefree. At the end of World War II, the Royal Way was in ruins. That epic war actually began here, in what was then the "Free City of Danzig." Following World War I, nobody could decide what to do with this influential and multiethnic city. So, rather than assign it to Germany or Poland, it was set apart as its own little autonomous state-let. In 1939, Danzig was 80 percent German-speaking—enough for Hitler to consider it his. And so, on September 1 of that year, the Nazis seized it in one day with relatively minor damage (though the attack on the Polish military garrison on the city's Westerplatte peninsula lasted a week).

But six years later, when the Soviets arrived (March 30, 1945), the city was left devastated. This was the first traditionally German city that the Red Army took on their march toward Berlin. And, while it was easy for the Soviets to seize the almost empty city, the commander then insisted that it be leveled, building by build-ing—in retaliation for all the pain the Nazis had caused in Russia. (Soviets didn't destroy nearby Gdynia, which they considered Pol-ish rather than German.) Soviet officers turned a blind eye as their soldiers raped and brutalized residents. An entire order of horrified nuns committed suicide by throwing themselves into the river.

It was only thanks to detailed drawings and photographs that these buildings could be so carefully reconstructed. Notice the cheap plaster facades done in the 1950s—rough times under com-munism, in the decade after World War II. (Most of the town's medieval brick was shipped to Warsaw for a communist-sponsored "rebuild the capital first" campaign.) While the fine facades were restored, the buildings behind the facades were completely rebuilt to modern standards.

Just beyond Uphagen House, **Cukiernia Sowa** ("The Owl," on the right at #13) is *the* place for cakes and coffee. Directly across the street, **Grycan** (at #73) has been a favorite for ice cream here for generations.

Just a few doors down, on the left, are some of the most striking **facades** along the Royal Way. The blue-and-white house with the three giant heads is from the 19th century, when the hot style was eclecticism—borrowing bits and pieces from various architectural eras. This was one of the few houses on the street that survived World War II.

At the next corner on the right is the huge, blocky, red **post office,** which doesn't quite fit with the skinny facades lining the rest of the street. Step inside. With doves fluttering under an airy glass atrium, the interior's a class act. Directly across the street, the candy shop **(Ciuciu Cukier Artist)** is often filled with children clamoring to see lollipop-making demos. Step in and inhale a universal whiff of childhood.

A few doors farther down, on the left at #62, pop into the **Millennium Gallery** amber shop (which would love to give you an educational amber polishing demo) to see the fascinating collection of old-timey photos, letting you directly compare Gdańsk's cityscape before and after the WWII destruction.

Above the next door, notice the colorful **scenes.** These are slices of life from 17th-century Gdańsk: drinking, talking, buying, playing music. The ship is a *koga,* a typical symbol of Hanseatic ports like Gdańsk.

Across the street and a few steps down are the fancy facades of three houses belonging to the very influential medieval **Ferber family,** which produced many burghers, mayors, and even a bishop. On the house with the little dog over the door (#29), look for the heads in the circular medallions. These are Caesars of Rome. At the top of the building is Mr. Ferber's answer to the constant question, "Why build such an elaborate house?"—*PRO INVIDIA,* "For the sake of envy."

A few doors down, on the right, is Gdańsk's most scenically situated milk bar, the recommended **Bar Mleczny Neptun.** Back in communist times, these humble cafeterias were subsidized to give workers an affordable place to eat out. To this day, they offer simple and very cheap grub.

Next door (at #35) is the **Russian Culture Center,** with Russian movies and art exhibits. With a complicated history—and many Poles now siding with Ukraine in their stand against Vladimir Putin's incursion into Ukrainian territory—this is a poignant address.

Before you stands the **Main Town Hall** (Ratusz Głównego Miasta) with its mighty brick clock tower. Consider climbing its

Gdańsk History

Visitors to Gdańsk are surprised at how "un-Polish" the city's history is. In this cultural melting pot of German, Dutch, and Flemish merchants (with a smattering of Italians and Scots), Poles were only a small part of the picture until the city became exclusively Polish after World War II. However, in Gdańsk, cultural backgrounds traditionally took a back seat to the bottom line. Wealthy Gdańsk was always known for its economic pragmatism—no matter who was in charge, merchants here made money.

Gdańsk is Poland's gateway to the waters of Europe, where its main river (the Vistula) meets the Baltic Sea. The town was first mentioned in the 10th century, and was seized in 1308 by the Teutonic Knights (who called it "Danzig"; for more on the Teutonic Knights, see page 290). The Knights encouraged other Germans to settle on the Baltic coast, and gradually turned Gdańsk into a wealthy city. In 1361, Gdańsk joined the Hanseatic League, a trade federation of mostly Germanic merchant towns that provided mutual security. By the 15th century, Gdańsk was a leading member of this mighty network, which virtually dominated trade in northern Europe (and also included Toruń, Kraków, Lübeck, Hamburg, Bremen, Bruges, Bergen, Tallinn, Novgorod, and nearly a hundred other cities).

In 1454, the people of Gdańsk rose up against the Teutonic Knights, burning down their castle and forcing them out of the city. Three years later, the Polish king borrowed money from wealthy Gdańsk families to hire Czech mercenaries to take the Teutonic Knights' main castle, Malbork (described in the next chapter). In exchange, the Gdańsk merchants were granted special privileges, including exclusive export rights. Gdańsk now acted as a middleman for much of the trade passing through Polish lands, and paid only a modest annual tribute to the Polish king.

The 16th and 17th centuries were Gdańsk's Golden Age. Now a part of the Polish kingdom, the city had access to an enormous hinterland of natural resources to export—yet it maintained a privileged, semi-independent status. Like Amsterdam, Gdańsk became a progressive and booming merchant city. Its mostly Germanic and Dutch burghers imported Dutch, Flemish, and Italian architects to give their homes an appropriately Hanseatic flourish. At a time of religious upheaval in the rest of Europe, Gdańsk became known for its tolerance—a place that opened its doors to all visitors (many Mennonites and Scottish religious refugees emigrated here). It was also a haven for great thinkers, including philosopher Arthur Schopenhauer and scientist Daniel Fahrenheit (who invented the mercury thermometer).

Along with the rest of Poland, Gdańsk declined in the late 18th century and became part of Prussia (today's northern Germany) during the Partitions. But the people of Gdańsk—even those of German heritage—had taken pride in their independence and weren't enthusiastic about being ruled from Berlin. After World War I, in a unique compromise to appease its complex ethnic makeup, Gdańsk did not fall under German or Polish control, but once again became an independent city-state: the Free City of Danzig (populated by 400,000 ethnic Germans and 15,000 Poles). The city, along with the so-called Polish Corridor connecting it to Polish lands, effectively cut off Germany from its northeastern territory. On September 1, 1939, Adolf Hitler started World War II when he invaded Gdańsk in order to bring it back into the German fold. Later, nearly 80 percent of the city was destroyed when the Soviets "liberated" it from Nazi control.

After World War II, Gdańsk officially became part of Poland, and was painstakingly reconstructed (mostly replicating the buildings of its Golden Age). In 1970, and again in 1980, the shipyard of Gdańsk witnessed strikes and demonstrations that would lead to the fall of European communism. Poland's great anticommunist hero and first postcommunist president, Lech Wałęsa, is Gdańsk's most famous resident, and still lives here. When he flies around the world to give talks, he leaves from Gdańsk's "Lech Wałęsa Airport."

A city with a recent past that's both tragic and uplifting, Gdańsk celebrated its 1,000th birthday in 1997. Very roughly, the city has spent about 700 years as an independent entity, and about 300 years under Germanic overlords (the Teutonic Knights, Prussia, and the Nazis). But today, Gdańsk is decidedly its own city. And, as if eager to prove it, Gdańsk is making big improvements at a stunning pace: new museums (the European Solidarity Center and World War II Museum), cultural facilities (the Shakespeare Theater), sports venues (a stadium that resembles a blob of amber, built for the 2012 Euro Cup tournament), and an ongoing surge of renovation and refurbishment that has the gables of the atmospheric Hanseatic quarter gleaming once again.

observation tower and visiting its superb interior, which features ornately decorated meeting rooms for the city council (described later).

• *Just beyond the Main Town Hall, ulica Długa widens and becomes...*

❺ The Long Market (Długi Targ)

Step from the Long Street into the Long Market, and do a slow, 360-degree spin to appreciate the amazing array of proud architecture here in a city center that rivals the magnificent Grand Place in Brussels. The centerpiece of this square is one of Gdańsk's most important landmarks, the statue of **Neptune**—god of the sea. He's a fitting symbol for a city that dominates the maritime life of Poland. Behind him is another worthwhile museum, the **Artus Court.** Step up to the magnificent door and study the golden relief just above, celebrating the Vistula River (in so many ways the lifeblood of the Polish nation): Lady Vistula is exhausted after her heroic journey, and is finally carried by Neptune to her ultimate destination, the Baltic Sea. (This is just a preview of the ornate art

that fills the interior of this fine building—described later.)

Midway down the Long Market (on the right, across from the Hard Rock Café) is a glass case with the **thermometer and barometer of Daniel Fahrenheit.** Although that scientist was born here, he did his groundbreaking work in Amsterdam.

• *At the end of the Long Market is the...*

❻ Green Gate (Zielona Brama)

This huge gate (named for the Green Bridge just beyond) was actually built as a residence for visiting kings...who usually preferred to stay back by Neptune instead (maybe because the river, just on the other side of this gate, stank). It might not have been good enough for kings and queens, but it's plenty fine for a former president: Lech Wałęsa's office is upstairs (see the plaque on the left side, *Biuro Lecha Wałęsy*). His windows, up in the gable, overlook the Long Market. A few steps down the skinny lane to the left is the endearing little **Historical Zone of the Free City of Gdańsk** museum, which explains the interwar period when "Danzig" was an independent and bicultural city-state (described later).

• *Now go through the gate, walk out onto the Green Bridge, anchor yourself in a niche on the left, and look downstream.*

❼ Riverfront Embankment

The Motława River—a side channel of the mighty Vistula—flows into the nearby Baltic Sea. This port was the source of Gdańsk's phenomenal Golden Age wealth. This embankment was jam-packed in its heyday, the 14th and 15th centuries. It was so crowded with boats that you would hardly have been able to see the water, and boats had to pay a time-based moorage fee for tying up to a post.

Look back at the Green Gate and notice that these bricks are much smaller than the locally-made ones we saw earlier on this walk. These bricks are Dutch: Boats from Holland would come here empty of cargo, but with a load of bricks for ballast. Traders filled their ships with goods for the return trip, leaving the bricks behind.

The old-fashioned **galleons** and other tour boats moored nearby depart hourly for a fun cruise to Westerplatte (where on September 1, 1939, Germans fired the first shots of World War II) and back. Though kitschy, the galleons are a fun way to get out on the water (details on page 274).

Across the river is **Granary Island** (Wyspa Spichrzów), where grain was stored until it could be taken away by ships. Before World War II, there were some 400 granaries here. Today, much of the island is still in ruins while developers make their plans. Recently, the city ringed the island with an inviting boardwalk, which offers a restful escape from the city and fine views across the narrow river to the embankment. In the summer, sometimes they erect a big Ferris wheel here. And someday there will be several more rebuilt granaries in this area (likely mixed with modern buildings) to match the ones you already see on either side of the bridge. The three rebuilt granaries downstream, in the distance on the next island, house exhibits for the National Maritime Museum (described later).

From your perch on the bridge, look down the embankment

(about 500 yards, on the left) and find the huge wooden **Crane (Żuraw)** bulging over the water. This monstrous 15th-century crane—a rare example of medieval port technology—was once used for loading and repairing ships...beginning a shipbuilding tradition that continued to the days of Lech Wałęsa. The crane mechanism was operated by several workers scrambling around in giant hamster wheels. Treading away to engage the gears and pulleys, they could lift 4 tons up 30 feet, or 2 tons up 90 feet.

• *Walk along the embankment about halfway to*

*the Crane, passing the lower embankment, with excursion boats heading to the Westerplatte monument. Pause when you reach the big brick building with green window frames and a tower. This red-brick fort houses the **Archaeological Museum** (described later). Its collection includes the five ancient stones in a small garden just outside its door (on the left). These are the **Prussian Hags**—mysterious sculptures from the second century A.D. (each described in posted plaques).*

Turn left through the gate in the middle of the brick building. You'll find yourself on the most charming lane in town...

❽ Mariacka Street

The calm, atmospheric "Mary's Street" leads from the embankment to St. Mary's Church. Stroll the length of it, enjoying the most romantic lane in Gdańsk. The **porches** extending out into the street, with access to cellars underneath, were a common feature in Gdańsk's Golden Age. For practical reasons, after the war, these were restored only on this street. Notice how the porches are bordered with fine stone relief panels and gargoyles attached to storm drains. If you get stuck there in a hard rainstorm, you'll understand why in Polish these are called "pukers." Enjoy a little amber comparison-shopping. As you stroll up to the towering brick St. Mary's Church, imagine the entire city like this cobbled lane of proud merchants' homes, with street music, delightful facades, and brick church towers high above.

Look up at the church tower viewpoint—filled with people who hiked 409 steps for the view. Our next stop is the church, which you'll enter on the far side under the tower. Walk around the left side of the church, appreciating the handmade 14th-century bricks on the right and the plain post-WWII facades on the left. (Reconstructing the Royal Way was better funded. Here, the priority was simply getting people housed again.) In the distance is the fancy facade of the Armory (where you'll head after visiting the church).

• *But first, go inside...*

❾ St. Mary's Church (Kościół Mariacki)

Of Gdańsk's 13 medieval red-brick churches, St. Mary's (rated ▲▲) is the one you must visit. It's the largest brick church in the world—with a footprint bigger than a football field (350 feet long and 210 feet wide), it can accommodate 20,000 standing worshippers.

Cost and Hours: 4 zł, 6 zł also includes tower climb—described later; Mon-Sat 8:30-18:30, Sun 11:00-12:00 & 13:00-18:30; Oct-April daily until 17:00; tower closed Dec-late March.

➔ **Self-Guided Tour:** Inside, sit directly under the fine carved and painted 17th-century Protestant pulpit, midway down the nave, to get oriented.

Overview: Built from 1343 to 1502 by the Teutonic Knights (who wanted a suitable centerpiece for their newly-captured main city), St. Mary's remains an important symbol of Gdańsk. The church started out Catholic, became Lutheran in the mid-1500s, and then became Catholic again after World War II. (Remember, Gdańsk was a Germanic city before World War II and part of the big postwar demographic shove, when Germans were sent west, and Poles from the east relocated here. Desperate, cold, and homeless, the new Polish residents moved into what was left of the German homes.) While the church was originally frescoed from top to bottom, the Lutherans whitewashed the entire place. Today, some of the 16th-century whitewash has been peeled back (behind the high altar—we'll see this area soon), revealing a bit of the original frescoes. The floor is paved with 500 gravestones of merchant families. Many of these were cracked when bombing sent the brick roof crashing down in 1945.

Most Gothic stone churches are built of stone in the basilica style—with a high nave in the middle, shorter aisles on the side,

and flying buttresses to support the weight. (Think of Paris' Notre-Dame.) But with no handy source of stone available locally, most Polish churches are built of brick, which won't work with the basilica design. So, like all Gdańsk churches, St. Mary's is a "hall church"—with three naves the same height and no exterior buttresses.

Also like other Gdańsk churches, St. Mary's gave refuge to the Polish people after the communist government declared martial law in 1981. When a riot broke out and violence seemed imminent, people flooded into churches, knowing that the ZOMO riot police wouldn't dare follow them inside.

Most of the church decorations are original. A few days before the Soviets arrived to "liberate" the city in 1945, locals—knowing what was in store—hid precious items in the countryside. Take some time now to see a few of the highlights.

• *From this spot, you can see most of what we'll visit in the church: As you face the altar, the astronomical clock is at 10 o'clock, the Ferber family medallion is at 1 o'clock, the Priests' Chapel is at 3 o'clock (under a tall, colorful window), and the magnificent 17th-century organ is directly behind you (it's played at each Mass and during free concerts on Fri in summer).*

Pulpit: For Protestants, the pulpit is important. Designed as

GDAŃSK & THE TRI-CITY

an impressive place from which to share the Word of God in the people's language, it's located midnave, so all can hear.

• *Opposite the pulpit is the moving...*

Priests' Chapel: The 1965 statue of Christ weeping commemorates 2,779 Polish chaplains executed by the Nazis because they were priests. See the grainy black-and-white photo of one about to be shot, above on the right.

• *Head up the nave to the...*

High Altar: The main altar, beautifully carved in 1517, is a triptych showing the coronation of Mary. She is surrounded by the Trinity: flanked by God and Jesus, with the dove representing the Holy Spirit overhead. The church's medieval stained glass was destroyed in 1945. Poland's biggest stained-glass window, behind the altar, is from 1980.

• *Start circling around the right side of the altar. Look right to find (high on a pillar) the big, opulent family marker.*

Ferber Family Medallion: The falling baby (under the crown) is Constantine Ferber. As a precocious child, li'l Constantine leaned out his window on the Royal Way to see the king's processional come through town. He slipped and fell, but landed in a salesman's barrel of fish. Constantine grew up to become the mayor of Gdańsk.

• *As you continue around behind the altar, search high above you, on the walls to your right, to spot those restored pre–Reformation frescoes. Directly behind the altar, under the big window, is the...*

Empty Glass Case: This case was designed to hold Hans Memling's *Last Judgment* painting, which used to be in this church, but is currently being held hostage by the National Museum (described on page 262). To counter the museum's claim that the church wasn't a good environment for such a precious work, the priest had this display case built—but that still wasn't enough to convince the museum to give the painting back. (You'll see a small replica of the painting in the rear of this church.)

• *Now circle back the way you came to the area in front of the main altar, and proceed straight ahead into the transept. High on the wall to your right, look for the...*

Astronomical Clock: This 42-foot-tall clock is supposedly the biggest wooden clock in the world. Below it is an elaborate circular calendar that, like a medieval computer, calculates on which day each saint's festival day falls in different years (see the little guy on the left, with the pointer). Above are zodiac signs and the time (back then, the big hand was all you needed). Way up on top, Adam and Eve are naked and ready to ring the bell. Adam's been swinging his clapper at the top of the hour since 1473...but sadly, the clock is broken.

• *A few steps in front of the clock is a modern chapel with the...*

Memorial to the Polish Victims of the 2010 Plane Crash: The gold-shrouded Black Madonna honors the 96 victims of an air disaster that killed much of Poland's government—including the president and first lady—during a terrible storm over Russia. The main tomb is for Maciej Płażyński, from Gdańsk, who was leader of the parliament. On the left, the jagged statue has bits of the wreckage and lists each victim by name.

• *In a small chapel in the rear corner of the church—on the far right with your back to the high altar—you'll find the...*

Pietà and Memling Replica: The *pietà*, carved of limestone and painted in 1410, is by the Master of Gdańsk. In the same room is a musty old copy of Memling's *Last Judgment*—the exquisite original once graced this very chapel. If you're not planning to go see it at the National Museum, you could read the description on page 263 now.

• *Next door are stairs leading to the...*

Church Tower: You can climb 409 steps to burn off some pierogi and earn a grand city view. It's a long hike (and you'll know it—every 10th step is numbered). But because the viewpoint is surrounded by a roof, the views are distant and may not be worth the effort. The first third is up a tight, medieval spiral staircase. Then you'll walk through the eerie, cavernous area between the roof and the ceiling, before huffing up steep concrete steps that surround the square tower (as you spiral up, up, up around the bells). Finally you'll climb a little metal ladder and pop out at the viewpoint.

• *Leaving the church, angle left and continue straight up ulica Piwna ("Beer Street") toward the sprightly facade of the Armory.*

❿ The Gdańsk Armory (Zbrojownia)

The 1605 armory, which we saw from a distance at the start of this walk, is one of the best examples of Dutch Renaissance architecture in Europe. Athena, the goddess of war and wisdom, stands in the center, amid motifs of war and ornamental pukers.

• *If you want to make your walk a loop, you're just a block away from where we started (to the left). But there's much more to see. Facing the Armory, turn right and start the second half of this walk.*

PART 2: THROUGH THE OLD TOWN TO THE SHIPYARDS

• *From here, we'll work our way out of the Main Town and head into the Old Town, toward Solidarity Square and the shipyards. We'll be walking along this street (which changes names a couple of times) nearly all the way. Keep in mind that this part of the walk ends at the European Solidarity Center's fine museum. You'll want plenty of time to tour the museum and linger over its exhibits, so if you're already pooped or it's getting late in the day, consider finishing this walk another time.*

From the Armory, head down Kołodziejska, which quickly becomes Węglarska. After two blocks (that is, one block before the big market hall), detour to the right down Świętojańska and use the side door to enter the brick church.

⓫ St. Nicholas Church (Kościół Św. Mikołaja)

Near the end of World War II, when the Soviet army reached Gdańsk on its march westward, they were given the order to burn all the churches. Only this one survived—because it happened to be dedicated to Russia's patron saint. As the best-preserved church in town, it has a more impressive interior than the others, with lavish black-and-gold Baroque altars.

• Backtrack out to the main street and continue along it, passing a row of seniors selling their grown and foraged edibles. Immediately after the church is Gdańsk's...

⓬ Market Hall

Built in 1896 and renovated in 2005, Gdańsk's market hall is fun to explore. Appreciate the delicate steel-and-glass canopy over-head. This is a totally untouristy scene: You'll see everything from skintight *Polska* T-shirts, to wedding gowns, to maternity wear. The meat is downstairs, and the veggies are outside on the adjacent square. As this was once the center of a monastic community, the basement has the graves of medieval Dominican monks, which were exposed when the building was refurbished: Peer over the glass railing, and you'll see some of those scant remains.

Across the street from the Market Hall, a round, red-brick **tower,** part of the city's protective wall back in 1400, marks the end of the Main Town and the beginning of the Old Town.

• Another block up the street, on the right, is the huge...

⓭ St. Catherine's Church (Kościół Św. Katarzyny)

"Katy," as locals call it, is the oldest church in Gdańsk. In May of 2006, a carelessly discarded cigarette caused the church roof to burst into flames. Local people ran into the church and pulled everything outside, so nothing valuable was damaged; even the carillon bells were saved. However, the roof and wooden frame were totally destroyed. The people of Gdańsk were determined to rebuild this important symbol of the city. Within days of the fire, fundraising concerts were held to scrape together most of the money needed to raise the roof once more. Step inside. On the left side of the gate leading to the nave, photos show bomb damage. Farther in, on the left, are vivid photos of the more recent conflagration. The interior is evocative, with still-bare-brick walls that almost seem intentional—as if they're trying for an industrial-mod look.

• The church hiding a block behind Katy—named for Catherine's daugh-

ter Bridget—has important ties to Solidarity and is worth a visit. Go around the right side of Katy and skirt the parking lot to find the entrance.

⓮ St. Bridget's Church (Kościół Św. Brygidy)

This was the home church of Lech Wałęsa during the tense days of the 1980s. The church and its priest, Henryk Jankowski, were particularly aggressive in supporting the ideals of Solidarity. Jankowski became a mouthpiece for the movement. In gratitude for the church's support, Wałęsa named his youngest daughter Brygida.

Cost and Hours: 2 zł, daily 10:00-18:00.

Visiting the Church: Head inside. For your visit, start at the high altar, then circle clockwise back to the entry.

The enormous, unfinished **high altar** is made entirely of amber—more than a thousand square feet of it. Features that are already in place include the Black Madonna of Częstochowa, a royal Polish eagle, and the Solidarity symbol (tucked below the Black Madonna). The structure, like a scaffold, holds pieces as they are completed and added to the ensemble. The video you may see playing overhead gives you a close-up look at the amber elements.

The wrought-iron gate of the adjacent **Chapel of Fatima** (right of main altar) recalls great battles and events in Polish history from 966 to 1939, with important dates boldly sparkling in gold. Some say the Polish Church is too political. But it was only through a politically-engaged Church that this culture survived the Partitions of Poland over a century and a half, plus the brutal anti-religious policies of the communist period. The national soul of the Polish people—whether religious or not—is tied up in the Catholic faith.

Henryk Jankowski's tomb—a white marble box with red trim—is a bit farther to the right. Jankowski was a key hero during Solidarity times; the tomb proclaims him *Kapelan Solidarności* ("Solidarity Chaplain"). But his public standing took a nosedive near the end of his life—thanks to ego-driven projects like his amber altar, as well as accusations of anti-Semitism and corruption. Forced to retire in 2007, Jankowski died in 2010. (An offering box is next to his tomb, if you'd like to donate to the amber altar project.)

In the rear corner, where a figure lies lifeless on the floor under a wall full of wooden crosses, is the tomb of Solidarity martyr **Jerzy Popiełuszko**. A courageous and famously outspoken Warsaw priest, in 1984 Popiełuszko was kidnapped, beaten, and murdered by the communist secret police. Notice that the figure's hands and feet are bound—as his body was found. The crosses are historic—each one was carried at various strikes against the communist regime. The communists believed they could break the spirit of the Poles with brutality—like the murder of Popiełuszko. But it only made the rebels stronger and more resolved to ultimately win their freedom. (Near the exit, on a monitor, a fascinating 12-minute video shows great moments of this church, with commentary by Lech Wałęsa himself.)

• *Return to the main street, turn right, and continue on. The big brick building ahead on the left, with the many windows, is the Great Mill. Walk past that and look down at the canal that once powered it.*

⓯ The Great Mill

This huge brick building dates from the 14th century. Look at the waterfalls and imagine standing here in 1400—with the mill's 18 wheels spinning 24/7, powering grindstones that produced 20 tons of flour a day. Like so much else here, the mill survived until 1945. Until recently it housed a shopping mall, but it may soon become home to one of the city's many museums.

The **park** just beyond the mill is worth a look. In the distance is the Old City Town Hall (Dutch Renaissance style, from 1595). The monument in the middle honors the 17th-century astronomer Jan Haweliusz. He's looking up at a giant, rust-colored wall with a map of the heavens. Haweliusz built the biggest telescopes of his era to better appreciate and understand the cosmos. Behind the mill stands the miller's home—its opulence indicates that, back in the Middle Ages, there was a lot of money in grinding. Just steps into the family-friendly park is a fountain that brings shrieks of joy to children on hot summer days.

• *To get to the **shipyards,** keep heading straight up Rajska. You'll pass the modern Madison shopping mall. After another long block, jog right, passing to the right of the big, ugly, and green 1970s–era skyscraper. On your right, marked by the famous red sign on the roof, is today's **Solidarity headquarters** (which remains the strongest trade union in Poland, with 700,000 members, and is also active in many other countries). Just in front of the Solidarity building, you may see two big chunks of **wall:** a piece of the Berlin Wall and a stretch of the shipyard wall that Lech Wałęsa scaled to get inside and lead the strike. The message: What happened behind one wall eventually led to the fall of the other Wall.*

From here, hike on (about 100 yards) to the finale of this walk.

⑯ Solidarity Square and the Shipyards

Three tall crosses mark Solidarity Square and the rust-colored European Solidarity Center (with an excellent museum). For the exciting story of how Polish shipbuilders set in motion events that led to the end of the USSR, turn to page 251.

Sights in Gdańsk

MAIN TOWN (GŁÓWNE MIASTO)

The following sights are all in the Main Town, listed roughly in the order you'll see them on the self-guided walk of the Royal Way.

Gdańsk Historical Museum

The Gdańsk Historical Museum has four excellent branches: the Amber Museum, Uphagen House, Main Town Hall, and Artus Court. Along with St. Mary's Church (described on page 238), these are the four most important interiors in the Main Town. All have the same hours, but you must buy a separate ticket for each.

Cost and Hours: 10 zł for Uphagen House and Artus Court, 12 zł for Amber Museum and Main Town Hall; hours fluctuate, but typically open mid-June-mid-Sept Mon-Thu 9:00-16:00, Fri-Sat 10:00-18:00, Sun 10:00-16:00; mid-Sept-mid-June Tue 10:00-13:00, Wed-Sat 10:00-16:00, Thu until 18:00, Sun 11:00-16:00, closed Mon.

Information: The museums share a phone number and website (central tel. 58-767 9100, www.mhmg.gda.pl).

▲Amber Museum (Muzeum Bursztynu)

Housed in a pair of connected brick towers (the former Prison Tower and Torture Chamber) just outside the Main Town's Golden

Gate, this museum has two oddly contradictory parts. One shows off Gdańsk's favorite local resource, amber, while the other focuses on implements of torture. You'll follow the one-way route through four exhibits on amber (with lots of stairs), and then walk the rampart to the other tower for a little torture (the 1.5-hour audioguide is overpriced at 25 zł). For a primer before you visit, read the "All About Amber" sidebar.

Visiting the Museum: The exhibit has four parts: First, head up to the **second floor** for a scientific look at amber. View inclusions (organic items trapped in resin) through a magnifying glass and microscope, and see dozens of samples showing the full rainbow of amber shades. Interactive video screens ex-

All About Amber

Poland's Baltic seaside is known as the Amber Coast. You can see amber *(bursztyn)* in Gdańsk's Amber Museum, in the collection at Malbork Castle (see the Pomerania chapter), and in shop windows everywhere. This fossilized tree resin originated here on the north coast of Poland 40 million years ago. It comes in as many different colors as Eskimos have words for snow: 300 distinct shades, from yellowish white to yellowish black, from opaque to transparent. (I didn't believe it either, until I toured Gdańsk's museum.) Darker-colored amber is generally mixed with ash and sand—making it more fragile, and generally less desirable. Lighter amber is mixed with gasses and air bubbles.

Amber has been popular since long before there were souvenir stands. Archaeologists have found Roman citizens (and their coins) buried with crosses made of amber. Almost 75 percent of the world's amber is mined in northern Poland, and it often simply washes up on the beaches after a winter storm. Some of the elaborate amber sculptures displayed at the museum are joined with "amber glue"—melted-down amber mixed with an adhesive agent. More recently, amber craftsmen are combining amber with silver to create artwork—a method dubbed the "Polish School."

Some Poles believe that, in addition to being good for the economy, amber is good for their health. A traditional cure for arthritis pain is to pour strong vodka over amber, let it set, and then rub it on sore joints. Other remedies call for mixing amber dust with honey or rose oil. It sounds superstitious, but users claim that it works.

plain the creation of amber. The **third-floor** exhibit explains the "Amber Route" (the ancient Celtic trade road connecting Gdańsk to Italy) and medicinal uses of the stuff, and displays a wide range of functional items made from amber—clocks, pipe stems, candlesticks, chandeliers, jewelry boxes, and much more. Take a whiff—what's that smell? It's a cathedral. Amber is an ingredient in incense. The **fourth floor** shows off more artistic items made of amber—sculptures, candelabras, beer steins, chessboards, and a model ship with delicate sails made of amber. At the **top floor,** you'll find a modern gallery showing more recent amber craftsmanship and displays about amber's role in fashion today.

Then, walking along the upper rampart level of the courtyard, you'll enter an exhibit about the building itself and the town's fortifications. This leads to the **Prison Tower** and the torture exhibit—with sound effects, scant artifacts, and mannequins helpfully demonstrating the grisly equipment.

▲Uphagen House (Dom Uphagena)

This interesting place, at ulica Długa 12, is your chance to glimpse what's behind the colorful facades lining this street. It's the only grand Gdańsk mansion rebuilt as it was before 1945. The model near the entry shows the three parts: dolled-up visitors' rooms in front, a corridor along the courtyard, and private rooms in the back. The finely decorated salon was used to show off for guests. Most of this furniture is original (saved from WWII bombs by locals who hid it in the countryside). Passing into the dining room, note the knee-high paintings of hunting and celebrations. Along the passage to the back, each room has a theme: butterflies in the smoking room, then flowers in the next room, then birds in the music room. In the private rooms at the back, the decor is simpler. Downstairs, you'll pass through the kitchen, the pantry, and a room with photos of the house before the war, which were used to reconstruct what you see today.

▲▲Main Town Hall (Ratusz Głównego Miasta)

This landmark building contains remarkable decorations from Gdańsk's Golden Age. You can also climb 293 concrete steps to

the top of the **tower** for commanding views (5 zł extra, mid-June-mid-Sept only).

Visiting the Main Town Hall: In the entry room, examine the photos showing this building at the end of World War II and ogle the finely-crafted spiral staircase. The ornately-carved wooden **door,** which we'll pass through in a minute, is all-original, from the 1600s. Above the door are two crosses under a crown. This seal of Gdańsk is being held—as it's often depicted—by a pair of lions. The felines are stubborn and independent, just like the citizens of Gdańsk.

The surface of the door is carved with images of crops. Around the frame of the door are mermen, reminding us that this agricultural bounty, like so many of Poland's resources, is transported on the Vistula and out through Gdańsk.

Go through the door into the **Red Hall,** where the Gdańsk city council met in the summertime. (The lavish fireplace, with another pair of lions holding the coat of arms of Gdańsk, was just for show. There's no chimney.) City council members would sit in the seats around the room, debating city policy. Marvel at the 17th-century inlaid wood panels (just above eye level) showing slices of local life. Paintings on the wall above represent the seven virtues that the burghers meeting in this room should possess. And the exquisite ceiling—with 25 paintings in total—is all about theology.

GDAŃSK & THE TRI-CITY

Including both Christian and pagan themes, the ceiling was meant to inspire the decision-makers in this room to make good choices. Study the oval painting in the middle (from 1607)—the museum's highlight. It shows the special place Gdańsk occupies between God, Poland, and the rest of the world. In the foreground, the citizens of Gdańsk go about their daily lives. Above them, high atop the arch, God's hand reaches down (from within clouds of Hebrew characters) and grasps the Main Town Hall's steeple. The rainbow arching above also symbolizes God's connection to Gdańsk. Mirroring that is the Vistula River, which begins in the mountains of southern Poland (on the right), runs through the country, and exits at the sea in Gdańsk (on the left, where the rainbow ends).

Continue into the less-impressive **Winter Hall,** with another fireplace (this one actually hooked up to a chimney) and another coat of arms held by lions. Keep going through the next room, into a room with photos of **WWII damage.** The twist of wood is all that's left of the main support for the spiral staircase (today reconstructed in the room where you entered). Ponder the inspiring ability of a city to be reborn after the tragedy of war.

Upstairs are some temporary exhibits and several examples of **Gdańsk-style furniture.** These pieces are characterized by three big, round feet along the front, lots of ornamentation, and usually a virtually impossible-to-find lock (sometimes hidden behind a movable decoration). You can also see a coin collection, from the days when Gdańsk had the elite privilege of minting its own currency.

Then head upstairs, to a fascinating exhibit about Gdańsk's time as a **"free city"** between the World Wars—when, because of its delicate ethnic mix of Poles and Germans, it was too precarious to assign it to either country. You'll see border checkpoints, uniforms, signs in German (the predominant language of "Danzig"), and reconstructed rooms (homes and shops) from the era. Near the end of this room, you have the option to climb up to the top of the tower. Otherwise, you'll take stairs down—with huge photos at each landing showing the city in ruins after World War II, then triumphantly being rebuilt—and into the cellars, where you'll wander through some pointless subterranean chambers before emerging back into the courtyard where you started.

▲▲Artus Court (Dwór Artusa)

In the Middle Ages, Gdańsk was home to many brotherhoods and guilds (like businessmen's clubs). For their meetings, the city provided this elaborately decorated hall, named for King Arthur—a medieval symbol for prestige and power. Just as in King Arthur's Court, this was a place where powerful and important people came together. Of many such halls in Baltic Europe, this is the only original one that survives (skip the dry and too-thorough audioguide; in tall, white, triple-arched building behind Neptune statue at Długi Targ 43).

Visiting the Artus Court: In the grand hall, various **cupboards** line the walls. Each organization that met here had a place to keep its important documents and office supplies. Suspended from the ceiling are seven giant **model ships** that depict Baltic vessels, symbolic of the city's connection to the sea.

In the far-back corner is the museum's highlight: a gigantic **stove** decorated with 520 colorful tiles featuring the faces of kings, queens, nobles, mayors, and burghers—a mix of Protestants and Catholics, as a reminder of Gdańsk's religious tolerance. Almost all the tiles are original, having survived WWII bombs.

Notice the huge **paintings** on the walls above, with 3-D animals emerging from flat frames. Hunting is a popular theme in local artwork. Like minting coins, hunting was a privilege usually reserved for royalty, but it was extended in special circumstances to the burghers of special towns...like Gdańsk. These "paintings" are new, digitally-generated reproductions of the originals, which were damaged in World War II.

The next room—actually in the next building—is a typical **front room** of the burghers' homes lining ulica Długa. Ogle the gorgeously-carved wooden staircase. Upstairs is a hall of knights— once again evoking Arthurian legend. If you've rented an audioguide, take it back up front to return it; otherwise, you can exit through the back.

Other Museums in the Main Town
Historical Zone of the Free City of Gdańsk
(Strefa Historyczna Wolne Miasto Gdańsk)

In a city so obsessed with its Golden Age and Solidarity history, this charming little collection illuminates a unique but often-overlooked chapter in the story of Gdańsk: The years between World Wars I and II, when—in an effort to find a workable compromise in this ethnically mixed city—Gdańsk was not part of Germany or Poland, but a self-governing "free city" *(wolne miasto)*. Like a holdover from medieval fiefdoms in modern times, the city-state of Gdańsk even issued its own currency and stamps. This modest museum earnestly shows off artifacts from the time—photos, stamps, maps, flags, promotional tourist leaflets, and other items from the free city, all marked with the Gdańsk symbol of two white crosses under a crown on a red shield. The brochure explains that four out of five people living in the free city identified themselves not as Germans or Poles, but as "Danzigers." While some might find the subject obscure, this endearing collection is a treat for WWII history buffs. Be sure to borrow the English translations at the entrance.

Cost and Hours: 8 zł, Tue-Sun 12:00-18:00, Sept-April until 17:00, closed Mon year-round, down the little alley just in front of the Green Gate at Warzywnicza 10A, tel. 58-320-2828, www.strefahistorycznawmg.pl.

Archaeological Museum (Muzeum Archeologiczne)

This recently-updated museum is worth a quick peek for those interested in archaeology. Highlights include distinctive urns with cute faces (which date from the Hallstatt Period and were discovered in slate graves around Gdańsk); Bronze and Iron Age tools; before-and-after photos of WWII Gdańsk; and a reconstructed 12th-century Viking-like Slavonic longboat. You can also climb the building's tower, with good views up Mariacka street toward St. Mary's Church.

Cost and Hours: Museum-8 zł (free on Sat), tower-5 zł; July-Aug Tue-Fri 9:00-17:00, Sat-Sun 10:00-17:00; Sept-June Tue and Thu-Fri 8:00-16:00, Wed 9:00-17:00, Sat-Sun 10:00-16:00; closed Mon year-round; ulica Mariacka 25, tel. 58-322-2100, www.archeologia.pl.

▲National Maritime Museum (Narodowe Muzeum Morskie)

Gdańsk's history and livelihood are tied to the sea. This collection, spread among several buildings on either side of the river, examines all aspects of this connection. Nautical types may get a thrill out of the creaky, sprawling museum, but most visitors find it little more than a convenient way to pass some time and enjoy a cruise across the river. The museum's lack of English information is frustrating; fortunately, some exhibits have descriptions you can borrow.

Cost and Hours: Each part of the museum has its own admission (6-8 zł; ask about combo-tickets). The Maritime Cultural Center is worth neither the time nor the money for grown-ups. It's open July-Aug daily 10:00-18:00; Sept-Oct and March-June Tue-Sun 10:00-16:00, closed Mon; Nov-Feb Tue-Sun 10:00-15:00, closed Mon; ulica Ołowianka 9, tel. 58-301-8611, www.cmm.pl.

Visiting the Museum: The exhibit has four parts. The first two parts—the Crane and Maritime Cultural Center—are on the Main Town side of the river. The landmark medieval **Crane** (Żuraw), Gdańsk's most important symbol, houses a humble exhibit on living in the city during its Golden Age (16th-17th centuries). For more on the Crane itself, see page 237.

The **Maritime Cultural Center,** a modern exhibit right next door to the Crane, is not worth the exercise unless you are leading a school group. For adults, the most interesting areas are on the third floor ("Working Boats," with examples of vessels from around the world) and the fourth floor (temporary exhibits).

The rest of the museum—the Old Granaries and the *Sołdek* steamship—is across the river on Ołowianka Island, which you can reach via the little **ferry** (named the *Motława*, like the river; 1.50 zł one-way). The ferry runs about every 15 minutes in peak season (during museum hours only), less frequently in shoulder season, and not at all in the winter.

Once on the island, visit the three rebuilt **Old Granaries** (Spichlerze). These make up the heart of the exhibit, tracing the history of Gdańsk—particu-

larly as it relates to the sea—from prehistoric days to the present. Models of the town and region help put things in perspective. Other exhibits cover underwater explora-tion, navigational aids, artifacts of the Polish seafaring tradition, peekaboo cross-sections of multilevel ships, and models of the modern-day shipyard where Solidarity was born. This place is home to more miniature ships than you ever thought you'd see, and the Nautical Gallery upstairs features endless rooms with paintings of boats.

Finally, crawl through the holds and scramble across the deck of a decommissioned steamship called the *Sołdek*, docked perma-nently across from the Crane (ship generally closed in winter). This was the first postwar vessel built at the Gdańsk shipyard. Below decks, you can see where the crew shoveled the coal; wander through a maze of pipes, gears, valves, gauges, and ladders; and visit the rooms where the sailors lived, slept, and ate. You can even play captain on the bridge.

SOLIDARITY (SOLIDARNOŚĆ) AND THE GDAŃSK SHIPYARD (STOCZNIA GDAŃSKA)

Gdańsk's single most memorable experience is exploring the ship-yard that witnessed the beginning of the end of communism's stranglehold on Eastern Europe. Taken together, the sights in this area are worth ▲▲▲. Here in the former industrial wasteland that Lech Wałęsa called the "cradle of freedom," this evocative site tells the story of the brave Polish shipyard workers who took on—and ultimately defeated—an Evil Empire. A visit to the Solidarity sights has two main parts: Solidarity Square (with the memorial and gate in front of the shipyard), and the outstanding museum inside the European Solidarity Center.

GDAŃSK & THE TRI-CITY

Getting to the Shipyard: These sights cluster around Solidarity Square (Plac Solidarności), at the north end of the Old Town, about a 20-minute walk from the Royal Way. For the most interesting approach, follow "Part 2" of my self-guided walk (earlier), which ends here.

Background: After the communists took over Eastern Europe at the end of World War II, oppressed peoples throughout the Soviet Bloc rose up in different ways. The most dramatic uprisings—Hungary's 1956 Uprising and Czechoslovakia's 1968 "Prague Spring"—were brutally crushed under the treads of Soviet tanks. The formula for freedom that finally succeeded was a patient, nearly decade-long series of strikes and protests spearheaded by Lech Wałęsa and his trade union, called Solidarność— "Solidarity." (The movement also benefited from good timing, as it coincided with the *perestroika* and *glasnost* policies of Soviet premier Mikhail Gorbachev.) While some American politicians might like to take credit for defeating communism, Wałęsa and his fellow workers were the ones fighting on the front lines, armed with nothing more than guts.

Solidarity Square (Plac Solidarności) and the Monument of the Fallen Shipyard Workers

The seeds of August 1980 were sown a decade before. Since becoming part of the Soviet Bloc, the Poles staged frequent strikes, protests, and uprisings to secure their rights, all of which were put down by the regime. But the bloodiest of these took place in December of 1970—a tragic event memorialized by the **three-crosses monument** that towers over what's now called Solidarity Square.

The 1970 strike was prompted by price hikes. The communist government set the prices for all products. As Poland endured drastic food shortages in the 1960s and 1970s, the regime frequently announced what it called "regulation of prices." Invariably, this meant an increase in the cost of essential foodstuffs. (To be able to claim "regulation" rather than "increase," the regime would symbolically lower prices for a few select items—but these were always nonessential luxuries, such as elevators and TV sets, which nobody could afford anyway.) The regime was usually smart enough to raise prices on January 1, when the people were fat and happy after Christmas, and too hungover to complain. But on December 12, 1970, bolstered by an ego-stoking visit by West German Chancellor Willy Brandt, Polish premier Władysław

Gomułka increased prices. The people of Poland—who cared more about the price of Christmas dinner than relations with Germany—struck back.

A wave of strikes and sit-ins spread along the heavily industrialized north coast of Poland, most notably in Gdańsk, Gdynia, and Szczecin. Thousands of angry demonstrators poured through the gate of this shipyard, marched into town, and set fire to the Communist Party Committee building. In an attempt to quell the riots, the government-run radio implored the people to go back to work. On the morning of December 17, workers showed up at shipyard gates across northern Poland, and were greeted by the army and police. Without provocation, the Polish army opened fire on the workers. While the official death toll for the massacre stands at 44, others say the true number is much higher. The monument, with a trio of 140-foot-tall crosses, honors those lost to the regime that December.

Go to the middle of the **wall** behind the crosses, to the monument of the worker wearing a flimsy plastic work helmet, attempting to shield himself from bullets. Behind him is a list—pockmarked with symbolic bullet holes—of workers murdered on that day. *Lat* means "years old"—many teenagers were among the dead. The quote at the top of the wall is from St. John Paul II, who was elected pope eight years after this tragedy. The pope was known for his clever way with words, and this very carefully phrased quote—which served as an inspiration to the Poles during their darkest hours—skewers the regime in a way subtle enough to still be tolerated: "Let thy spirit descend, and renew the face of the earth—of *this* earth" (that is, Poland). Below that is the dedication: "They gave their lives so you can live decently."

Stretching to the left of this center wall are plaques representing labor unions from around Poland—and around the world (look for the Chinese characters)—expressing solidarity with these workers. To the right is an enormous Bible verse: "May the Lord give strength to his people. May the Lord bless his people with the gift of peace" (Psalms 29:11).

Inspired by the brave sacrifice of their true comrades, shipyard workers rose up here in August of 1980, formulating the "21 Points" of a new union called Solidarity. Their demands included the right to strike and form unions, the freeing of political prisoners, and an increase in wages. The 21 Points are listed in Polish on the panel at the far end of the right wall, marked *21 X TAK* ("21 times yes"). An unwritten precondition to any agreement was the right for the workers of 1980 to build a memorial to their comrades slain in 1970. The government agreed, marking the first time a communist regime ever allowed a monument to be built to honor its own victims. Wałęsa called it a harpoon in the heart of the com-

Lech Wałęsa

In 1980, the world was turned on its ear by a walrus-mustachioed shipyard electrician. Within three years, this seemingly run-of-the-mill Pole had precipitated the collapse of communism, led a massive 10-million-member trade union with enormous political impact, been named *Time* magazine's Man of the Year, and won a Nobel Peace Prize.

Lech Wałęsa was born in Popowo, Poland in 1943. After working as a car mechanic and serving two years in the army, he became an electrician at the Gdańsk Shipyard in 1967. Like many Poles, Wałęsa felt stifled by the communist government, and was infuriated that a system that was supposed to be for the workers clearly wasn't serving them.

When the shipyard massacre took place in December of 1970 (see page 251), Wałęsa was at the forefront of the protests. He was marked as a dissident, and in 1976, he was fired. Wałęsa hopped from job to job and was occasionally unemployed—under communism, a rock-bottom status reserved for only the most despicable derelicts. But he soldiered on, fighting for the creation of a trade union and building up quite a file with the secret police.

In August 1980, Wałęsa heard news of the beginnings of the Gdańsk strike and raced to the shipyard. In an act that has since become the stuff of legend, Wałęsa scaled the shipyard wall to get inside.

Before long, Wałęsa's dynamic personality won him the unofficial role of the workers' leader and spokesman. He negotiated with the regime to hash out the August Agreements, becoming a rock star-type hero during the so-called 16 Months of Hope... until martial law came crashing down in December 1981. Wałęsa was arrested and interned for 11 months in a country house. After

munists. The towering monument, with three crucified anchors on top, was designed, engineered, and built by shipyard workers. The monument was finished just four months after the historic agreement was signed.

• *Now continue to the gate and peer through into the birthplace of Eastern European freedom.*

Gdańsk Shipyard (Stocznia Gdańska) Gate #2

When a Pole named Karol Wojtyła was elected pope in 1978—and visited his homeland in 1979—he inspired his 40 million countrymen to believe that impossible dreams can come true. Prices being released, he continued to struggle underground, becoming a symbol of anticommunist sentiment.

Finally, the dedication of Wałęsa and Solidarity paid off, and Polish communism dissolved—with Wałęsa rising from the ashes as the country's first postcommunist president. But the skills that made Wałęsa a rousing success at leading an uprising didn't translate well to the president's office. Wałęsa proved to be a stubborn, headstrong politician, frequently clashing with the parliament. He squabbled with his own party, declaring a "war at the top" of Solidarity and rotating higher-ups to prevent corruption and keep the party fresh. He also didn't choose his advisors well, enlisting several staffers who wound up immersed in scandal. His overconfidence was his Achilles' heel, and his governing style verged on authoritarian.

Unrefined and none too interested in scripted speeches, Wałęsa was a simple man who preferred playing ping-pong with his buddies to attending formal state functions. Though lacking a formal education, Wałęsa had unsurpassed drive and charisma... but that's not enough to lead a country—especially during an impossibly complicated, fast-changing time.

Wałęsa was defeated at the polls, by the Poles, in 1995, and when he ran again in 2000, he received a humiliating one percent of the vote. Since leaving office, Wałęsa has kept a lower profile, but still delivers speeches worldwide. Many poor Poles grumble that Lech, who started life simple like them, has forgotten the little people. But his fans point out that he gives much of his income to charity. And on his lapel, he still always wears a pin featuring the Black Madonna of Częstochowa—the most important symbol of Polish Catholicism.

Poles say there are at least two Lech Wałęsas: the young, bombastic, working-class idealist Lech, at the forefront of the Solidarity strikes, who will always have a special place in their hearts; and the failed President Wałęsa, who got in over his head and tarnished his legacy.

continued to go up, and the workers continued to rise up. By the summer of 1980, it was clear that the dam was about to break.

In August, Anna Walentynowicz—a Gdańsk crane operator and known dissident—was fired unceremoniously just short of her retirement. This sparked a strike in the Gdańsk Shipyard (then called the Lenin Shipyard) on August 14, 1980. An electrician named Lech Wałęsa had been fired as an agitator years before and wasn't allowed into the yard. But on hearing news of the strike, Wałęsa went to the shipyard and climbed over the wall to get inside. The strike now had a leader.

These were not soldiers, nor were they idealistic flower children. The strike participants were gritty, salt-of-the-earth manual laborers: forklift operators, welders, electricians, machinists. Imagine being one of the 16,000 workers who stayed here for 18 days during the strike—hungry, cold, sleeping on sheets of Styrofoam, inspired by the new Polish pope, excited about finally standing up to the regime... and terrified that at any moment

you might be gunned down, like your friends had been a decade before. Workers, afraid to leave the shipyard, communicated with the outside world through this gate—wives and brothers showed up here and asked for a loved one, and those inside spread the word until the striker came forward. Occasionally, a truck pulled up inside the gate, with Lech Wałęsa standing atop its cab with a megaphone. Facing the thousands of people assembled outside the gate, Wałęsa gave progress reports on the negotiations and pleaded for supplies. The people of Gdańsk responded, bringing armfuls of bread and other food to keep the workers going. Solidarity.

During the strike, two items hung on the fence. One of them (which still hangs there today) was a picture of Pope John Paul II—a reminder to believe in your dreams and have faith in God (for more on the Pope and his role in Solidarity, see page 54). The other item was a makeshift list of the strikers' 21 Points—demands scrawled in red paint and black pencil on pieces of plywood.

• *Walk around the right end of the gate and enter the former shipyard.*

The shipyard churned out over a thousand ships from 1948 to 1990, employing 16,000 workers. About 60 percent of these ships were exported to the USSR—and so, when the Soviet Bloc broke apart in the 1990s, they lost a huge market. Today the facilities employ closer to 1,200 workers...who now make windmills.

Before entering the museum, take a look around. This part of the shipyard, long abandoned, is being redeveloped into a **"Young City"** (Młode Miasto)—envisioned as a new city center for Gdańsk, with shopping, restaurants, offices, and homes. Rusting shipbuilding equipment has been torn down, and old brick buildings are being converted into gentrified flats. The nearby boulevard called Nowa Wałowa will be the spine connecting this area to the rest of the city. Farther east, the harborfront will also be rejuvenated, creating a glitzy marina and extending the city's delightful waterfront people zone to the north (see www.ycgdansk.com). Fortunately, the shipyard gate, monument, and other important sites from the Solidarity strikes—now considered historical monuments—will remain.

• *The massive, rust-colored European Solidarity Center, which faces Solidarity Square, houses the museum where we'll learn the rest of the story.*

▲▲▲European Solidarity Center
(Europejskie Centrum Solidarności)

Europe's single best sight about the end of communism is made even more powerful by its location: in the very heart of the place

where those events occurred. Filling just one small corner of a huge, purpose-built educational facility, the permanent exhibition uses larger-than-life photographs, archival footage, actual artifacts, interactive touchscreens, and a state-of-the-art audioguide to eloquently tell the story of the end of Eastern European communism.

Cost and Hours: 17 zł, includes audioguide, daily 10:00-20:00, Oct-April until 18:00, last entry one hour before closing, Plac Solidarności 1, tel. 506-195-673, www.ecs.gda.pl.

➋ Self-Guided Tour: First, appreciate the architecture of the **building** itself. From the outside, it's designed to resemble the rusted hull of a giant ship—seemingly gloomy and depressing. But step inside to find an interior flooded with light, which cultivates a surprising variety of life—in the form of lush gardens that make the place feel like a very expensive greenhouse. You can interpret this symbolism a number of ways: Something that seems dull and dreary from the outside (the Soviet Bloc, the shipyards themselves, what have you) can be full of brightness, life, and optimism inside.

In the lobby, buy your ticket and pick up the essential, included audioguide. The exhibit has much to see, and some of it is arranged in a conceptual way that can be tricky to understand without a full grasp of the history. I've outlined the basics in this self-guided tour, but the audioguide can illuminate more details—including translations of films and eyewitness testimony from participants in the history.

• *The permanent exhibit fills seven lettered rooms—each with its own theme—on two floors. From the lush lobby, head up the escalator and into...*

The Birth of Solidarity (Room A): This room picks up right in the middle of the dynamic story we just learned out on the square. It's August of 1980, and the shipyard workers are rising up. You step straight into a busy shipyard: punch clocks, workers' lockers, and—up on the ceiling—hundreds of plastic helmets. A big **map** in the middle of the room shows the extent of the shipyard in 1980. Inside the cab of the **crane,** you can watch an interview with spunky Anna Walentynowicz, whose firing led to the first round of strikes. Nearby stands a **truck;** Lech Wałęsa would stand on top

GDAŃSK & THE TRI-CITY

of the cab of a truck like this one to address the nervous locals who had amassed outside the shipyard gate, awaiting further news.

In the middle of the room, carefully protected under glass, are those original **plywood panels** onto which the strikers scrawled their 21 demands, then lashed to the gate. Just beyond that, a giant wall of photos and a map illustrate how the strikes that began here spread like a virus across Poland. At the far end of the room, behind the partition, stand **two tables** that were used during the talks to end the strikes (each one with several actual items from that era, under glass).

After 18 days of protests, the communist authorities finally agreed to negotiate. On the afternoon of August 31, 1980, the Governmental Commission and the Inter-Factory Strike Committee (MKS) came together and signed the August Agreements, which legalized Solidarity—the first time any communist government permitted a workers' union. As Lech Wałęsa sat at a big table and signed the agreement, other union reps tape-recorded the proceedings and played them later at their own factories to prove that the unthinkable had happened. Take a moment to linger over the rousing **film** that plays on the far wall, which begins with the strike, carries through with the tense negotiations that a brash young Lech Wałęsa held with the authorities, and ends with the triumphant acceptance of the strikers' demands. Lech Wałęsa rides on the shoulders of well-wishers out to the gate to spread the good news.

• Back by the original 21 demands, enter the next exhibit...

The Power of the Powerless (Room B): This section traces the roots of the 1980 strikes, which were preceded by several far less successful protests. It all begins with a kiss: a giant photograph of Russian premier Leonid Brezhnev mouth-kissing the Polish premier Edward Gierek, with the caption **"Brotherly Friendship."** Soviet premiers and their satellite leaders really did greet each other "in the French manner," as a symbolic gesture of their communist brotherhood.

Working your way through the exhibit, you'll see the door to a **prison cell**—a reminder of the intimidation tactics used by the Soviets in the 1940s and 1950s to deal with their opponents as they exerted their rule over the lands they had liberated from the Nazis.

The typical **communist-era apartment** is painfully humble. After the war, much of Poland had been destroyed, and population shifts led to housing shortages. People had to make do with tiny spaces and ramshackle furnishings. Communist propaganda blares from both the radio and the TV.

A map shows **"red Europe"** (the USSR plus the satellites of Poland, Czechoslovakia, Hungary, and East Germany), and a **timeline** traces some of the smaller Soviet Bloc protests that led up to Solidarity: in East Germany in 1953, in Budapest and Poznań in 1956, the "Prague Spring" of 1968, and other 1968 protests in Poland.

In the wake of these uprisings, the communist authorities cracked down even harder. Peek into the **interrogation room,** with a wall of file cabinets and a lowly stool illuminated by a bright spotlight. (Notice that the white Polish eagle on the seal above the desk is missing its golden crown—during communism, the Poles were allowed to keep the eagle, but its crown was removed.)

The next exhibit presents a day-by-day rundown of the **1970 strikes,** from December 14 to 22, which resulted in the massacre of the workers who are honored by the monument in front of this building. A wall of mug shots gives way to exhibits chronicling the steady rise of dissent groups through the 1970s, culminating in the June 1976 protests in the city of Radom (prompted, like so many other uprisings, by unilateral price hikes).

• *Loop back through Room A, and proceed straight ahead into...*

Solidarity and Hope (Room C): While the government didn't take the August Agreements very seriously, the Poles did... and before long, 10 million of them—one out of every four, or effectively half the nation's workforce—joined Solidarity. So began what's often called the **"16 Months of Hope."** Newly legal, Solidarity continued to stage strikes and make its opposition known. Slick Solidarity posters and children's art convey the childlike enthusiasm with which the Poles seized their hard-won kernels of freedom. The communist authorities' hold on the Polish people began to slip. Support and aid from the outside world poured in, but the rest of the Soviet Bloc looked on nervously, and the Warsaw Pact army assembled at the Polish border and glared at the uprisers. The threat of invasion hung heavy in the air.

• *Exiting this room, head up the staircase and into...*

At War with Society (Room D): You're greeted by a wall of TV screens delivering a stern message. On Sunday morning, December 13, 1981, the Polish head of state, **General Wojciech Jaruzelski**—wearing his trademark dark glasses—appeared on national TV and announced the introduction of **martial law.** Solidarity was outlawed, and its leaders were arrested. Frightened Poles heard the announcement and looked out their windows to see Polish Army tanks rumbling through the snowy streets. (On the opposite wall, see footage of tanks and heavily armed soldiers intimidating their countrymen into compliance.) Jaruzelski claimed that he imposed martial law to prevent the Soviets from invading. Today, many historians question whether martial law was really necessary, though Jaruzelski remained unremorseful through his death in 2014.

Continuing deeper into the exhibit, you come to a **prisoner transport.** Climb up inside to watch chilling scenes of riots, demonstrations, and crackdowns by the ZOMO riot police. In one gruesome scene, a demonstrator is quite intentionally—and practically in slow motion—run over by a truck. From here, pass through a gauntlet of *milicja* riot-gear shields to see the truck crashing through a gate. Overhead are the uniforms of miners from the **Wujek mine** who were massacred on December 16, 1981 (their names are projected on the pile of coal below).

Martial law was a tragic, terrifying, and bleak time for the Polish people. It didn't, however, kill the Solidarity movement, which continued its fight after going underground. Passing prison cells, you'll see a wall plastered with handmade, underground posters and graffiti. Notice how in this era, **Solidarity propaganda** is much more primitive; circle around the other side of the wall to see several presses that were actually used in clandestine Solidarity print shops during this time. The outside world sent messages of support as well as supplies—represented by the big wall of cardboard boxes. This approval also came in the form of a Nobel Peace Prize for Lech Wałęsa in 1983; you'll see video clips of his wife accepting the award on his behalf (Wałęsa feared that if he traveled abroad to claim it, he would not be allowed back into the country).

• *But even in these darkest days, there were glimmers of hope. Enter...*

The Road to Democracy (Room E): By the time the Pope visited his homeland again in 1983, martial law had finally been lifted, and Solidarity—still technically illegal—was gaining momentum, gradually pecking away at the communists. Step into the small inner room with footage of the **Pope's third pilgrimage** to his homeland in 1987, by which time (thanks in no small part to his inspirational role in the ongoing revolution) the tide was turning.

Step into the room with the big, white **roundtable.** With the moral support of the pope and the entire Western world, the brave Poles were the first European country to throw off the shackles of communism when, in the spring of 1989, the "Roundtable Talks" led to the opening up of elections. (If you look through the viewfinders of the TV cameras in the corners, you'll see footage of those meetings.) The government arrogantly called for parliamentary elections, reserving 65 percent of seats for themselves.

In the next room, you can see Solidarity's strategy in those **elections:** On the right wall are posters showing Lech Wałęsa with each candidate. Another popular "get out the vote" measure was the huge poster of Gary Cooper—an icon of America, which the Poles deeply respect and viewed as their friendly cousin across the Atlantic—except that, instead of a pistol, he's packing a ballot. Rousing reminders like this inspired huge voter turnout. The communists' plan backfired, as virtually every open seat went to Solidarity. It was the first time ever that opposition candidates had taken office in the Soviet Bloc. On the wall straight ahead, flashing a V-for-*wiktoria* sign, is a huge photo of Tadeusz Mazowiecki—an early leader of Solidarity, who became prime minister on June 4, 1989.

• *For the glorious aftermath, head into the final room.*

The Triumph of Freedom (Room F): This room is dominated by a gigantic **map of Eastern Europe.** A countdown clock on the right ticks off the departure of each country from communist clutches, as the Soviet Bloc "decomposes." You'll see how the success of Solidarity in Poland—and the ragtag determination of a scruffy band of shipyard workers right here in Gdańsk—inspired people all over Eastern Europe. By the winter of 1989, the Hungarians had opened their borders, the Berlin Wall had crumbled, and the Czechs and Slovaks had staged their Velvet Revolution. (Small viewing stations that circle the room reveal the detailed story for each country's own road to freedom.) Lech Wałęsa—the shipyard electrician who started it all by jumping over a wall—became the first president of postcommunist Poland. And a year later, in Poland's first true elections since World War II, 29 different parties won seats in the parliament. It was a free-election free-for-all.

In the middle of the room stands a white wall with **inspirational quotes** from St. John Paul II and Václav Havel—the Czech poet-turned-protester-turned-prisoner-turned-president—which are repeated in several languages. On the huge wall, the **Solidarity "graffiti"** is actually made up of thousands of little notes left behind by visitors to the museum. Feel free to grab a piece of paper and a pen and record your own reflections.

• *Finally, head downstairs and find the...*

St. John Paul II Room (Room G): Many visitors find that touring this museum—with vivid reminders of a dramatic and pivotal moment in history that took place in their own lifetimes and was brought about not by armies or presidents, but by everyday people—puts them in an emotional state of mind. Designed for silent reflection, this room overlooks the monument to those workers who were gunned down in 1970.

• *For an epilogue, if you're not already pooped, continue deeper into the former shipyard to see one more important landmark from 1980. The path leads to a low-profile, red-brick building, the...*

Sala BHP

This is the building where the communists sat down across the table from Lech Wałęsa and his team and worked out a compromise (as seen in the videos inside the European Solidarity Center). Entering, turn left to view a series of photos that illustrate Solidarity history; these are all the more poignant because they lack the bombastic presentation of the glitzy museum. The images speak for themselves. The other side of the building (right from the entrance) is the actual hall where those fateful meetings took place, with a long table set up on the stage.

Cost and Hours: Free, daily 10:00-18:00, Oct-April until 16:00, www.salabhp.pl.

NORTH OF THE MAIN TOWN
Museum of the Second World War
Since 2007, Gdańsk has been preparing this expansive, architecturally striking, world-class museum just east of the Solidarity shipyard. Collecting thousands of artifacts (from intimate belongings of wartime victims, to tanks and railway cars), it was originally designed to present an ambitiously global, yet personal, perspective on the war that began right at Gdańsk's doorstep. But as it neared completion, politicians from the nationalistic Law and Justice Party deemed it too pacifistic and "not Polish enough," demanding changes to make it more singularly patriotic. Political wrangling ensued to determine who controlled the museum's content. With this delay, it's unclear when the museum will open (likely in 2017 or 2018; for details, ask at the TI or see www.muzeum1939.pl). But when it does—and if its original design is preserved—it will likely be regarded one of Europe's definitive World War II museums.

SOUTH OF THE MAIN TOWN
A 10- to 15-minute walk south of the Main Town, these sights round out your Gdańsk experience. They're most worthwhile to those with a special interest in each one's subject matter: art, theater, and kids who love archaeology.

National Museum in Gdańsk
(Muzeum Narodowe w Gdańsku)
This art collection, housed in what was a 15th-century Franciscan monastery, is worth ▲▲ to art lovers for one reason: Hans Memling's glorious *Last Judgment* triptych altarpiece, one of the two most important pieces of art to be seen in Poland (the other is Leonardo da Vinci's *Lady with an Ermine,* usually in Kraków's Czartoryski Museum). If you're not a purist, you can settle for seeing the much smaller replica in St. Mary's Church. But if medieval art is your bag, make the 10-minute walk here from the Main Town.

Cost and Hours: 10 zł; May-Sept Tue-Sun 10:00-17:00 (Thu 12:00-19:00 in June-Aug); Oct-April Tue-Fri 9:00-16:00, Sat-Sun 10:00-17:00; closed Mon year-round; last entry 45 minutes before closing; walk 10 minutes due south from ulica Długa's Golden Gate, after passing the Shakespeare Theater take the pedestrian underpass beneath the big cross street, then continue down the busy street until you see signs for the museum; ulica Toruńska 1, tel. 58-301-7061, www.mng.gda.pl.

Visiting the Museum: From the entry, the **altarpiece by Hans Memling** (c. 1440-1494) is at the top of the stairs and to the right. The history of the painting is as interesting as the work itself. It was commissioned in the mid-15th century by the Medicis' banker in Florence, Angelo di Jacopo Tani. The ship delivering the painting from Belgium to Florence was hijacked by a Gdańsk pirate, who brought the altarpiece to his hometown to be displayed in St. Mary's Church. For centuries, kings, emperors, and czars admired it from afar, until Napoleon seized it in the early 19th century and took it to Paris to hang in the Louvre. Gdańsk finally got the painting back, only to have it exiled again—this time into St. Petersburg's Hermitage Museum—after World War II. On its return to Gdańsk in 1956, this museum claimed it—though St. Mary's wants it back.

Have a close look at Memling's well-traveled work. It's the end of the world, and Christ rides in on a rainbow to judge humankind. Angels blow reveille, waking the dead, who rise from their graves. The winged archangel Michael—dressed for battle and wielding the cross like a weapon—weighs the grace in each person, sending them either to the fires of hell (right panel) or up the sparkling-crystal stairway to heaven (left).

It takes all 70 square feet of paneling to contain this awesome scene. Jam-packed with dozens of bodies and a Bible's worth of symbolism, and executed with astonishing detail, the painting can keep even a nonart lover occupied. Notice the serene, happy expressions of the righteous, as they're greeted by St. Peter (with his giant key) and clothed by angels. And pity the condemned, their faces filled with terror and sorrow as they're tortured by grotesque devils more horrifying than anything Hollywood could devise.

Tune in to the exquisite details: the angels' robes, the devils' genetic-mutant features, the portrait of the man in the scale (a Medici banker), Michael's peacock wings. Get as close as you can to the globe at Christ's feet and Michael's shining breastplate: You can just make out the whole scene in mirror reflection. Then back up and take it all in—three panels connected by a necklace of bodies that curves downward through hell, crosses the earth, then rises up to the towers of the New Jerusalem. On the back side of the triptych are reverent portraits of the painting's patron, Angelo Tani, and his new bride, Catarina.

Beyond the Memling, the remainder of the collection isn't too thrilling. The rest of the upstairs has more Flemish and Dutch art, as well as paintings from Gdańsk's Golden Age and various works by Polish artists. The ground floor features a cavernous, all-white cloister filled with Gothic altarpiece sculptures, gold and silver wares, majolica and Delft porcelain, and characteristic Gdańsk-style furniture.

Gdańsk Shakespeare Theater (Teatr Szekspirowski)

Gdańsk has a long and proud tradition of staging plays by Shakespeare. As early as the 17th century, theater troupes from England would come to this cosmopolitan trading city to perform. In 1993, local actors revived the tradition with an annual Gdańsk Shakespeare Festival. And in 2014, the city built the state-of-the-art Gdańsk Shakespeare Theater to honor its connection to the Bard.

The building's minimalist, black-brick, blocky architecture—with a few symbolic faux-buttresses to echo the gables of the surrounding buildings—was criticized for not blending in very well with its surroundings. But the celebration of theater that takes place inside is welcomed by all. The main theater can be modified to create three different types of performance spaces (proscenium, thrust stage, and theater in the round)—and even has a retractable roof to wash the actors with direct sunlight.

If you want to take a peek, the building is on ulica Zbytki—just follow Pcztowa street south from the middle of ulica Długa.

Tours and Performances: Theater lovers can take a one-hour guided tour of the building for 15 zł. Call or check their website for details on the tour and upcoming performances (tel. 58-351-0101, www.teatrszekspirowski.pl).

Shakespeare contributes only a tiny piece of the theater's full lineup—it plays host to a wide variety of performances and festivals throughout the year. You're most likely to find Shakespeare performed in English during the annual Shakespeare Festival, which is typically in the summer (www.shakespearefestival.pl).

"Blue Lamb" Archaeological Education Center (Centrum Edukacji Archeologicznej "Blękitny Baranek")

Hiding far from the Main Town, on Granary Island, this kid-friendly exhibit re-creates the atmosphere of medieval Gdańsk. Occupying a rebuilt granary called the "Blue Lamb," its highlight is a full-scale replica of an atmospheric medieval street, populated by mannequins whose features are based on actual human remains. Also telling the tale are artifacts from the period, a selection of films (subtitled in English), and touchscreens that provide some background. Though information is a bit sparse (especially along the medieval street), the collection tries hard not to be just another fuddy-duddy, dusty old museum, making it popular with kids on field trips.

Cost and Hours: 10 zł, Tue-Sun 10:00-17:00, July-Aug until 18:00, closed Mon year-round, ulica Chmielna 53, tel. 58-320-3188, www.archeologia.pl.

OUTER GDAŃSK

These two sights—worthwhile only to those with a particular interest in them—are each within the city limits of Gdańsk, but they take some serious time to see round-trip.

Oliwa Cathedral (Katedra Oliwska)

The suburb of Oliwa, at the northern edge of Gdańsk, is home to this visually striking church. The quirky, elongated facade hides a surprisingly long and skinny nave. The ornately decorated 18th-century organ over the main entrance features angels and stars that move around when the organ is played. While locals are proud of this place, it's hard to justify the effort it takes to get out here. Skip it unless you just love Polish churches or you're going to a concert.

Concerts: The animated organ performs its 20-minute show frequently, especially in summer (in high season, concerts at the top of most hours—confirm schedule online or at Gdańsk TI before making the trip, www.archikatedraoliwa.pl). Note that on Sundays and holidays, there are no concerts before 15:00.

Getting There: Oliwa is about six miles northwest of central Gdańsk, on the way to Sopot and Gdynia. To reach Oliwa from Gdańsk's main train station, you have two options: Ride **tram #6** or **#12**, get off at Oliwski Park, and walk a few minutes through the park to the church (about 30 minutes total); or take an **SKM commuter train** to the Gdańsk Oliwa stop (15 minutes), then walk 15 minutes (or take a 10-zł taxi ride) to Oliwski Park and the cathedral.

Westerplatte

World War II began on September 1, 1939, when Adolf Hitler sent the warship *Schleswig-Holstein* to attack this Polish munitions depot, which was guarding Gdańsk's harbor. Though it may give serious WWII history buffs goosebumps, most visitors will find little to see here aside from a modest museum, a towering monument, and some old bunkers.

Getting There: The most enjoyable approach is on a cruise—either on a modern boat, or on the fun old-fashioned galleons (45 minutes each way; see page 274). You can also take **bus #138** from the main train station (about 30 minutes).

Shopping in Gdańsk

The big story in Gdańsk is amber *(bursztyn)*, a fossil resin available in all shades, shapes, and sizes (see the "All About Amber" sidebar, earlier). While you'll see amber sold all over town, the best place to browse and buy is along the atmospheric ulica Mariacka (between the Motława River and St. Mary's Church). This pretty street, with old-fashioned balconies and dozens of display cases, is fun to wander even if you're not a shopper. Other good places to buy amber are along the riverfront embankment and on ulica Długa. To avoid rip-offs—such as amber that's been melted and reshaped—always buy it from a shop, not from someone standing on the street. (But note that most shops also have a display case and salesperson out front, which are perfectly legit.) Prices everywhere are about the same, so instead of seeking out a specific place, just window shop until you see what you want. Styles range from gaudy necklaces with huge globs of amber, to tasteful smaller pendants in silver settings, to cheap trinkets. All shades of amber—from near-white to dark brown—cost about the same, but you'll pay more for inclusions (bugs or other objects stuck in the amber).

Gdańsk also has several modern shopping malls, most of them in the Old Town or near the main train station. The walk between the Main Town and the Solidarity shipyard goes past some of the best malls (see page 227).

Sleeping in Gdańsk

The high season is generally May through September; at all these places, you'll pay a bit less in the off-season (Oct-April). Many hotels are booked up (mostly with German tourists) in peak season (mid-June-mid-Sept)—reserve ahead.

ACROSS THE RIVER

These hotels are across the river from the Main Town. That puts you a bit farther from the sightseeing action, but it's a relatively short walk (no more than 10 minutes from any of these).

$$$$ Hotel Podewils is the top choice for a friendly splurge. Filling a storybook-cute house from 1728, overlooking the marina and across the river from a fine panorama of the Gdańsk embankment, it's classy. The public spaces and 10 rooms have all the modern amenities, but with plush, almost Baroque, decor (air-con, Szafarnia 2, tel. 58-300-9560, www.podewils.pl, gdansk@podewils.pl).

$$ Hotel Królewski, in a beautifully renovated red-brick granary, offers 30 stylish rooms sitting right along the river, facing classic Gdańsk embankment views. It's just beyond the three granaries of the National Maritime Museum, across the river from the Crane. The Polish Baltic Philharmonic is right next door, so you may be serenaded by a rehearsal or performance (apartments, try asking for a view room for no extra charge, elevator, good restaurant, ulica Ołowianka 1, tel. 58-326-1111, www.hotelkrolewski.pl, office@hotelkrolewski.pl). To get into town, hop on the ferry across the river offered by the Maritime Museum; if it's not run-

Sleep Code

Hotels are classified based on the average price of a standard double room with breakfast in high season.

$$$$	**Splurge:** Most rooms over 550 zł
$$$	**Pricier:** 400-550 zł
$$	**Moderate:** 250-400 zł
$	**Budget:** 100-250 zł
¢	**Backpacker:** Under 100 zł
RS%	**Rick Steves discount**

Unless otherwise noted, credit cards are accepted, hotel staff speak basic English, and free Wi-Fi is available. Comparison-shop by checking prices at several hotels (on each hotel's own website, on a booking site, or by email). For the best deal, *book directly with the hotel.* Ask for a discount if paying in cash; if the listing includes **RS%**, request a Rick Steves discount.

ning, it's a scenic 15-minute walk along the river, past the marina, and over the bridge into the Main Town.

$$ Willa Litarion, run by the Owsikowski family, sits on the back side of a charmingly restored row of colorful houses on the island just across the river from the main drag. It's tall and skinny, with no elevator, and faces a gloomy parking lot, but it's a handy location at a decent price. Each of the 13 small rooms is different, but all are artsy and mod (pay parking garage, ulica Spichrzowa 18, tel. 58-320-2553, www.litarion.pl, recepcja@litarion.pl). Several other, similar (but less appealing) "villas" line this same street—if you're in a pinch for a room, this is a handy place to go ringing doorbells.

At the Academy of Music: Two places hide in the back of the big Academy of Music building (Akademia Muzyczna), a 10-minute walk from the sights in a nondescript residential neighborhood. They're difficult to find at first, but the prices are worth the hunt. **$$ Dom Muzyka** rents 87 simple, tidy rooms. Their "deluxe" rooms, mostly twins, are bigger and overlook the quiet courtyard; most of the standard rooms face a busy street but have good windows and air-conditioning (apartments, elevator, popular with tour groups, good restaurant, free and easy parking, ulica Łąkowa 1, tel. 58-326-0600, www.dommuzyka.pl, biuro@dommuzyka.pl). In the same complex, **$ Dom Sonata** is a tempting budget option. Its 60 rooms—nearly as nice as at Dom Muzyka, but with fewer hotelesque amenities—house students for most of the year, but are rented out to tourists from July through September (breakfast extra, air-con, elevator, ulica Łąkowa 1, tel. 58-300-9260, www.domsonata.com.pl, domsonata@amuz.gda.pl). To get here from the Main Town's Green Gate, cross the two bridges, then walk a long block along the modern commercial building, and turn right just before the park (on Łąkowa, across from the big brick church). Walk to the end of this block, and before the busy road, go through the gate just before the big yellow-brick building on the right. Once inside the gate checkpoint, the hotel is around the back of the yellow building, the door farthest down. If you get lost, just ask people, "Hotel?"

IN THE MAIN TOWN

The Main Town is convenient for sightseeing, but can come with nighttime noise—particularly in summer, when loud bars and discos keep things lively. Request a quiet room...and pack earplugs.

$$$ Hotel Wolne Miasto ("Free City") offers rich, wood-carved public spaces with photos of old Gdańsk and 68 elegant rooms on the edge of the Main Town, just two blocks from the main drag. It's above a popular disco that gets noisy on weekends (Thu-Sat nights), so it's especially important to request a quieter room when you reserve (elevator, ulica Świętego Ducha 2, tel. 58-322-2442, www.hotelwm.pl, rezerwacja@hotelwm.pl).

$$$ Hotel Admirał is simply practical: a big, impersonal, business-class place with 44 nicely decorated rooms tucked in a quiet residential alley at the north end of the embankment, just a few steps off the old fish market. Their rates are soft, so this place is worth considering if you can get a good deal (air-con, elevator, Tobiasza 9, tel. 58-320-0320, www.admiralhotel.pl, recepcja@admiralhotel.pl).

$$ Gotyk House, a good value, is run with warmth and pride by the Rybicki family. Owner Andrzej is an energetic armchair historian who works hard to make his little hotel comfortable while still respecting the sanctity of what's supposedly Gdańsk's oldest house. The chimes from St. Mary's Church, next door, provide a pleasant soundtrack. The cellar houses a minuscule gingerbread museum and small shrine to Copernicus (whose longtime lover may have lived here). The seven straightforward rooms share a tiny breakfast room, so you'll have to tell them what time you'd like to eat (tight public spaces, ulica Mariacka 1, tel. 58-301-8567, mobile 516-141-133, www.gotykhouse.eu, reservation@gotykhouse.eu).

$$ Aparthotel Neptun lacks personality, but owns a great location—on a slightly dreary side street between delightful Mariacka and bustling Długi Targ ("Long Square"). While it's just a few steps to most of the town's big sights, it's just far enough away to avoid the crowds and the weekend noise. The 30 rooms and apartments are modern, efficient, well-equipped, and forgettable...but well-priced for the central location (breakfast extra, elevator, Grzaska 1, mobile 604-466-466, www.aparthotelgdansk.com, info@aparthotelgdansk.com).

¢-$$ Stay Inn, a self-declared "hostel with vibe," is fresh and young, but still feels practical. The location couldn't be more central—facing the side of St. Mary's Church, right in the heart of the Main Town—and though the street it's on is quieter than most, a downstairs pub can be noisy on weekends. It combines 29 beds in small 5- to 8-bed dorms with 10 private rooms that are as hotelesque as any in this price range. The dorm dwellers and fancier folks alike share the same kitchen/lounge/breakfast room. Everything feels tidy and well-designed; it lacks the grungy party personality of some hostels, so it's well worth considering even for nonhostelers (elevator, bike rental, Piwna 28, tel. 58-354-1543, www.stayinngdansk.com, booking@stayinngdansk.com).

Eating in Gdańsk

In addition to traditional Polish fare, Gdańsk has some excellent Baltic seafood. Herring *(śledź)* is popular here, as is cod *(dorsz)*. Natives brag that their salmon *(łosoś)* is better than Norway's. For a stiff drink, sample *Goldwasser* (similar to Goldschlager). This sweet and strong liqueur, flecked with actual gold, was supposedly invented here in Gdańsk. The following options are all in the Main Town, within three blocks of the Royal Way.

BUDGET RESTAURANTS IN THE CITY CENTER

These places are affordable, tasty, quick, and wonderfully convenient—on or very near the Royal Way (ulica Długa). They're worth considering even if you're not on a tight budget.

$ **Bar pod Rybą** ("Under the Fish") is nirvana for fans of baked potatoes *(pieczony ziemniak)*. They offer more than 20 varieties, piled high with a wide variety of toppings and sauces, from Mexican beef to herring to Polish cheeses. They also serve fish dishes with salad and potatoes, making this a cheap place to sample local seafood. The tasteful decor—walls lined with old bottles, antique wooden hangers, and old street signs—is squeezed into a single cozy room packed with happy eaters. In the summer, order inside, and they'll bring your food to you at an outdoor table (daily 10:00-22:00, ulica Piwna 61, tel. 58-305-1307).

$ **Bar Mleczny Neptun** is your handiest milk-bar option in the Main Town. A hearty meal, including a drink, runs about $5. This popular place has outdoor seating along the most scenic stretch of the main drag, and an upstairs dining room overlooking it all. The items on the counter are for display—point to what you want, and they'll dish it up fresh (Mon-Fri 7:30-19:30, Sat-Sun 10:00-19:00, may have shorter hours off-season, free Wi-Fi, ulica Długa 33, tel. 58-301-4988). For more on milk bars, see page 16.

$ **Pijalnia Wódki i Piwa,** part of a popular Polish chain, hides half a block behind the Hard Rock Café (on Kuśnierska). This little

Gdańsk Hotels & Restaurants

Accommodations

1. Hotel Podewils
2. Hotel Królewski
3. Willa Litarion
4. Dom Muzyka & Dom Sonata Hotels
5. Hotel Wolne Miasto
6. Hotel Admiral
7. Gotyk House
8. Aparthotel Neptun
9. Stay Inn

Eateries

10. Bar pod Rybą
11. Bar Mleczny Neptun
12. Pijalnia Wódki i Piwa
13. Bar Turystyczny
14. Baryłka, Kamienica Goldwasser & Sushi 77
15. Lao Thai
16. Targ Rybny/Fischmarkt
17. Restauracja Kubicki

Other

18. Galeon Lew & Czerna Perła Boats to Westerplatte
19. Żegluga Gdańska Boats to Westerplatte
20. ZTM "Ferry Trams" to Hel & Sopot

MŁODY MIASTO DEVELOPMENT ZONE ("YOUNG CITY")

WWII MUSEUM (under construction)

KROSNA

OLEJARNA

TANECZNA

STAROMIEJSKIE

Targ Rybny

River

STRAGANIARSKA

GROBLA

ŚWIĘTOJAŃSKA

DŁUGIE POBRZEŻE

MARITIME CULTURAL CENTER

SS SOŁDEK

NATIONAL MARITIME MUSEUM

TOWN

THE CRANE

ARCHAEOLOGICAL MUSEUM

MARIACKA

GOTYK HOUSE

ARTUS COURT

FIVE LITTLE LADIES

EMBANKMENT

Motława

CHMIELNA

MOTŁAWSKA

SZAFARNIA

Long Market (Długi Targ)

HISTORICAL ZONE OF FREE CITY OF GDAŃSK

GREEN GATE

To "Blue Lamb" Archaeological Center & National Museum

STAGIEWNA

Granary Island

ŁĄKOWA

Shuttle from Cruise Port

200 Meters

200 Yards

vodka-and-herring bar takes you back to the 1970s. Pop in to study the retro decor: ads from the 1970s and photos of the lines that people routinely endured. The place is literally wallpapered with pages from the "Tribune of the Masses" newspaper infamous for its propaganda that passed for news. They play pop hits from the last years of communism. The menu is fun, accessible, and simple: 4 zł for vodka or other drinks, and 8 zł for herring or other bar nibbles (open daily 9:00-late).

$ Bar Turystyczny is misnamed—not just for tourists, it has become beloved by locals as the central area's favorite milk bar. Easy to miss on the way between the Main Town and the Solidarity sights, it's always jammed (Mon-Fri 8:00-18:00, Sat-Sun 9:00-17:00, Szeroka 8, tel. 58/301-6013).

ON THE RIVERFRONT EMBANKMENT

Perhaps the most appealing dining zone in Gdańsk stretches along the riverfront embankment near the Crane. On a balmy summer evening, the outdoor tables here are enticing. This area is popular—consider scouting a table during your sightseeing, and reserve your choice for dinner later that night. While these places are mostly interchangeable, I've listed a few to consider, in the order you'll reach them as you walk north along the embankment.

$$ Baryłka ("Barrel") is a simpler, more affordable alternative to some of the pricier places along here. While the outdoor seating is enticing, the elegant upstairs dining room, with windows overlooking the river, is also appealing (daily 9:00-24:00, Długie Pobrzeże 24, tel. 58-301-4938).

$$$$ Kamienica Goldwasser offers high-quality Polish and international cuisine. Choose between cozy, romantic indoor seating on several levels, or scenic outdoor seating (daily 10:00-24:00, occasional live music, Długie Pobrzeże 22, tel. 58-301-8878).

$$$ Sushi 77, serving up a wide selection of surprisingly good sushi right next to the Crane, is a refreshing break from ye olde Polish food. Choose between the outdoor tables bathed in red light, or the mod interior (daily 12:00-23:00, Długie Pobrzeże 30, tel. 58-682-1823).

Past the Crane

About 100 yards past the Crane, near the old fish market (Targ Rybny), cluster several more options.

$$ Lao Thai is a modern space right along the embankment, selling surprisingly high-quality, yet still affordable, Thai cuisine (daily 12:00-22:00, ulica Targ Rybny 11, tel. 58/305-2525).

$$$ Targ Rybny/Fischmarkt ("The Fish Market") has less appealing outdoor seating that overlooks a park and parking lot. But the warm, mellow-yellow nautical ambience inside is pleasant, making this a good bad-weather option. It features classy but not stuffy service, and an emphasis on fish (daily 10:00-23:00, ulica Targ Rybny 6C, tel. 58-320-9011).

$$ Restauracja Kubicki, along the water just past the Hilton, has a long history (since 1918), but a recent remodel has kept the atmosphere—and its food—feeling fresh. This is a good choice for high-quality Polish and international cuisine in a fun, sophisticated-but-not-stuffy interior that's a clever mix of old and new (daily 12:00-23:00, Wartka 5, tel. 58-301-0050).

Gdańsk Connections

BY TRAIN

Gdańsk is well-connected to the Tri-City via the commuter SKM trains (explained later, under "Getting Around the Tri-City"). It's also connected to Warsaw and Kraków by the high-speed EIC line (which requires reservations). Given the distance between Gdańsk and other Polish destinations, also consider domestic flights: LOT has easy flights between Gdańsk and Kraków or Warsaw for about the same price as a train ticket.

From Gdańsk by Train to: Hel (town on Hel Peninsula, 3/day direct July-Aug only, 2 hours; otherwise about hourly with change in Gdynia), **Malbork** (2/hour, about half are express EIC trains that take 30 minutes, the rest are slower regional trains that take around 45 minutes), **Toruń** (4/day direct, 2.5 hours; more with a change in Bydgoszcz, 3 hours), **Warsaw** (hourly, 3 hours on express EIC train), **Kraków** (6/day direct, 5.5 hours, 1 more with change in

Warsaw; plus 10-hour night train), **Berlin** (1/day direct, 6 hours; 3/day, 7.5 hours, change in Poznań.

BY BOAT

Various boats depart from Gdańsk's embankment to nearby destinations, including **Westerplatte** (the monument marking where World War II started) and **Hel** (the beachy peninsula, described below). While boats also run sporadically to Sopot and Gdynia, the train is better for those trips (described under "Getting Around the Tri-City," later). As these boat schedules tend to change from year to year, confirm your plans carefully at the TI. All boat trips are weather permitting, especially the faster hydrofoils. In shoulder season (April-June and Sept-Oct), even though most boats stop running from Gdańsk, several routes still run between Sopot, Gdynia, and Hel. Boats generally don't run in winter (Nov-March).

To Westerplatte: To travel by boat to the monument at Westerplatte, you have three options. The most enjoyable one is to ride the replica **17th-century galleons,** either the *Galeon Lew* ("Lion Galleon") or the *Czarna Perła* ("Black Pearl"). These over-the-top, touristy boats depart hourly from the embankment just outside the Green Gate for a lazy 1.5-hour round-trip cruise to Westerplatte and back. (You can choose to get off at Westerplatte and take a later boat back.) Both of them have English commentary on the way there and live nautical music on the return trip (if you've ever wanted to hear "What Shall We Do with a Drunken Sailor?" in Polish, here's your chance). It's not exactly pretty—you'll see more industry than scenery—but it's a fun excuse to set sail, even if you don't care about Westerplatte (40 zł round-trip, 30 zł one-way, the two boats take turns departing at the top of each hour 10:00-19:00 in July-Aug, fewer departures May-June and Sept, from the embankment near the Crane, mobile 601-629-191, www.galeony.pl). Two other, duller alternatives leave from right nearby: big, modern **Żegluga Gdańska** boats (www.zegluga.pl); or much cheaper but less frequent city-run **ZTM "ferry trams"** *(tramwaj wodny),* which depart from the embankment on the south side of the bridge (3-4/day).

To Hel: Various boats zip out to Hel in two hours during the summer. Though the specifics change from year to year, this route is most likely run by Żegluga Gdańska (May-June weekends only, July-Aug 3/day, 35 zł each way, www.zegluga.pl).

BY CRUISE SHIP

A few cruise ships (under 800 passengers) dock in **Gdańsk,** near the Westerplatte monument (described earlier; connected to the center by 45-minute pleasure-boat trip or 30-minute ride on bus #138). But most cruises advertising a stop in Gdańsk actually dock in the nearby town of **Gdynia.** For details on this town—and what to do if you arrive there—see page 279.

The Tri-City (Trójmiasto)

Gdańsk is the anchor of the three-part metropolitan region known as the Tri-City (Trójmiasto). The other two parts are as different as night and day: Sopot, a swanky resort town, and Gdynia, a practical, nose-to-the-grindstone business center. The Tri-City as a whole is home to bustling industry and a sprawling university, with several campuses and plenty of well-dressed, English-speaking students. Beyond the Tri-City, the long, skinny Hel Peninsula—a sparsely populated strip of fishing villages and fun-loving beaches—arches dramatically into the Baltic Sea.

Sopot—boasting sandy beaches, tons of tourists, and a certain elegance—is clearly the most appealing day-trip option. Gdynia offers a glimpse into workaday Poland, but leaves most visitors cold. Hel, which requires the better part of a day to visit, is worthwhile only if you've got perfect summer weather and a desire to lie on the beach.

GETTING AROUND THE TRI-CITY

Gdańsk, Sopot, and Gdynia are connected by regional commuter trains (*kolejka,* operated by SKM) as well as by trains of Poland's national railway (operated by PKP). Tickets for one system can't be used on the other. While trains for the two systems chug along the same tracks, they use different (but nearby) platforms/stations. For example, in Sopot, the SKM station is a few hundred feet before the PKP station. Regional SKM trains are much more frequent than long-distance PKP trains—they go in each direction about every 10-15 minutes (less frequently after 19:30). Trains to Hel are always operated by PKP.

In Gdańsk, two SKM train stations flank the major sights: the main train station ("Gdańsk Główny" on schedules, platforms 3-5) and, a few blocks south, Gdańsk Śródmieście (in the middle of the busy street in front of the National Museum). Buy tickets at the machine marked *SKM Bilety* (English instructions). Prices are based on the distance but are typically cheap (figure 6 zł one-way for the 35-minute trip from Gdańsk to Gdynia). Tickets purchased

Gdańsk Day Trips

from a machine come already validated, but if you buy one from a kiosk, you'll need to stamp it in the easy-to-miss yellow slots under the boards with SKM information.

Each city has multiple stops. Remember, in Gdańsk, use either Gdańsk Główny (the main station) or Gdańsk Śródmieście; for Sopot, use the stop called simply Sopot; and for Gdynia, it's Gdynia Główna (the main station).

For a more romantic—and much slower—approach, consider the boat (see "Gdańsk Connections," earlier).

Sopot

Sopot (SOH-poht), dubbed the "Nice of the North," was a celebrated haunt of beautiful people during the 1920s and 1930s, and it remains a popular beach getaway to this day.

Sopot was created in the early 19th century by Napoleon's doctor, Jean Georges Haffner, who believed Baltic Sea water to be therapeutic. By the 1890s, it had become a fashionable seaside resort. This gambling center boasted enough high-roller casinos to garner comparisons to Monte Carlo.

The casinos are gone, but the health resorts remain, and you'll still see more well-dressed people here per capita than just about anywhere else in the country. While it's not quite Cannes, Sopot feels relatively high class, which is unusual in otherwise unpretentious Poland. But even so, a childlike spirit of summer-vacation fun pervades this St-Tropez-on-the-Baltic, making it an all-around enjoyable place.

You can get the gist of Sopot in just a couple of hours. Zip in on the train, follow the main drag to the sea, wander the pier, get your feet wet at the beach, then head back to Gdańsk. Why not come here in the late afternoon, enjoy those last few rays of sunshine, stay for dinner, then take a twilight stroll on the pier?

Orientation to Sopot

The main pedestrian drag, Monte Cassino Heroes street (ulica Bohaterów Monte Cassino), leads to the Molo, the longest pleasure pier in Europe. From the Molo, a broad, sandy beach stretches in each direction. Running parallel to the surf is a tree-lined, people-filled path made for strolling.

Tourist Information: The TI is near the base of the Molo at Plac Zdrojowy 2 (daily 10:00-18:00, mobile 790-280-884, www.sopot.pl).

Arrival in Sopot: From the SKM station, exit to the left and walk down the street. After a block, you'll see the PKP train station on your left. Continue on to the can't-miss-it main drag, ulica Bohaterów Monte Cassino (marked by the big red-brick church steeple). Follow it to the right, down to the seaside.

Sights in Sopot

▲Monte Cassino Heroes Street
(Ulica Bohaterów Monte Cassino)

Nicknamed "Monciak" (MOHN-chak) by locals, this in-love-with-life promenade may well be Poland's most manicured street (and is named in honor of the Polish soldiers who helped the Allies pry Italy's Monte Cassino monastery from Nazi forces during World War II). Especially after all the suburban and industrial dreck you passed through to get here, it's easy to be charmed by this pretty drag. The street is lined with happy tourists, trendy cafés, al fresco restaurants, movie theaters, and late-19th-century facades (known for their wooden balconies).

The most popular building along here (on the left, about halfway down) is the so-called **Crooked House** (Krzywy Domek), a trippy, Gaudí-inspired building that looks like it's melting. Hard-partying Poles prefer to call it the "Drunken House," and say that when it looks straight, it's time to stop drinking.

Molo (Pier)

At more than 1,600 feet long, this is Europe's longest wooden entertainment pier. While you won't find any amusement-park rides, you will be surrounded by vendors, artists, and Poles having the time of their lives. Buy a *gofry* (Belgian waffle topped with whipped cream and fruit) or an oversized cloud of *wata cukrowa* (cotton candy), grab your partner's hand, and stroll with gusto (7.50 zł, free Oct-April, open long hours daily, www.molo.sopot.pl).

Climb to the top of the Art Nouveau lighthouse for a waterfront panorama. Scan the horizon for sailboats and tankers. Any pirate ships? For a jarring reality check, look over to Gdańsk. Barely visible from the Molo are two of the most important sites in 20th-century history: the towering monument at Westerplatte, where World War II started, and the cranes rising up from the Gdańsk Shipyard, where Solidarity was born and European communism began its long goodbye.

In spring and fall, the Molo is a favorite venue for pole vaulting—or is that Pole vaulting?

The Beach

Yes, Poland has beaches. Nice ones. When I heard Sopot compared to places like Nice, I'll admit that I scoffed. But when I saw those stretches of inviting sand as far as the eye can see, I wished I'd packed my swim trunks. (You could walk from Gdańsk all the way to Gdynia on beaches like this.) The sand is finer than anything I've seen in Croatia...though the water's not exactly crystal-clear. Most of the beach is public, except for a small private stretch in front of the Grand Hotel Sopot. Year-round, it's crammed with locals. At these northern latitudes, the season for bathing is brief and crowded.

Overlooking the beach next to the Molo is the **Grand Hotel Sopot.** It was renovated to top-class status just recently, but its history goes way back. They could charge admission for room #226, a multiroom suite that has hosted the likes of Adolf Hitler, Marlene Dietrich, and Fidel Castro (but not all at the same time). With all the trappings of Sopot's belle époque—dark wood, plush upholstery, antique furniture—this room had me imagining Hitler sitting at the desk, looking out to sea, and plotting the course of World War II.

Gdynia

Compared to its flashier sister cities, straightforward Gdynia (guh-DIN-yah) has retained a more working-class vibe, still in touch with its salty, fishing-village roots. Gdynia is less historic than Gdańsk or Sopot, as it was mostly built in the 1920s to be Poland's main harbor after Gdańsk became a free city. Although nowhere as attractive as Gdańsk or Sopot, Gdynia has an authentic feel and a lovely waterfront promenade (www.gdynia.pl).

Gdynia is a major business center, and—thanks to its youthful, progressive city government—has edged ahead of the rest of Poland in transitioning from communism. It enjoys one of the highest income levels in the country. Many of the crumbling downtown buildings have been renovated, and Gdynia is becoming known for its top-tier shopping—all the big designers have boutiques here. If a local woman has been shopping on Świętojańska street in Gdynia, it means that she's got some serious zloty.

Because Gdańsk's port is relatively shallow, the biggest cruise ships must put in at Gdynia...leaving confused tourists to poke around town looking for some medieval quaintness, before coming to their senses and heading for Gdańsk. Gdynia is also home to a major military harbor and an important NATO base.

To get a taste of Gdynia, take the SKM train to the Gdynia Główna station, follow signs to *wyjście do miasta*, cross the busy street, and walk 15 minutes down Starowiejska. When you come to the intersection with the broad Świętojańska street, turn right (in the direction the big statue is looking) and walk two blocks to the tree-lined park on the left. Head through the park to the Southern Pier (Molo Południowe). This concrete slab—not at all as charming as Sopot's wooden-boardwalk version—features a modern shopping mall and a smattering of sights, including an aquarium and a pair of permanently moored museum boats.

The big sightseeing draw in Gdynia is at the fairly distant Nabrzeże Francuskie (French Quay, where cruise ships arrive—handy for cruisers but a taxi ride away for tourists coming on the train). Here you'll find the new **Emigration Museum,** telling the story of Poles who left through Gdynia to find a better life in the New World. High-tech, interactive exhibits help bring the story to life (10 zł, Tue 12:00-20:00, Wed-Sun 10:00-18:00, closed Mon, www.polska1.pl). To get here, you can ride bus #119, #133, #137, or #147 from along Władysława IV avenue (between the train station and the waterfront) to the Dworzec Morski/Muzeum Emigracji stop.

ARRIVING BY CRUISE IN GDYNIA

Many Northern European cruises include a stop at "Gdańsk"; most of these actually put in at Gdynia's sprawling port. And, while Gydnia's town center is relatively manicured and pleasant, its port area is the opposite—like a Soviet Bloc bodybuilder, it's muscular and hairy. Cruise ships are shuffled among hardworking industrial piers that make the area feel uninviting. Three of the port's many piers are used for cruises: Most ships—especially large ones—dock at **Nabrzeże Francuskie** (French Quay). Some smaller ships may use the distant **Nabrzeże Stanów Zjednoczonych** (United States Quay) or the very central **Nabrzeże Pomorskie** (Pomeranian Quay, part of the Southern Pier, an easy walk from the center). Port information: www.port.gdynia.pl.

Unfortunately, there are no **ATMs** or money-exchange options at or near the cruise-ship berths, but cash machines are plentiful in downtown Gdynia.

To get from your cruise ship to Gdańsk, the best option is a **shuttle bus-plus-train connection.** First, ride your cruise line's shuttle bus into downtown Gdynia (5-minute trip; price depends on the cruise line). The shuttle drops you off at Skwer Kościuski; from here, it's a 10-minute walk (gradually uphill) to the train station. Start by walking away from the water on the broad, parklike boulevard. After the street becomes ulica 10 Lutego (you'll pass the TI on your right), it curves to the right; once you're around the corner, use the crosswalk to reach the train station (marked *Dworzec Podmiejski*). From here you can ride the handy *kolejka* commuter train into Gdańsk (runs every 10-15 minutes, 35 minutes; for details on this train, see "Getting Around the Tri-City," earlier). You can either get off at the Gdańsk Główny stop (main train station—see "Arrival in Gdańsk—By Train," on page 224), or stay on one more stop to Gdańsk Śródmieście (a slightly shorter walk to the start of my self-guided walk). Returning on the train, you want the Gdynia Główna stop.

Taxi drivers line up to meet arriving cruise ships. Cabbies here tend to overcharge, but if they use the meter, these are the legitimate rates: 20 zł to Gdynia's train station (*Dworzec*, DVOH-zhets); 125 zł to Gdańsk's Main Town; and 60-80 zł to Sopot. Taxi drivers generally take euros, though their off-the-cuff exchange rate may not be favorable.

For more details on Gdynia's port—and several others on the Baltic, North Sea, and beyond—pick up the *Rick Steves Northern European Cruise Ports* guidebook.

Hel Peninsula (Mierzeja Helska)

Out on the edge of things, this slender peninsula juts 20 miles into the ocean, providing a sunny retreat from the big cities—even as it shelters them from Baltic winds. Trees line the peninsula, and the northern edge is one long, sandy, ever-shifting beach.

On hot summer days, Hel is a great place to frolic in the sun with Poles. Sunbathing and windsurfing are practically religions here. Small resort villages line Hel Peninsula: Władysławowo (at the base), Chałupy, Kuźnica, Jastarnia, Jurata, and—at the tip—a town also called Hel. Beaches right near the towns can be crowded in peak season, but you're never more than a short walk away from your own stretch of sand. There are few permanent residents, and the waterfront is shared by budget campgrounds, hotels hosting middle-class families, and mansions of Poland's rich and famous (former president Aleksander Kwaśniewski has a summer home here).

The easiest way to go to Hel—aside from coveting thy neighbor's wife—is by boat (see "Gdańsk Connections," earlier). Trains from Gdańsk also reach Hel (summer only), and from Gdynia, you can take a train, bus, or minibus. But overland transit is crowded and slow—especially in summer, when Hel is notorious for its hellish traffic jams.

POMERANIA

Malbork Castle • Toruń

The northwestern part of Poland—known as Pomerania (Pomorze)—has nothing to do with excitable little dogs, but it does offer two attractions worth singling out. Malbork, the biggest Gothic castle in Europe, is one of the best castles in Eastern Europe. Farther south, the Gothic town of Toruń—the birthplace of Copernicus, and a favorite spot of every proud Pole—holds hundreds of red-brick buildings...and, it seems, even more varieties of tasty gingerbread.

PLANNING YOUR TIME

Malbork works well as a side-trip from Gdańsk (frequent trains, 30-45 minutes each way), and it's also on the main train line from Gdańsk to Warsaw. While Toruń doesn't merit a long detour, it's worth a stroll or an overnight if you want to sample a smaller Polish city. Unfortunately, Toruń is on a different train line than Malbork—if you visit both in one day, it'll be a very long one. Ideally, if traveling round-trip from Warsaw, see one of these destinations coming to Gdańsk, and visit the other on the way back. Or do Malbork as a side-trip from Gdańsk, then visit Toruń on the way to or from Warsaw.

Malbork Castle

Malbork Castle is soaked in history. The biggest brick castle in the world, the largest castle of the Gothic period, and one of Europe's most imposing fortresses, it sits smugly on a marshy plain at the edge of the town of Malbork, 35 miles southeast of Gdańsk. This was the headquarters of the notorious Teutonic Knights, a Germanic band of ex-Crusaders who dominated northern Poland in the Middle Ages.

GETTING THERE

Malbork is on the train line between Gdańsk and Warsaw. Coming by train from Gdańsk, you'll enjoy views of the castle on your right as you cross the Nogat River. Store your luggage at the station's lockers and head into town.

To get from the station to the castle, consider taking a **taxi** (shouldn't cost more than about 10 zł, though corrupt cabbies charge twice that—ask for an estimate before you get in). Or you can **walk** 15 minutes to the castle: Leave the station to the right, walk straight, and go through the pedestrian underpass beneath the busy road (by the red staircase). When you emerge on the other side, follow the busy road (noticing peek-a-boo views on your right of the castle's main tower) and take your first right turn (onto Kościuszki, the main shopping street). On Kościuszki, you'll pass the fancy pink building housing the TI on the right. Near the bottom of Kościuszki, at the fountain and the McDonald's, jog right, then bear left over two moats to find the ticket office (marked *kasa*).

ORIENTATION TO MALBORK CASTLE

Cost and Hours: Mid-April-Sept—40 zł, open Tue-Sun 9:00-19:00; Oct-mid-April—30 zł, open Tue-Sun 10:00-15:00; closed Mon year-round; grounds stay open an hour later than the castle; tel. 55-647-0978, www.zamek.malbork.pl.

Tours: You are technically required to enter the castle with a three-hour **guided tour** or an audioguide, but this is rarely enforced—you can usually just walk in. (If they do enforce this rule, simply enter with a Polish group—tours leave from the ticket booth every 15 minutes—and split off on your own once inside.) My self-guided tour covers the basics.

Your ticket includes a good **audioguide,** but supply is limited—they often run out during peak times (11:00-15:00). Try to get one if you can—it lets you wander aimlessly through this fascinating place, keying in *audio-tour stop* numbers as you explore.

In the summer, ask about free **English tours** (often 2-3/

POMERANIA

day). Any time of year, you can pay 210 zł for a private English tour (book a few days ahead, tel. 55-647-0978, kasa@zamek. malbork.pl). If you show up and there's no scheduled English tour, ask whether an English-speaking guide is available. Then take the initiative, play "tour organizer," and gather a group of frustrated English speakers to split the cost of a private tour.

Eating: Several cheap food stands cluster outside the castle (by the river). For a meal inside the castle complex, the **$$$ Gothic Café,** under the stairs to the armory in the Middle Castle, is a serious restaurant with a renowned chef. Dishing up traditional Polish food inspired by old dishes once served here, it's handy for its lunch deal that includes a main dish and soup. You can eat in the busy cellar or out in the garden (tel. 55-647-0889, www.gothic.com.pl).

Best Views: The views of massive Malbork are stunning—especially at sunset, when its red brick glows. Be sure to walk out across the footbridge over the Nogat River. The most scenic part of the castle is probably the twin-turreted, riverside Bridge Gate, which used to be connected by a bridge to the opposite bank.

BACKGROUND

When the Teutonic Knights were invited to Polish lands in the 13th century to convert neighboring pagans, they found the perfect site for their new capital here, on the bank of the Nogat River. Construction began in 1274. After the Teutonic Knights conquered Gdańsk in 1308, the order moved its official headquarters from Venice to Malbork, where they remained for nearly 150 years. They called the castle Marienburg, the "Castle of Mary," in honor of the order's patron saint.

At its peak in the early 1400s, Malbork was both the imposing home of a seemingly unstoppable army and Europe's final bastion of chivalric ideals. Surrounded by swamplands, with only one gate in need of defense, it was a tough nut to crack. Malbork Castle was never taken by force in the Middle Ages, though it had to withstand various sieges by the Poles during the Thirteen Years' War (1454-1466)—including a campaign that lasted more than three years. Finally, in 1457, the Polish king gained control of Malbork by buying off Czech mercenaries guarding the castle. Malbork became a Polish royal residence for 300 years. But when Poland was partitioned in the late 18th century, this region went back into

German hands. The castle became a barracks, windows were sealed up, delicate vaulting was damaged, bricks were quarried for new buildings, and Malbork deteriorated.

In the late 19th century, Romantic German artists and poets rediscovered the place. An architect named Konrad Steinbrecht devoted 40 years of his life to Malbork, painstakingly restoring the palace to its medieval splendor. A half-century later, the Nazis used the castle to house POWs. Hitler—who, like many Germans, had a soft spot for Malbork's history—gave the order to defend it to the last man. About half of it was destroyed by the Soviet army, who saw it as a symbol of long-standing German domination. But it was restored once again, and today Malbork has been returned to its Teutonic glory.

❍ SELF-GUIDED TOUR

The official tour of Malbork lasts about three hours. While there's plenty to see, my self-guided tour shows you the highlights at your own pace. Use the map on the next page to navigate and jump around as needed. The castle complex is a bit of a maze, with various entrances and exits for each room, often behind closed (but unlocked) doors. Don't be shy about grabbing a medieval doorknob and letting yourself in.

Lower Castle and Entrance Gate

Just past the ticket taker, step through the front gate and stand on the castle's drawbridge. Look up at one of Europe's most intimidating fortresses—home to the Grand Master, monks, and knights of the Teutonic Order.

Above the door to the brick gate is a sculpture of the Virgin Mary with Baby Jesus...next to a shield and helmet. The two messages to visitors: This castle is protected by Mary, and the Teutonic Knights are here to convert pagans—by force, if necessary.

From the drawbridge, look right to observe the formidable fortifications. The rooster-capped tower (which contains a toilet) is connected by a sky bridge to the fancy Gothic 14th-century facade of the brick infirmary—kept at a distance for disease control.

Pass through the gate, into the entry area. Imagine the gate behind you closing. Look up to see wooden chutes where archers are preparing to rain arrows down on you. Your last thought: Maybe we should have left the Teutonic Knights alone, after all.

Before you're pierced by arrows, read the castle's history in its walls: The foundation is made of huge stones brought from Sweden, which are rare in these marshy lands. But most of the castle, like so many other buildings in northern Poland, was built with handmade red brick. Throughout the castle, the darker-colored, rougher brick is original, and the lighter-colored, smoother brick

Malbork Castle

ST. JOHN

TERRACES

N
o
g
a
t

To Town &
Train Station

PIASTOWSKA

❼

HIGH
CASTLE

❻

TICKET OFFICE
(MEET TOURS)

❽

BRIDGE
GATE

DRAW-
BRIDGE

STAROŚCIŃSKA

WC

❷   ❺ ❹

❸

MIDDLE
CASTLE

❶

To
Best
Views

DRAW-
BRIDGE

FOOD
STANDS

ENTRANCE
GATE

R
i
v
e
r

LOWER
CASTLE

SOUVENIR
SHOP

100 Meters

100 Yards

POMERANIA

❶ Amber Collection (downstairs)
❷ Armory (upstairs) & Gothic
    Café (downstairs)
❸ "Boiler Room" (downstairs)
    & Grand Refectory (upstairs)
❹ Grand Master's Palace

❺ Grand Master Statues
❻ Well
❼ Dansker Tower
❽ St. Mary's Church

was used during later restorations (in the 19th century, and again after World War II). Marvel at the ironclad doors and the heavy portcullis.

Venture through two more enclosed spaces, watching for the holes in the wall (for more guards and soldiers). The Teutonic Knights connected nearby lakes to create a system of canals, forming a moat around the castle that could be crossed only by this drawbridge. Ponder the fact that you have to go through five separate, well-defended gates to reach the...

Middle Castle (Zamek Średni)

This part of Malbork, built at an uphill incline to make it even more imposing, was designed to impress. Knights and monks lived here.

Let's get oriented: To your left is the east wing, where visiting monks would sleep. Today this houses the Amber Collection (ground floor) and the armory (upstairs). To the right (west) as you enter the main courtyard is the Grand Refectory (closer to the entrance) and the Grand Master's Palace (the taller, squarer building at the far end).

• *Before we move on, this is a good time to read up on the history of the Teutonic Knights (see sidebar). When you're ready to continue, enter the ground floor of the building on the left (at audio-tour stop #15; remember, don't be shy about opening closed doors), and visit the...*

Amber Collection

This exhibit will make jewelry shoppers salivate. For a primer, read the "All About Amber" sidebar on page 246. You'll start 42 million years ago and follow the story of amber. Begin at the huge chunks of raw amber and the illuminated display of inclusions (bugs and other organic objects stuck in the amber, à la *Jurassic Park*). Some of the ancient amber artifacts displayed here are up to 3,000 years old. These were found in graves, put there by people who thought amber would help the deceased enter a better world. Wandering the hall, you'll see all manner of amber creations: boxes, brooches, necklaces, chess sets, pipes, miniature ships, wine glasses, and belts for skinny-waisted, fashion-conscious women. Look for two truly exquisite pieces: a small casket and an altar. Many of the finely decorated jewelry boxes and chests have ivory, silver, or shell inlays—better for contrast than gold. The portable religious shrines and altars allowed travelers to remain reverent on the road and still pack light. Find the amber crucifix. This is a small replica of a six-foot-tall amber and silver cross, presented to St. John Paul II by the people of Gdańsk. Another exhibit case contains necklaces displaying the full range of amber colors, from opaque white at the top, to transparent yellow in the middle, to virtually black at the bottom.

• *Go back outside and turn left, to the wooden staircase above the recommended Gothic Café. Go up that staircase, and several more inside, to the top-floor...*

Armory

This is a small armory for such a massive castle. In its two rooms you'll see an impressive array of swords, armor, and other armaments. Look for the 600-year-old "hand-and-a-half" swords—too big to be held in one hand. At the end, in the display of cannons, pikes, and spears, find the giant shield. These shields could be lined up to form a portable "wall" to protect the knights. Downstairs, the suit of armor from the Hussars—Polish horseback knights—came with wings, which created a terrifying sound when the horses were galloping.

• *Head back outside (noticing the handy and rare WC straight ahead). Cross the main courtyard going downhill and enter the smaller courtyard through the passage next to the stubby, dark-wood-topped tower. Find the dark, steep, and unlabeled steps down into the...*

"Boiler Room"

The Teutonic Knights had a surprisingly sophisticated method for heating this huge complex. You see a furnace down below and a holding area for hot rocks above. The radiant heat given off by the rocks spread through the vents without also filling them with smoke (illustrated by a chart on the wall). This is one of 11 such "boiler rooms" in the castle complex. As you tour the rest of the castle, keep an eye out for little saucer-sized heating vents in the floor.

• *Climb back up the stairs, take an immediate left through a tiny arch, and then go left again, up through the door labeled #5 (not down, which takes you out of the castle). This leads into the...*

Grand Master's Palace

This was one of the grandest royal residences in medieval Europe, used in later times by Polish kings and German *Kaisers.* (Today it's sometimes used for special exhibitions.)

• *Walk through the kitchen into the big and bright...*

   Grand Refectory: With remarkable palm vaulting and grand frescoes, this dining hall hosted feasts for up to 400 people to celebrate a military victory or to impress visiting dignitaries. Notice the 36 heating vents—which are directly above the boiler room you just visited—designed to keep the VIPs warm.

• *From here, climb the stairs into the...*

Private Rooms of the Grand Master: Though the Teutonic Order dictated that the monks sleep in dormitories, the Grand Master made an exception for himself—with a suite of private rooms that came with his own toilet (with a river view) and his own chapel, dedicated to St. Catherine. Exploring the Top Knight's residence, appreciate the show-off decor (including some 15th-century original frescoes of wine leaves and grapes). His private bedroom was decorated with frescoes of four virgins—female martyrs. The passage outside the private rooms came with a washbasin, as anyone wanting an audience with the Grand Master had to wash both his hands and his feet.

Next, enter the private dining room, the **Winter Refectory,** with fewer windows (better insulation) and little manhole-like openings in the floor where the "central heating" entered the room. The adjacent **Summer Refectory** had big stained-glass windows. With all the delicate vaulting supported by a single pillar in the middle, this room was clearly not designed with defense in mind. In fact, medieval Polish armies focused their attacks on this room. On one legendary occasion, the attackers—tipped off by a spy— knew that an important meeting was going on here and fired a cannonball into the room. It just missed the pillar. (You can see where the cannonball hit the wall, just above the fireplace.) The ceiling eventually did collapse during World War II.

• *Back out in the courtyard, look for the four...*

Grand Master Statues

Though this was a religious order, these powerful guys look more like kings than monks. From left to right, shake hands with Hermann von Salza (who was Grand Master when the Teutonic Knights came to Poland); Siegfried von Feuchtwangen (who actually moved the T. K. capital from Venice to Malbork, and who conquered Gdańsk for the Knights—oops, can't shake his hand, which was supposedly chopped off by Soviet troops); Winrich von Kniprode (who oversaw Malbork's Golden Age and turned it into a castle fit for a king); and Markgraf Albrecht von Hohenzollern (the last Grand Master before the order dissolved and converted to Protestantism).

• *To the right of the statues, continue into the High Castle by passing over the...*

Drawbridge

As you cross, notice the extensive system of fortifications and moats protecting the innermost part of the castle just ahead. Check

The Teutonic Knights

The Order of the Teutonic Knights began in the Holy Land in 1191, during the Third Crusade. These German militarized monks built hospitals and cared for injured knights. When the Crusades ended in the 12th century, the Knights returned to Europe and reorganized as a chivalric order of Christian mercenaries—pagan-killers for hire.

In 1226, a northern Polish duke called in the Teutonic Knights to subdue a tribe of pagans who had been attacking his lands. Clad in their white cloaks with skinny black crosses, the Teutonic Knights spent 60 years "saving" the pagans by turning them into serfs or brutally massacring them.

Job done, the Teutonic Knights decided to stick around. With the support of the pope and the Holy Roman Emperor (who were swayed by the Knights' religious zeal), the Knights built one of Europe's biggest and most imposing fortresses: Malbork. In 1308, they seized large parts of northern Poland (including Gdańsk), cutting off Polish access to the Baltic Sea. The Knights grew rich from Hanseatic trade, specializing in amber, grain, and timber. By the late 14th century, the Teutonic Knights had grown to become Europe's largest-ever monastic state and were threatening to overtake Lithuania.

Inspired by a mutual desire to oust the Teutonic Knights, the Poles and the Lithuanians teamed up. In 1386, Polish Princess Jadwiga married Lithuanian Prince Władysław Jagiełło, kick-starting a grand new dynasty: the Jagiellonians.

Every Pole knows the date July 15, 1410: the Battle of Grunwald. King Władysław Jagiełło and Lithuanian Grand Duke Vytautas the Great led a ragtag army of some 40,000 soldiers—Lithuanians, Poles, other Slavs, and even speedy Tatar horsemen—against 27,000 Teutonic Knights. At the end of the day, some 18,000 Poles and Lithuanians were dead—but so were half of the Teutonic Knights, and the other half had been captured. Poland and Lithuania were victorious.

The Battle of Grunwald marked the beginning of the end for the Teutonic Knights, who were finally defeated during the Thirteen Years' War (1454-1466). The order officially dissolved in 1575, when they converted to Protestantism and much of their land was folded into Prussia. Later, 19th-century Polish Romantics reimagined the Teutonic Knights as an early symbol of Germanic oppression—poignant among Poles, who suffered through a new round of German abuse in World War II. Some conspiracy theorists believe the Teutonic Knights are still very much active...but that's another story.

out the cracks in the walls (on right)—an increasing threat to this ever-settling castle set on marshy, unstable terrain. On the left is a collection of stone catapult balls that were actually fired at this castle when it was under siege. (Look high above to see the dents such stones can make.) The passage ahead is lined with holes (for surveillance) and with chutes up above (to pour scalding water or pitch on unwanted visitors). It's not quite straight—so a cannon fired here would hit the side wall of the passage, rather than enter the High Castle and its central courtyard. Which is what you're about to do now.

High Castle (Zamek Wysoki)

This is the heart of the castle, and its oldest section. From this spot, the Teutonic Knights governed their vast realm—the largest monk-ruled territory in European history. As much a monastery as a fortress, the High Castle was off-limits to all but 60 monks of the Teutonic Order and their servants. (The knights stayed in the Middle Castle.) Here you'll find the monks' dormitories, chapels, church, and refectory. As this was the nerve center of the Teutonic Knights—the T. K. HQ—it was also their last line of defense. They stored enormous amounts of food here in case of a siege.

In the middle of the High Castle courtyard is a **well**—an essential part of any inner castle, especially one as prone to sieges as Malbork. At the top is a sculpture of a pelican. Because this noble bird was believed to kill itself to feed its young (notice that it's piercing its own chest with its beak), it was often used in the Middle Ages as a symbol for the self-sacrifice of Jesus.

• *Take some time to explore the...*

High Castle—Ground Floor

Work clockwise around the courtyard from where you entered. A door leads to the prison (with small "solitary confinement" cells near the entrance). Along the next wall of the cloister is a post-WWII photo of bombed-out Malbork. Just adjacent, hiding in the far corner, is an exhibit on stained-glass windows from the castle church. Somewhere around here, you should see a demonstration of how medieval money was made. The Teutonic Knights minted their own coins—and you can buy your very own freshly minted replica today.

• *Continuing around the courtyard, you'll find the...*

Kitchen: This exhibit—with a long table piled with typical ingredients from that time—really gives you a feel for medieval monastery life. The monks who lived here ate three meals a day, along with lots of beer (made here) and wine (imported from France, Italy, and Hungary). A cellar under the kitchen was used as a primitive refrigerator—big chunks of ice were cut from the frozen

POMERANIA

river in winter, stored in the basement, and used to keep food cool in summer. Behind the long table, see the big dumbwaiter (with five shelves for hot dishes), which connects this kitchen with the refectory upstairs. Step into the giant stove and look up the biggest chimney in the castle.

• *Now go back out into the courtyard and climb up the stairs near where you first entered.*

High Castle—Middle Floor

• *From the top of the stairs, the first door on the left (with the colorfully painted arch) leads to the most important room of the High Castle, the...*

Chapter Room: Monks gathered here after Mass, and it was also the site for meetings of Teutonic Knights from around the countryside. If a Grand Master was killed in battle, the new one would be elected here. Carvings above each chair indicated the status of the man who sat there. The big chair belonged to the Grand Master. Notice the little windows above his chair, connecting this room to the church next door. Ecclesiastical music would filter in through these windows; imagine the voices of 60 monks bouncing around with these acoustics.

While monks are usually thought to pursue simple lives, the elegant vaulting in this room is anything but plain. The 14th-century frescoes (restored in the 19th century) depict Grand Masters. In the floor are more vents for the central heating.

• *Leave the Chapter Room and walk straight ahead, imagining the monk-filled corridors of Teutonic times. The first door on the right is the...*

Treasury: As you explore the five rooms of the tax collector and the house administrator, notice the wide variety of safes and other lock boxes. Documents, amber, and coins were kept behind heavily armored and well-locked doors.

• *Continue around the cloister. At the end of the corridor, spot the little devil at the bottom of the vaulting (on the right, about eye level). He's pulling his beard and crossing his legs—pointing you down the long corridor leading about 50 yards away from the cloister to the...*

Dansker Tower: From the devil's grimace, you might have guessed that this tower houses the latrine. Four wooden toilet stalls filled this big room. Where one is missing, you can look down to see how the "toilets" simply dropped the waste into the moat. For obvious sanitary (and olfactory) reasons, this potty tower is set apart from the main part of the castle. The bins above the toilets were filled with cabbage leaves, to be used by the T. K. as TP (and as an organic form of Preparation H). This tower could also serve as a final measure of defense—it's easier to defend than the entire castle. Food was stored above, just in case. More info on this grand castle WC is on the wall.

• *Return down the long corridor. Before the end, on the right-hand side of the long passage, a door leads into the...*

Church Exhibition: Once dormitories for the monks, these three rooms now display a wide range of relics from the church. In the last room, on the far wall, is the artistic highlight of the castle: a finely carved and painted three-panel altarpiece from about 1500 featuring the coronation of Mary. Mary's face is mesmerizing. Characteristic of the late Gothic period, the robes seem to fly unrealistically (as if they were bent metal).

• *Back out in the main cloister, turn right, and continue to the end, arriving at the...*

Golden Gate: This elaborate doorway—covered in protective glass—marks the entrance to **St. Mary's Church.** Before en-

tering, examine this rare original door. Ringed with detailed carvings from the New Testament, and symbolic messages about how monks of the Teutonic Order should live their lives, it's a marvelous example of late-13th-century art. At the bottom-left end of the arch, find the five wise virgins who, having filled their lamps with oil and conserved it wisely, are headed to heaven. On the right, the five foolish virgins who overslept and used up all their oil are damned, much to their dismay. Step inside the church to appreciate a glorious Gothic interior—recently reopened after a lengthy restoration. The highlight is the dramatic 25-foot-tall Madonna.

• *Back outside, go through the narrow door next to the Golden Gate (on the right) and hike up the tight spiral staircase to the final set of exhibits.*

High Castle—Top Floor

Walk through an exhibit about the illustrious guests of the castle. At the end, descend into the monks' common room (left, at the

bottom of the stairs). Over the fireplace is a relief depicting the Teutonic Knights fighting the pagans. To the left and above (see the stone windows) is a balcony where musicians entertained the monks after a meal. The next, very long room, with seven pillars, is the refectory, where the monks ate in silence. Along the right-hand wall are lockable storage boxes for tableware. At the end of this room, just beyond another ornate fireplace, notice the grated hole in the wall. This is where the dumbwaiter comes up from the kitchen (which we saw below). Beyond this room is an exhibit about the architectural renovation of the castle.

• *Your Malbork tour ends here. You leave the way you came. En route, you can walk around terraces lining the inner moat, between the castle walls (stairs lead down off the drawbridge, by the catapult balls). It's hardly a must-see, but it's pleasant enough, with the Grand Master's garden, a cemetery for monks, and the remains of the small St. Anne's Chapel (with Grand Master tombs).*

MALBORK CONNECTIONS

From Malbork by Train to: Gdańsk (2/hour, about half are express EIC trains that take 30 minutes, the rest are slower regional trains that take around 45 minutes), **Toruń** (about every 2 hours, 2.5 hours, change in Iława), **Warsaw** (hourly, 2.5 hours).

Toruń

Toruń (TOH-roon) is a pretty, lazy Gothic town conveniently located about halfway between Warsaw and Gdańsk. It's worth a couple of hours to stroll the lively streets, ogle the huge red-brick buildings, and savor the flavor of perhaps Poland's most livable city.

With about 210,000 residents and 30,000 students (at Copernicus University), Toruń is a thriving burg. Like Kraków (and unlike most other Polish cities), Toruń escaped destruction during World War II and remains well-preserved today. Locals brag that their city is a "mini Kraków." But that sells both cities short. Toruń lacks Kraków's over-the-top romanticism, and its sights are quickly exhausted. On the other hand, Toruń may well be Poland's most user-friendly city: tidy streets with a sensible grid plan (and English signposts to keep you on track), wide pedestrian boulevards crammed with locals who greet each other like they're long-lost friends, and an easygoing ambience that seems to say, "Hey—relax." And, while it has its share of tourists, Toruń feels more off-the-beaten-path than the other Polish destinations in this book.

Toruń clings fiercely to its two claims to fame: It's the proud birthplace of the astronomer Copernicus (Mikołaj Kopernik), and home to a dizzying variety of gingerbread treats (*piernika;* pyer-NEE-kah).

Orientation to Toruń

Everything in Toruń worth seeing is in the walled Old Town, climbing up a gentle hill from the Vistula River. The broad, traffic-free main drag, ulica Szeroka (called Różana at the entrance of town) bisects the Old Town, running parallel to the river. The **TI** is on the main square, behind the Old Town Hall (closed Sun off-season, Rynek Staromiejski 25, tel. 56-621-0930, www.it.torun.pl).

ARRIVAL IN TORUŃ

Toruń's main train station (called Toruń Główny) is across the river from the Old Town, about a mile away. The main hall has ticket windows, an ATM, and lockers. (The TI also stores bags for a small fee.)

To reach the Old Town, you have two options: If you go out the door from the main hall, you'll spot **taxis** waiting to take you into town (the trip costs around 15-20 zł). To take the **bus,** buy a ticket from the *RUCH* kiosk, then take the pedestrian underpass outside (look for *wyjście do miasta* sign and bus icon) and find the bus stop for bus #22, #25, or #27. Take the bus to Plac Rapackiego, the first stop after the long bridge. To return to the station, catch bus #22, #25, or #27 across the busy road from where you got off.

Toruń Walk

This brief self-guided walk takes you through the heart of Toruń. With no stops, you could do it in less than 30 minutes.

• *From the Plac Rapackiego bus stop, head into town through the passageways under the colorful buildings. Within a block, you're at the bustling...*

Old Town Market Square (Rynek Staromiejski): This square is surrounded by huge brick buildings and outdoor restaurants buzzing with lively locals. The **Old Town Hall** (Ratusz Staromiejski) fills the middle of the square, as was often the case in medieval Hanseatic towns. Its fine museum and climbable tower are Toruń's main sights worth visiting (described later, under "Sights in Toruń"). The building with the pointy spires on the right (across from the Old Town Hall) is the **Artus Court,** where the medieval town council and merchants' guilds met. While the town was founded in 1231, the current building is Neo-Gothic, dating from the 19th century.

The guy playing his violin in front of the Old Town Hall is a

Toruń

ETHNOGRAPHIC PARK

To Main Bus Station

100 Meters
100 Yards

OLD TOWN

New Market Square

FRANCISZKAŃSKA
CHURCH OF VIRGIN MARY
PANNY MARII   Old Town Market Square
CHURCH OF HOLY SPIRIT
TOWN HALL MUSEUM & TOWER
COPERNICUS STATUE
ULIKA SZEROKA
WIELKE GARBARY
Plac Rapackiego
RÓŻANA
PIERNIKI GINGERBREAD SHOP
CASTLE RUINS
B
#22, 25 & 27
WALK BEGINS
MIKOŁAJA KOPERNIKA
GINGERBREAD MUSEUM
CATHEDRAL OF TWO ST. JOHNS
TOWN WALLS
RABIAŃSKA   COPERNICUS HOUSE
TOILET TOWER
KLASZTORNA GATE
BULWAR FILADELFIJSKI
ŻEGLARSKA GATE
BANKOWA
MOSTOWA GATE
RIVERSIDE PROMENADE
River
Vistula
PIŁSUDSKIEGO BRIDGE
To Main Train Station (Toruń Glowny)

❶ Hotel Karczma "Spichrz"
❷ Hotel Retman

POMERANIA

rafter *(retman)*—one of the medieval lumberjacks who lashed tree trunks together and floated them down the Vistula to Gdańsk. This particular rafter came to Toruń when the town was infested with frogs. He wooed them with his violin and marched them out of town. (Hmm...sounds like a certain pied piper....)

The bigger statue, at the other end of the Old Town Hall, depicts **Mikołaj Kopernik,** better known as Nicolaus Copernicus (1473-1543). This Toruń-born son of aristocrats turned the world on its ear when he suggested that the sun, not the earth, is the center of the universe (the "heliocentric theory"). Toruń is serious about this local boy done good—he's the town mascot, as well as the namesake of the local university. Among its fields of study, Copernicus U. has a healthy astronomy program. There's a planetarium in the Old Town (just past the far corner of the square) and a giant radio telescope on the town outskirts. Despite all the local fuss over Copernicus, there's some dispute about his ethnicity; he was born in Toruń, all right, but at a time when it was the predominantly German town of "Thorn." So is he Polish or German? (For more on Copernicus, visit his birth house—now a modest museum on the astronomer—just two blocks away and described later, under "Sights in Toruń".)

Copernicus faces a shiny donkey at the corner of **Szeroka** and Żeglarska streets. We'll venture down Żeglarska first, and then return to walk down Szeroka. By the way, that shiny donkey with a sharp ridge on his back, while happy today, recalls a humiliating punishment. Centuries ago, delinquents and petty criminals needing to be set straight would be forced to straddle this donkey—after townspeople had tied heavy stones to their feet, weighing them down painfully.

• *But you're on vacation and, rather than humiliation, you get gingerbread. Head down Żeglarska to #25 (on the right).*

Pierniki (Gingerbread) Shop: For Poles, Toruń is synonymous with **gingerbread** *(piernika)*—you'll smell its sweet scent all over town. This Toruń treat can be topped with different kinds of jams or glazes, and/or dipped in chocolate. This shop has a fun system: All the varieties cost the same, so you can create just the mix you like by pointing. *Róża* is rose, *malina* is raspberry, *czarna porzeczka* is black currant, *morela* is apricot, and—of course—*czekolada* is chocolate.

• *A few steps down and across the street is the...*

Cathedral of Two Saint Johns (Katedra Św. Jana Chrzciciela i Jana Ewangelisty): Dedicated in the 12th century to John the Baptist and John the Evangelist, this is the parish church of the Old Town. From the street, notice the architectural heaviness: This marshy land lacked big stones, so instead of flying buttresses, they designed a bulky and sturdy brick structure so they could build big. Stepping inside, you find pure Gothic architecture. The gravestones of big shots pave the floor. Each trade guild had its own chapel. To the left of the altar, notice the finely restored 13th-century *Last Judgment*. In the rear of the church (on the right) is the baptismal font where, in 1473, Copernicus was baptized.

• *Having satisfied your ginger tooth and seen the town's most important church, head back to the square and that painful donkey, turn right, and join the human stream down the appropriately named...*

Ulica Szeroka ("Wide Street"): This enjoyable pedestrian promenade leads through the heart of town. Embedded in the paving bricks are the coats of arms of Toruń's medieval trading partners. And on each side of the street is an eclectic commotion of fun facades.

About 30 yards before the road forks at the stately, white Empik building, look down narrow Przedzamcze street to the right to see fragments of the town wall. This marks the border between the Old Town and the New Town (chartered only about 30 years later—both in the 13th century). While these areas are collectively known today as the unified "Old Town," they were quite different in the Middle Ages—each with its own market square, and separated by a wall. (If you're curious to see the New Town Square and

Town Hall, take the left fork at the Empik building and walk two blocks up ulica Królowej Jadwigi.)

• *Turn right down Przedzamcze, bear left at the parking lot, and continue under the stubby, standalone brick gate to the...*

Toruń Castle Ruins: This castle, built by the Teutonic Knights who were so influential in northern Poland in the Middle Ages (see page 290), was destroyed in the 15th century by the locals—who, aside from a heap of bricks, left only the tower that housed the Teutonic toilets. The ruins have nothing much to offer, but what survives is one of the better toilet towers in Europe—which was connected to the castle by an elevated walkway and located far enough away to keep things hygienic. The old mill next to the toilet is now a hotel named 1231, for the date the Teutonic Order arrived here.

• *Our walk is over. You can backtrack the way you came and explore more of the city (including the sights listed next). Or you can take a quick riverside stroll: Go under the toilet tower and down to the Vistula River, turn right, and stroll along the castle and 14th-century city walls back to your starting point. The road is called Bulwar Filadelfijski—for Toruń's sister city in Pennsylvania.*

Sights in Toruń

Toruń is more about strolling than it is about sightseeing—the town's museums are underwhelming. Aside from its half-dozen red-brick churches (any of which are worth dropping into), the following attractions are worth considering on a rainy day.

▲City Hall Museum and Tower

Like Kraków's Cloth Hall, this building, dominating the town square, was a general market. It served as the heart of the city. Today it offers the only chance in town to see historic artifacts. It gives a good history of the Teutonic Knights, who first came to Toruń in 1231. You'll see intimate bits and pieces of history—from pewter tankards to old gingerbread molds—that show the richness of this traders' city. Another wing of the ground floor is filled with medieval church art saved from the region's churches. Much of it is pre-Reformation Catholic art, with lots of Marys (the patron of the Teutonic Order) and a close-up look at some 14th-century stained glass. The royal halls upstairs feature portraits and fine 17th-century inlaid wooden doors. The 130-foot-tall tower can be climbed (on narrow wooden steps) for great views over the city center.

Cost and Hours: 11 zł apiece for museum and tower, 17-zł combo-ticket for both, free on Wed; Tue-Sun 10:00-18:00, Oct-April until 16:00, closed Mon year-round; Rynek Staromiejski 1, tel. 56-660-5612, www.muzeum.torun.pl.

POMERANIA

Gingerbread Museum (Muzeum Piernika)

This fun attraction—by far Toruń's liveliest—is an actual working gingerbread bakery of yore. Barefoot, costumed medieval bakers walk you through the traditional process of rolling, cutting out, baking, and tasting your own batch of gingerbread cookies (30-40 minutes, start to finish). After aging for 12 weeks to achieve the proper consistency, the dough bakes for only 12 minutes—or, according to the medieval bakers, about 50 Hail Marys.

Cost and Hours: 14 zł, daily 10:00-18:00, Polish tours start at the top of each hour, English demonstrations most likely at 13:00 and 16:00, can be crowded in peak times—call ahead to confirm schedule and reserve a spot, 2 blocks toward the river from Old Town Market Square at Rabiańska 9, tel. 56-663-6617, www.muzeumpiernika.pl.

Copernicus House (Dom Kopernika)

Filling a pair of beautiful, gabled brick buildings, this dull, over-priced little museum celebrates the hero of Toruń. As much about medieval Toruń as about the famous astronomer, and sprawling over several floors in the two buildings, the exhibits loosely explain Nicolaus Copernicus' life and achievements.

The displays are copies of important documents and paintings and models of his instruments. The second part of the exhibit is an 18-minute slideshow with recorded commentary about medieval Toruń, with a model of the city that lights up dramatically at appropriate moments (plays on the half-hour, in English by request).

Cost and Hours: Museum only-11 zł, model/slideshow only-13 zł, 20-zł combo-ticket for both, free on Wed; Tue-Sun 10:00-18:00, Oct-April until 16:00, closed Mon year-round; Kopernika 15, tel. 56-662-7038, www.muzeum.torun.pl.

Sleeping in Toruń

$$ Hotel Karczma "Spichrz" ("Granary") is a fresh, atmospheric hotel in a renovated old granary. Its 23 rooms and public spaces are a fun blend of old and new—with huge wooden beams around every corner and the aroma of the restaurant's wood-fired grill wafting through the halls. It's comfortable, central, well-priced, and a little kitschy (tall people may not appreciate low ceilings and beams, elevator, a block off the main drag toward the river at ulica Mostowa 1, tel. 56-657-1140, www.spichrz.pl, hotel@spichrz.pl). The restaurant is also good.

$ Hotel Retman ("Rafter") has 29 older but nicely appointed rooms over a restaurant just down the street from the Gingerbread Museum (ulica Rabiańska 15, tel. 56-657-4460, www.hotel-retman.pl, recepcja@hotelretman.pl).

Toruń Connections

Toruń is a handy stopover on the way between Warsaw and Gdańsk.

From Toruń by Train to: Warsaw (every 2 hours direct, 2.5 hours on express IC train), **Gdańsk** (4/day, 2.5 hours; additional options with a change in Bydgoszcz, 3 hours), **Malbork** (about every 2 hours, 2.5 hours, change in Iława), **Kraków** (1/day direct, 6.5 hours; better to change at Warsaw's Zachodnia station: 7/day, 6 hours), **Berlin** (4/day, 6 hours, change in Poznań).

POMERANIA

PRACTICALITIES

This section covers just the basics on traveling in Poland (for much more information, see *Rick Steves Eastern Europe*). You'll find free advice on specific topics at www.ricksteves.com/tips.

Money

Poland uses a currency called the złoty: 4 Polish złoty (zł) = about $1. To roughly convert Polish złoty into dollars, divide by four (e.g., 40 zł = about $10, 100 zł = about $25, 200 zł = about $50).

The standard way for travelers to get złoty is to withdraw money from an ATM (known as a *Bankomat* in Poland) using a debit or credit card, ideally with a Visa or MasterCard logo. Before departing, call your bank or credit-card company: Confirm that your card(s) will work overseas, ask about international transaction fees, and alert them that you'll be making withdrawals in Europe.

Also ask for the PIN number for your credit card—you may need it for Europe's "chip-and-PIN" payment machines (see below; allow time for your bank to mail your PIN to you). To keep your valuables safe, wear a money belt.

Dealing with "Chip and PIN": Newer credit and debit cards have chips that authenticate and secure transactions. In Europe, the cardholder inserts the chip card into the payment machine slot, then enters a PIN. (In the US, you provide a signature.) Any American card, whether with a chip or an old-fashioned magnetic stripe, will work at Europe's hotels, restaurants, and shops. But some self-service chip-and-PIN payment machines—such as those at train stations, toll roads, or unattended gas pumps—may not accept your card, even if you know the PIN. If your card won't work, look for a cashier who can process the transaction manually—or pay in cash.

Dynamic Currency Conversion: If merchants or hoteliers offer to convert your purchase price into dollars (called dynamic currency conversion, or DCC), refuse this "service." You'll pay extra for the expensive convenience of seeing your charge in dollars. If an ATM offers to "lock in" or "guarantee" your conversion rate, choose "proceed without conversion." Other prompts might state, "You can be charged in dollars: Press YES for dollars, NO for złoty." Always choose the local currency.

Staying Connected

The simplest solution is to bring your own device—mobile phone, tablet, or laptop—and use it just as you would at home (following the tips below, such as connecting to free Wi-Fi whenever possible).

To call Poland from a US or Canadian number: Whether you're phoning from a landline, your own mobile phone, or a Skype account, you're making an international call. Dial 011-48 and then the phone number. (011 is our international access code; 48 is Poland's country code.) If dialing from a mobile phone, you can enter + in place of the international access code—press and hold the 0 key.

To call Poland from a European country: Dial 00-48 followed by the phone number. (00 is Europe's international access code.)

To call within Poland: Just dial the whole number.

To call from Poland to another country: Dial 00 followed by the country code (for example, 1 for the US or Canada), then the area code and number. If you're calling European countries whose phone numbers begin with 0, you'll usually have to omit that 0 when you dial.

Tips: If you bring your own mobile phone, consider getting an international plan; most providers offer a global calling plan that cuts the per-minute cost of phone calls and texts, and a flat-fee data plan.

Use Wi-Fi whenever possible. Most hotels and many cafés offer free Wi-Fi, and you'll likely also find it at tourist information offices, major museums, and public-transit hubs. With Wi-Fi you can use your phone or tablet to make free or inexpensive domestic and international calls via a calling app such as Skype, FaceTime, or Google+ Hangouts. When you can't find Wi-Fi, you can use your cellular network to connect to the Internet, send texts, or make voice calls. When you're done, avoid further charges by manually switching off "data roaming" or "cellular data."

To make calls without a mobile phone, your best bet is to buy a prepaid phone card to use at a public phone booth. Sold locally at newsstands, these are reasonable for calls within Poland; they work for international calls as well, but can be expensive. Be aware that public pay phones are getting harder to find. (Cheap international phone cards that work with a PIN code, which are common in many European countries, generally aren't available in Poland.)

Calling from your hotel-room phone is usually expensive—

Sleep Code

Hotels are classified based on the average price of a standard double room with breakfast in high season.

$$$$	**Splurge:** Most rooms over 550 zł
$$$	**Pricier:** 400-550 zł
$$	**Moderate:** 250-400 zł
$	**Budget:** 100-250 zł
¢	**Backpacker:** Under 100 zł
RS%	**Rick Steves discount**

Unless otherwise noted, credit cards are accepted, hotel staff speak basic English, and free Wi-Fi is available. Comparison-shop by checking prices at several hotels (on each hotel's own website, on a booking site, or by email). For the best deal, *book directly with the hotel.* Ask for a discount if paying in cash; if the listing includes **RS%,** request a Rick Steves discount.

ask the rates before you dial. For more on phoning, see www. ricksteves.com/phoning. For a one-hour talk on "Traveling with a Mobile Device," see www.ricksteves.com/travel-talks.

Sleeping

I've categorized my recommended accommodations based on price, indicated with a dollar-sign rating (see sidebar). In Poland, you can choose from a variety of stylish and charming hotels and guest-houses. Hotel prices are roughly on par with midrange Western European countries. You can uncover some bargains, but I think it's worth paying a little more for comfort and a good location.

Reserve rooms as soon as your itinerary is set. For the best rates, book directly with the hotel using their official website (not a booking agency's site). If there's no secure reservation form, or for complicated requests, send an email with the following information: number and type of rooms; number of nights; arrival date; departure date; and any special requests. Use the European style for writing dates: day/month/year. Hoteliers typically ask for your credit-card number as a deposit.

Some hotels are willing to make a deal to attract guests: Try emailing several hotels to ask for their best price. In general, hotel prices can soften if you do any of the following: offer to pay cash, stay at least three nights, or travel off-season.

Eating

I've categorized my recommended eateries based on price, indicated with a dollar-sign rating (see sidebar). Poland offers good food for relatively little money. Polish cuisine has a reputation for being heavy and hearty, with lots of pork, potatoes, and cabbage...

PRACTICALITIES

Restaurant Price Code

I've assigned each eatery a price category, based on the average cost of a typical main course. Drinks, desserts, and splurge items (steak and seafood) can raise the price considerably.

$$$$	**Splurge:** Most main courses over 60 zł
$$$	**Pricier:** 45-60 zł
$$	**Moderate:** 25-45 zł
$	**Budget:** Under 25 zł

In Poland, a milk bar or takeout spot is **$**; a basic sit-down eatery is **$$**; a casual but more upscale restaurant is **$$$**; and a swanky splurge is **$$$$**.

which is true. But the food here is also delicious, with more variety than you might expect. For all the details about Polish food, see page 17. Ethnic restaurants provide a welcome change of pace. Seek out Italian, Indian, sushi, and other alternatives (I've recommended several in this book).

Tipping: Good service is relaxed (slow to an American). You won't get the bill until you ask for it: *"Rachunek?"* (rah-KHOO-nehk). To tip at restaurants that have a waitstaff, round up the bill 5 to 10 percent if you're happy with the service.

Transportation

Public transportation is the best way to connect the cities in this book.

By Train: Poland has an extensive, if dated, rail network; you can reach most towns and cities by train. Since point-to-point tickets are affordable, a rail pass won't likely save you money (but to review your options, see www.ricksteves.com/rail). To research train schedules and fares, visit the Polish rail site, www.rozklad-pkp.pl, or Germany's excellent online timetable, www.bahn.com. While most short-haul journeys don't require a seat reservation, you must reserve for some high-speed trains (such as the Kraków-Warsaw or Warsaw-Gdańsk express). It's also smart to reserve a sleeping berth if you're taking a night train. For more tips, see "Train Station Lingo" on page 5.

By Bus: PolskiBus runs bus routes throughout Poland (www.polskibus.com).

By Car: It's cheaper to arrange most car rentals from the US. If you're planning a multicountry itinerary by car, be aware of often-astronomical international drop-off fees. For tips on your insurance options, see www.ricksteves.com/cdw. Bring your driver's license. It's also required to carry an International Driving Permit (IDP), available at your local AAA office ($20 plus two passport-type photos, www.aaa.com). For route planning, consult www.viamichelin.com.

Poland is building a network of new expressways, but they're far from complete (you'll pay tolls to take completed segments—take a toll ticket as you enter the expressway, then pay when you get off, based on how far you've traveled). Locals travel long distances on two-lane country roads. Since each lane is about a lane and a half wide, passing is commonplace. Slower drivers should keep to the far-right of their lane, and not be surprised when faster cars zip past them. A car is a worthless headache in cities—park it safely (get tips from your hotel).

You're required to have your headlights on whenever you're driving—even in broad daylight, and seat belts are mandatory. Road etiquette is similar to that in the US. Ask your car-rental company for details, or check the US State Department website (www.travel.state.gov, search for Poland in the "Learn about your destination" box, then click on "Travel and Transportation").

By Plane: Consider covering long distances on a budget flight, which can be cheaper (and much faster) than a train. Poland's national carrier, LOT Airlines (www.lot.com), generally charges reasonable fares for short-distance trips. Or try some no-frills carriers, such as www.wizzair.com, www.easyjet.com, and www.ryanair.com. To compare several budget airlines, see www.skyscanner.com.

Helpful Hints

Emergency Help: For any emergency—whether **medical** or **police**—dial 112. For passport problems, call the **US Embassy** in Warsaw (tel. 022-504-2784, after-hours emergency tel. 022-504-2000) or the **US Consulate** in Kraków (tel. 012-424-5100); or the **Canadian Embassy** in Warsaw (tel. 022-584-3100).

If you have a minor illness, do as the locals do and go to a pharmacist for advice. Or ask at your hotel for help—they'll know of the nearest medical and emergency services. For other concerns, get advice from your hotelier.

Theft or Loss: To replace a passport, you'll need to go in person to an embassy or consulate (see above). Cancel and replace your credit and debit cards by calling these 24-hour US numbers collect: Visa—tel. 303/967-1096, MasterCard—tel. 636/722-7111, American Express—tel. 336/393-1111. In Poland, to make a collect call to the US, dial 00-800-111-1111; press zero or stay on the line for an operator. File a police report either on the spot or within a day or two; you'll need it to submit an insurance claim for lost or stolen rail passes or travel gear, and it can help with replacing your passport or credit and debit cards. For more information, see www.ricksteves.com/help.

PRACTICALITIES

Time: Poland uses the 24-hour clock. It's the same through 12:00 noon, then keep going: 13:00, 14:00, and so on. Poland, like most of continental Europe, is six/nine hours ahead of the East/West Coasts of the US.

Dress Code: At churches, a modest dress code (no bare shoulders or shorts) is encouraged.

Holidays and Festivals: Poland celebrates many holidays, which can close sights and attract crowds (book hotel rooms ahead). For information on holidays and festivals, check Poland's website: www.poland.travel. For a simple list showing major—though not all—events, see www.ricksteves.com/festivals.

Numbers and Stumblers: What Americans call the second floor of a building is the first floor in Europe. Europeans write dates as day/month/year, so Christmas 2019 is 25/12/19. Commas are decimal points and vice versa—a dollar and a half is 1,50, and there are 5.280 feet in a mile. Poland uses the metric system: A kilogram is 2.2 pounds; a liter is about a quart; and a kilometer is six-tenths of a mile.

Resources from Rick Steves

This Snapshot guide is excerpted from the latest edition of *Rick Steves Eastern Europe*, which is one of many titles in my ever-expanding series of guidebooks on European travel. I also produce a public television series, *Rick Steves' Europe*, and a public radio show, *Travel with Rick Steves*. My website, www.ricksteves.com, offers free travel information, a forum for travelers' comments, guidebook updates, my travel blog, an online travel store, and information on European rail passes and our tours of Europe. If you're bringing a mobile device, my free Rick Steves Audio Europe app features podcasts of my radio shows and travel interviews about Poland. You can get Rick Steves Audio Europe via Apple's App Store, Google Play, or the Amazon Appstore. For more information, see www.ricksteves.com/audioeurope.

Additional Resources

Tourist Information: www.poland.travel
Passports and Red Tape: www.travel.state.gov
Packing List: www.ricksteves.com/packing
Travel Insurance: www.ricksteves.com/insurance
Cheap Flights: www.kayak.com or www.google.com/flights
Airplane Carry-on Restrictions: www.tsa.gov/travelers
Updates for This Book: www.ricksteves.com/update

How Was Your Trip?

To share your tips, concerns, and discoveries after using this book, please fill out the survey at www.ricksteves.com/feedback. Thanks in advance—it helps a lot.

INDEX

Start your trip at

Our website enhances this book and turns

Explore Europe

At ricksteves.com you can browse through thousands of articles, videos, photos and radio interviews, plus find a wealth of money-saving travel tips for planning your dream trip. And with our mobile-friendly website, you can easily access all this great travel information anywhere you go.

TV Shows

Preview the places you'll visit by watching entire half-hour episodes of Rick Steves' Europe (choose from all 100 shows) on-demand, for free.

your travel dreams into affordable reality

Radio Interviews

Enjoy ready access to Rick's vast library of radio interviews covering travel

tips and cultural insights that relate specifically to your Europe travel plans.

Travel Forums

Learn, ask, share! Our online community of savvy travelers is a great resource for first-time travelers to Europe, as well as seasoned pros. You'll find forums on each country, plus travel tips and restaurant/hotel reviews. You can even ask one of our well-traveled staff to chime in with an opinion.

Travel News

Subscribe to our free Travel News e-newsletter, and get monthly updates from Rick on what's happening in Europe.

Audio Europe™

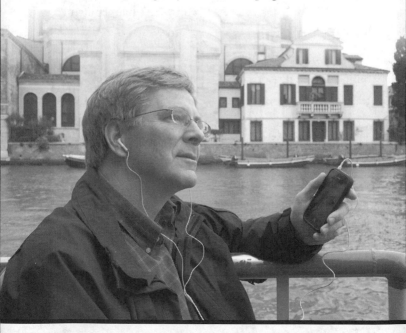

Pack Light and Right

Gear up for your next adventure at ricksteves.com

Light Luggage

Pack light and right with Rick Steves' affordable, custom-designed rolling carry-on bags, backpacks, day packs and shoulder bags.

Accessories

From packing cubes to moneybelts and beyond, Rick has personally selected the travel goodies that will help your trip go smoother.

Experience maximum Europe

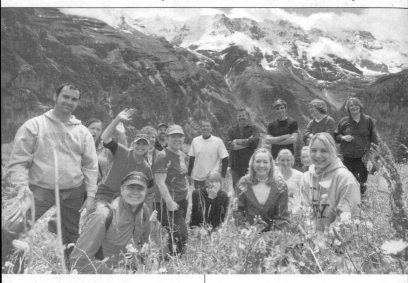

Save time and energy

This guidebook is your independent-travel toolkit. But for all it delivers, it's still up to you to devote the time and energy it takes to manage the preparation and logistics that are essential for a happy trip. If that's a hassle, there's a solution.

Rick Steves Tours

A Rick Steves tour takes you to Europe's most interesting places with great

great tours, too!

with minimum stress

guides and small groups of 28 or less. We follow Rick's favorite itineraries, ride in comfy buses, stay in family-run hotels, and bring you intimately close to the Europe you've traveled so far to see. Most importantly, we take away the logistical headaches so you can focus on the fun.

travelers—nearly half of them repeat customers— along with us on four dozen different itineraries, from Ireland to Italy to Istanbul. Is a Rick Steves tour the right fit for your travel dreams? Find out at ricksteves.com, where you can also request Rick's latest tour catalog. Europe is best experienced with happy travel partners. We hope you can join us.

Join the fun

This year we'll take thousands of free-spirited

A Guide for Every Trip

BEST OF GUIDES

Full color easy-to-scan format, focusing on Europe's most popular destinations and sights.

Best of France
Best of Germany
Best of England
Best of Europe
Best of Ireland
Best of Italy
Best of Spain

COMPREHENSIVE GUIDES

City, country, and regional guides with detailed coverage for a multi-week trip exploring the most iconic sights and venturing off the beaten track.

Amsterdam & the Netherlands
Barcelona
Belgium: Bruges, Brussels, Antwerp & Ghent
Berlin
Budapest
Croatia & Slovenia
Eastern Europe
England
Florence & Tuscany
France
Germany
Great Britain
Greece: Athens & the Peloponnese
Iceland
Ireland
Istanbul
Italy
London
Paris
Portugal
Prague & the Czech Republic
Provence & the French Riviera
Rome
Scandinavia
Scotland
Spain
Switzerland
Venice
Vienna, Salzburg & Tirol

THE BEST OF ROME

ome, Italy's capital, is studded with
man remnants and floodlit-fountain
uares. From the Vatican to the Colos-
m, with crazy traffic in between, Rome
onderful, huge, and exhausting. The
vds, the heat, and the weighty history

of the Eternal City where Caesars walked
can make tourists wilt. Recharge by taking siestas, gelato breaks, and after-dark
walks, strolling from one atmospheric
square to another in the refreshing evening air.

red **Pantheon**—which
gest dome until the
rly 2,000 years old
day over 1,500).

of Athens in the Vat-
odies the humanistic
nce.

gladiators fought
another, entertaining
.

is Rome ristorante,
rds at **St. Peter's**
k seriously.
in, toss in a coin

Rick Steves guidebooks are published by Avalon Travel,
an imprint of Perseus Books, a Hachette Book Group company.

POCKET GUIDES

Compact, full color city guides with the essentials for shorter trips.

Amsterdam	Paris
Athens	Prague
Barcelona	Rome
Florence	Venice
Italy's Cinque Terre	Vienna
London	
Munich & Salzburg	

SNAPSHOT GUIDES

Focused single-destination coverage.

Basque Country: Spain & France
Copenhagen & the Best of Denmark
Dublin
Dubrovnik
Edinburgh
Hill Towns of Central Italy
Krakow, Warsaw & Gdansk
Lisbon
Loire Valley
Madrid & Toledo
Milan & the Italian Lakes District
Naples & the Amalfi Coast
Northern Ireland
Normandy
Norway
Reykjavik
Sevilla, Granada & Southern Spain
St. Petersburg, Helsinki & Tallinn
Stockholm

CRUISE PORTS GUIDES

Reference for cruise ports of call.

Mediterranean Cruise Ports
Northern European Cruise Ports

Complete your library with...

TRAVEL SKILLS & CULTURE

Study up on travel skills and gain insight on history and culture.

Europe 101
European Christmas
European Easter
European Festivals
Europe Through the Back Door
Postcards from Europe
Travel as a Political Act

PHRASE BOOKS & DICTIONARIES

French
French, Italian & German
German
Italian
Portuguese
Spanish

PLANNING MAPS

Britain, Ireland & London
Europe
France & Paris
Germany, Austria & Switzerland
Ireland
Italy
Spain & Portugal

ABOUT THE AUTHORS

RICK STEVES

Since 1973, Rick has spent about four months a year exploring Europe. His mission: to empower Americans to have European trips that are fun, affordable, and culturally broadening. Rick produces a best-selling guidebook series, a public television series, and a public radio show, and organizes small-group tours that take over 20,000 travelers to Europe annually. He does all of this with the help of a hardworking, well-traveled staff of 100 at Rick Steves' Europe in Edmonds, Washington, near Seattle. When not on the road, Rick is active in his church and with advocacy groups focused on economic justice, drug policy reform, and ending hunger. To recharge, Rick plays piano, relaxes at his family cabin in the Cascade Mountains, and spends time with his partner Trish, son Andy, and daughter Jackie. Find out more about Rick at www.ricksteves.com and on Facebook.

CAMERON HEWITT

Cameron was born in Denver and grew up in central Ohio. The Polish nursery rhymes and gentle spirit of his grandfather, Jan Paweł Dąbrowski, instilled in him a deep affection for the Slavic world. After college, a back-packing trip reignited Cameron's interest in Eastern (ahem, "Central") Europe, and he's enjoyed annual trips to the region ever since. Since moving to Seattle and joining Rick Steves' Europe (where he serves as content manager) in 2000, Cameron has traveled to more than 35 European countries, contributing to guidebooks, tours, radio and television shows, and other media. Cameron married his high school sweetheart (and favorite travel partner), Shawna, and enjoys taking pictures, trying new restaurants, and planning his next trip.